fifth edition

Classroom Assessment

What Teachers Need to Know

W. James Popham

Professor Emeritus, UCLA

Boston ■ New York ■ San Francisco
Mexico City ■ Montreal ■ Toronto ■ London ■ Madrid ■ Munich ■ Paris
Hong Kong ■ Singapore ■ Tokyo ■ Cape Town ■ Sydney

Senior Editor: Arnis E. Burvikovs
Series Editorial Assistant: Erin Reilly
Marketing Manager: Erica DeLuca
Production Editor: Annette Joseph
Editorial Production Service: Lynda Griffiths
Composition Buyer: Linda Cox
Manufacturing Buyer: Megan Cochran
Electronic Composition: Denise Hoffman
Interior Design: Denise Hoffman
Cover Designer: Kristina Mose-Libon

For related titles and support materials, visit our online catalog at www.ablongman.com.

Between the time website information is gathered and then published, it is not unusual for some sites to have closed. Also, the transcription of URLs can result in typographical errors. The publisher would appreciate notification where these errors occur so that they may be corrected in subsequent editions.

Library of Congress Cataloging-in-Publication Data

Popham, W. James
    Classroom assessment : what teachers need to know / W. James Popham. — 5th ed.
        p.   cm.
    ISBN 0-205-51075-2
        1. Educational tests and measurements.   2. Examinations—Design and
    construction.   3. Examinations—Validity.   I. Title.
    LB3051.P6142 2007
    371.26—dc22

                                                                2006052016

ISBN 978-0-205-51075-7

Printed in the United States of America

10 9 8 7 6 5 4 3 2 1   RRD-VA   11 10 09 08 07

Text credit: Sections of Chapter 14 are based on an essay by the author originally published in the Winter 1991 issue of *Educational Measurement: Issues and Practices,* pp. 12–15. Copyright 1991 by the National Council on Measurement in Education. Adapted by permission of the publisher.

Cartoons: Joan King

For Sarah:
Former Teacher, Former Principal,
Current Colleague, Current and Future Spouse

W. James Popham has spent the bulk of his educational career as a teacher. His first teaching assignment, for example, was in a small eastern Oregon high school where he taught English and social studies while serving as yearbook advisor, class sponsor, and unpaid tennis coach. The recompense meshed well with the quality of his coaching.

Most of Dr. Popham's teaching career took place at UCLA where, for nearly 30 years, he taught courses in instructional methods for prospective teachers as well as courses in evaluation and measurement for graduate students. At UCLA he won several distinguished teaching awards. In January 2000, he was recognized by *UCLA Today* as one of UCLA's top 20 professors of the 20th century.

Because at UCLA he was acutely aware of the perishability of professors who failed to publish, he spent his non-teaching hours affixing words to paper. The result: over 25 books, 200 journal articles, 50 research reports, and 175 papers presented before research societies.

His most recent books are *Assessment for Educational Leaders* (2006), Allyn & Bacon; *The Truth About Testing: An Educator's Call to Action* (2001) and *Test Better, Teach Better: The Instructional Role of Assessment* (2003), ASCD; and *America's "Failing" Schools: How Parents and Teachers Can Cope with No Child Left Behind* (2005) and *Mastering Assessment: A Self-Service System for Educators* (2006), RoutledgeFalmer. He encourages purchase of these books because he regards their semi-annual royalties as psychologically reassuring.

In 1968, Dr. Popham established IOX Assessment Associates, an R&D group that formerly created statewide student achievement tests for a dozen states. He has personally passed all of those tests, largely because of his unlimited access to the tests' answer keys.

contents

3 Validity   48

4 Absence-of-Bias   73

5 Deciding What to Assess and How to Assess It   101

6 Selected-Response Tests   125

7 Constructed-Response Tests   149

8 Performance Assessment   172

9 Portfolio Assessment   195

10 Affective Assessment   214

11 Improving Teacher-Developed Assessments   237

12 Instructionally Oriented Assessment   255

13 Making Sense Out of Standardized Test Scores   281

14 Appropriate and Inappropriate Test-Preparation Practices   307

15 Evaluating Teaching and Grading Students   324

f e a t u r e s

Today's teachers teach their students. And today's teachers test their students. But the way today's teachers teach and test their students is dramatically different from how it was a few decades ago. The reason for the difference is easy to identify. Teachers find themselves currently operating in an educational arena completely dominated by accountability tests. Those accountability tests are being used to evaluate schools. And, as you know, this is where teachers do their teaching and testing.

If a school's students score high on a state's accountability tests, the school's staff is thought to be doing an effective instructional job. If, however, a school's students score poorly on a state's accountability tests, then the opposite conclusion is reached. Today's teachers, therefore, find themselves on the receiving end of relentless pressures to "raise those test scores!"

Moreover, those score-boosting pressures were ratcheted up dramatically in early 2002 when President George W. Bush signed a federal law calling for the nationwide expansion of educational accountability programs. The cornerstone of each state's federally mandated accountability program must be students' performances on standardized statewide accountability tests. Every U.S. public school, then, is to be evaluated primarily according to how well its students score on these accountability tests. A teacher whose classroom conduct is not affected by these developments is a teacher whose contact with reality is definitely debatable. But, as I said earlier, it wasn't always this way.

Eons ago, I was a high school teacher in eastern Oregon. It was so long ago, indeed, my friends contend that Oregon must still have been a territory. Way back then, we administered standardized achievement tests to our students. But students' scores on those tests really made little difference in how we taught our students or how we tested them. Pressure to raise our students' scores on those external achievement exams was nonexistent. We taught and we tested as we saw fit. But, of course, the world of education is different today—much different.

This is a book about classroom assessment. Its aim is to help teachers do a good job of testing their students so, as a consequence, those teachers can do a better job of teaching their students. But the ubiquitous presence of accountability testing in our nation's public schools these days has altered the educational playing field dramatically. Classroom teachers' teaching and testing practices that might have been perfectly acceptable as recently as the 1980s must now be altered completely. Significant statewide accountability testing, and its use to evaluate schools, has changed all this.

All right. I hope I've been able to build a reasonably compelling case that the accountability context in which teachers function now exerts a major influence on how teachers teach—and on how teachers test. I hope I've convinced you of this view because my beliefs about the impact of today's accountability testing on teachers' lives has led me to a major thematic emphasis for this, the fifth edition of *Classroom Assessment: What Teachers Need to Know.*

Even when I began to write the first edition of this book, well over a decade ago, there was a substantial amount of accountability testing going on in this country. But when President Bush signed the No Child Left Behind Act on January 8, 2002, the impact of accountability testing on the day-in, day-out conduct of classroom teachers simply skyrocketed. Thus, here's the thematic question I'll try to address in this fifth edition:

How can classroom assessment most effectively benefit students when carried out in a context dominated by accountability tests?

For an author to write a book about classroom assessment these days without recognizing the likely impact of accountability testing is, in my view, irresponsible. Thus, whenever it seems germane, I'm going to level with you about how your classroom assessment, and your classroom teaching, is likely to be influenced by the presence of an influential state-level accountability test. And, just in case you don't already know it, *all* state-level accountability tests are influential.

We'll also dig into some of the most assessment-relevant features of the No Child Left Behind Act because this significant federal statute has dramatically elevated the stakes associated with educational accountability testing. You need to learn what makes the accountability framework of that law tick. And you'll find that those ticking noises sound frighteningly like a time-bomb!

As in past editions, this new one is attentive to the *instructional* payoffs of well-designed classroom tests. Whenever I can, I've attempted to highlight the implications that testing has on teaching. There's even a section in each chapter entitled But What Does This Have to Do with Teaching? In these sections, I try to spell out the instructional implications of a chapter's content. There's also a chapter dealing explicitly with the dividends teachers can obtain from instructionally oriented assessment. I think you'll find it (Chapter 12) illuminating.

You will also encounter in each chapter a description of a fictitious teacher in a classroom situation that's related to one or more of the topics treated in the chapter. These are called Decision Time features. Each Decision Time is concluded with a decision that must be made by the teacher who is being described. You're then requested to put yourself in the place of the teacher and decide how you would proceed. These vignettes are intended to set a series of practice problems squarely on your plate, then see how you might munch on them.

Considerable attention is also given in this fifth edition to an important audience for teachers—namely, *parents*. Teachers often need to explain assessment-related topics to parents, such as why a child scored a certain way on a standardized test or the way classroom exams are related to the grades a child receives. So, in every chapter you'll find a feature entitled Parent Talk. In these Parent Talks, I've described a situation in which a teacher needs to explain something about assessment to parents. I then tell you what I would have said to the parents if I had been the teacher in that situation. What I hope you'll do, then, is decide how *you* would respond in that same situation. In fact, you might say *aloud* (in private, if you have any sense) what you'd tell parents. Either paraphrase my words or whip out better words of your own. Teachers who can talk sensibly to parents about assessment-related concerns will find they're able to establish more effective educational rapport with parents. Such teachers will get along far better with parents than will teachers who convey to parents the idea that assessment is an exotic measurement mystery, well beyond the perceptive powers of mere parents.

I've added several chunks of new and important content to this fifth edition. I've also tossed in some new cartoons so that every chapter now has its very own cartoon. Frankly, in previous editions there was some fairly blatant cartoon-envy on the part of several cartoonless chapters.

There are 15 chapters designed to take you on a tour of the key measurement concepts needed by classroom teachers. Each chapter could have been twice as long if the audience had been prospective measurement specialists. Instead, a deliberate effort was made to strip away superfluous information so you're left with only the need-to-know content, not the nice-to-know content.

I realize all too well that you're not likely to regard the contents of a book on assessment as enthralling. For myself, if I had the choice of whether I would read any assessment book or a cracking good espionage novel, I'd shove the assessment book into second place in a millisecond. In recognition of your probable response to the book's content, I've tried to lighten the load with cartoons and an occasional dash of levity. If you had to write 15 chapters about assessment, I suspect you would also get more than a little whimsical. If you don't find the light style to be acceptable, simply frown during the funny parts.

An important feature in the fifth edition of this book is a serious attempt by me (your affable author) to inform you (an unsuspecting educator awaiting a relaxing measurement massage) about a serious problem these days. That problem, and it's one that is causing all sorts of educational harm to children, is the use of *inappropriate* standardized achievement tests to judge the success of teachers' efforts. This issue is addressed in the final chapter. (I'm trying to entice you to keep reading till the book's end!) You'll learn in Chapter 15 why the use of certain kinds of students' standardized test scores to evaluate a school staff's effectiveness is quite wrongheaded.

Another key feature of this edition of *Classroom Assessment* is a glossary of assessment terms. Anytime I thought there was a word or phrase you might wish to refer to later, I tossed it into the Glossary and whipped up a brief definition. That's where you'll also find the definitions of any words or phrases identified by *boldfaced italics* in the text.

Now, here are just a few words about the layout of the book. Every chapter contains several elements intended to foster a stick-to-your-ribs mastery of its content. You'll find the following at the close of most chapters:

■ A succinct isolation of *what teachers really need to know* about the chapter's content
■ A general *summary* of the chapter's contents
■ A set of *self-check* exercises

■ A *self-check* key that provides answers to all of the self-check exercises as well as, in a few instances, an elaboration of the concepts addressed by the exercises

■ A set of *Pondertime* questions designed to get you pondering up a storm about key concepts in the chapter

■ *Additional Stuff*—a set of additional books and articles that can extend your understanding of the chapter's content

■ *Nonprint Stuff,* such as videotapes or audiotapes, that expand on the chapter's concepts

■ *Cyber Stuff*—a useful feature for the fifth edition identifying relevant websites for readers who are not seriously cowed by computers. If you can use a computer, you can whip yourself into a www frenzy with these websites.

I personally visited and exited from all of the websites I've listed—just a few weeks before sending the revised manuscript off to the publishers. When I did so, they were all working well. I hope they still are.

mylabschool   MyLabSchool is a collection of online tools for student success in the course, in licensure exams, and the teaching career. Visit www.mylabschool.com to access the following: **video clips** from real classrooms, with opportunities for students to reflect on the videos and offer their own thoughts and suggestions for applying theory to practice; an extensive archive of **text and multimedia cases** that provide valuable perspectives on real classrooms and real teaching challenges; Allyn & Bacon's **Lesson and Portfolio Builder** application, which includes an integrated state standards correlation tool; help with research papers using **Research Navigator™,** which provides access to three exclusive databases of credible and reliable source material including EBSCO's ContentSelect Academic Journal Database, New York Times Search by Subject Archive, and "Best of the Web" Link Library. MyLabSchool also includes a **Careers** section with resources for Praxis exams and licensure preparation, professional portfolio development, job search, and interview techniques.

An online Instructor's Manual with additional teaching resources and a video with several assessment vignettes are also available to adopters. Please contact your local representative for more information.

There's one final new wrinkle in this fifth edition, and you'll find it nicely nestled on a new website developed just for this book at www.ablongman.com/popham5e. This website will provide additional exercises for the book's 15 chapters. Most folks now have easy access to a computer. This surely wasn't the case when the first edition of *Classroom Assessment* wandered into the world. In an attempt to take advantage of our current computers-everywhere environment, I've cranked out a series of exercises I believe will reinforce your understanding of what I'm jabbering about in the book. I've referred to it as *Extra Electronic Exercises for Classroom Assessment* (E^3CA), and I think you'll find it a useful way to snare a clump of closure regarding each chapter's contents.

These days, teachers who don't know most of what this book contains are going into educational battle without suitable weaponry. Good luck in grappling with the assessment topics you'll be greeting on subsequent pages.

To my colleagues who reviewed this latest edition I offer my wholehearted thanks: Nancy Cerezo, Saint Leo University; Karen E. Eifler, University of Portland; Jerrie Smith Jackson, Our Lady of the Lake University; Terry H. Stepka, Arkansas State University; and James Valle, Millersville University of Pennsylvania.

I am most grateful to Dolly Bulquerin, word-processor nonpareil, who prepared the first edition of *Classroom Assessment*, then guided the transformation of that first edition into a second life, a third life, a fourth life, and, finally, transformed edition number four into this new revision. I suspect those efforts clearly make Dolly a revisionist midwife.

W. J. P.

Why Do Teachers Need to Know about Assessment?

Teachers teach students. That hardly constitutes a breakthrough insight. Just as preachers preach and flyers fly—teachers teach. That's why they're called teachers.

But what is a bit less obvious is that teachers teach because they *like* to teach. Primary teachers like to teach little people. High school teachers like to teach bigger people. Most high school teachers like to teach about a particular subject matter. (Have you ever seen how mathematics teachers' eyes get misty when they introduce their students to the raptures of the Pythagorean theorem?) Yes, most teachers love to teach. It is because they enjoy what they do that they waded through a medley of preservice teacher education courses, conquered the challenges of student teaching, and hopped the myriad hurdles of the certification process. Teachers overcame these obstacles in order to earn annual salaries that, particularly during the first few years, are laughably low. Yes, there's little doubt that teachers enjoy teaching.

Although teachers like to *teach*, they rarely like to *test*. Yet, here you are— beginning a book about testing. How can I, the author, ever entice you, the reader, to become interested in testing when your heart has already been given to teaching? The answer is really quite straightforward. Teachers who can test well will be better teachers. Effective testing will enhance a teacher's instructional effectiveness. Really!

If you're willing to suspend any preconceptions about testing while you're reading this book, particularly any negative ones, I'll make a pledge to you. If you tackle this text with even half the enthusiasm you might bring to a teaching assignment, I promise you'll discover how *testing will make you a much better teacher*. And, because I've been a teacher for over 50 years, it's a promise I'll keep. Teachers definitely should not break promises to teachers. Teachers' promises to administrators, on the other hand, should be regarded as eminently renegotiable.

But before I attempt to convince you, ever so subtly, that testing can be a boon to teaching, I want you to get a fix on your own *current* views about educational testing. And, because this is a book about testing, what better way to have you learn about those attitudes than to have you take a self-test I devised just for readers of this book?

So, on the adjacent page (it's on the *right* from where you're currently reading!) you'll find a brief self-test similar to the ones you've surely encountered in many widely read magazines. I saw one such self-test in a health magazine recently. It was entitled "How Long Will You Live? A Self-Test." Frankly, I was afraid to try it. As one gets older, one becomes more cautious.

But you have nothing to fear by taking the self-test I've whipped up for you. To emphasize its brevity, I have entitled it "A Terse Self-Test about Testing." It is an example of a Likert inventory. Later, in Chapter 10, you'll learn more about Likert inventories—you'll learn, that is, if you continue reading this spellbinding book. And if you're not planning to do so, then put the book down *immediately*. I am disinclined to allow potential *quitters* to read any further. Quitters are, by definition, people inclined to quit. This book was written for *finishers*. All right (if you're still reading, that is), take a crack at page 3's teensy self-test. The way to interpret your responses is given as a footnote at the bottom of page 4. Just for a change of pace, I proposed to Allyn and Bacon, the book's publisher, that we start putting footnotes at the *top* of each page. As is often the case with a publisher's representatives, the Allyn and Bacon folks smiled winningly—while ignoring my innovative suggestion.

■ Federal Laws Rule

Anyone who has completed even an introductory course in U.S. Government knows that while state laws can overturn the laws enacted by local communities, federal laws can overturn state laws. When it comes to the art of overturning, federal folks hold all the trump cards.

Any consideration of educational testing these days cannot be sensibly undertaken without recognizing the existence of an enormously important federal statute—namely, the No Child Left Behind (NCLB) Act, signed into law by President George W. Bush on January 8, 2002. That law, actually the most recent reauthorization of the Elementary and Secondary Education Act (ESEA) first passed by Congress in 1965, contains a series of significant *test-based* accountability provisions. Because those provisions are certain to have a substantial impact on the way testing goes on in U.S. public schools, you need to become familiar with the chief features of the NCLB Act as it was originally created. (I've added that last little qualifier about the law's *original* form because it seems likely to me that the NCLB Act will soon be meaningfully modified. Therefore, I suggest that, because even publishers as skillful as Allyn and Bacon cannot revise their textbooks in hours, you find out if the NCLB Act has been substantially altered at the time you tussle with this textbook.)

A Terse Self-Test about Testing

Directions: For each of the statements below, use the following answer key to indicate how you react to the statement:

SA = Strongly Agree	A = Agree	U = Uncertain	D = Disagree	SD = Strongly Disagree

There are no right or wrong answers, so please answer frankly by circling the appropriate response for each statement.

1. The chief reason that teachers should give classroom tests is to determine students' grades.　SA　A　U　D　SD

2. Teachers should typically plan instruction focused on the skills or knowledge represented by a test.　SA　A　U　D　SD

3. In their classroom tests, teachers should only use items that can be scored objectively.　SA　A　U　D　SD

4. There are other legitimate indicators of a teacher's instructional effectiveness besides students' test scores.　SA　A　U　D　SD

5. A teacher has no business measuring students' confidence in their ability to do schoolwork.　SA　A　U　D　SD

6. Nationally standardized achievement tests should never be used to supply evidence about how well teachers are instructing children.　SA　A　U　D　SD

7. Teachers really don't need to determine the reliability of their own classroom tests.　SA　A　U　D　SD

8. It is impossible to judge the quality of students' written compositions with any meaningful accuracy.　SA　A　U　D　SD

9. The enormous pressure to boost students' scores on important tests permits teachers to employ almost any sort of score-improvement preparation activities.　SA　A　U　D　SD

10. Significant classroom tests should almost always be constructed prior to a teacher's instructional planning.　SA　A　U　D　SD

Here's a thumbnail sketch of the major test-related features of the NCLB Act. First, it calls for much more state-level testing. No later than the close of the school year that started in 2005, standardized achievement tests in reading and mathematics were to be given annually to all U.S. public school students in grades 3 through 8 and once more in high school. That's more than twice the amount of student testing required by an earlier reauthorization of ESEA.

Next, based chiefly on students' scores on these tests, a school or district may be identified as "in need of improvement" if its students fail to show that they are making *adequate yearly progress (AYP)*. AYP requires schools (and districts) to increase substantially the number of students who score at "proficient-or-better" levels on a state's NCLB tests. Although each state is allowed to devise its own time line regarding the amount of AYP improvement that each school must periodically make (and to come up with its own definition of *proficiency*), the NCLB Act has set a target that 100 percent of all students must earn test scores at proficient-or-above levels by 12 years following the law's enactment. This federal requirement that all students will be proficient by the end of the school year starting in 2013, of course, translates into the need for substantial improvements in students' scores on NCLB tests. If schools fail to achieve their test-based AYP targets, those schools will be identified as inadequate. If those schools that receive ESEA funds fail their AYP targets for two consecutive years, they are placed on an improvement track laden with increasingly severe sanctions.

Clearly, the NCLB Act's accountability provisions are making America's educators do a substantial amount of squirming. That's because there is enormous pressure on the nation's teachers to raise their school's NCLB test scores. Few educators relish the opportunity to be teachers or administrators in a "failing" school and therefore be regarded themselves as failures. Thus, the demands to boost students' performances on NCLB tests will influence many teachers' day-to-day instructional decisions for the foreseeable future.

And that's why I'm going to address this issue head-on throughout the following pages. Testing—*and teaching*—following the passage of the NCLB Act are certain to be different than testing—*and teaching*—before the law's enactment. Today's public school teachers are now obliged to take part in an education game whose rules have been dramatically altered because of a significant federal law. The NCLB Act, almost literally, seems to countermand almost everything it touches.

Self-Test Interpretation Guide: For statements 2, 4, 6, 7, and 10, use the following scoring key: SA = 5, A = 4, U = 3, D = 2, and SD = 1. For statements 1, 3, 5, 8, and 9, use the following scoring key: SA = 1, A = 2, U = 3, D = 4, and SD = 5. The highest possible total score is 50; the lowest possible total score is 10. The higher your total score, the more sensible is your view of educational testing. After finishing this book, you might wish to retake this terse self-test (without looking at your earlier answers, of course). If you come up with a postbook score that's substantially *lower* than your prebook score, you and I should *both* be worried.

■ Assessment versus Testing

So far, I've been contrasting teaching to testing when, if you'll glance at this book's cover, you'll find that it's supposed to be a book about assessment. If you're alert, you've already started to wonder—What's this author trying to pull off? Am I going to learn about *testing* or *assessment*? Is *assessment* simply a more fashionable word for *testing*? In short, what's he up to? These are reasonable questions, and I'll now try to supply you with a set of compelling, confidence-engendering answers.

Almost everyone knows about the kinds of tests typically encountered in school. Most of today's adults, indeed, were on the receiving end of a hoard of teacher-dispensed tests during their own days in school. There were final exams, midterm exams, end-of-unit tests, pop quizzes, and (in the interest of equity) mom quizzes. All of those tests had one thing in common. They represented the teacher's attempt to get a fix on how much the teacher's students had learned. More accurately, such tests were employed to determine a student's status with respect to the knowledge or skills the teacher was attempting to promote. This is an altogether praiseworthy endeavor for teachers—to find out how much students know. If teachers are reasonably sure about what their students currently know, then teachers can more accurately tailor instructional activities to promote what their students need to learn.

The sorts of tests referred to in the preceding paragraph, such as the quizzes and examinations most of us took in school, have historically been paper-and-pencil instruments. When I was a student, many years ago, the three most common forms of tests I encountered were essay tests, multiple-choice tests, and true-false tests. Until the past decade or so, those three kinds of tests were, by far, the most prevalent sorts of tests found in classrooms.

In recent years, however, educators have been urged to broaden their conception of testing so students' status is determined via a wider variety of measuring devices—a variety extending well beyond traditional paper-and-pencil tests. The reason teachers have been challenged to expand their repertoire of testing techniques is not merely for the sake of variety. Rather, thoughtful educators have recognized there are a number of important kinds of student learning not measured most appropriately by paper-and-pencil tests. If, for example, a teacher wants to determine how well students can function orally in a job-interview situation, it's pretty clear that a true-false test doesn't cut it.

Thus, because there are many worthwhile learning outcomes not best measured by paper-and-pencil tests, and because when most people use the word *test* they automatically think of traditional paper-and-pencil tests, the term *assessment* has been increasingly adopted by many educators and measurement specialists. Assessment is a broader descriptor of the kinds of educational measuring teachers do—a descriptor that, while certainly including traditional paper-and-pencil tests, covers many more kinds of measurement procedures. Here is a working definition of *assessment* as it is used in an educational context:

> Educational assessment is a formal attempt to determine students' status with respect to educational variables of interest.

Lest you be put off by this fairly foreboding definition, let's briefly consider its chief elements. Note that the kind of assessment we're talking about is aimed at determining the status of students regarding "educational variables of interest." *Variables* are merely things that vary. (I suspect you could have figured this out all on your own!) In education, for example, we find that students vary in how much they know about a subject, how skilled they are in performing such operations as long division, and how positive their attitudes are toward school. Those are the sorts of variables with which a teacher is typically concerned, thus they are the "variables of interest" teachers typically measure. If the teacher's instructional focus is on the industrial revolution, then the teacher may wish to assess how much students know about the industrial revolution. In that case, the variable of interest would be the degree of students' knowledge regarding the industrial revolution. If the teacher is interested in how confident students are regarding their own written composition skills, then students' composition confidence would be a variable of interest. Educational assessment deals with such variables.

Our working definition also indicates that educational assessment constitutes a "formal" attempt to get a fix on students' status. As human beings, we make all sorts of informal determinations regarding people's status. For example, we may conclude that the woman who cut into the supermarket line ahead of us is rude, or that the man who keeps stumbling as he climbs a set of stairs is clumsy. But these are informal status determinations. Teachers, too, make informal judgments about their students. For instance, a teacher might conclude that a student, based on the student's glum demeanor during the first few moments of class, is definitely grumpy. Such informal appraisals, although they may be useful to teachers, should not be regarded as educational assessment.

When I was a high school teacher, for example, I employed informal judgment to conclude that Raymond Gonty, one of the seniors in my U.S. Government class, was not really interested in what I was teaching. I reached this conclusion chiefly because Raymond usually slept during class. I became more firmly convinced, however, when he began arriving at class carrying a pillow!

The kind of educational assessment you'll be reading about in this book is formal—that is, it's a deliberate effort to determine a student's status regarding such variables as the student's knowledge, skills, or attitudes. The kind of educational assessment you'll be considering is more than a teacher's "impressions." Rather, you'll be learning about systematic ways to get a fix on a student's status.

Assessment, therefore, is a broad and relatively nonrestrictive label for the kinds of testing and measuring teachers must do. It is a label to help remind educators that the measurement of students' status should include far more than paper-and-pencil instruments. Assessment is a word that embraces diverse kinds of tests and measurements. In the remaining pages, you'll find that although I'll use the term *assessment*, I'll often use the words **test** and **measurement**. I'll not be trying to make any subtle distinctions at those times. Instead, I'm probably just tired of using the A-word.

■ Why Should Teachers Know about Assessment? Yesteryear's Answers

Let's play a bit of time travel. Suppose you were magically transported back to the 1950s or 1960s. And, as long as we're in a let's-pretend mode, imagine you're a new teacher taking part in a fall orientation for first-year teachers in a large school district. The thematic topic of the particular session you're attending is Why Should Teachers Know about Testing? The session's lecturer, Professor Tess Tumm, is supplying the audience with a set of traditional answers to this thematic question based on how teachers actually can use classroom tests. Because you are a docile new teacher (remember, this is imaginary), you are compliantly taking notes to help guide you during the coming school year.

What I'm suggesting, as you've probably guessed, is that there are a number of fairly traditional answers to the question of why teachers should learn about assessment. Those answers have been around for several decades. There is also a set of more current answers to the question of why teachers should know about assessment. Let's give tradition its due and, initially, consider four time-honored answers to the question of why teachers should know about testing. Although these reasons for knowing about classroom assessment may have been around for a while, they're still compelling because they are rooted in the realities of what skilled teachers can do with classroom assessment. These four reasons may well have been the major points treated by Professor Tumm during our imaginary orientation session of yesteryear.

Diagnosing Students' Strengths and Weaknesses

One important reason that teachers assess students is to determine an individual student's weaknesses and strengths. If you're an elementary teacher, you need to know how well Giselle is comprehending what she reads so, if she's having certain difficulties, you can address those problems instructionally. Student weaknesses, once identified via assessment, can be the focus of future instruction.

On the flip side of the issue, teachers need to know what their students' prior accomplishments are. If Jaime is already truly proficient in solving simultaneous equations, it's a waste of Jaime's time to make him plow through practice piles of such equations. When I was growing up, the expression "That's like carrying coal to Newcastle" was used to disparage any scheme that reeked of redundancy. (I always assumed that coal mining was a big deal in Newcastle.) Well, teachers who relentlessly keep instructing students regarding knowledge or skills that the students have already mastered are definitely lugging coal lumps to Newcastle. Assessment can allow teachers to identify students' current strengths and, as a consequence, can help teachers avoid superfluous and wasteful instruction.

Thus, by measuring students' current status, teachers can discern (1) where to put their instructional energies to ameliorate a student's weaknesses and (2) what already mastered skills or knowledge can be instructionally avoided. Such diagnostic assessment is particularly useful for a teacher's planning if the assessment is carried out at the beginning of an instructional sequence. This kind of early diagnosis is often referred to as *preassessment* because it is assessment that takes place prior to the teacher's initiation of instruction.

Monitoring Students' Progress

A second, related answer to the question, Why should teachers assess? is that such assessments help teachers determine whether their students are making satisfactory progress. Sometimes, of course, it's easy for teachers to tell whether their students are or are not progressing satisfactorily. I can still recall, with suitable embarrassment, the absolutely scintillating lesson I provided as a high school English teacher on the topic of Modifying Gerunds with Possessives. It was a lesson designed for a full-class period, and I was confident that at its conclusion my students would not only understand the topic but also be able to explain to others why one of the following sentences contains an appropriate pronoun and one does not:

Improper
Pronoun   *Gerund*
↓   ↓

☹ **Sentence 1:** I really appreciate you sending the brownies.

Proper
Pronoun   *Gerund*
↓   ↓

☺ **Sentence 2:** I really appreciate your sending the brownies.

At the end of a bravura 40-minute lesson, replete with all sorts of real-life examples and a host of on-target practice activities, I was certain I had effectively taught students that because a gerund was a noun-form of a verb, any modifiers of such gerunds, including pronouns, must be possessive. And yet, at the end of the lesson, when I looked into my students' baffled faces, I realized that my optimism was unwarranted. After asking several students to explain to me the essence of what I'd been talking about, I quickly discerned that my lesson about gerund modification was not an award-winning effort. Most of my students couldn't distinguish between a gerund and a geranium.

Although teachers can occasionally discern informally, as I did, that their students aren't making satisfactory progress, more often than not we find teachers' believing their students are progressing quite well. (Note in the previous sentence that the modifier of the gerund *believing* is the possessive form of *teachers*. Yes, I'm still trying.) It's only human nature for teachers to believe they're teaching well and their students are learning well. But unless teachers systematically monitor students' progress via some type of assessment, there's too much chance teachers will improperly conclude progress is taking place when, in fact, such progress is not.

A useful function of classroom assessment, therefore, is to determine whether students are moving satisfactorily toward the instructional outcomes the teacher is seeking to promote. If progress for all students is satisfactory, of course, then the teacher need make no instructional changes. If progress for most students is satisfactory, but a few students are falling behind, then some separate doses of remedial assistance would seem to be in order. If progress for most students is inadequate, then the teacher should substantially modify whatever instructional approach is being used because, it is all too clear, this approach is not working. Progress monitoring is a time-honored and altogether sensible use of classroom assessment.

I've run into a number of teachers in recent years who refer to this use of assessment as "dip-sticking." When I think back to the days that I occasionally used a dip-stick to determine if my second-hand automobile was running low on oil (as it typically was), that label definitely rings true.

A teacher needs to monitor students' progress via classroom assessment because, more often than you'd think, the teacher can stop instructing on a certain topic well in advance of what the teacher anticipated. Suppose, for instance, you're attempting to get your students to acquire a certain skill, and you've set aside two weeks to promote their mastery of the skill. If you monitor students' progress with an assessment after only a week, however, and discover your students have already mastered the skill, you should simply scrap your week-two plans and smilingly move on to the next topic.

Another way of thinking about the monitoring of student progress is that it positions teachers to use the results of classroom tests for making *formative assessments* of their instructional procedures—that is, evaluations intended to improve unsuccessful yet still modifiable instruction. *Summative assessments,* in contrast, refer to tests whose purpose is to make a final success/failure decision about a relatively unmodifiable set of instructional activities. In a review of research studies focused on the instructional payoffs of formatively oriented classroom assessments, two British investigators (Black and Wiliam, 1998) concluded that the use of progress-monitoring classroom assessments can promote striking gains in student learning on *external* exams.

The range of typical improvements in student learning reported by these investigators was such that at the *least* positive level, an average student whose classes featured formative assessments displayed the same achievement as a student in the top 35 percent of students in classes without such formative assessments. And at the *most* positive end of the effect-size range, there were learning gains in classes using formative assessments that, had they been seen in all of a nation's classes, would have raised the score of that nation from the middle of a pack of 40 or so nations to one of the top 5 nations in the world. The British researchers concluded their review of empirical studies about classroom assessments with the assertion that "there is a body of firm evidence that formative assessment is an essential component of classroom work and that its development can raise standards of achievement" (Black and Wiliam, 1998, p. 148).

Based on their conclusions regarding the major instructional dividends of formatively oriented classroom assessments, members of Britain's Assessment Reform Group introduced the idea of classroom assessment *for* learning—in contrast to assessment *of* learning. They describe this approach as follows:

> *Assessment for learning is any assessment for which the first priority in its design and practice is to serve the purpose of promoting pupils' learning. It thus differs from assessment designed primarily to serve the purpose of accountability, or of ranking, or of certifying competence.* (Black et al., 2002)

More recently, Stiggins (2004) has pushed assessment *for* learning as the cornerstone of effective classroom measurement.

Assigning Grades

If I were somehow able to carry out an instant nationwide survey of beginning teachers and asked them, "What is the most important function of classroom assessment?" I know what answer I'd get from most of the surveyed teachers. They'd immediately respond: *to give grades.*

That's certainly what I thought testing was all about when I taught in public schools. To be honest (confession, I am told, is good for the soul), the *only* reason I tested my students was to give them grades. I've talked to hundreds of teachers during the past few years, and I've been dismayed at how many of them continue to regard testing's exclusive function to be grade giving. A third reason, therefore, that teachers assess students is to assemble the evidence necessary to give their students grades. Most school systems are structured so the end-of-course or end-of-year grades a student earns constitute the beginnings of a record of the student's personal accomplishments—a record destined to follow the student throughout life. Thus, it is imperative teachers not assign grades capriciously. Whether we like it or not, students' grades are important.

The best way to assign grades properly is to collect evidence of a student's accomplishments so the teacher will have access to ample information before deciding whether to dish out an A, B, C, D, or F to a student. Some school systems employ less traditional student grading systems—for example, the use of descriptive verbal reports that are relayed to parents. Yet, whatever the reporting system used, it is clear the teacher's assessment activities can provide the evidence necessary to make sensible student-by-student appraisals. The more frequent and varied the evidence of student accomplishments, the more judiciously the teacher can assign to students the grades they deserve.

Determining One's Own Instructional Effectiveness

A fourth and final reason teachers have traditionally been told they should test students is that students' test performances can help teachers infer how effective teaching has been. Suppose a teacher sets out to have students master a set of worthwhile skills and knowledge regarding Topic X during a three-week instructional unit. Prior to instruction, a brief test indicated students knew almost nothing about Topic X, but after the unit was concluded, a more lengthy test revealed students had mastered most of the skills and knowledge addressed during the Topic X unit.

Because the comparison of students' pretest and posttest results indicated the teacher's students had acquired ample knowledge and skills regarding Topic X, the teacher has a solid chunk of evidence that the instructional approach being used appears to be working. If the teacher's instruction seems to be promoting the desired outcomes, then it probably shouldn't be altered much.

On the other hand, let's say a teacher's Topic X pretest-to-posttest results for students suggest students' progress has been piffling. After comparing results on the end-of-instruction posttest to students' performance on the preinstruction test, it appears students barely knew more than they knew before the instruction commenced. Such trivial student growth should suggest to the teacher that modifications in the instructional activities seem warranted when teaching Topic X again next term or next year.

I'm not suggesting students' pretest-to-posttest results are the only way for teachers to tell whether they're flying or flopping, but students' end-of-instruction performances on assessment devices constitute a particularly compelling indication of whether teachers should retain, alter, or jettison their current instructional procedures.

In review, then, we've considered four fairly traditional answers to the question of why teachers should assess students. Here they are again:

Traditional Reasons That Teachers Assess Students
- To diagnose students' strengths and weaknesses
- To monitor students' progress
- To assign grades to students
- To determine instructional effectiveness

You will notice that each of these four uses of educational assessment is directly related to *helping the teacher make a decision*. When a teacher assesses students' strengths and weaknesses, the teacher uses test results to *decide* what instructional objectives to pursue. When a teacher assesses students' progress, the teacher uses test results to *decide* whether certain parts of the ongoing instructional program need to be altered. When a teacher assesses students to help assign grades, the teacher uses students' performances to *decide* which students get which grades. And, finally, when a teacher uses pretest-to-posttest assessment results to indicate how effective an instructional sequence has been, the teacher is trying to *decide* whether the instructional sequence needs to be overhauled. Teachers should never assess students without a clear understanding of what the decision is that will be informed by results of the assessment. The chief function of educational assessment, you see, is to improve the quality of educational decision making.

Taken in concert, the four traditional reasons just described should incline teachers to assess up a storm in their classrooms. But these days even more reasons can be given regarding why teachers need to know about assessment.

■ Why Should Teachers Know about Assessment? Today's Answers

In addition to the four traditional reasons teachers need to know about assessment, there are three new reasons that should incline teachers to dive into the assessment pool. Having emerged during the past decade or so, these are compelling reasons why today's teachers dare not be ignorant regarding educational assessment. Let's consider three new roles for educational assessment and see why these new functions of educational testing should incline you to pump up your assessment knowledge.

Influencing Public Perceptions of Educational Effectiveness

When I was a high school teacher a long while ago, teachers were required to give nationally standardized achievement tests. But, to be honest, no one really paid much attention to the test results. My fellow teachers perused the test-score reports, but were rarely influenced by them. The public was essentially oblivious of the testing process and altogether disinterested in the results unless, of course, parents received a report that their child was performing below expectations. Testing took place in the fifties and sixties, but it was no big deal.

During the seventies and eighties, however, a modest journalistic wrinkle changed all that. Newspaper editors began to publish statewide educational test results on a district-by-district and even school-by-school basis. Citizens could see how their school or district stacked up in comparison to other schools or districts in the state. Districts and schools were *ranked* from top to bottom.

From a news perspective, the publishing of test results was a genuine coup. The test scores were inexpensive to obtain, and readers were really interested in the scores. Residents of low-ranked districts could complain; residents of high-ranked districts could crow. More importantly, because there are no other handy indices of educational effectiveness around, test results became the measuring-stick by which citizens reached conclusions about how well their schools were doing. There are

Decision Time

Pressure from "Higher Ups"

Laura Lund has been teaching second-graders at Horace Mann Elementary School for the past three years. During that period, Laura has become increasingly convinced that "developmentally appropriate instruction" is what she wants in her classroom. Developmentally appropriate instruction takes place when the instructional activities for children are not only matched with the typical developmental level of children in that grade but also matched with the particular developmental level of each child. Because of her growing commitment to developmental appropriateness, and its clear implications for individualized instruction, Laura's students now no longer receive, in unison, the same kinds of massed practice drills in reading and mathematics Laura provided earlier in her career.

Having discovered what kinds of changes are taking place in Laura's second grade, however, the third-grade and fourth-grade teachers in her school have registered great concern over what they regard as less attention to academics, at least less attention of the traditional sort. Because state NCLB tests are given to all third- and fourth-grade students each spring, Laura's colleagues are afraid their students will not perform well on those tests because they will not be skilled at the end of the second grade.

A year or so earlier, when Laura was teaching her second grade in a fairly traditional manner, it was widely recognized that most of her students went on to the third grade with a solid mastery of reading and mathematics. Now, however, the school's third- and fourth-grade teachers fear that "Horace Mann's NCLB test scores may plummet."

As Laura sees it, she has to decide whether to (1) revert to her former instructional practices or (2) maintain her stress on developmentally appropriate instruction. In either case, she realizes that she has to try to justify her action to her colleagues.

 If you were Laura Lund, what would your decision be?

many reports of realtors trying to peddle homes to prospective buyers on the basis that a house was located "in a school district with excellent test scores."

However, if the public's perceptions of educators' prowess were influenced by students' test performances *prior* to the NCLB Act, the public's ideas about educational quality will now be almost totally dependent on NCLB test scores. Indeed, one of the provisions of that federal law is that parents and the public be provided with annual report cards regarding the caliber of a state's school districts and the individual schools within those districts. The dominant determiner of a school's quality, as reflected on those report cards, is to be whether a school's students score well enough on the state's NCLB tests to pass or to fail its annual AYP targets.

Let me be as clear as I can possibly be about this topic, because I think it is a terrifically important one. As matters stand, the NCLB Act is the law of the land. And students' performances on the tests mandated by that statute, as long as the law remains essentially in its current form, will be the primary evidence that the public relies on to judge the quality of schools. This will soon be all too clear to teachers whose students must be tested under provisions of the new law. However, students' performances on a state's NCLB tests will influence the way that *all* teachers are evaluated—even if a particular teacher's own students never come near an NCLB test. Here's how that will happen.

Suppose you teach ninth-grade social studies, so your ninth-graders aren't required to take an NCLB test. Suppose you're a second-grade teacher, so your students aren't required to take an NCLB test. Suppose you're a high school teacher who teaches subjects and grade levels where no NCLB tests are required. In all these "suppose" situations, *your* students won't be NCLB-tested. However, the public's perception of *your* personal effectiveness will most certainly be influenced by the scores of *your* school's students on the NCLB tests that are required for such schools. Let's be honest—Do you want to be a teacher in a "failing" school? Do you want your students' parents to regard *you* as ineffective because you do your teaching in a sub-par school? I doubt it.

The reality is that the performance of any school's students on NCLB tests will splash over on every teacher in that school. If you teach in a school that's regarded as successful, then you will be seen as a member of an effective educational team. The opposite is also true. Unless the NCLB Act is substantially altered, no public school teacher will be able to remain isolated from its impact.

And, as I'll try to point out later in the book, the nature of a school's success on high-stakes external assessments such as the NCLB tests, will (and, indeed, *should*) have an impact on the sorts of classroom assessments you personally choose to employ. We live in an era when public perceptions of schooling are more important than some educators might prefer. Yet, like it or not, that's the reality today's teachers must face.

Helping Evaluate Teachers

Teaching skill is coming under increasing scrutiny these days. With the push for more rigorous evaluation of a classroom teacher's performance, we now see many teacher appraisal systems in which students' test performances constitute one key category of evidence being used to evaluate teachers. Sometimes, teachers are directed to assemble pretest and posttest data that can be used to infer how much learning by students was promoted by the teacher. And, of course, teachers whose students are *required* to take annual NCLB tests understand all too well that their students' scores on those tests will play a prominent role in teacher evaluation—that is, in the evaluation of *their* teaching.

Experienced teachers will be quick to tell you that the caliber of students' test performances is dramatically influenced by the caliber of the students being tested. It should be apparent that a teacher who is blessed with a flock of bright students will almost always get better test results than a teacher who must work with a less able group of students. Nonetheless, a number of statewide and districtwide teacher evaluation systems now call for teachers to assemble tangible evidence of student accomplishments based on classroom assessment. It is clear, therefore, today's teachers need to know enough about educational assessment so they can corral compelling evidence regarding their own students' growth.

Clarifying Teachers' Instructional Intentions

For many years, educational tests were regarded as instructional afterthoughts. Once an instructional unit was over, the teacher got busy cranking out a test. Tests were rarely created before instruction was initiated. Instead, tests were devised *after* instruction to fulfill some of the traditional functions of educational assessment described earlier in the chapter—for example, the assignment of grades.

Today, however, many educational measuring instruments have become high-stakes tests. A *high-stakes test* is an assessment for which important consequences ride on the test's results. One example of an educational high-stakes tests would be a statewide basic skills test that must be mastered before a student graduates. (Note that the important consequences are for the test taker.) Another example would be a districtwide achievement test whose results are publicized so local taxpayers' judgments about educational effectiveness are influenced by the test results. (Note that in this second case the important consequences apply to the educators who prepared the students, not the test takers themselves.)

An NCLB test will fall into this second category of high-stakes tests. Because students' performances on these tests will so powerfully influence the way people regard a school staff's quality, NCLB tests will be genuinely high stakes in nature. You should know, however, there is nothing in the NCLB Act that requires diploma denial or that obliges students to be held back at grade level if they fail to perform well enough on an NCLB test. This federal law imposes no penalties on individual students who score badly. A *state's* decision can transform an NCLB test into one that has an adverse impact on a particular student. Many people continue to be confused by this, for they assume the NCLB Act requires diploma-denial or promotion-denial testing. It's just not so.

Insofar as important consequences are directly linked to assessment results, the content of such high-stakes tests tends to be emphasized instructionally by teachers. Because teachers want their students to perform well on high-stakes tests (for the students' own good and/or for the teacher's benefit), high-stakes tests tend to serve as the curricular magnet seen in Figure 1.1.

Figure 1.1 ■ The Curricular Impact of High-Stakes Tests

On some educational grounds, teachers might prefer that tests did not influence instruction so directly, but the reality is that high-stakes assessment will definitely have an impact on classroom instructional practices. Because this curricular influence is certain to be present, it will be in teachers' and students' best interests if the nature of the upcoming assessment is sufficiently well understood so the teacher can organize the most effective, on-target instruction possible. (Later in the book, we will consider the deficits of teaching exclusively toward assessment targets.) In a sense, however, the more that teachers understand what the innards of a test are, the more effectively they can use this understanding to clarify what's to be sought instructionally.

Even the low-stakes classroom tests routinely employed by teachers can be used to help teachers clarify their instructional targets. Tests should obviously not, then, be instructional afterthoughts. Rather, classroom assessment instruments should always be prepared *prior* to any instructional planning in order for the teacher to better understand what is being sought of students and, therefore, what to incorporate in instructional activities for students. Assessment instruments prepared prior to instruction concretely exemplify a teacher's instructional intentions and, as a consequence, clarify those intentions. Clarified instructional intentions characteristically lead to more effective instructional decisions by the teacher. The better you understand where you're going, the more efficiently you can get there.

To reiterate, we've now looked at three reasons today's teachers, unlike their counterparts of a few decades ago, need to know about assessment. These reasons are supplemental to, not in place of, the previously considered traditional reasons teachers assess students. Here are the three new reasons for teachers' familiarization with educational assessment:

Today's Reasons for Teachers to Know about Assessment

- Test results determine public perceptions of educational effectiveness.
- Students' assessment performances are increasingly seen as part of the teacher evaluation process.
- As clarifiers of instructional intentions, assessment devices can improve instructional quality.

These reasons are also linked to decisions. For instance, when citizens use test results to reach judgments about a school district's effectiveness, those judgments can play a major role in determining what level of taxpayer support will be provided. There are also decisions on the line when students' test scores are used as evidence to evaluate teachers. Such decisions as whether the teacher should be granted tenure or receive merit-pay awards are illustrative of the kinds of decisions that can ride, at least in part, on the results of educational assessments. Finally, from the teacher's perspective, when tests serve as clarifiers of the teacher's instructional intentions, the teacher can make better decisions about how to put together an instructional program likely to help students attain the instructional intentions represented by the assessment. With these three current roles of educational assessment, as was true with the four more traditional roles of educational assessment, test results should contribute to educational *decisions*.

■ What Do Classroom Teachers Really Need to Know about Assessment?

Whether you are already a teacher or are preparing to become a teacher, you really do need to know about educational assessment. But the field of educational assessment contains huge chunks of information. In fact, some educators devote their entire careers to assessment. Clearly, there's more to educational assessment than you probably care to know. The question is, What should *classroom teachers* know about assessment?

The title of this book suggests an answer—namely, *Classroom Assessment: What Teachers Need to Know.* The key word in the title, at least for purposes of this discussion, is *need.* There are oodles of fascinating things about assessment you might learn. You'd even find a few of them interesting (not all that many, I suspect). But to help your students learn, you really don't *need* to know a host of assessment esoterica. This book about educational assessment is deliberately focused on only those things that you really *must know* in order to promote your students' learning most effectively. I am altogether reluctant to clutter your head with a galaxy of nice-to-know but nonessential knowledge about educational assessment. Such nice-to-know content often crowds out the need-to-know content. There is, after all, only so much skull space available.

As a preview, I want to describe briefly what you will have learned by the time you reach the book's index. (I have never had much confidence in any book's index as a teaching tool, so if you haven't learned what's needed by that time—it's too late.) It may be easier for you to get a handle on what you'll be reading if you realize you'll be covering topics dealing chiefly with:

1. Constructing your own assessment instruments
2. Using assessment instruments constructed by others
3. Planning instruction based on instructionally illuminating assessments

Creating Classroom Assessment Devices

Let's start with the kinds of classroom assessment devices you will personally need to create. The chief thing you will learn in this book is how to construct a wide variety of assessment instruments you can use as part of your day-to-day classroom instruction. You really do need to know how to determine what your students have learned—for example, whether they comprehend what they have read. You really do need to know how to get a fix on your students' educationally relevant attitudes—such as how positively disposed your students are toward the subject(s) you're teaching. Thus, you are going to be learning about how to create classroom assessment approaches to measure students' *achievement* (that is, the knowledge and/or skills students acquire) as well as students' *affect* (that is, the educationally pertinent attitudes, interests, and values influenced by school).

As suggested earlier, the kinds of classroom assessment procedures you'll be learning about will extend well beyond traditional paper-and-pencil testing instruments. You may even learn about several assessment approaches with which you are currently unfamiliar.

In a related vein, you will also learn how to judge the quality of the assessment devices *you* create. And, at the same time, you will learn how to judge the quality of assessment devices created by others. Those "others" might be your own colleagues or, perhaps, the folks who devise large-scale assessment instruments. It may seem presumptuous for me to suggest that you, a classroom teacher (in practice or in preparation), could be judging the efforts of folks who create nationally standardized educational tests. But you'll discover from this book that you will, indeed, possess the knowledge and skill necessary to distinguish between tawdry and terrific practices by those who create such large-scale educational tests. In particular, you can use your new knowledge to judge the quality of the NCLB tests being used in your state. Those tests are going to be so important that, if you are teaching in a state whose NCLB tests are educationally unsound, you definitely need to know it.

Fundamentally, educational assessment rests on a foundation of common sense. Once you learn the technical vocabulary of assessment, you'll be able to identify departures from commonsensical assessment practices, whether those departures are seen in your own tests, in the tests of a teacher down the hall, or in the tests created by state or national assessment specialists. In short, after you finish this book, you really need not be deferent to any "measurement experts." You'll know enough to spot serious shortcomings in their work.

In the very next chapter, for example, you will learn about three criteria you can use to evaluate all educational tests. Those criteria apply with equal force to tests you might develop as well as to tests that are commercially developed. Once you get the hang of how to evaluate tests, you can apply this skill in many settings.

Interpreting Standardized Test Results

Because your students will often be assessed with nationally standardized or state-developed tests, you will need to know how to interpret the results of such tests. In general, commercially developed educational tests focus either on students' *achievement,* which, as noted earlier, deals with the knowledge and skills that students have acquired, or on *aptitude,* which is a term used to describe a student's learning *potential.* You should know, however, that the term *aptitude* is definitely falling from grace these days. In the old days, when I was a tyke, people talked about intelligence. As a prospective teacher, I learned all about the intelligence quotient (IQ), which was a numerical way of indicating the degree to which a particular individual's intellectual abilities exceeded or fell short of conventional expectations for such individuals.

But "intelligence" has fallen decisively out of favor with educators during the past few decades. The term *intelligence* conveys the notion that students possess an inborn potential schools can do little to influence. Yet, the so-called intelligence tests, widely used until recently, usually measured what students had learned at school or, more importantly, what students had learned at home. Thus, the term *aptitude* has been increasingly used rather than *intelligence* in order to convey a notion of a student's academic potential. But even the term *aptitude* tends to create the perception there is some sort of innate cap on one's potential. Because of this perception, we now find that the commercial test makers who formerly created so-called intelligence tests, and then renamed them aptitude tests, are looking for a

but what does this have to do with
Teaching?

This chapter contains over a half-dozen reasons teachers need to learn about assessment. Actually, there are *seven* reasons in the chapter, and that's one more reason than a half-dozen. (Notice how low-level the arithmetic in this book is going to be!)

But let me single out the *two* reasons I think, *from an instructional perspective,* all teachers need to know about testing. The first of these reasons is the last of the seven reasons cited in the chapter—namely, the *instructional-planning payoffs* teachers can get from a more clear understanding of what they're trying to have their students accomplish. Because a properly constructed classroom test can truly exemplify what a teacher is trying to achieve, the resulting *clarity of intention* helps teachers make more astute decisions when they plan their instruction.

When I recall my own early years as a high school teacher, I remember how often I simply whipped together lesson plans that *seemed* somewhat instructional. Yet, my planning was almost never guided by a truly clearheaded notion of what knowledge, skills, or attitudes I wanted my students to possess when the instruction was over. If I had relied on my classroom tests to clarify what I wanted my students to become, I'm certain my lessons would have been far better focused on intended instructional outcomes.

The second reason I think all teachers should become more astute regarding assessment is also instructionally rooted. It's the second of the four traditional reasons considered in the chapter—namely, so teachers can *monitor students' progress.* If teachers use students' assessed levels of achievement to determine whether the current instructional plan is splendid or sucko, then teachers' changes in lessons can, if warranted, be made. Without the evidence yielded by classroom formative assessments, a teacher will often fail to spot instructional inadequacies. As Black and Wiliam, the British investigators, made quite clear, the instructional dividends from monitoring students' progress can be striking. And their views were based on solid research investigations, not wishful yearnings. My grandparents came to the United States from Great Britain, so I typically groove on anything that's asserted with a British accent. But, then, doesn't everyone?

less negatively loaded descriptor. Interestingly, the tests themselves, although they've been relabeled, haven't really changed all that much.

At any rate, you'll learn how to make sense out of the kinds of reports regarding student performance released by those who conduct large-scale assessments. You will need this knowledge not only to inform your own decisions about classroom instruction but also to interpret students' test performances to parents who may demand answers to questions such as, "What does my son's standardized test performance at 40th percentile really mean?" or "If my fifth-grade daughter earned a grade-equivalent score at the eighth-grade level on this year's standardized achievement test, why shouldn't she be promoted?" In short, you'll learn how to interpret students' performances on both *achievement tests* and *aptitude tests.*

Instructionally Illuminating Assessment

Earlier, it was suggested that because assessment devices exemplify a teacher's instructional intentions, those assessment instruments can clarify the teacher's instructional decision making. You'll learn more about how the link between testing and teaching can prove beneficial to your students because you can provide more on-target and effective instruction.

On the other hand, you'll also learn how some teachers inappropriately prepare their students for tests, particularly for high-stakes tests. You will learn about ways of judging whether a given test-preparation practice is (1) in students' best interests from an educational perspective and (2) in educators' best interests from an ethical perspective. In short, you'll learn about the increasingly important relationship between instruction and assessment.

Parent Talk

Mr. and Mrs. Smothers are attending a back-to-school night at a middle school where their daughter, Cathy, is a fifth-grader. After briefly leafing through Cathy's math portfolio and language arts portfolio, they get around to the real reason they've come to school. Mrs. Smothers, looking more than a little belligerent, says, "Cathy tells us she gets several teacher-made tests in class every week. All that testing can't be necessary. It obviously takes away the time you spend teaching her! Why is there so darn much testing in your class?"

 If I were you, here's how I'd respond to Mrs. Smothers:

"I suppose that it might seem to you there's too much testing going on in my class, and I can understand your concern about testing-time taking away from teaching-time. But let me explain how the time my students spend doing classroom assessments really leads to much *better* use of instructional time.

"You see, the way I use classroom assessment is to make sure my instruction is on target and, most importantly, that I don't waste the children's time. Last month, for instance, we started a new unit in social studies and I gave students a short pretest to find out what they already knew. To my delight, I discovered that almost all of the students—including Cathy—knew well over half of what I had been planning to teach.

"Based on the pretest's results, I was able to shorten the social studies unit substantially, and spend the extra time giving students more practice on their map-interpretation skills. You probably saw some of the maps Cathy was interpreting as part of her homework assignments.

"Mr. and Mrs. Smothers, I want Cathy's time in class to be as well spent as possible. And to make sure of that, I use formal and informal classroom tests to be certain that I'm teaching her, and her classmates, what they really need to learn."

 Now, how would you respond to Mrs. Smothers?

Later, you'll learn about a way to build classroom assessments so that they'll have a decisively positive impact on how well you teach. *Tests,* if deliberately created with instruction in mind, *can boost your personal success as a teacher.* We'll dig into that topic in Chapter 12.

There's one other issue that I'd like to bring to your attention—namely, the possibility (after you've finished the book) of your helping *parents* learn more about educational assessment. And why, you might ask, should a teacher be messing around trying to promote parental measurement moxie? It's a good question. And the answer is this: Parents who are *assessment literate* will be better able to *help you help their children learn* more successfully.

You see, most parents know little more about testing than what they can recall, often vaguely, from their own classroom days as students. But the nature of classroom testing has changed dramatically since that time. Not only are there new approaches to assessment being used in classrooms (all of which you'll learn about in this scintillating book), but students' test scores are also being used to judge the success of teachers' instructional efforts. You'll learn in Chapter 15 that, in many instances, this is a dumb idea. If you and your students' parents truly understand the fundamentals of educational assessment, you can work together in many ways that will benefit your students. Assessment-literate parents can be a potent force to counter the serious misuses of educational tests we see so often today. And, if you are teaching in a state whose officials have opted to use instructionally insensitive NCLB tests, you'll find that assessment-literate parents can be a potent political force who might, if you're lucky, help get better NCLB tests installed in your state.

■ A Three-Chapter Preview

Because the next three chapters in the book are highly related, I'm going to do a little previewing of what you'll be encountering in those chapters. Later in the book, you'll learn all sorts of nifty ways to assess your students. Not only will you learn how to create a variety of traditional paper-and-pencil tests, such as the true-false and multiple-choice instruments, but you'll also discover how to generate many of the alternative forms of educational assessment receiving so much attention these days. To illustrate, you will learn how to create really demanding performance tests, student portfolios, and assessment devices that can gauge your students' attitudes and interests. But when you read about these assessment approaches in later chapters, it will make it easier for you to determine their worth *to you* if you know how to evaluate the quality of educational assessment approaches. The next three chapters give you the concepts you will need to do such evaluating.

If you're evaluating a test—whether it's your own test, a test developed by another teacher, or a test distributed by a commercial test publisher—you will need some criteria to help you decide whether the test should be wildly applauded or, instead, sent swiftly to a paper shredder.

Judging educational tests, in fact, is fundamentally no different from evaluating brownies. If, for example, you are ever called on to serve as a judge in a brownie bake-off, you'll need some evaluative criteria to use when you appraise

Table 1.1 ■ Potential Criteria for Brownie Judging

Criterion	Optimal Status
■ Fudginess	Should reek of chocolate flavor—so much, indeed, as to be considered fundamentally fudgelike.
■ Chewiness	Must be so chewy as to approximate munching on a lump of fudge-flavored Silly Putty.
■ Acceptable Additives	Although sliced walnuts and extra chocolate chips are praiseworthy, shredded raw brussels sprouts are not.

the merits of the contending brownies. I realize your preferences may differ from mine, but if I were chief justice in a brownie-judging extravaganza, I would employ the three evaluative criteria presented in Table 1.1. If you are a brownie aficionado and prefer other evaluative criteria, I can overlook such preferences. You may, for example, adore nut-free and high-rise brownies. However, I have no personal interest in establishing a meaningful brownie-bond with you.

When we evaluate just about anything, we employ explicit or implicit evaluative criteria to determine quality. And although there may be substantial disagreements among brownie devotees regarding the criteria to employ when appraising their favorite baked goods, there are far fewer disputes when it comes to judging the quality of educational assessment devices. In the next three chapters, we're going to look at the three widely accepted criteria that are used to evaluate educational assessment procedures. Two of the criteria have been around for a long while. The third is a relative newcomer, having figured in the evaluation of educational tests only during the last couple of decades.

In Table 1.2 are the three criteria we'll be considering in the next three chapters. The capsule description of each criterion presented in the table will let you

Table 1.2 ■ A Preview of the Three Test-Evaluation Criteria to Be Considered in Chapters 2, 3, and 4

Criterion	Brief Description
■ Reliability	Reliability represents the *consistency* with which an assessment procedure measures whatever it's measuring.
■ Validity	Validity reflects the defensibility of the *score-based inference* made on the basis of an educational assessment procedure.
■ Absence-of-Bias	Absence-of-bias signifies the degree to which assessment procedures are free of elements that would *offend* or *penalize* students on the basis of students' gender, ethnicity, and so on.

know what's coming. After considering each of these three criteria in its very own chapter, I'll level with you regarding what classroom teachers *really* need to know about the three criteria. In other words, I'll toss out my personal opinion regarding whether you should establish an intimate relationship or merely a nodding acquaintance with each criterion.

Of all the things you will learn from reading this book, and there will be lots of them, the topics treated in the next three chapters are regarded by psychometricians as the most important. (*Psychometrician,* by the way, is simply a ritzy descriptor for a measurement specialist.) Chapters 2, 3, and 4 will familiarize you with the pivotal criteria by which assessment specialists tell whether educational assessment procedures are stellar or stupid. But because this book is focused on classroom assessment, we'll be looking at the content of the next three chapters in relation to *educational decisions* that must be made by classroom teachers. I promise not to mess around with psychometric abstractions merely because they induce theoretical thrills.

■ Chapter Summary

In this first chapter, the emphasis was on why teachers really need to know about assessment. Early in the chapter, the accountability provisions of the NCLB Act were briefly described because this federal law's impact on most teachers' instructional and assessment decisions is profound. *Educational assessment* was defined as a formal attempt to determine students' status with respect to educational variables of interest. Much of the chapter was devoted to a consideration of why teachers must become knowledgeable regarding educational assessment. Based on teachers' classroom activities, four traditional reasons were given for why teachers assess—namely, to (1) diagnose students' strengths and weaknesses, (2) monitor students' progress, (3) assign grades, and (4) determine a teacher's own instructional effectiveness. Based on recent uses of educational assessment results, three more current reasons teachers need to know about instruction were identified. Those more recent functions of educational tests are to (1) influence public perceptions of educational effectiveness, (2) help evaluate teachers, and (3) clarify teachers' instructional intentions. Regardless of the specific application of test results, however, it was emphasized that teachers should use the results of assessments *to make better decisions.* That's really the only excuse for taking up students' time with assessment.

The chapter identified three major outcomes to be attained by those reading the book—namely, becoming more knowledgeable about how to (1) construct and evaluate their own classroom tests, (2) interpret results of standardized tests, and (3) teach students to master what's assessed in classroom and high-stakes tests. It was also suggested that an assessment-literate teacher should attempt to promote parents' assessment literacy. The chapter was concluded by a preview of three test-evaluation criteria to be considered in the next three chapters.

Self-Check

This was the book's first chapter. If you're not sure I'm correct, you may wish to check the table of contents. As an initial chapter, it was decisively heavier on pep talk and previewing than on solid assessment-related content. However, to help you get in the groove for the postchapter merriment associated with future chapters, I've included a brief self-check exercise section so you can become familiar with what will be coming up at the end of every chapter. An answer key for all such self-check exercises is provided immediately after the discussion questions (entitled Pondertime to encourage you to devote meaningful time to pondering) and immediately before the references section (entitled Additional Stuff because it is, in fact, additional stuff). The answer key will be presented in slightly smaller type to make you pay careful attention and to make your eyes hurt.

1. Without referring to the text, and using your own words (although, if you're stuck, you can borrow some of mine), how would you define *educational assessment?*

   _____

   _____

   _____

2. An educational *test* is a term that's been around for a long time. Why was it suggested in the chapter that educational *assessment* is the preferred descriptor these days?

   _____

   _____

   _____

3. Review the following list of six fictitious quotes from classroom teachers and decide which four quotations represent the *traditional* reasons that teachers are likely to give in response to the question, Why should you, as a teacher, test your students?
   a. "Because I need to base my students' grades on something other than smiling faces."
   b. "Because I can figure out, before I begin to teach, what my students already know and don't know."
   c. "Because testing takes up classroom time, and I have so many classroom hours to fill and so little content to cover."
   d. "Because I can tell whether my pupils have learned, hence whether I've taught well."

    e. "Because I can see what kinds of progress my students are making, and can give more instruction to those who need it."

    f. "Because I want to learn more about what kinds of pronouns to use when modifying gerunds."

4. (*Note:* The following self-check exercise represents the book's very first multiple-choice item. It will surely not be its last.)

    Which of the following four statements does *not* represent one of the *current* reasons cited in the chapter that today's teacher should either learn about educational assessment or be considered a consummate cluck?

    a. Educational measuring devices, as clarifications for instructional intentions, can improve instructional quality.

    b. Student performances on high-stakes tests substantially influence public perceptions of educational effectiveness.

    c. Today's teacher evaluation systems increasingly incorporate students' performances on educational assessment devices.

    d. Educational assessment devices are now being used to advertise young people's fashionwear.

(Remember, a Self-Check Key is always provided following the Pondertime questions.)

? Pondertime

Here are a few assessment-related questions for you to ponder. Such pondering can be done in public, as in a class discussion, or in private, as in by yourself. A recent survey of pondering practices in Pennsylvania indicated that public pondering was preferred over private pondering, even by consenting adults, almost two to one. (There was a sampling error for the survey of ±100%.)

1. Why do you think we have witnessed such an increased interest in educational assessment during the past decade or so?

2. In many states, prospective teachers are not required to take any courses dealing with educational assessment. Why do you think this is so?

3. What kind of rights, if any, does the public have regarding educational assessment?

4. Recalling your personal days in school, what level of expertise do you think your own teachers possessed regarding educational assessment?

5. Do you think the movement to discourage the use of the terms *intelligence* and *aptitude* is appropriate? Why?

6. Do you believe that classroom teachers will derive any advantages from promoting parental assessment literacy? If so, what might those advantages be?

Self-Check Key

1. Any reasonable paraphrase of the following definition, given on page 6, will be acceptable: "Educational assessment is a formal attempt to determine students' status with respect to educational variables of interest."

2. Two related reasons were given—namely, that (1) the phrase *educational test* conjures up notions of only paper-and-pencil instruments and (2) many worthwhile educational outcomes are not best assessed by paper-and-pencil tests.

3. Choices a, b, d, and e are winners. Choices c and f, therefore, are losers.

4. If you did not choose d for this warm-up, giveaway item, you are hereby sentenced to a rereading of the entire first chapter.

■ Additional Stuff

Allensworth, Elaine M. (2005). "Dropout Rates After High-Stakes Testing in Elementary School: A Study of the Contradictory Effects of Chicago's Efforts to End Social Promotion." *Educational Evaluation and Policy Analysis, 27*, no. 4 (Winter): 341–364.

Black, Paul, Christine Harrison, Clare Lee, Bethan Marshall, and Dylan Wiliam. (2002). *Working Inside the Black Box*. London: King's College, London.

Black, Paul, and Dylan Wiliam. (1998). "Inside the Black Box: Raising Standards through Classroom Assessment." *Phi Delta Kappan, 80*, no. 2 (October): 139–148.

Egan, Kieran. (2003). "Testing What for What?" *Educational Leadership, 61*, no. 3 (November): 27–30.

Harvard Education Press. (2003). *Spotlight on High-Stakes Testing (*from the Editors of the Harvard Education Letter). Cambridge, MA: Author.

Kozol, Jonathan. (2006). "Standardized Testing: The Do-or-Die Agenda." *Principal, 85*, no. 4 (March/April): 18–23.

Goldberg, Mark. (2005). "Test Mess 2: Are We Doing Better a Year Later?" *Phi Delta Kappan, 86*, no. 5 (January): 389–395.

Kim, James S., and Gail. L. Sunderman. (2005). "Measuring Academic Proficiency Under the No Child Left Behind Act: Implications for Educational Equity." *Educational Researcher, 34*, no. 8 (November): 3–13.

Popham, W. James. (2001). *The Truth About Testing: An Educator's Call to Action*. Alexandria, VA: Association for Supervision and Curriculum Development.

Popham, W. James. (2005). *America's "Failing" Schools: How Parents and Teachers Can Cope with No Child Left Behind*. New York: RoutledgeFalmer.

Stiggins, Richard J. (2004). *Student-Involved Assessment FOR Learning* (4th ed.). Columbus, OH: Merrill Prentice-Hall.

■ Nonprint Stuff

Northwest Regional Educational Laboratory. *Understanding the Meaning and Importance of Quality Classroom Assessment* (Videotape #NREL-2). Los Angeles: IOX Assessment Associates.

■ Cyber Stuff

■ *The Council of Chief State School Officers (CCSSO)* is a nationwide, nonprofit organization of public officials who lead K–12 education in the 50 states. This website is a rich resource for those who wish to monitor state-level assessment activities throughout the United States. The website also contains a host of practical guidelines regarding how states can satisfy the accountability requirements of the No Child Left Behind Act. www.ccsso.org

■ *IOX Assessment Associates*, established in 1968, offers a website describing a variety of staff-development and parent-education videotapes, many of which deal with assessment-related issues. The website also contains a number of essays focusing on assessment topics. A highlight of the website is a photo of the author of this book (that's right, the one you're currently reading) as a Cub Scout. I was, at that age, quite adorable. www.ioxassessment.com

■ *The No Child Left Behind* website of the U.S. Department of Education provides a clear description of the basics of the NCLB Act, signed into law by President Bush on January 8, 2002. The website contains a wealth of information that parents of school-age children will find useful. A continually updated news center offers users of the site a range of NCLB-related information emanating from the office of the Secretary of Education. www.nclb.gov

Companion Website

To access chapter objectives, practice tests, weblinks, and flashcards, visit the companion website at **www.ablongman.com/popham5e.**

mylabschool
Where the classroom comes to life!

MyLabSchool is a collection of online tools for your success in this course, your licensure exams, and your teaching career. Discover where the classroom comes to life by visiting **www.mylabschool.com** to access the following resources:

■ Video clips from real classrooms

■ An archive of real-life cases

■ Help with your research papers using Research Navigator™

■ Career Center with resources for:
    Praxis exams and licensure preparation
    Professional portfolio development
    Job search and interview techniques
    Lesson planning with state standard correlations

2

Reliability of Assessment

R eliability is such a cherished commodity. We all want our automobiles, washing machines, and spouses to be reliable. The term *reliability* simply reeks of solid goodness. It conjures up visions of meat loaf, mashed potatoes, and a mother's love. Clearly, reliability is an attribute to be sought.

In the realm of educational assessment, reliability is also a desired attribute. We definitely want our educational assessments to be reliable. In matters related to measurement, however, reliability has a very restricted meaning. When you encounter the term *reliability* in any assessment context, you should draw a mental equal sign between *reliability* and *consistency*, because reliability refers to the consistency with which a test measures whatever it's measuring:

Reliability = Consistency

From a classroom teacher's perspective, there are two important ways the concept of reliability can rub up against your day-to-day activities. First, there's the possibility your own classroom assessments might lack sufficient reliability to be doing a good job for you and your students. Second, if your students are obliged to complete any sort of commercially published standardized tests, you're apt to find a parent or two who might want to discuss the adequacy of those standardized tests. And reliability, as noted in the previous chapter's preview, such as for your state's NCLB tests, is an evaluative criterion by which external standardized tests are judged. You may need to know enough about reliability's wrinkles so you'll be able to talk sensibly with parents about the way reliability is employed to judge the quality of standardized tests.

The *Standards for Educational and Psychological Testing* (AERA, 1999), a joint publication of the American Educational Research Association, the American Psychological Association, and the National Council on Measurement in Education, is generally conceded to be the most important document governing educational assessment procedures because it reflects the opinions of leading assessment experts about educational and psychological testing. If you were to read page 25 of the 1999 *Standards*, you'd find solid support for the idea that assessment reliability equals assessment consistency. But the authors of the *Standards* also send a clear message that most experienced teachers already know—namely, a given child's test performances vary.

> *The usefulness of behavioral measurement presupposes that individuals and groups exhibit some degree of stability in their behavior. However, successive samples of behavior from the same person are rarely identical in all pertinent aspects. An individual's performances, products, and responses to sets of test questions vary in their quality or character from one occasion to another, even under strictly controlled conditions. This variation is reflected in the examinee's scores. The causes of this variability are generally unrelated to the purposes of measurement. An examinee may try harder, may make luckier guesses, be more alert, feel less anxious, or enjoy better health on one occasion than another. An examinee may have knowledge, experience, or understanding that is more relevant to some tasks than to others in the domain sampled by the test. Some individuals may exhibit less variation in their scores than others, but no examinee is completely consistent. Because of this variation and, in some instances, because of subjectivity in the scoring process, an individual's obtained score and the average score of a group will always reflect at least a small amount of measurement error. (AERA, 1999)*

Another way of thinking about reliability is that it refers to the extent to which students' scores on tests are free from errors of measurement.

But consistency, in educational assessment, appears in three varieties, not merely one. In other words, there are three different ways to think about consistency of measurement. To assume that these three kinds of consistency are interchangeable is erroneous. Let's consider each of the three varieties of consistency you're apt to encounter in educational assessment. Table 2.1 previews the three types of reliability evidence you'll be considering in the chapter.

Table 2.1 ■ Three Types of Reliability Evidence

Type of Reliability Evidence	Brief Description
■ Stability (Test-Retest)	Consistency of results among different testing occasions
■ Alternate Form	Consistency of results among two or more different forms of a test
■ Internal Consistency	Consistency in the way an assessment instrument's items function

■ Stability Reliability

The first kind of reliability we'll be looking at is called *stability reliability*. This conception of reliability often comes to people's minds when someone asserts that reliability equals consistency. Stability, as a form of reliability, refers to consistency of test results over time. We want our educational assessments of students to yield similar results even if the tests were administered on different occasions. For example, suppose you gave your students a midterm exam on Tuesday, but later in the afternoon a masked thief (1) snatched your briefcase containing the students' test papers, (2) jumped into a waiting armored personnel-carrier, and (3) escaped to an adjacent state or nation. The next day, after describing to your students how their examinations were purloined by a masked personnel-carrier person, you ask them to retake the midterm exam. Because there have been no intervening events of significance, such as more instruction from you on the topics covered by the examination, you would expect your students' Wednesday examination scores to be fairly similar to their Tuesday examination scores. And that's what the *stability* conception of test reliability refers to—consistency over time. If the Wednesday scores aren't comparable to the Tuesday scores, then your midterm exam would be judged to have little stability reliability.

To get a fix on how stable an assessment's results are over time, we usually test students on one occasion, wait a week or two, then retest them with the same instrument. For that reason, stability reliability is often referred to as *test-retest reliability*. (In fact, because measurement specialists typically use the descriptors *stability reliability* and *test-retest reliability* interchangeably, you are hereby allowed to do the same thing. Simply choose which of the two labels you prefer.) It is important, however, that no significant events that might alter students' performances on the second assessment occasion have taken place between the two testing occasions. For instance, suppose the test you are administering assessed students' knowledge regarding World War II. If a widely viewed television mini-series about World War II is presented during the interval between the initial test and the retest, it is likely the performances of the students who watched the mini-series will be higher on the second test because of their exposure to test-relevant information in the mini-series. Thus, for test-retest results to be interpreted accurately, it is imperative that no significant performance-influencing events occur during the between-assessments interval.

Typically, a *correlation coefficient* is computed between students' test scores on the two assessment occasions—that is, the initial test and the retest. A correlation coefficient reflects the degree of similarity between students' scores on the two tests. If you've already taken a statistics course, you probably know about correlation coefficients. If not, for purposes of this discussion you can think of a correlation coefficient as a numerical indicator (ranging from +1.0 to −1.0) that reflects the degree to which individuals' performances on two sets of test scores are related. A correlation coefficient (signified by r) near 1.0 indicates a strong relationship. A correlation coefficient near 0 indicates a weak relationship. Thus, if the test-retest r for two sets of students' test scores were .84, this would indicate stu-

Decision Time

Quibbling over Quizzes

Wayne Wong's first-year teaching assignment is a group of 28 fifth-grade students in an inner-city elementary school. Because Wayne believes in the importance of frequent assessments as motivational devices for his students, he typically administers one or more surprise quizzes per week to his students. Admittedly, after the first month or so, very few of Wayne's fifth-graders are really "surprised" when Wayne whips out one of his unannounced quizzes. Students' scores on the quizzes are used by Wayne to compute each student's six-weeks' grades.

Mrs. Halverson, the principal of Wayne's school, has visited his class on numerous occasions. Mrs. Halverson believes that it is her "special responsibility" to see that first-year teachers receive adequate instructional support.

Mrs. Halverson has recently completed a master's degree from the local branch of the state university. As part of her coursework, she was required to take a class in "educational measurement." She earned an A. Because the professor for that course stressed the importance of "reliability as a crucial ingredient of solid educational tests," Mrs. Halverson has been pressing Wayne to compute some form of reliability evidence for his surprise quizzes. Wayne has been resisting her suggestion because, in his view, he administers so many quizzes that the computation of reliability indices for the quizzes would surely be a time-consuming pain. He believes that if he's forced to fuss with reliability estimates for each quiz, he'll reduce the number of quizzes he uses. And, because he thinks students' perceptions that they may be quizzed really stimulates them to be prepared, he is reluctant to lessen the number of quizzes he gives. Even after hearing Wayne's position, however, Mrs. Halverson seems unwilling to bend.

If you were Wayne Wong and were faced with this problem, what would your decision be?

dents' relative test performances on the two testing occasions were quite similar. If the test-retest r were only .23, this would indicate the test yielded performances on the two occasions weren't all that similar. If there's a high reliability coefficient, it doesn't necessarily signify students' scores on the two tests are identical. Rather, it signifies students' *relative* performances on the initial test (relative, that is, to the other students' scores) are similar to their relative performances on the retest.

Another procedure for calculating the stability of students' performances on the same test administered on two assessment occasions is to determine the percentage of classifications regarding students that were consistent over time. Such a *classification-consistency* approach to the determination of a test's stability reliability might be used, for instance, when a teacher was deciding which students would be exempted from further study about Topic *X*. To illustrate, if the teacher establishes an 80% correct level as the degree of proficiency required in order to exempt students from further Topic X study, then on a test-retest basis the teacher would simply determine the percentage of students who were classified the same way on the two assessment occasions. The focus in such an approach would not be on the specific scores a student earned, but only on whether the *same classification* was made about the student. Thus, if Jill Jones earned an 84% correct score on the first testing occasion and a 99% correct score on the second testing occasion, Jill would be exempted from further Topic X study in both cases because she had surpassed the 80% correct standard both times. The classifications for Jill would be consistent, so the teacher's decisions about Jill would also be consistent. However, if Harry Harvey received a score of 65% correct on the first testing occasion and a score of 82% correct on the second testing occasion, different classifications on the two occasions would lead to different decisions being made about Harry's need to keep plugging away at Topic X. To determine the percentage of a test's classification consistency, you would simply make the kinds of calculations seen in Table 2.2.

Whether you use a correlational approach or a classification-consistency approach to the determination of a test's consistency over time, it is apparent you'll need to test students twice in order to determine the test's stability. If a test is yielding rather unstable results between two occasions, it's really difficult to put much confidence in that test's results. Just think about it—if you can't tell whether your students have really performed wonderfully or woefully on a test because their scores might vary depending on the day you test them, how can you proceed to make sensible instructional decisions about those students?

Realistically, of course, why would a sane, nonsadistic classroom teacher administer the identical test to the same students on two different testing occasions? It's pretty tough to come up with a decent answer to that question. What's most important for teachers to realize is that there always is a meaningful level of *instability* between students' performances on two different testing occasions, *even if the very same test is used*. And this realization, of course, should disincline teachers to treat a student's test score as though it is a superscientific representation of the student's achievement level.

Table 2.2 ■ An Illustration of How Classification-Consistency Stability Is Determined

A. Percent of students identified as exempt from further study on both assessment occasions	=	42%
B. Percent of students identified as requiring further study on both assessment occasions	=	46%
C. Percent of students classified differently on the two occasions	=	12%
D. Percentage of the test's classification-consistency (A + B)	=	88%

■ Alternate-Form Reliability

The second of our three kinds of reliability evidence for educational assessment instruments focuses on the consistency between two forms of a test—forms that are supposedly equivalent. *Alternate-form reliability* deals with the question of whether two or more allegedly equivalent test forms are, in fact, equivalent.

In the classroom, teachers rarely have reason to generate two forms of a particular assessment instrument. Multiple forms of educational tests are more commonly encountered in high-stakes assessment situations, such as when students must pass basic skills tests before receiving diplomas. In such settings, students who fail an examination when it is initially administered are usually given other opportunities to pass the examination. Clearly, to make the assessment process fair, the challenge of assessment hurdle faced by individuals when they took the initial test must be the same as the challenge of assessment hurdle faced by individuals when they take the makeup examination. Alternate-form reliability evidence bears on the comparability of two (or more) test forms.

Multiple test forms are apt to be found whenever educators fear that if the same test were simply reused, students who had access to subsequent administrations of the test would be advantaged because those later test takers would have learned about the test's contents, and thus have an edge over the first-time test takers. Typically, therefore, in a variety of high-stakes settings such as (1) those involving high school diploma tests or (2) the certification examinations governing entry to a profession, multiple test forms are employed.

To determine the degree of alternate-form consistency, procedural approaches are employed that are in some ways similar to those used for the determination of stability reliability. First, the two test forms are administered to the same individuals. Ideally, there would be little or no delay between the administration of the two test forms. For example, suppose you were interested in determining the comparability of two forms of a district-developed language arts examination. Let's say you could round up 100 suitable students. Because the examination requires only 20 to 25 minutes to complete, you could administer both forms of the language arts test (Form A and Form B) to each of the 100 students during a single period. To eliminate the impact of the order in which the tests were completed by students, you could ask 50 of the students to complete Form A, then Form B. The remaining students would be directed to take Form B first, then Form A.

Once you obtain each student's scores on the two forms, you could compute a correlation coefficient reflecting the relationship between students' performances on the two forms. As with stability reliability, the closer the alternate-form correlation coefficient is to 1.0, the more agreement there is between students' relative scores on the two forms. Alternatively, you could use the kind of classification-consistency approach for the determination of alternate-form reliability that was described earlier for stability reliability. To illustrate, you could decide on a level of performance that would lead to different classifications for students, then simply calculate the percentage of identically classified students on the basis of the two test forms. For instance, if a pass/fail cutoff score of 65% correct had been chosen, then you would simply add up (1) the percent of students who passed both times (that is, scored 65% or better) and (2) the percent of students who failed both times (that is, scored 64% or lower). The addition of those two percentages yields a classification-consistency estimate of alternate-form reliability for the two test forms under consideration.

As you can see, although both species of reliability we've considered thus far are related—in the sense that both deal with consistency—they represent very different conceptions of consistency. Stability (test-retest) reliability deals with consistency over time for a single examination. Alternate-form reliability deals with the consistency of challenge inherent in two or more supposedly equivalent forms of the same examination.

Alternate-form reliability is not established by proclamation. Rather, evidence must be gathered regarding the between-form consistency of the test forms under scrutiny. Accordingly, if you're ever reviewing a commercially published or state-developed test that claims to have equivalent forms available, be sure you inspect the evidence that those claims of equivalence are supported. Determine how the evidence of alternate-form comparability was gathered—that is, under what circumstances. Make sure that what's described makes sense to you.

Later in the book (Chapter 13), we'll consider a procedure known as *item response theory* that, whenever large numbers of students are tested, can be employed to adjust students' scores on different forms of tests not actually equivalent in difficulty. For purposes of our current discussion, however, simply remember that alternate-form reliability is a special form of consistency dealing with the comparability of two or more test forms.

■ Internal Consistency Reliability

The final entrant in our reliability sweepstakes is called *internal consistency reliability*. It really is quite a different creature than stability and alternate-form reliability. Internal consistency does not focus on the consistency of students' scores on a test. Rather, internal consistency deals with the extent to which the *items* in an educational assessment instrument are functioning in a consistent fashion.

Whereas stability and alternate-form reliability require two administrations of a test, internal consistency reliability can be computed on the basis of only a single test administration. It is for this reason, one suspects, we tend to encounter internal consistency estimates of reliability far more frequently than we encounter its two reliability brethren. Yet, as you will see, internal consistency reliability is quite a different commodity than stability and alternate-form reliability.

Internal consistency reliability reflects the degree to which the items on a test are functioning in a consistent manner—that is, the degree to which the test's items are functioning *homogeneously*. Many educational tests are designed to measure a single variable, such as students' "reading achievement" or their "attitude toward school." If a test's items are all truly measuring a single variable, then each of the test's items ought to be doing fundamentally the same assessment job. To the extent the test's items are tapping the same variable, of course, the responses to those items by students will tend to be quite similar. For example, if all the items in a 20-item test on problem solving do, in fact, measure one's problem-solving ability, then students who are skilled problem solvers should get most of the 20 test's items right, whereas unskilled problem solvers should miss most of the test's 20 items. The more homogeneous the responses yielded by a test's items, the higher will be the test's internal consistency.

There are several different formulae around for computing a test's internal consistency.[1] Each formula is intended to yield a numerical estimate reflective of the extent to which the assessment procedure's items are functioning homogeneously.

For tests containing items on which a student can be right or wrong, such as a multiple-choice item, the most commonly used internal consistency approaches are the *Kuder-Richardson* procedures (usually referred to as the K-R formulae). For tests containing items on which students can be given different numbers of points, such as essay items, the most common internal consistency approach is called Cronbach's *coefficient alpha* after its originator Lee J. Cronbach. Incidentally, if you want to impress your colleagues with your newfound and altogether exotic assessment vocabulary, you might want to know that test items scored right or wrong (such as true-false items) are called *dichotomous* items, while those that yield multiple scores (such as essay items) are called *polytomous* items. Try to work *polytomous* into a casual conversation around the watercooler. Its intimidation power is awesome.

Parent Talk

One of your strongest students, Raphael Hobbs, has recently received his scores on a nationally standardized achievement test used in your school district. Raphael's subtest percentile scores (in comparison to the test's norm group) were the following:

Subject	Percentile
Language Arts	85th
Mathematics	92nd
Science	91st
Social Studies	51st

Raphael's father, a retired U.S. Air Force colonel, has called for an after-school conference with you about the test results. He has used his home computer and the Internet to discover that the internal consistency reliabilities on all four subtests, as published in the test's technical manual, are higher than .93. When he telephoned you to set up the conference, he said he couldn't see how the four subtests could all be reliable when Raphael's score on the social studies subtest was so "out of whack" with the other three subtests. He wants you to explain how this could happen.

 If I were you, here's how I'd respond to Colonel Hobbs:

"First off, Colonel Hobbs, I'm delighted that you've taken the time to look into the standardized test we're using in the district. Not many parents are willing to expend the energy to do so.

"I'd like to deal immediately with the issue you raised on the phone regarding the reliability of the four subtests, then discuss Raphael's social studies result. You may already know some of what I'll be talking about because of your access to the Internet, but here goes.

"Assessment reliability refers to the *consistency* of measurement. But there are very different ways that test developers look at measurement consistency. The reliability estimates that are supplied for Raphael's standardized test, as you pointed out, are called internal consistency correlation coefficients. Those correlations tell us whether the items on a particular subtest are performing in the same way—that is, whether they seem to be measuring the same thing.

"The internal consistency reliability for all four subtests is quite good. But this kind of reliability evidence doesn't tell us anything about how Raphael would score if he took the test again or if he took a different form of the same test. We don't know, in other words, whether his performance would be stable across time or would be consistent across different test forms.

"What we do see in Raphael's case is a social studies performance that is decisively different from his performance on the other three subtests. I've checked his grades for the past few years and I've seen that his grades in social studies are routinely just as high as his other grades. So those grades do cast some doubt on the meaningfulness of the lower test performance in social studies.

"Whatever's measured on the social studies subtest seems to be measured by a set of homogeneous items. That doesn't mean, however, the content of the social studies subtest meshes with the social studies Raphael's been taught here in our district. To me, Colonel, I think it's less likely to be a case of measurement unreliability than it is to be a problem of content mismatch between what the standardized examination tests and what we try to teach Raphael.

"I recommend that you, Mrs. Hobbs, and I monitor Raphael's performance in social studies during the school year so that we can really see if we're dealing with a learning problem or with an assessment inaccuracy."

 Now, how would you respond to Colonel Hobbs?

Incidentally, other things being equal, the more items there are in an educational assessment device, the more reliable it will tend to be. To illustrate, if you set out to measure a student's mathematics achievement with a 100-item test dealing with various aspects of mathematics, you're apt to get a more reliable fix on a student's mathematical prowess than if you asked students to solve only 1 lengthy mathematical word problem. The more times you ladle out a taste from a pot of soup, the more accurate will be your estimate of what the soup's ingredients are. One ladleful might fool you. Twenty ladlesful will give you a much better idea of what's in the pot. In general, then, more items on educational assessment devices will yield more reliable estimates than will fewer items.

■ Three Coins in the Reliability Fountain

You've now seen that there are three different ways of conceptualizing the manner in which the consistency of a test's results are described. Consistency of measurement is a requisite for making much sense out of a test's results. If the test yields inconsistent results, of course, how can teachers make sensible decisions based on what appears to be a capricious assessment procedure? Yet, as we have seen, reliability evidence comes in three flavors. It is up to you to make sure the reliability evidence supplied with a test is consonant with the use to which the test's results will be put—that is, the decision linked to the test's results. Although there is surely a relationship among the three kinds of reliability evidence we've been discussing, the following is unarguably true:

$$\text{Stability Reliability} \neq \text{Alternate-Form Reliability} \neq \text{Internal Consistency Reliability}$$

To illustrate, suppose you were a teacher in a school district where a high school diploma test had been developed by an assistant superintendent in collaboration with a committee of district teachers. The assistant superintendent has claimed the test's three different forms are essentially interchangeable because each form, when field-tested, yielded a Kuder-Richardson coefficient of .88 or higher. "The three test forms," claimed the assistant superintendent at a recent school board meeting, "are reliable and, therefore, equivalent." You now know better.

If the assistant superintendent really wanted to know about between-form comparability, then the kind of reliability evidence needed would be alternate-form reliability, not internal consistency. (Incidentally, I do not recommend that you rise at the school board meeting to publicly repudiate the assistant superintendent's motley mastery of measurement reliability. Simply send the assistant superintendent a copy of this book, designating the pages to be read. And send it anonymously.)

Yet, even those educators who know something about reliability and its importance will sometimes unthinkingly mush the three brands of reliability together. They'll see a K-R reliability coefficient of .90 and assume the test is not only internally consistent but that it will also produce stable results. That's not necessarily so.

■ The Standard Error of Measurement

Before bidding adieu to reliability and all its raptures, there's one other thing you need to know about consistency of measurement. So far, the kinds of reliability evidence we've been considering deal with the reliability of a *group* of students' scores. For a few paragraphs, I want to turn your attention to the consistency with which we measure an *individual's* performance. The index used in educational assessment to describe the consistency of a particular person's performance(s) is referred to as the ***standard error of measurement***. Sometimes a test's standard error of measurement is identified as the test's SEM.

You should think of the standard error of measurement as a reflection of the consistency of an individual's scores if a given assessment procedure were administered to that individual again, and again, and again. However, as a practical matter, it is impossible to readminister the same test innumerable times to the same students because such students would revolt or, if exceedingly acquiescent, soon swoon from exhaustion. (Swooning, these days, is rarely seen—except on television.) Accordingly, we need to *estimate* how much variability there would be if we were able to readminister a given assessment procedure many times to the same individual. The standard error of measurement is much like the plus or minus "sampling errors" so frequently given in the media these days for various sorts of national polls. We are told that "89% of telephone interviewees indicated they would consider shredded brussels sprouts in brownies to be repugnant" (±3% margin of error).

Other things being equal, the higher the reliability of a test, the smaller the standard error of measurement will be. For all commercially published tests, a technical manual is available that gives you the standard error of measurement for the test. Sometimes, if you ever have an occasion to check out a test's standard error, you'll find it's much larger than you might have suspected. As is true of sampling errors for surveys, what you'd prefer to have is small, not large, standard errors of measurement.

In many realms of life, big is better. Most folks like big bank accounts, houses with ample square footage, and basketball players who tower over other folks. But with standard errors of measurement, the reverse is true. Smaller standard errors of measurements signify more accurate assessment.

I don't want you to think that a test's standard error of measurement is computed by employing some type of measurement mysticism. Accordingly, presented here is the formula assessment folks use in order to obtain a standard error of measurement. If, however, you don't really care if the standard error of measurement was spawned on Mysticism Mountain, just skip the formula as well as the explanatory paragraph that follows it.

$$s_e = s_x \sqrt{1 - r_{xx}}$$

where s_e = standard error of measurement

s_x = standard deviation of the test scores

r_{xx} = the reliability of the test

Take a look at the formula for just a moment (especially if you get kicks out of formula looking), and you'll see that the size of a particular test's standard error of measurement (s_e) depends on two factors. First, there's the standard deviation (s_x) of the test's scores—that is, how spread out those scores are. The greater the spread in scores, the lower the scores' standard deviation will be. Second, there's the coefficient representing the test's reliability (r_{xx}). Now, if you consider what's going on in this formula, you'll see that the *larger* the standard deviation (score spread), the larger the standard error of measurement. Similarly, the *smaller* the reliability coefficient, the larger the standard error of measurement. So, in general, you see a test will have a smaller standard error of measurement if the test's scores are not too widely spread out and if the test is more reliable. A smaller standard error of measurement, as I've recently pointed out, signifies that a student's score is more accurately reflective of the student's "true" performance level.[2]

The standard error of measurement is an important concept because it reminds teachers about the *imprecision* of the test scores an individual student receives. Novice teachers often ascribe unwarranted precision to a student's test results. I can remember all too vividly making this mistake myself when I began teaching. While getting ready for my first group of students, I saw when inspecting student files that one of my students, Sally Palmer, had taken a group intelligence test. (Such tests were popular in those days.) Sally had earned a score of 126. For the next year, I was absolutely convinced that Sally was not merely above average in her intellectual abilities. Rather, I was certain that her IQ was *exactly* 126. I was too ignorant about assessment to realize there may have been a sizeable standard error of measurement associated with the intelligence test Sally had taken. Her "true" IQ score might have been substantially lower or higher. I doubt, if Sally had retaken the same intelligence test 10 different times, she'd ever get another score of precisely 126. But, in my naivete, I blissfully assumed Sally's intellectual ability was dead-center 126. The standard error of measurement helps remind teachers that the scores earned by students on commercial *or* classroom tests are not so darned exact.

There's one place a typical teacher is apt to find standard errors of measurement useful, and it is directly linked to the way students' performances on a state's NCLB tests are reported. By law, a state must classify a student's performance in at least one of three levels: *basic*, *proficient*, or *advanced*. In most instances, a student is given one of these three (or more) labels depending on the student's test scores. So, for instance, on a 60-item NCLB test in mathematics, the following classification scheme might have been adopted:

Student's Mathematics Classification	Student's NCLB Mathematics Test Score
Advanced	54–60
Proficient	44–53
Basic	37–43
Below Basic	36 and below

Now, let's suppose one of your students scores *near the cutoff* for one of this fictitious state's NCLB classifications. To illustrate, suppose your student had answered 53 of the 60 items correctly, and was therefore classified as a *proficient* student. Well, if the NCLB test has a rather large standard error of measurement, you recognize it's quite likely your *proficient* student really might have been an *advanced* student who, because of the test's inaccuracy, didn't earn the necessary extra point. This is the kind of information you can relay to both the student and to the student's parents. But to do so, of course, you need to possess at least a rudimentary idea about where a standard error of measurement comes from and how it works.

■ What Do Classroom Teachers Really Need to Know about Reliability?

What do you, as a teacher or teacher in preparation, truly need to know about reliability? Do you, for example, need to gather data from your own classroom assessment procedures so you can actually calculate reliability coefficients? If so, do you need to collect all three varieties of reliability evidence? My answers may surprise you. I think you need to know what reliability is, but I don't think you'll have much call to use it with your own tests—you won't, that is, unless certain of your tests are extraordinarily significant. And I haven't run into classroom tests, even rocko-socko final examinations, that I would consider sufficiently significant to warrant your whipping up a reliability extravaganza. In general, if you construct your own classroom tests with care, those tests will be sufficiently reliable for the decisions you will base on the tests' results.

You need to know about what reliability is because you may be called on to explain to parents the meaning of a student's standardized test scores, and you'll want to know how reliable the test is. You need to know what the test manual's

but what does this have to do with
Teaching?

Students' questions can sometimes get under a teacher's skin. For example, a student once asked me a question that, in time, forced me to completely rethink what I believed about reliability—at least insofar as it made a difference in a classroom teacher's behavior. "Why," the student asked, "is reliability *really* important for classroom teachers to know?"

The incident occurred during the early seventies. I can still recall where the student was sitting (the back-right corner of an open-square desk arrangement). I had only recently begun teaching measurement courses at UCLA, and I was "going by the book"; in other words, I was following the course's textbook almost unthinkingly.

You see, as a graduate student myself, I had never taken any coursework dealing with testing. My doctoral studies dealt with curriculum and instruction, not measurement. I wanted to learn ways of instructing prospective teachers about how to whip up winning instructional plans and deliver them with panache. But, after graduate school, I soon began to recognize that what was *tested* on important tests invariably influenced what was *taught* by most teachers. I began to read all about educational measurement so I could teach the introductory measurement course in the UCLA Graduate School of Education. Frankly, I was somewhat intimidated by the psychometric shroud testing experts sometimes use to surround their sandbox. Thus, as a beginner in the field of measurement, I rarely strayed from the "truths" contained in traditional measurement textbooks.

I can't recall my answer to that 1970s student, but I'm sure it must have been somewhat insipid. You see, I was merely mouthing a traditional view of reliability as a key attribute of good tests. In my own mind, at that moment, I really didn't have an answer to her *Why* question. But her question kept bothering me—actually for several years. Then I finally rethought the realistic value of reliability as a concept for classroom teachers. As you'll see in this chapter's wrap-up, I now downplay reliability's importance for busy teachers. But I suspect I still might be dishing out the same old psychometric party line about reliability—if it hadn't been for this one student's perceptive question. One of those psychometrically sanctioned truths was "reliability is a good thing." Accordingly, I was in the midst of a lecture extolling the extreme goodness of reliability when this memorable student, a woman who was at the time teaching sixth-graders while also working on her master's degree, said, "I can't see any practical reason for teachers to know about reliability or to go to the trouble of computing all these reliability coefficients you've just described. Why should we?"

Teachers *do* need to make sure they evaluate their students' test performances with consistency, especially if students are supplying essay responses or other sorts of performances that can't be scored objectively. But, as a general rule, classroom teachers need *not* devote their valuable time to reliability exotica. In reality, reliability has precious little to do with a classroom teacher's *teaching*. But this doesn't make key notions about reliability totally irrelevant to the concerns of classroom teachers. It's just that reliability is way, way less germane than how to whomp up a winning lesson plan for tomorrow's class!

authors are talking about and to be wary of those who secure one type of reliability evidence—for instance, a form of internal consistency evidence (because it's the easiest to obtain)—then try to proclaim this form of reliability evidence provides an indication of the test's stability or the comparability of its multiple forms. In short, you need to be at least knowledgeable about the fundamental meaning of reliability, but I do not suggest you make your own classroom tests pass any sort of reliability muster.

Reliability is a central concept in measurement. As you'll see in the next chapter, if an assessment procedure fails to yield consistent results, it is almost impossible to make any accurate inferences about what a student's score signifies. Inconsistent measurement is, at least much of the time, almost certain to be inaccurate measurement. Thus, you should realize that as the stakes associated with an assessment procedure become higher, there will typically be more attention given to establishing that the assessment procedure is, indeed, reliable. If you're evaluating an important test developed by others and you see that only skimpy attention has been given to the establishment of reliability, you should be critical of the test because evidence regarding an essential attribute of an educational test is missing.

I also think you ought to possess at least an intuitive understanding of what a standard error of measurement is. Such an understanding will come in handy when you're explaining to students, or their parents, how to make sense of a student's scores on such high-stakes external exams as your state's NCLB tests.

The other thing you should know about reliability is it comes in three brands—three kinds of evidence about a test's consistency *that are not interchangeable*. Don't let someone foist a set of internal consistency results on you and suggest that these results tell you anything of importance about stability. Don't let anyone tell you that a stability reliability coefficient indicates anything about the equivalence of a test's multiple forms. Although the three types of reliability evidence are related, they really are fairly distinctive kinds of creatures, something along the lines of second or third cousins.

What I'm trying to suggest is that classroom teachers, as professionals in the field of education, need to understand that an important attribute of educational assessment procedures is reliability. The higher the stakes associated with a test's use, the more the educators should attend to the assessment procedure's reliability. Reliability is such a key criterion by which psychometricians evaluate tests that you really ought to know what it is, even if you don't use it on a daily basis.

The situation regarding your knowledge about reliability is somewhat analogous to a health professional's knowledge about blood pressure and how blood pressure influences one's health. Even though only a small proportion of health professionals work directly with patients' blood pressure on a day-by-day basis, there are few health professionals who don't know at least the fundamentals of how one's blood pressure can influence a person's health.

I don't think you should devote any time to calculating the reliability of your own classroom tests, but I think you should have a general knowledge about what it is and why it's important. Besides, computing too many reliability coefficients for your own classroom tests might give you high blood pressure.

■ Chapter Summary

This chapter focused on the reliability of educational assessment procedures. *Reliability* refers to the consistency with which a test measures whatever it's measuring—that is, the absence of measurement errors that would distort a student's score.

There are three distinct types of reliability evidence. *Stability (test-retest) reliability* refers to the consistency of students' scores over time. Stability reliability is usually represented by a test-retest coefficient of correlation between students' scores on two occasions, but can be indicated by the degree of classification consistency displayed for students on two measurement occasions. *Alternate-form reliability* refers to the consistency of results between two or more forms of the same test. Alternate-form reliability is usually represented by the correlation of students' scores on two different test forms, but can also be reflected by classification-consistency percentages. *Internal consistency* represents the degree of homogeneity in an assessment procedure's items. Common indices of internal consistency are the Kuder-Richardson formulae as well as Cronbach's coefficient *alpha*. The three forms of reliability evidence should *not* be used interchangeably, but should be sought if relevant to the educational purpose to which an assessment procedure is being put—that is, the kind of educational decision linked to the assessment's results.

The standard error of measurement supplies an indication of the consistency of an individual's score by estimating person-score consistency from evidence of group-score consistency. The standard error of measurement is interpreted in a manner similar to the plus or minus sampling-error estimates often provided with national surveys. Classroom teachers are advised to become generally familiar with the key notions of reliability, but not to subject their own classroom tests to reliability analyses unless the tests are extraordinarily important.

Self-Check

For this chapter's first set of self-check exercises, you can see how well you've mastered the distinctions among the three kinds of reliability evidence that were described in the chapter. Please consider each of the reliability situations described here, then decide whether the question following the description is best answered by stability reliability (S), alternate-form reliability (AF), or internal consistency reliability (IC). There are 10 exercises. See if you can answer all 10 correctly.

S   AF   IC   **1.** An obsessive-compulsive teacher, having read this chapter and dismissed its recommendation that classroom teachers not gather reliability evidence regarding their own tests, routinely computes a K-R coefficient for all his quizzes and major exams. What brand of reliability evidence is he trying to get?

S   AF   IC   2. A commercially developed science achievement test has been recently published. The test's publishers produce evidence to show that if students score well on one of the test's three forms, they will also tend to score well on the other two forms. What kind of reliability evidence is this?

S   AF   IC   3. A state-developed composition test for tenth-grade students requires students to write four short essays. Cronbach's coefficient *alpha* has been applied because each of the essays is to be scored on a 1, 2, 3, 4, 5, or 6 basis. What sort of reliability evidence is being sought here?

S   AF   IC   4. A self-report inventory focusing on students' vocational interests was field-tested by being administered to 1,000 students in late March and again in mid-April. The inventory's developers wanted to see if students' vocational interests shifted over a three-week period. What brand of reliability evidence was the focus of the field-test?

S   AF   IC   5. A committee of teachers and central office administrators have been developing a basic skills test the district's high school students will need to pass if they are to receive an "endorsed" diploma. The test is computer administered and can be taken any time students wish during their senior year. What kind of reliability evidence would be most important because of the different times students can take the test?

S   AF   IC   6. Suppose you were trying to show that the items constituting an educational assessment procedure all measured the same underlying trait. What sort of reliability evidence should you attempt to secure?

S   AF   IC   7. A chemistry teacher has created four new versions of her final exam because she believes some students may have "gained access" to her old single-version exam. She decides she wants to see if all four new versions of the examination are providing students with the same kind of challenge. What sort of reliability evidence should she gather?

S   AF   IC   8. Suppose a commercial test developer wanted to see if students' scores on a new "oral communication" assessment procedure remained the same irrespective of when the student completed the assessment. What kind of reliability evidence would be most pertinent in this instance?

S   AF   IC   9. Although a university professor has developed three forms of the same attitudinal inventory, the professor is most interested in the extent to which each set of items on each of the three forms are measuring the same attitudinal dimension. What kind of reliability evidence should the professor be securing for each of the forms?

S   AF   IC   **10.** A new nationally standardized reading achievement test for junior high school students has been created, but the test's developers want to make sure that the three forms of the new test are performing in essentially the same way. What sort of reliability evidence should they snare?

Now that you've displayed your ability to distinguish among the three varieties of reliability evidence, let's see how you do with a pair of tougher exercises. These are open-ended exercises, so use your own words in responding.

11. What is the purpose of the standard error of measurement?

_____

_____

12. If one of your students has scored one point lower than the score needed on an NCLB test to exempt that student from a district-mandated summer school program, how would you use the notion of a test's standard error of measurement to explain to the student's parents why their child still must go to summer school?

_____

_____

(A Reminder: A Self-Check Key follows the Pondertime questions. You'd be wise to review the Self-Check Key because for many chapters—this one, for instance—there's neat new stuff presented there. Please note this subtle motivational ploy to get you to snuggle up to the Self-Check Keys.)

 Pondertime

1. Why do you think, although reliability is such a central concept in the appraisal of educational assessment devices, I've recommended classroom teachers generally not mess around with the determination of reliability for the tests they personally develop?

2. If an educational assessment procedure has a relatively small standard error of estimate, it's likely the assessment procedure is relatively reliable. Why do you think this is so?

3. What kinds of educational assessment procedures do you think should definitely require the assembly of reliability evidence? Why?

4. Should an educator have a favorite kind of reliability evidence among the three varieties we've considered? Why?

5. What is your reaction to *classification consistency* as an approach to the determination of reliability?

Self-Check Key

1. IC	3. IC	5. S	7. AF	9. IC
2. AF	4. S	6. IC	8. S	10. AF

11. The standard error of measurement provides an estimate of how much variability there would be if a student took the examination on another occasion. In a sense, therefore, the standard error of measurement offers test users a notion of the confidence that can be put in the accuracy of an individual's test performance. Unlike the three kinds of reliability evidence that deal with *group* test performances, the standard error of measurement focuses on the consistency of an *individual's* performance on a test.

12. Educational measurement is not flawlessly accurate, and NCLB tests can also be inaccurate. Typically, educational tests are constructed so they are as accurate as they can be, and this point should be stressed with the student's parents. To clarify the imprecision of *all* such tests, if the standard error of measurement is reasonably small, then student misclassifications are less likely. If the standard error of measurement is fairly hefty, then the parents need to be told that, *regrettably*, there's a genuine possibility their child may have been misclassified. However, there's no way to tell for sure. Indeed, the student's "true" score might *not* have been higher but, in contrast, might actually be much lower. The smaller the test's standard error of measurement, the easier this explanation is likely to be.

Endnotes

1. Please note the use of the Latin plural for formula. Because I once completed two years of Latin in high school and three years in college, I have vowed to use Latin at least once per month to make those five years seem less wasted. Any ninny could have said *formulas.*

2. You should recognize that because there are different kinds of reliability coefficients used to reflect a test's consistency, the size of a test's standard error of measurement will depend on the *particular* reliability coefficient that's used when calculating a standard error of measurement.

■ Additional Stuff

American Educational Research Association. (1999). *Standards for Educational and Psychological Testing.* Washington, DC: Author.

Frisbie, David A. (2005). "Presidential Address: Measurement 101: Some Fundamentals Revisited." *Educational Measurement: Issues and Practice, 24,* no. 5 (Fall): 21–28.

McMillan, James H. (2004). *Classroom Assessment: Principles and Practice for Effective Instruction* (3rd ed.). Boston: Allyn and Bacon.

■ Cyber Stuff

- *The American Educational Research Association (AERA)* is an international scholarly association devoted to the field of educational research. A large organization, AERA's members are divided into various divisions. Division D, for instance, is concerned with measurement and research methodology. The website contains recent newsletters of its divisions, including the most recent Division D electronic newsletter. www.aera.net

- *The National Council on Measurement in Education (NCME)* is a nonprofit organization committed to scientific, educational, and literary purposes as they relate to the field of educational assessment. This website describes the chief activities of the organization, especially at its annual meeting held each spring. Featured prominently at the NCME annual meeting are numerous empirical and analytical presentations, many of which deal with such routine topics as measurement reliability and validity. By securing a copy of the program for the annual meeting via this website, a visitor can write to presenters, requesting electronic copies of papers pertaining to the requestor's interests. NCME is the scholarly society most directly concerned with educational assessment, but in recent years its concerns have become more focused on such practical issues as how to build and administer better educational tests. www.ncme.org

Companion Website

To access chapter objectives, practice tests, weblinks, and flashcards, visit the companion website at **www.ablongman.com/popham5e.**

mylabschool™
Where the classroom comes to life!

MyLabSchool is a collection of online tools for your success in this course, your licensure exams, and your teaching career. Discover where the classroom comes to life by visiting **www.mylabschool.com** to access the following resources:

- Video clips from real classrooms
- An archive of real-life cases
- Help with your research papers using Research Navigator™
- Career Center with resources for:
    Praxis exams and licensure preparation
    Professional portfolio development
    Job search and interview techniques
    Lesson planning with state standard correlations

chapter 3

Validity

We'll be looking at *validity* in this chapter. Validity is, hands down, the most significant concept in assessment. In order to appreciate the reasons validity is so all-fired important, however, one first needs to understand why it is educators carry out assessments in the first place. Thus, let's set the stage a bit for your consideration of validity by explaining why educators frequently find themselves obliged to mess around with measurement.

Before you eagerly plunge into this important chapter, however, I need to issue a heads-up warning. This chapter on validity contains some fairly unusual concepts—that is, ideas you're not apt to see on Saturday night television or even encounter in your local newspaper's "Letters to the Editor" section.

Don't become put off by these new concepts. When you've finished the chapter, having smilingly succeeded on its end-of-chapter Self-Check, you'll be better able to focus on the really necessary ideas about validity. The really necessary ideas, when all the hotsy-totsy terminology has been stripped away, are simply gussied-up applications of common sense. Thus, be patient and plug away at Chapter 3. When it's over, you'll be a better person for having done so. And you'll know tons more about validity.

■ A Quest for Defensible Inferences

As noted in Chapter 1, we assess students because we want to determine a student's status with respect to an educationally relevant variable. One kind of variable of relevance to teachers is a variable that can be altered as a consequence of instruction. Such a variable would be how much students have learned about world history. Another educationally relevant variable is one that can influence the way a teacher decides to instruct students. This sort of variable might be students' attitudes toward the study of whatever content the teacher is dealing with.

The more that teachers know about their students' status with respect to certain educationally relevant variables, the better will be the educational decisions made regarding those students. To illustrate, if a junior high school teacher knows that Lee Lacey is a weak reader and has truly negative attitudes toward reading, the teacher will probably decide *not* to send Lee trotting off to the school library to tackle an independent research project based on self-directed reading. Similarly, if a mathematics teacher discovers early in the school year that her students know much more about mathematics than she had previously suspected, the teacher is apt to decide the class will tackle more advanced topics than originally planned. Teachers use the results of assessments to make decisions about students. But appropriate educational decisions depend on the *accuracy of educational assessment.* That's because, quite obviously, accurate assessments will improve the quality of decisions, whereas inaccurate assessments will do the opposite. And this is where validity comes in.

Teachers often need to know how well their students have mastered a *curricular aim*—for example, a skill or body of knowledge that students are supposed to learn. A curricular aim is also referred to these days as a **content standard.** To illustrate, if we set out to determine how well students can comprehend what they have read, it is obviously impractical to find out how well students can read *everything.* There's too much out there to read. Nonetheless, teachers would like to get an accurate fix on how well a particular student can handle the full array of relevant reading tasks implied by a particular curricular aim. Because it is impossible to see how well students can perform with respect to the entire array of skills or knowledge embodied in a curricular aim, we have to fall back on a *sampling* strategy. Thus, when we measure students, we try to sample their mastery of a curricular aim in a representative manner so that, based on students' performance on the sample, we can infer what their status is with respect to their mastery of the entire curricular aim. In Figure 3.1, this relationship is portrayed graphically. Note that we start with a curricular aim. In Figure 3.1, that's the oval at the left. The left-hand oval

Figure 3.1 ■ An Illustration of How We Infer a Student's Status with Respect to a Curricular Aim from the Student's Performance on an Educational Test that Samples the Aim

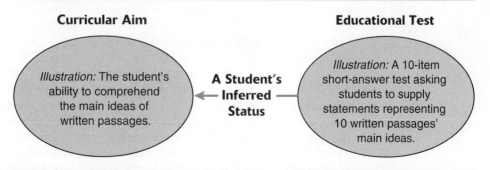

Decision Time

Group-Influenced Grading

A junior high school English teacher, Cecilia Celina, has recently installed cooperative learning groups in all five of her classes. The groups are organized so that, although there are individual grades earned by students based on each student's specific accomplishments, there is also a group-based grade that is dependent on the average performance of a student's group. Cecilia decides 60% of a student's grade will be based on the student's individual effort and 40% of the student's grade will be based on the collective efforts of the student's group. This 60–40 split is used when she grades students' written examinations as well as when she grades a group's oral presentation to the rest of the class.

Several of Cecilia's fellow teachers have been interested in her use of cooperative learning because they are considering the possibility of employing it in their own classes. One of those teachers, Fred Florie, is uncomfortable about Cecilia's 60–40 split of grading weights. Fred believes that Cecilia cannot arrive at a valid estimate of an individual student's accomplishment when there's 40% of the student's grade based on the efforts of other students. Cecilia responds that this aggregated grading practice is one of the key features of cooperative learning because it is the contribution of the group grade that motivates the students in a group to help one another learn. In most of her groups, for example, she finds students willingly help other group members prepare for important examinations.

As she considers Fred's concerns, Cecilia concludes he is most troubled about the validity of the inferences she makes about her students' achievements. In her mind, however, she separates an estimate of a student's accomplishments from the grade she gives a student.

Cecilia believes she has three decision options facing her. As she sees it, she can (1) leave matters as they are, (2) delete all group-based contributions to an individual student's grade, or (3) modify the 60–40 split.

 If you were Cecilia, what would your decision be?

represents, for illustration purposes, a curricular aim in reading consisting of a student's ability to comprehend the main ideas of written passages. The oval at the right in Figure 3.1 represents an educational assessment approach—in this instance a 10-item test—that we use to make an *inference* about a student. If you prefer, you can think of a test-based inference simply as an *interpretation* of what the test results signify. The inference concerns the student's status with respect to the entire curricular aim (the oval at the left). If this inference is accurate, then the resultant educational decisions are likely to be more defensible because those decisions will be based on a correct estimate regarding the student's actual status.

It is the *validity of a score-based inference* that's at issue when measurement folks deal with validity. Tests, themselves, do not possess validity. Educational tests are used so educators can make inferences about a student's status. If high scores lead to one kind of inference, low scores typically lead to an opposite inference. Moreover, because validity hinges on the accuracy of our inferences about students' status with respect to a curricular aim, it is technically inaccurate to talk about "the validity of a test." A well-constructed test, if used with the wrong group of students or if administered under unsuitable circumstances, can lead to a set of unsound and thoroughly invalid inferences. Test-based inferences may or may not be valid. It is the test-based inference with which teachers ought to be concerned.

In real life, however, you'll find a fair number of educators talking about the "validity of a test." Perhaps they really understand it's the validity of score-based inferences that is at issue, and they're simply using a short-cut descriptor. Based on my experience, it's more likely they really don't know that the focus of validity should be on test-based inferences, not on tests themselves.

Now that you know what's really at issue in the case of validity, if you ever hear a colleague talking about "a test's validity," you'll have to decide whether you should preserve that colleague's dignity by letting such psychometric shortcomings go unchallenged. I suggest that, unless there are really critical decisions on the line—decisions that would have an important educational impact on students—you keep your insights regarding validation to yourself. (When I first truly comprehended what was going on with the validity of test-based inferences, I shared this knowledge rather aggressively with several fellow teachers and, thereby, meaningfully miffed them. No one, after all, likes a psychometric smart aleck.)

■ Validity Evidence

Teachers make scads of decisions, sometimes on a minute-by-minute basis. Teachers decide whether to ask questions of their students and, if questions are to be asked, which student gets which question. Most of a teacher's *instructional* decisions are based to a large extent on the teacher's judgment about students' achievement levels. For instance, if a third-grade teacher concludes most of her students are able to read independently, then the teacher may decide to use independent reading as a key element in a social studies lesson. The teacher's judgment about students' reading abilities is based on evidence of some sort—gathered either formally or informally.

The major contribution of classroom assessment to a teacher's decision making is it provides reasonably accurate evidence about students' status. Although teachers are often forced to make inferences about students' knowledge, skills, or attitudes on the basis of informal observations, such unsystematic observations sometimes lead teachers to make invalid inferences about a particular student's status. I'm not knocking teachers' informal observational skills, mind you, for I certainly relied on my own informal observations when I was in the classroom. Frequently, however, I was off the mark! More than once, I saw what I wanted to see by inferring that my students possessed knowledge and skills they really didn't have. Later, when students tackled a midterm or final exam, I discovered that the conclusions I had drawn from my observation-based judgments were far too generous.

Classroom assessments, if they're truly going to help teachers make solid instructional decisions, should allow a teacher to arrive at valid inferences (interpretations) about students. And, more often than not, because a classroom assessment can be carefully structured, an assessment-based inference is going to be more valid than an inference made while the teacher is focused on other concerns.

The only reason teachers should assess their students is to make better educational decisions about those students. Thus, when you think about validity, remember it is not some abstruse measurement mystery, knowable only to those who've labored in validity vineyards for eons. Rather, validity centers on the accuracy of the inferences teachers make about their students.

Even though there are different ways of determining whether test-based inferences are apt to be valid, the overriding focus is on the *accuracy of an assessment-based inference*. It usually helps to think about validity as an overall evaluation of the degree to which a specific interpretation of a test's results is supported. People who develop important tests, such as college admissions exams, often try to build a **validity argument** in which they assemble evidence and analyses to show their tests permit the inferences (interpretations) being claimed.

As a teacher or a teacher in preparation, you may wonder why you have to devote any time at all to different kinds of validity evidence. I appreciate this concern, but I think it's important you understand at least the chief kinds of evidence bearing on the validity of a score-based inference. I promise to give most attention to the sort of validity evidence with which classroom teachers should be chiefly concerned.

In the last chapter, we saw that there are three kinds of reliability evidence that can be used to help us decide how consistently a test is measuring what it's measuring. Well, and this should come as no surprise, there are also three kinds of evidence that can be used to help educators determine whether their score-based inferences are valid. Rarely will one set of evidence be so compelling that, all by itself, the evidence assures us our score-based inference is truly accurate. More commonly, several different sets of validity evidence and several different kinds of validity evidence are needed for educators to be really comfortable about the test-based inferences they make. Putting it another way, in order to develop a powerful validity argument, it is almost always necessary to collect *varied* kinds of validity evidence.

When I was preparing to be a high school teacher, many years ago, my teacher education classmates and I were told that "validity refers to the degree to which a test measures what it purports to measure." (I really grooved on that definition because it gave me an opportunity to use the word *purport*. Prior to that time, I didn't have too many occasions to do so.) Although, by modern standards, the traditional definition of validity is pretty antiquated, it still contains a solid seed of truth. If a test *truly* measures what it sets out to measure, then it's likely the inferences we make about students based on their test performances will be valid. Valid test-based interpretations will be made because we will typically interpret students' performances according to what the test's developers set out to measure.

In some instances we find educators making meaningful modifications in the sorts of assessments they use with children who have physical or cognitive disabilities. We'll look into that issue in the next chapter, particularly as it has been reshaped by the NCLB Act. However, I want you to think about an assessment procedure in which a reading achievement test is read aloud to a blind child. Let's say that the child, having heard the test's reading passages and each multiple-choice options be read aloud, scores very well. Does this permit us to make a valid inference that the blind child can *read?* No, even though it is a reading test involved, a more valid inference is that the child can derive substantial meaning from read-aloud material. It's an important skill for visually impaired children, and it's a skill that ought to be nurtured. But it isn't *reading*. Validity resides in a test-based inference, not in the test itself.

Let's take a look, now, at the three most common kinds of evidence you are apt to encounter in determining whether the inference one makes from an educational assessment procedure is valid. Having looked at the three varieties of validity evidence, I'll give you my opinion about what classroom teachers *really* need to know about validity and what kinds of validity evidence, if any, teachers need to gather regarding their own tests. Table 3.1 previews the three types of validity evidence we'll be considering in the remainder of the chapter.

■ Content-Related Evidence of Validity

Remembering that the more evidence of validity we have, the better we'll know how much confidence to place in our score-based inferences, let's look at the first variety of validity evidence: content-related evidence of validity.

Content-related evidence of validity (often described simply as *content validity*) refers to the adequacy with which the content of a test represents the content of the curricular aim about which inferences are to be made. When the idea of content representatives was first dealt with by educational measurement folks several decades ago, the focus was dominantly on achievement examinations, such as a test of students' knowledge of history. If educators thought that eighth-grade students ought to know 124 specific facts about history, then the more of those 124 facts represented in a test, the more evidence there was of content validity.

Table 3.1 ■ Three Types of Validity Evidence

Type of Validity Evidence	Brief Description
■ Content Related	The extent to which an assessment procedure adequately represents the content of the curricular aim being measured
■ Criterion Related	The degree to which performance on an assessment procedure accurately predicts a student's performance on an external criterion
■ Construct Related	The extent to which empirical evidence confirms that an inferred construct exists and that a given assessment procedure is measuring the inferred construct accurately

These days, however, the notion of *content* refers to much more than factual knowledge. The content of curricular aims in which teachers are interested can embrace knowledge (such as historical facts), skills (such as higher-order thinking competencies), or attitudes (such as students' dispositions toward the study of science). Content, therefore, should be conceived of broadly. When we determine the content representativeness of a test, the content in the curricular aim being sampled can consist of whatever is in that curricular aim. Remember, the curricular aims for most classroom tests consist of the skills and knowledge included in a teacher's goals for a certain instructional period.

During the past decade or so, the term *content standard* has become a common way to describe the skills and knowledge educators want their students to learn. Almost all states currently have an officially approved set of content standards for each of the major subject areas taught in that state's public schools. Teachers, too, sometimes pursue additional content standards (or curricular aims) associated with the particular grade level or subjects they teach.

But what is adequate representativeness of a set of content standards and what isn't? Although this is clearly a situation in which more representativeness is better than less representativeness, let's illustrate varying levels with which a curricular aim can be represented by a test. Take a look at Figure 3.2 where you see an illustrative curricular aim (represented by the shaded rectangle) and the items from different tests (represented by the dots). As the test items coincide less adequately with the curricular aim, the weaker is the content-related evidence of validity.

Figure 3.2 ■ Varying Degrees to Which a Test's Items Represent the Curricular Aim about Which Score-Based Inferences Are to Be Made

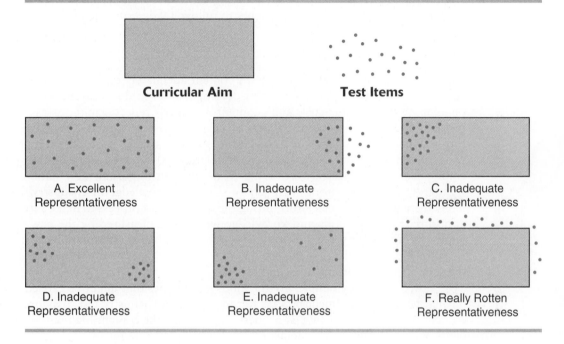

For example, in Illustration A of Figure 3.2, we see that the test's items effectively sample the full range of the curricular aim's content represented by the shaded rectangle. In Illustration B, however, note that some of the test's items don't even coincide with the curricular aim's content, and that those items falling in the curricular aim don't cover it well. Even in Illustration C, where all the test's items measure content included in the curricular aim, the breadth of coverage for the curricular aim is insufficient.

Trying to put a bit of reality into those rectangles and dots, think about an Algebra I teacher who is trying to measure his students' mastery of a semester's worth of content by creating a truly comprehensive final examination. Based chiefly on students' performances on the final examination, he will assign grades that will influence whether his students can advance to Algebra II. Let's assume the content the teacher addressed instructionally in Algebra I—that is, the algebraic skills and knowledge taught during the Algebra I course—is truly prerequisite to Algebra II. Then, if the curricular aims representing the Algebra I content are *not* satisfactorily represented by the teacher's final examination, the teacher's score-based interpretations about students' end-of-course algebraic capabilities and his resultant decisions about students' readiness for Algebra II are apt to be in error. If teachers' educational decisions hinge on students' status regarding a curricular aim's content, then those decisions are likely to be flawed if inferences about students' mastery of the curricular aim are based on a test that doesn't adequately represent the curricular aim's content.

How do educators go about gathering content-related evidence of validity? Well, there are generally two approaches to follow. I'll describe each briefly.

Developmental Care

One way of trying to make sure a test's content adequately taps the content of a curricular aim is to employ a set of test-development procedures carefully focused on assuring that the curricular aim's content is properly reflected in the assessment procedure itself. The higher the stakes associated with the test's use, the more effort is typically devoted to making certain the assessment procedure's content properly represents the content in the curricular aim(s) involved. For example, if a commercial test publisher were trying to develop an important new nationally standardized test measuring high school students' knowledge of chemistry, it is likely there would be much effort during the development process to make sure the appropriate sorts of skills and knowledge were being measured by the new test. Similarly, because of the significance of a state's NCLB tests, substantial attention is typically given to the task of verifying that the test's content suitably represents the state's most important curricular aims.

Listed here, for example, are the kinds of activities that might be carried out during the test-development process for an important chemistry test to assure the content covered by the new test properly represents "the content high school students ought to know about chemistry."

Possible Developmental Activities to Enhance a High-Stakes Chemistry Test's Content Representativeness

- A panel of national content experts, individually by mail or during extended face-to-face sessions, recommends the knowledge and skills that should be measured by the new test.
- The proposed content of the new test is systematically contrasted with a list of topics derived from a careful analysis of the content included in the five leading textbooks used in the nation's high school chemistry classes.
- A group of high school chemistry teachers, each judged to be a "teacher of the year" in his or her own state, provides suggestions regarding the key topics (that is, knowledge and skills) to be measured by the new test.
- Several college professors, conceded to be international authorities regarding the teaching of chemistry, having independently reviewed the content suggestions of others for the new test, offer recommendations for additions, deletions, and modifications.
- State and national associations of secondary school chemistry teachers provide reviews of the proposed content to be measured by the new test.

With lower-stakes tests, such as the kind of quiz that a high school chemistry teacher might give after a one-week unit, less elaborate content reviews are obviously warranted. Even classroom teachers, however, can be attentive to the content representativeness of their tests. For openers, teachers can do so by *giving deliberate consideration* to whether the content of their classroom tests reflects the instructional objectives supposedly being measured by those tests. For instance, whatever the test is, a teacher can deliberately try to identify the nature of the curricular aim the test is supposed to represent. Remember, the test itself should not be the focus of the teacher's concern. Rather, the test should be regarded as simply a "stand in" for a curricular aim—that is, the set of skills and/or knowledge embraced by the teacher's instructional objectives.

To illustrate, if a teacher of tenth-grade English wants to create a final examination for a one-semester course, the teacher should first try to identify all the important skills and knowledge to be taught during the semester. An outline of such content, or even a simple listing of topics, will usually suffice. Then, after identifying the content of the curricular aims covering the English course's key content, the teacher can create an assessment instrument that attempts to represent the identified content properly.

As you can see, the important consideration here is that the teacher makes a careful effort to conceptualize the nature of a curricular aim, then tries to see if the test being constructed actually contains content that is appropriately representative of the content in the curricular aim. Unfortunately, many teachers generate tests without any regard whatsoever for curricular aims. Rather than trying to figure out what knowledge, skills, or attitudes should be promoted instructionally, some teachers simply start churning out test items. Before long, a test is born—a test that, more often than not, does a pretty poor job of sampling the skills and knowledge about which the teacher should make inferences.

We have seen, then, that one way of supplying content-related evidence of validity is to deliberately incorporate test-development activities that increase the likelihood of representative content coverage. Having done so, these procedures should be carefully documented. It is this documentation, in fact, that constitutes an important form of content-related evidence of validity. The more important the test, the more it is that test-development activities should be documented. For most teachers' classroom assessments, I don't believe any such documentation is requisite.

External Reviews

A second form of content-related evidence of validity for educational assessment procedures involves the assembly of judges who rate the content appropriateness of a given test in relationship to the curricular aim the test allegedly represents. For high-stakes tests, such as a state's NCLB tests or a state-developed examination that must be passed before a student receives a high school diploma, these content reviews are typically quite systematic. For run-of-the-mill classroom tests, such external reviews are usually far more informal. For instance, when one teacher asks a colleague to scrutinize the content coverage of a midterm exam, that's a version of this second approach to reviewing a test's content. Clearly, the care with which external reviews of an assessment procedure's content are conducted depends on the consequences associated with students' performances. The more significant the consequences, the more elaborate the external content-review process. Let's look at a couple of examples to illustrate this point.

Suppose state department of education officials decide to construct a state-wide assessment program in which all sixth-grade students who fail to achieve a specified level of competence in language arts or mathematics must take part in state-designed, but locally delivered, after-school remediation programs. Once the items for the new assessment program are developed (and those items might be fairly traditional or quite innovative), a panel of 20 content reviewers for language arts and a panel of 20 content reviewers for mathematics then consider the test's items. Such reviewers, typically, are subject-matter experts who have substantial familiarity with the content involved.

Using the mathematics portion of the test for illustrative purposes, the 20 members of the Mathematics Content Review Panel might be asked to render a yes/no judgment for *each* of the test's items in response to a question such as this:

An Illustrative Item-Judgment Question for Content-Review Panelists

Does this item appropriately measure mathematics knowledge and/or skill(s) that, because of the content's significance to the student's further study, should, if unmastered, result in after-school remedial instruction for the student?

Note that the illustrative question is a two-component question. Not only should the mathematical knowledge and/or skill involved, if unmastered, require after-school remedial instruction for the student, but also the item being judged must "appropriately measure" this knowledge and/or skill. In other words, the knowledge and/or skill must be sufficiently important to warrant remedial instruction on the part of the student *and* the knowledge and/or skill must be properly measured by the item. If the content of an item is important *and* if the content of the item is also properly measured, the content review panelists should supply a *yes* judgment for the item. If either an item's content is not significant, or if the content is badly measured by the item, then the content review panelists should supply a *no* judgment for the item.

By calculating the percentage of panelists who rate each item positively, an index of content-related evidence of validity can be obtained for each item. To illustrate the process, suppose we had a five-item subtest whose five items received the following positive per-item ratings from a content-review panel: Item One, 72%; Item Two, 92%; Item Three, 88%; Item Four, 98%; and Item Five, 100%. The average positive content per-item ratings for the entire test, then, would be 90%. The higher the average per-item ratings provided by a test's content reviewers, the stronger the content-related evidence of validity. This first kind of item-by-item judgment for reviewers represents an attempt to isolate (and eliminate) items whose content is insufficiently related to the curricular aim being measured.

In addition to the content-review panelists' ratings of the individual items, the panel can also be asked to judge how well the test's items represent the domain of content that *should* be assessed in order to determine whether a student is assigned to the after-school remediation extravaganza. Presented here is an example of how such a question for content-review panelists might be phrased.

An Illustrative Content-Coverage Question for Content-Review Panelists

First, try to identify mentally the full range of mathematics knowledge and/or skills you believe to be so important that, if not mastered, should result in a student's being assigned to after-school remediation classes. Then, having mentally identified that domain of mathematics knowledge and/or skills, please estimate the percent of the domain represented by the set of test items you just reviewed. What percent is it?   _____%

If a content panel's review of a test's content coverage yields an average response to such a question of, say, 85%, that's not bad. If, however, the content-review panel's average response to the content coverage question is only 45%, this indicates there is a solid chunk of important content not being measured by the test's items. For high-stakes tests, external reviewers' average responses to an item-by-item content question for all items and their average responses to a content coverage question for the whole test constitute solid indicators of judgmentally derived content-related evidence of validity. The more positive the evidence, the greater confidence one can have in making score-based inferences about a student's status with respect to the curricular aims being measured.

Although it would be possible for classroom teachers to go through the same content-review machinations just described for their own classroom assessments, I know of no sane teacher who would want to expend this much energy to review the content of a typical classroom test. Instead, a teacher might ask another teacher to look over a test's items and to render judgments akin to those asked of a content-review panel. Because it takes time to provide such judgments, however, a pair of teachers might trade the task of reviewing the content of each other's classroom assessments. ("You scratch my back/review my test, and I'll scratch/review yours.")

One of the significant dividends resulting from having a fellow teacher review the content of your classroom tests is that the prospect of having such a review will usually lead to a proactive inclusion of more representative content coverage in your tests. The more carefully you consider your test's content coverage early on, the more likely the test's content coverage will be appropriate.

In review, we have considered one kind of validity evidence—namely, content-related evidence of validity—that can be used to support the defensibility of score-based inferences about a student's status with respect to curricular aims. We've discussed this form of validity evidence in some detail because, as you will see, it is the most important form of validity evidence classroom teachers need to be concerned with when they judge their own classroom assessment procedures.

■ Criterion-Related Evidence of Validity

The second form of validity evidence you're apt to encounter when working with educational tests is referred to as ***criterion-related evidence of validity.*** As was true with content-related evidence of validity, this kind of evidence helps educators decide how much confidence can be placed in a score-based inference about a student's status with respect to one or more curricular aims. Yet, a decisively different evidence-collection strategy is used when we gather criterion-related evidence of validity. Moreover, criterion-related evidence of validity is collected only in situations where educators are using an assessment procedure to *predict* how well students will perform on some subsequent ***criterion variable.***

The easiest way to understand what this second kind of validity evidence looks like is to describe the most common educational setting in which it is collected—namely, the relationship between students' scores on (1) an aptitude test and (2) the grades those students subsequently earn. An *aptitude test,* as noted in Chapter 1, is an assessment device that is used in order to predict how well a student will perform at some later point. For example, many high school students complete a scholastic aptitude test (such as the SAT) when they're still in high school. The test is supposed to be predictive of how well those students are apt to perform in college. More specifically, students' scores on the aptitude test are employed to predict students' grade-point averages (GPAs) in college. It is assumed that those students who score well on the aptitude test will earn higher GPAs in college than those students who score poorly on the aptitude test.

In Figure 3.3, we see the classic kind of relationship between a predictor test and the criterion it is supposed to predict. As you can see, a test is used to predict students' subsequent performance on a criterion. The criterion could be GPAs, on-the-job proficiency ratings, annual income, or some other performance variable in which we are interested. Most of the time in the field of education, we are concerned with a criterion that deals directly with educational matters. Thus, grades earned in later years are often employed as a criterion. Teachers could also be interested in such "citizenship" criteria as the number of times students vote after completing high school (a positive criterion) or the number of misdemeanors or felonies that are subsequently committed by students (a negative criterion).

Figure 3.3 ■ The Typical Setting in Which Criterion-Related Evidence of Validity Is Sought

If we know a predictor test is working pretty well, we can use its results to help us make educational decisions about students. For example, if you discovered that Cliff Carver scored very poorly on a scholastic aptitude test while in high school, but Cliff's heart is set on attending college, you could devise a set of supplemental instructional activities so that he could try to acquire the needed

Parent Talk

Mrs. Billings, the mother of one of your students, is this year's president of your school's parent-teacher organization (PTO). As a consequence of her office, she's been reading a variety of journal articles dealing with educational issues. After every PTO meeting, or so it seems to you, Mrs. Billings asks you to comment on one of the articles she's read. Tonight, she asks you to explain what is meant by the phrase content standards and to tell her how your classroom tests are related, if at all, to content standards. She says that the author of one article she read argued that "if teachers' tests didn't measure national content standards, the tests wouldn't be valid."

 If I were you, here's how I'd respond to Mrs. Billings:

"You've really identified an important topic for tonight, Mrs. Billings. Content standards are regarded by many of the country's educators as a key factor in how we organize our national education effort. Put simply, a *content standard* describes the knowledge or skill we want our students to master. You might think of a content standard as today's label for what used to be called an instructional objective. What's most imperative, of course, is that teachers focus their instructional efforts on *appropriate* content standards.

"As you may know, our state has already established a series of content standards at all grade levels in language arts, mathematics, social studies, and science. Each of these state-approved sets of content standards is based, more or less, on a set of content standards originally developed by the national subject-matter association involved—for example, the National Council of Teachers of Mathematics. So, in a sense, teachers in our school can consider both the state-sanctioned standards as well as those devised by the national content associations. Most of the school's teachers have looked at both sets of content standards.

"Teachers look over these content standards when they engage in an activity we call *test sharing*. Each teacher has at least one other colleague look over all the teacher's major classroom assessments to make sure that most of the significant content standards have been addressed. It's really an attempt to gather content-related evidence of validity for the tests we use here.

"Those teachers whose tests do not seem to address the content standards satisfactorily are encouraged to revise their tests so the content standards are more suitably covered. It really seems to work well for us. We've used the system for a couple of years now, and the teachers uniformly think our assessment coverage of key skills and knowledge is far better."

 Now, how would you respond to Mrs. Billings?

academic skills and knowledge before he leaves high school. Test results, on predictor tests as well as on any educational assessment procedures, should always be used to make better educational decisions.

In some cases, however, psychometricians can't afford to wait the length of time that's needed between the administration of the predictor test and the gathering of the data regarding the criterion. For example, if the staff of a commercial testing company is developing a new academic aptitude test to predict high school students' GPAs at the end of college, the company's staff members might administer the new *high school* aptitude test to *college seniors* only a month or so before they earned their baccalaureate degrees. The correlation between the aptitude test scores and the students' final college GPAs would be referred to as *concurrent* criterion-related evidence of validity. Clearly, such evidence is far less compelling than properly gathered *predictive* criterion-related evidence of validity (that is, when a meaningful length of time has elapsed between the predictor test and the collection of the criterion data).

What teachers need to realize about the accuracy of scholastic predictor tests such as the ones we've been discussing is that those tests are far from perfect. Sometimes the criterion that's being predicted isn't all that reliable itself. (How accurate were *your* college grades?) For instance, the correlations between students' scores on academic aptitude tests and their subsequent grades rarely exceed .50. A correlation coefficient of .50 indicates that, although the test predicts to some degree how students will subsequently perform, there are many other factors (such as motivation, study habits, and interpersonal skills) that play a major role in the grades a student earns. In fact, the best predictor of students' future grades is not their scores on aptitude tests; it is students' earlier grades. Previous grades more accurately reflect the full range of important grade-influencing factors, such as perseverance, that are not directly assessable via aptitude assessment devices.

Statistically, if you want to determine what proportion of students' performances on a criterion variable (such as college grades) is meaningfully related to students' scores on a predictor test (such as the ACT or SAT), you must *square* the correlation coefficient between the predictor and criterion variables. Thus, if the coefficient is .50, simply square it—that is, multiply it times itself—and you end up with .50 times .50 = .25. This signifies that about 25 percent of students' college grades can be explained by their scores on the aptitude test. Factors such as motivation and study habits account for the other 75 percent.

■ Construct-Related Evidence of Validity

The last of our three varieties of validity evidence is the most esoteric, yet the most comprehensive. It is referred to as **construct-related evidence of validity.** Construct-related evidence of validity was originally used when psychologists were trying to measure such elusive and covert constructs as individuals' "anxiety" and "perseveration tendencies." Because these variables were clearly hypothetical constructs, if a test was created that could accurately be used to get a fix on a person's level of anxiety, then evidence could also be assembled that (1) the inferred construct was sensible and (2) the test measured this construct with some accuracy.

But most of the variables educators try to assess are every bit as covert as anxiety and perseveration tendencies. When we talk about a student's "mathematical competence" or a student's "reading comprehension capabilities," there's nothing overt about those variables. Based on the student's observed behavior in class or on tests, we make judgments about what the student's mathematical skills and reading prowess are. Although routine educational variables are less exotic than one's anxiety and perseveration tendencies, a student's knowledge of history and scientific thinking skills are equally hidden.

The way construct-related evidence of validity is assembled for a test is really quite straightforward. First, based on our understanding of how the hypothetical construct that we're measuring works, we make one or more formal hypotheses about students' performances on the test for which we're gathering construct-related evidence of validity. Second, we gather empirical evidence to see whether the hypothesis (or hypotheses) is confirmed. If it is, we have assembled evidence that the test is measuring what it's supposed to be measuring. As a consequence, we are more apt to be able to draw valid score-based inferences when students take the test.

Construct-related evidence of validity for educational tests is typically gathered by way of a series of studies, not one whopper "it-settles-the-issue-once-and-for-all" investigation. There are three types of strategies most commonly used in construct-related evidence studies. (Have you noticed how often psychometricians toss things into three categories? It's unsettling.) We'll take a brief peek at all three approaches to the collection of construct-related evidence of validity.

Intervention Studies

One kind of investigation that provides construct-related evidence of validity is an *intervention study*. In an intervention study, we hypothesize that students will respond differently to the assessment instrument after having received some type of treatment (or intervention). For example, let's say a group of teachers developed an essay examination they believed tapped students' "higher-order mathematical skills." It would be hypothesized that students would receive markedly higher scores on the examination after a six-week intensive summer workshop on the topic Messing about with Higher-Order Mathematical Thinking than the scores those same students earned before the six-week workshop. If the hypothesis is confirmed—in other words, if students' postworkshop scores are higher than their preworkshop scores—then this constitutes one chunk of construct-related evidence of validity for the examination under consideration.

Differential-Population Studies

A second kind of investigation that can be used to provide construct-related evidence of validity is a *differential-population study*. In this kind of study, based on our knowledge of the construct being measured, we hypothesize that individuals representing distinctly different populations will score differently on the assessment procedure under consideration. To illustrate, suppose a new oral test of students' bilingual proficiency in English and Spanish had been created. If we could locate three groups of students who were (1) fluent in English but not Spanish, (2) fluent in Spanish but not English, and (3) fluent in Spanish and English, we could predict that the bilingually fluent speakers ought to decisively outperform their monolingual counterparts. If our hypothesis is confirmed when we carry out an actual study, that's more construct-related evidence to support an inference about students' status based on their test performances.

Related-Measures Studies

A third kind of empirical investigation providing construct-related evidence of validity is referred to as a *related-measures study.* In a related-measures study, we hypothesize that a given kind of relationship will be present between students' scores on the assessment device we're scrutinizing and their scores on a related (or unrelated) assessment device. To illustrate, if we churned out a brand new test of students' ability to comprehend what they read, we could hypothesize that students' scores on the new reading test would be positively correlated with their scores on an already established and widely used reading achievement test. To the extent that our hypothesis is confirmed, we have assembled more construct-related evidence of validity supporting the validity of our score-based inference (using the new test's results) about a student's reading skill.

When it is hypothesized that two sets of test scores *should* be related, and evidence is collected to show that positive relationship, this is referred to as *convergent evidence* of validity. For example, suppose you were a U.S. history teacher and you used a final exam to cover the period from the Civil War to the present. If another teacher of U.S. history in your school also had a final exam covering the same period, you'd predict the students who scored well on your final exam would also do well on your colleague's final exam. (Your dazzling students should dazzle on his exam and your clunky students should clunk on his exam.) If you went to the trouble of actually doing this (and, of course, why would you?), this would be a form of convergent validity evidence.

In contrast, suppose as a test-crazed U.S. history teacher you tried to compare your students' final exam scores to their scores on a final exam in an algebra class. You'd predict a weaker relationship between your students' final exam scores in your history class and their final exam scores in the algebra class. This lower relationship is referred to as *discriminant evidence* of validity. It simply means that if your test is assessing what you think it is, then scores on your test ought to relate weakly to results of tests designed to measure other constructs. (This sort of test comparison, too, would be an unsound use of your time.)

An increasing number of psychometricians believe that construct-related evidence of validity actually encompasses the other two forms of validity evidence. Remember, construct-related evidence of validity draws on empirical evidence to support the proposition that an inferred, unobservable construct exists and, moreover, is measured by the assessment instrument under consideration. Well, *criterion-related* evidence of validity is certainly empirical, and deals with the existence of a predictor construct. Therefore, such evidence would seem to be subsumed as a form of construct-related evidence. Similarly, to the extent that empirical *content-related* evidence of validity is gathered, as is the case when measurement specialists obtain quantifiable content ratings from review panelists, this too constitutes a form of support for the contention that the unobservable construct under consideration (for example, a set of basic skills needed by high school graduates) has been suitably measured. In short, depending on how you look at the first two forms of validity evidence we treated, they might well be regarded as special instances of construct-related evidence of validity.

■ Sanctioned and Unsanctioned Forms of Validity Evidence

Validity, as implied in the outset of the chapter, is the linchpin of educational measurement. If teachers can't draw valid score-based inferences about students, there's simply no reason to measure students in the first place. However, because validity is such a central notion in educational assessment, some folks have attached specialized meanings to it that, although helpful at some level, also may introduce confusion.

One of these is *face validity,* a notion that has been around for a number of decades. All that is meant by face validity is the *appearance* of a test seems to coincide with the use to which the test is being put. To illustrate, if an assessment procedure is supposed to measure a student's actual ability to function collaboratively with a group of other students, then a true-false test that focused exclusively on abstract principles of group dynamics would not appear to be face valid. But, appearance can be deceiving, as has been noted in a variety of ways, such as "not being able to judge a book by its cover." Thus, even though an assessment procedure may *appear* to be consonant with the assessment procedure's mission, we must still assemble evidence that inclines us to put confidence in the score-based inference we arrive at by using the test. If an assessment procedure has no face validity, we're less inclined to assume the assessment procedure is doing its job. Yet, even in those circumstances, we still need to assemble one or more of the three sanctioned varieties of validity evidence to help us know how much confidence, if any, we can put in a score-based interpretation derived from using the assessment procedure.

Another more recently introduced variant of validity is something known as consequential validity. *Consequential validity* refers to whether the *uses* of test results are valid. If, for example, a test's results are inappropriately employed to deny students a reasonable expectation, such as progressing to the next grade level, the test may be said to be consequentially invalid because its results had been used improperly. Yet, *whereas educators should obviously be attentive to the consequences of test use,* the notion of consequential validity is apt to confuse the central thrust of validity—namely, to confirm or disconfirm the defensibility of the score-based inferences we make about our students. If we make accurate inferences about students' status based on a test, yet rely on those inferences to make terrible educational decisions, our test will have negative consequences. But it was the *use* to which we put our valid score-based inferences that is deplorable. The score-based *inference* was right on the mark. "Consequential validity" might be a decent way to remind educators of the importance of consequences when tests are used; it isn't a *bona fide* form of validity evidence. I recommend that you don't employ this potentially confusion-inducing label.

The safest course of action for an educator who wants to remain clearheaded about validity is to rely on the most current version of the *Standards for Educational and Psychological Testing* referred to in the previous chapter. The most recent version of those important *Standards* is the 1999 edition. By incorporating key concepts of the 1999 *Standards* in this fifth edition of my classroom assessment book, I've tried to make the book absolutely *au courant*. (This is either a French phrase for up-to-date or a scone with small raisins.) Be on watch for the next revision of the *Standards*.

■ The Relationship between Reliability and Validity

If convincing evidence is gathered that a test is permitting valid score-based inferences, we can be assured the test is also yielding reasonably reliable scores. In other words, valid score-based inferences almost certainly guarantee that consistent test results are present. The reverse, however, is not true. If a test yields reliable results, it may or may not yield valid score-based inferences. A test, for example, could be measuring with remarkable consistency a construct the test developer never even contemplated measuring. For instance, although the test developer thought an assessment procedure was measuring students' punctuation skills, what was actually measured was students' general intellectual ability which, not comprisingly, splashes over into how well students can punctuate. Inconsistent results will invariably preclude the validity of score-based inferences. Evidence of valid score-based inferences almost certainly requires that consistency of measurement is present.

■ What Do Classroom Teachers Really Need to Know about Validity?

Well, we've spent a fair number of words worrying about the validity of score-based inferences. How much, if anything, do classroom teachers really need to know about validity? Do classroom teachers need to collect validity evidence for their own tests? If so, what kind(s)?

As with reliability, I think a classroom teacher needs to understand what the essential nature of the three kinds of validity evidence is, but I don't think classroom teachers need to go into a frenzy of evidence gathering regarding validity. Clearly, if you're a teacher or a teacher in preparation, you'll be far too busy in your classroom trying to keep ahead of the students to spend much time in assembling validity evidence. I do recommend, however, that for your more important tests, you devote at least some *attention* to content-related evidence of validity. As suggested in the chapter, giving serious thought to the content of an assessment domain being represented by a test is a good first step. Having a colleague review your tests' content is also an effective way to help make sure that your classroom

but what does this have to do with
Teaching?

Most teachers I talk to believe, mistakenly, that their classroom tests are pretty spiffy assessment instruments. Recently I asked five teachers whom I know, "Do you think your classroom tests are pretty spiffy assessment instruments?" Three of the five teachers said, "Yes." One said, "No." And one asked, "What does 'spiffy' mean?" (I counted this as a negative response.) Thus, based on my extensive opinion poll, I can support my contention that *most* teachers think their classroom tests are pretty good—that is, spiffy.

And that's where the concept of *validity* impinges on teaching. Many teachers, you see, believe their classroom assessments produce results that are really rather accurate. Many teachers, in fact, actually think "their tests are valid." The idea that validity resides in tests themselves is a prevalent misconception among the nation's educators. And, unfortunately, when teachers think that their *tests* are valid, then teachers begin to place unwarranted confidence in the scores their students attain on those "valid" tests.

What this chapter has been stressing, restressing, and re-restressing is the idea that validity applies to test-based interpretations, not the tests themselves. Moreover, for teachers to be confident their score-based inferences are valid, it's usually necessary to assemble some compelling evidence (three kinds of evidence are treated in the chapter) to support the accuracy of a teacher's score-based inferences.

And because teaching decisions are often based on a teacher's estimate of students' current achievement levels, then it is apparent that unwarranted confidence in those test-based estimates can sometimes lead to faulty interpretations and, as a result, to unsound instructional decisions.

If teachers accept the chapter's central contention that validity of test-based inferences requires teachers to make a *judgment* about the accuracy of those test-based inferences, and that compelling data are needed in order for a teacher to be supersure test-based *judgments* about students' achievement levels are on target, then teachers will more likely recognize that their instructional decisions are often based on a fairly fragile assessment foundation.

In today's high-stakes environment, it is even more important that teachers regard validity as a judgment-derived commodity. For example, suppose your state's officially approved curriculum contains scads of content standards. Because *scads* represents a large number (and is rarely encountered in its singular form), your state clearly has a great many content standards to be taught—and tested. Now let's suppose your state's annual NCLB tests are intended to assess students' mastery of those scads of content standards in a few hours of testing. Well, if that's the situation, do you really think there is apt to be great accuracy in the following statement by an elected state official? "Mastery of all our state's content standards can be determined on the basis of students' scores on our state's valid NCLB tests." Even elected state officials, you see, can make mistakes in their judgment. For one thing, there are too many content standards for students' "mastery" to be determined. Second (and you know this by now), tests aren't valid.

tests represent satisfactorily the content you're trying to promote, and that your score-based inferences about your students' status are not miles off the mark.

Regarding the other two forms of validity evidence, however, I urge little more than a reasonable understanding of what those kinds of evidence are. If you're ever asked to help scrutinize a high-stakes educational test, you'll want to know enough about such versions of validity evidence so you're not intimidated when measurement specialists start reciting their "odes to validity."

Perhaps the most important thing classroom teachers need to understand about validity is it does *not* reside in a test itself. Rather, it is a score-based inference that is either accurate or inaccurate. And because score-based inferences reflect judgments made by people, some of those judgments will be in error. Validity is a far more elusive critter than is usually thought. Indeed, valid score-based inferences in the field of education might properly be placed on our nation's endangered species list.

■ Chapter Summary

The focus of Chapter 3 was on three forms of validity evidence that can be used to support a validity argument. *Content-related evidence* provides a picture of the extent to which an assessment procedure suitably samples the content of the curricular aim it represents. *Criterion-related evidence* of validity deals with the degree to which an exam accurately predicts a student's subsequent status. *Construct-related evidence* of validity deals with the assembly of empirical evidence that a hypothetical construct, such as a student's ability to generate written compositions, is accurately assessed.

The relationship between validity evidence and reliability evidence was considered, as were certain unsanctioned forms of validity. It was suggested that, in general, more validity evidence is better than less, but that classroom teachers need to be realistic in how much evidence of validity to secure for their own tests. A recommendation was given to have teachers become familiar with all three forms of evidence, but to focus only on content-related evidence of validity for their own classroom assessment procedures. Most importantly, it was stressed that teachers recognize validity as a judgmental inference about the interpretation of students' test performances—not an attribute of tests themselves.

 ## Self-Check

For the first five self-check exercises, you'll be given four-option multiple-choice items in which you're asked to identify the kind of validity evidence that's described or to indicate that "None of the above" is the best response. Notice that the inclusion of the None-of-the-above option increases the difficulty of the items because, had there only been three evidence categories, you could simply choose the *best* answer from the three. With the None-of-the-above option, you have to decide whether there's any validity evidence there at all. After the first five multiple-choice items, you'll be getting five short-answer items.

1. A fifth-grade classroom teacher is concerned about whether he's measuring the appropriate content in his end-of-the-year final examination. Accordingly, he decides to see how well his students' end-of-the-year exam scores predict students' grades earned *at the end of the sixth grade*. He waits one year, then computes a correlation coefficient between his students' fifth-grade final exam scores and the end-of-year grades supplied by their sixth-grade teachers. What kind of evidence is the teacher assembling?
   a. Content-related evidence of validity
   b. Criterion-related evidence of validity
   c. Construct-related evidence of validity
   d. None of the above

2. Having created two forms of a final examination for her physics course, a teacher wishes to verify that the two forms are presenting equidifficult challenges to her students. She has her students take one form of the examination on a Wednesday and the second form of the examination on a Friday. She then correlates students' scores on the two forms. What kind of evidence is the teacher assembling?
   a. Content-related evidence of validity
   b. Criterion-related evidence of validity
   c. Construct-related evidence of validity
   d. None of the above

3. A school district measurement specialist has been studying a newly developed test of children's thinking skills as a potential assessment instrument to be used in the district. Because effective thinkers are supposed to be flexible, the developers of the new test provide evidence there is a negative relationship between students' test scores and their scores on a rigidity test. (The higher the scores on the rigidity test, the less flexible the student is supposed to be.) What kind of evidence are the developers of the thinking skills test providing?
   a. Content-related evidence of validity
   b. Criterion-related evidence of validity
   c. Construct-related evidence of validity
   d. None of the above

4. For all of his major classroom assessments, a history teacher asks the district's social studies supervisor to review the draft assessment instruments to make sure that they're covering the right knowledge and skills. Although most of the time the supervisor approves the proposed tests as is, on a few occasions the supervisor has identified content-coverage gaps. What kind of evidence is the teacher assembling?
   a. Content-related evidence of validity
   b. Criterion-related evidence of validity
   c. Construct-related evidence of validity
   d. None of the above

5. A third-grade teacher is concerned that her language arts tests are covering content that is too heterogenous. Accordingly, she computes an internal con-

sistency correlation coefficient for each test so she can establish the degree of content homogeneity represented in those tests. The resultant coefficients tend to range between .80 and .90. What kind of evidence is the teacher assembling?

a. Content-related evidence of validity
b. Criterion-related evidence of validity
c. Construct-related evidence of validity
d. None of the above

6. In your own words, describe the essence of *content-related evidence of validity.*

_____

_____

7. In your own words, describe the essence of *criterion-related evidence of validity.*

_____

_____

8. In your own words, describe the essence of *construct-related evidence of validity.*

_____

_____

9. What, in a nutshell, is the essential relationship between validity and reliability?

_____

_____

10. Why is it incorrect to say that "a test is valid" or to say that "a classroom assessment procedure is valid"?

_____

_____

? Pondertime

1. Why do you think validity is such a central concept in educational assessment?

2. It was suggested that some measurement specialists regard all forms of validity evidence as construct-related validity evidence. Do you agree? If so, or if not, why?

3. What, if anything, do you think school board members need to know about assessment validity?

4. What, if anything, do you think run-of-the-society citizens need to know about assessment validity?

5. What kind(s) of validity evidence do *you* think classroom teachers need to assemble regarding their classroom assessment devices?

6. What is your opinion of "consequential validity"?

Self-Check Key

Here are the correct answers for the first five self-check exercises: 1:b, 2:d (it's alternate-form reliability evidence she's gathering), 3:c, 4:a, 5:d (this is a quest for reliability evidence, not validity evidence).

6. You should have said something that resembles the brief description provided in Table 3.1.

7. You should have done what it says in number 6 above.

8. You should have done what it says in number 7 above that it says you should have done in number 6 above.

9. In a walnut shell (walnuts go great in brownies), if a test is reliable, it may or may not yield valid score-based inferences; if the test yields valid score-based inferences, it is almost certainly reliable.

10. Validity, in the case of classroom assessment procedures or any kind of test, refers not to the measurement itself, but to the validity of score-based inferences. More technically, we are trying to see if our test-based inferences about students' status with respect to a curricular aim are valid.

■ Additional Stuff

American Educational Research Association. (1999). *Standards for Educational and Psychological Testing.* Washington, DC: Author.

Cizek, Gregory J. (2003). *Detecting and Preventing Classroom Cheating: Promoting Integrity in Assessment.* Thousand Oaks, CA: Corwin Press.

Frisbie, David A. (2005). "Presidential Address: Measurement 101: Some Fundamentals Revisited." *Educational Measurement: Issues and Practice, 24,* no. 5 (Fall): 21–28.

Lane, Suzanne, and Clement A. Stone. (2002). "Strategies for Examining the Consequences of Assessment and Accountability Programs." *Educational Measurement: Issues and Practice, 21,* no. 1 (Spring): 25–30.

Popham, W. James. (1997). "Consequential Validity: Right Concern—Wrong Concept." *Educational Measurement: Issues and Practice, 16,* no. 2 (Summer): 9–13.

Shepard, Lorrie A. (1997). "The Centrality of Test Use and Consequences for Test Validity." *Educational Measurement: Issues and Practice, 16,* no. 2 (Summer): 5–8, 13, 24.

■ Nonprint Stuff

PSARAS Foundation and South Carolina Department of Education. (2002). (W. James Popham, Narrator). *Educational Tests: Misunderstood Measuring Sticks* (Videotape SCTV-10; SCTV-25). Columbia, SC: Author.

■ Cyber Stuff

- *The National Center for Research on Evaluation, Standards, and Student Testing (CRESST)* is headquartered at UCLA, but is jointly staffed by CRESST partners from a number of major universities and testing organizations. Funded by the U.S. Department of Education, the thrust of most CRESST projects over the years has been toward research on assessment and evaluation topics related to K–12 education. Ongoing CRESST projects are featured as well as a rich collection of CRESST-produced reports, newsletters, and policy briefs. www.cresst.org

To access chapter objectives, practice tests, weblinks, and flashcards, visit the companion website at **www.ablongman.com/popham5e.**

MyLabSchool is a collection of online tools for your success in this course, your licensure exams, and your teaching career. Discover where the classroom comes to life by visiting **www.mylabschool.com** to access the following resources:

- Video clips from real classrooms
- An archive of real-life cases
- Help with your research papers using Research Navigator™
- Career Center with resources for:
    Praxis exams and licensure preparation
    Professional portfolio development
    Job search and interview techniques
    Lesson planning with state standard correlations

Absence-of-Bias

T he last of the "big three" criteria for evaluating educational assessment devices is, in contrast to reliability and validity, a new kid on the block. During the past couple of decades, educators have increasingly recognized that the tests they use are often biased against particular groups of students. As a consequence, students in those groups do not perform as well on a test, not because the students are less able, but because there are features in the test that distort the nature of the students' performances.

Assessment bias refers to qualities of an assessment instrument that offend or unfairly penalize a group of students because of students' gender, race, ethnicity, socioeconomic status, religion, or other such group-defining characteristics. Most teachers are sufficiently familiar with the idea of test bias these days that, at least in a general way, they recognize what's being talked about when someone says, "That test was biased." In this chapter, however, we'll take a deeper look at what test bias is—and what it isn't. Moreover, we'll consider some procedures that can help classroom teachers recognize whether bias is present in assessment procedures and, as a consequence, can help reduce or eradicate bias in teachers' own classroom tests. Finally, we'll tackle a particularly difficult issue—namely, how to reduce bias when assessing students with disabilities.

Because the other two criteria for evaluating educational tests—reliability and validity—are "good things," we're going to use the expression *absence-of-bias* to describe the third evaluative criterion. When bias is absent in tests, this is also a "good thing." Before looking at procedures to promote the absence-of-bias in educational assessment procedures, let's first look more directly at what we're trying to eliminate. In other words, let's look at assessment bias.

■ The Nature of Assessment Bias

As indicated earlier, assessment bias is present when there are elements in an assessment procedure that distort a student's performance merely because of the student's personal characteristics, such as gender, ethnicity, and so on. Most of the time, we think about distortions that tend to lower the scores of students because those students are members of particular subgroups. For example, suppose officials in State *X* installed a high-stakes mathematics test to be passed before students receive an "honors" diploma. If the mathematics test contained many word problems based on competitive sports examples about which boys were more familiar than girls, then girls might perform less well on the test than boys. The lower performance by girls would not occur because girls were less skilled in mathematics, but because they were less familiar with the sports contexts in which the word problems were placed. The mathematics test, therefore, appears to be biased against girls. On the other hand, it could also be said the mathematics test is biased in favor of boys. In the case of assessment bias, what we're worried about is distortions of students' test performances—either unwarranted increases or unwarranted decreases.

Let's try another illustration. Suppose that a scholastic aptitude test featured test items based on five lengthy reading selections, two of which were based on content more likely to be known to members of a particular religious group. If, because of familiarity with the content of the two selections, members of the religious group outperformed others, this would be a distortion in their test performances. There would be an assessment bias in their favor.

If you think carefully about the issue we're considering, you'll realize assessment bias, because it distorts students' performances, interferes with the validity of the score-based inferences we draw from our assessment procedures. But, because assessment bias constitutes such a distinctive threat to the validity of test-based inferences, and a threat that can be directly addressed, it is usually regarded as a separate criterion when evaluating educational tests. To the extent that bias is present, for the groups of students against whom the test is biased, valid score-based inferences are not apt to be forthcoming.

Let's look, now, at two forms of assessment bias—that is, two ways in which the test performances of individuals in particular groups can be distorted. It was noted earlier in the chapter that assessment bias is present if an educational assessment procedure offends or unfairly penalizes students because of their membership in a gender, racial, ethnic, religious, or similar subgroup. We'll consider both of these forms of assessment bias.

Offensiveness

An assessment procedure is biased if its content (for example, its items) is *offensive* to a subgroup of students. Such offensiveness often occurs when negative stereotypes of certain subgroup members are presented in a test. For instance, suppose that in all of an exam's items we saw males portrayed in high-paying and prestigious positions (e.g., attorneys and physicians) and we saw women portrayed in low-paying and unprestigious positions (e.g., housewives and clerks). Because at least some female students will, quite appropriately, be offended by this gender inequality, their resultant distress may lead to less than optimal performances on the exam and, as a consequence, scores that do not accurately represent their capabilities. (Angry women, or angry men, aren't the best test takers.)

Other kinds of offensive content includes slurs, blatant or implied, based on stereotypic negatives about how members of particular ethnic or religious groups behave. This kind of offensive content, of course, can distract students in the offended group so they end up focusing more on the offensiveness of a given item than on accurately displaying their own abilities on subsequent items.

Although most of the nation's major test-development agencies now employ item-writing and item-review procedures designed to eliminate such offensive content, one encounters far too many examples of offensive content in less carefully developed teacher-made tests. It is not that teachers deliberately set out to offend any of their students. Rather, many teachers have simply not thought carefully about whether the content of their classroom assessment procedures might cause distress for any of their students. Later in the chapter, we'll consider some practical ways of eradicating offensive content in teachers' classroom assessment procedures.

Unfair Penalization

A second factor contributing to assessment bias is content in a test that may cause *unfair penalization* for a student based on the student's ethnicity, gender, race, religion, and so on. Let's consider for a moment what an "unfair" penalty really is.

Unfair penalization arises when a student's test performance is distorted because of content that, although not offensive, disadvantages the student because of the student's group membership. The previously cited example about girls' unfamiliarity with certain competitive sports would be an illustration of what an unfair penalty would be. As another example, suppose an assessment procedure includes content apt to be known only to children from affluent families. Let's say an assessment procedure is installed to see how well students can "collaboratively problem solve" in groups, and the assessment activity culminates when the teacher gives students a new problem to analyze collaboratively in a group discussion. If the content of the new problem deals with a series of locally presented operas and symphonies likely to have been attended only by those whose parents can afford such performances' hefty ticket prices, then students from less affluent families will be unfairly penalized because there was probably much less dinner conversation about the local operas and symphonies. Students from lower socioeconomic strata might perform less well on the "collaborative problem solving" assessment enterprise not because they are less skilled at collaborative problem solving, but because they are unfamiliar with the upper-crust content of the particular assessment procedure being employed to gauge students' collaborative problem-solving skills.

Some penalties, of course, are as fair as they can be. If you're a classroom teacher who's generated a test on a unit you've been teaching, and some students perform poorly simply because they didn't pay attention in class or didn't do their

Decision Time

Choose Your Language, Children!

Jaime Jemez teaches mathematics in Wilson Junior High School. He has done so for the past 10 years and is generally regarded as an excellent instructor. In the past few years, however, the student population at Wilson Junior High has been undergoing some dramatic shifts. Whereas there were relatively few Hispanic students in the past, almost 30% of the student population is now Hispanic. Moreover, almost half of those students arrived in the United States less than 2 years ago. Most of the newly arrived students in Jaime's classes came from Mexico and Central America.

Because English is a second language for most of these Hispanic students, and because many of the newly arrived students still have a difficult time with written English, Jaime has been wondering if his mathematics examinations are biased against many of the Hispanic students in his classes. Because Jaime reads and writes Spanish fluently, he has been considering whether he should provide Spanish-language versions of his more important examinations. Although such a decision would result in some extra work for him, Jaime believes that language-choice tests would reduce the bias in his assessment procedures for students whose initial language was Spanish.

Jaime is also aware that the demographics of the district are still shifting and that an increasing number of Southeast Asian students are beginning to show up in his classes. He is afraid that if he starts providing Spanish-language versions of his tests, perhaps he will need to provide the tests in other languages as well. However, he is fluent only in Spanish and English.

 If you were Jaime, what would your decision be?

homework assignments, their lousy performance on your test is eminently fair. Their "penalty," in fact, simply reeks of fairness. Poor performances on an assessment procedure need not signify the resultant penalty to the student (such as a low grade) is unfair. Many of the students I taught in high school and college richly deserved the low grades I gave them.

Unfair penalization arises only when it is not the student's ability that leads to poor performance but, rather, the student's group membership. If, because of the student's gender, ethnicity, and so on, the content of the test distorts how the student would otherwise have performed, then a solid case of assessment bias is at hand. As was true in the case of offensiveness of test content, we sometimes find classroom teachers who haven't thought carefully about whether their assessment procedures' content gives all students an equal chance to perform well. We'll soon consider some ways for classroom teachers to ferret out test content that might unfairly penalize certain of their students.

■ Disparate Impact and Assessment Bias

It is sometimes the case that when a statewide, high-stakes test is originally installed, its impact on different ethnic groups will be disparate. For example, African American students or Hispanic students may perform less well than non-Hispanic White students. Does this *disparate impact* mean the test is biased? Not necessarily. However, if a test has a disparate impact on members of a particular racial, gender, or religious subgroup, this disparate impact certainly warrants further scrutiny to see if the test is actually biased. Disparate impact does not equal assessment bias.

Let me tell you about an experience I had in the late seventies that drove this point home so I never forgot it. I was working in a southern state to help its state officials develop a series of statewide tests that, ultimately, would be used to deny diplomas to students who failed to pass the twelfth-grade level of the test. Having field-tested all of the potential items for the tests on several thousand children in the state, we had assembled a committee of 25 teachers from throughout the state, roughly half of whom were African American, to review the field-test results. The function of the committee was to see if there were any items that should be discarded. For a number of the items, the African American children in the statewide tryout had performed significantly less well than the other children. Yet, almost any time it was proposed that such items be jettisoned because of such a disparate impact, it was the African American teachers who said, "Our children need to know what's in that item. It deals with important content. Don't you *dare* toss that item out!"

Those African American teachers were saying, in no uncertain terms, that African American children, just as non-African American children, *should* know what was being tested by those items, even if a disparate impact was currently present. The teachers wanted to make sure that if African American youngsters could not currently perform well enough on those items, the presence of the items in the test would allow such deficits to be identified and, as a consequence, to be remediated. The teachers wanted to make sure that *future* disparate impacts would be eliminated.

If an assessment procedure leads to a differential impact on a particular group of students, then it is imperative to discern if the assessment procedure is biased. But if the assessment procedure does not offend or unfairly penalize any student subgroups, then the most likely explanation of disparate impact is prior instructional inadequacies for the low-performing group. In other words, there's nothing wrong with the test, but there was definitely something wrong with the quality of education previously provided to the subgroup of students who scored poorly on the examination.

It is well known, of course, that genuine equality of education has not always been present in every locale. Thus, it should come as no surprise that some tests will, in particular settings, have a disparate impact on certain subgroups. But this does not necessarily signify the tests are biased. It may well be the tests are helping identify prior inequities in instruction that should be ameliorated.

Let's conclude our consideration of assessment bias by dealing with two strategies for eliminating or, at least, markedly reducing the extent to which unsuitable content on assessment devices can distort certain students' scores. Such distortions, of course, erode the validity of the score-based inference educators arrive at when they use such assessment devices. And rotten inferences about students' status, of course, usually lead to rotten decisions about those students.

■ Judgmental Approaches

One particularly useful way to identify any aspects of an assessment procedure that may be biased is to call on content-knowledgeable reviewers to *judgmentally scrutinize* the assessment procedure, item by item, to see if any items offend or unfairly penalize certain subgroups of students. When any important, high-stakes test is developed these days, it is customary to have a bias review panel consider its items in order to isolate and discard any that may contribute to assessment bias. After seeing how such a procedure is implemented for high-stakes tests, we'll consider how classroom teachers can carry out the essential features of judgmental bias-detection reviews for their own assessment procedures.

Bias Review Panels

For high-stakes tests such as a state's NCLB exams, a bias review panel of, say, 15 to 25 reviewers is typically assembled. Each of the reviewers is conversant with the content of the test being reviewed. For example, if a sixth-grade NCLB language arts test were under development, the bias review committee might be comprised mostly of sixth-grade teachers along with a few district-level language arts curriculum specialists or university professors. The panel should be composed exclusively, or almost exclusively, of individuals from the subgroups who might be adversely impacted by the test. In other words, if the test is to be administered to minority students who are Asian American, Native American, African American, and Hispanic American, there should be representatives of each of those groups on the panel. There should also be a mix of male and female panelists so that panelists can attend to possible gender bias in items.

After the bias review panel is assembled, its members should be provided with a thorough orientation regarding the meaning of assessment bias—perhaps along the lines of the discussion earlier in this chapter. Ideally, panelists should be given some guided practice in reviewing several assessment items deliberately designed to illustrate specific deficits—for instance, content that is offensive or content that unfairly penalizes certain subgroups. Discussions of such illustrative items usually help clarify the panel's understanding of assessment bias.

A Per-Item Absence-of-Bias Judgment

After the orientation, the bias review panelists should be asked to respond to a question such as the following for *each* of the test's items:

An Illustrative Absence-of-Bias Item Question for Bias Review Panelists

Might this item offend or unfairly penalize any group of students on the basis of personal characteristics, such as gender, ethnicity, religion, or race?

Panelists are to respond *yes* or *no* to each item using this question. Note the illustrative question does not ask panelists to judge whether an item *would* offend or unfairly penalize. Rather, the question asks whether an item *might* offend or unfairly penalize. In other words, if there's a *chance* the item might be biased, bias review panelists are to answer *yes* to the absence-of-bias question. Had the item-bias question used *would* instead of *might*, I hope you can see this renders it a less stringent form of per-item scrutiny.

The percentage of *no* judgments per item is then calculated so an average per-item absence-of-bias index (for the whole panel) can be computed for each item and, thereafter, for the entire test. The more *no* judgments panelists supply, the less bias they think is present in the items. If the test is still under development, items are generally discarded that are judged to be biased by several panelists. Because panelists are usually encouraged to indicate (via a brief written comment) why an item appears to be biased, it is often the case that an item will be discarded because of a *single* panelist's judgment if it is apparent this panelist spotted a deficit in the item that had been overlooked by other panelists.

An Overall Absence-of-Bias Judgment

Although having a bias review panel scrutinize the individual items in an assessment device is critical, there's always the chance the *items in aggregate* may be biased, particularly with respect to the degree to which they might offend certain students. For instance, as the bias review panelists consider the individual items, they may find few problems. Yet, when considered as a collectivity, the items may prove to be offensive. Suppose, for example, in an extensive series of mathematics word problems, the individuals depicted were almost always females. Although this gender disproportion was not apparent from panelists' reviews of individual items, it could be discerned from panelists' responses to an overall absence-of-bias question such as the following:

An Illustrative Overall Absence-of-Bias Question for Bias Review Panelists

Considering all of the items in the assessment device you just reviewed, do the items, taken as a whole, offend or unfairly penalize any group of students on the basis of personal characteristics, such as gender, ethnicity, religion, or race?

Similar to the item-by-item judgments of panelists, the percent of *no* responses by panelists to this overall absence-of-bias question can provide a useful index of whether the assessment procedure is biased. As with the individual item judgments, bias review panelists who respond *yes* to an overall absence-of-bias question are usually asked to indicate why. Typically, the deficits identified in response to this overall question can be corrected rather readily. For instance, in the previous example about too many females being described in the mathematics word problems, all that needs to be done is a bit of gender changing (verbally rather than surgically).

In review, then, judgmental scrutiny of an assessment procedure's items, separately or *in toto*, can prove effective in identifying items that contribute to assessment bias. Such items should be modified or eliminated.

■ Empirical Approaches

If a high-stakes educational test is to be administered to a large number of students, it is typically possible to gather tryout evidence regarding the performance of different groups of students on individual items, then review any items for potential bias for which there are substantial disparities between the performances of different groups. There are a number of different technical procedures for identifying items on which subgroups perform differently. Generally, these procedures are characterized as *differential item functioning (DIF)* procedures because the analyses are used to identify items that function differently for one group (for example, girls) than for another (for example, boys). There are numerous DIF analysis procedures now available for use in detecting potentially biased items.

Even after an item has been identified as a differentially functioning item, this does not automatically mean the item is biased. Recalling our discussion of the difference between assessment bias and disparate impact, it is still necessary to scrutinize a differentially functioning item to see if it is biased or, instead, is detecting the effects of prior instructional inadequacies for a particular group of students. In most large-scale test-development projects these days, even after all items have been subjected to the judgmental scrutiny of a bias review panel, items identified as functioning differentially are "flagged" for a second look by bias reviewers (for example, by the earlier bias review panel or perhaps by a different bias review panel). Only those items that are, at this point, judgmentally identified as biased are excised from the test.

To reiterate, large numbers of students are required in order for empirical bias-reduction approaches to work. Several hundred responses per item for each subgroup under scrutiny are needed before a reasonably accurate estimate of an item's differential functioning can be made.

■ Bias Detection in the Classroom

If you're an experienced teacher or are preparing to be a teacher, what can you do about assessment bias in your own classroom? I have a deceptively simple but, I believe, accurate answer to this question. The answer is: *Become sensitive to the existence of assessment bias and the need to eliminate it.*

You'll remember there are three big-bopper evaluative criteria you've been urged to use in evaluating any kind of educational assessment—namely, reliability, validity, and absence-of-bias. Bias really can be a serious shortcoming of your own tests. As indicated earlier, a test that's biased won't allow you to make valid inferences about your students' learning levels. And if your inferences are invalid, who cares if you're making those inferences reliably? Absence-of-bias, in short, is significant stuff.

Okay, let's assume you've made a commitment to be sensitive to the possibility of bias in your own classroom assessments. How do you go about it? I recommend that you always review your own assessments, insofar as you can, from the perspective of the students you have in your classes—students whose experiences will frequently be decisively different from your own. Even if you're a Hispanic American and you have a dozen Hispanic American students, this does *not* mean that their backgrounds parallel yours.

What you need to do is *think seriously* about the impact that differing experiential backgrounds will have on the way students respond to your classroom assessments. You'll obviously not always be able to "get inside the heads" of the many different students you have, but try to.

My first teaching job was in a rural high school in an eastern Oregon town with a population of 1,500 people. I had grown up in a fairly large city and had no knowledge about farming or ranching. To me, a "range" was a kitchen appliance on which one cooked meals. In retrospect, I'm certain that many of my classroom tests contained "city" content that might have confused my students. I'll bet anything that many of my early test items unfairly penalized some of the boys and girls who had rarely, if ever, left their farms or ranches to visit more metropolitan areas. And, given the size of our tiny town, almost any place on earth was "more metropolitan." But assessment bias was something I simply didn't think about back then. I hope you will.

Parent Talk

Assume that you are White and were raised in a middle-class environment. During your fourth year of teaching, you've been transferred to an inner-city elementary school in which you teach a class of 27 fifth-graders, half of whom are African Americans. Suppose that Mrs. Johnson, a mother of one of your students, telephones you after school to complain about her son's test results in your class. Mrs. Johnson says, "George always got good grades until he came to your class. But on your tests, he always scores low. I think it's because your tests are biased against Black children!"

▶ *If I were you, here's how I'd respond to Mrs. Johnson:*

"First, Mrs. Johnson, I really appreciate your calling about George's progress. We both want the very best for him, and now that you've phoned, I hope we can work together in his best interest.

"About George's test performance, I realize he hasn't done all that well on most of the tests. But I'm afraid it isn't because of test bias. Because this is my first year in this school, and because about half of my fifth-graders are African American, I was really worried that, as a White person, I *might* be developing tests that were biased against some of my students.

"So, during my first week on the job, I asked Ms. Fleming—another fifth-grade teacher who's African American—if she'd review my tests for possible bias. She agreed and she's been kind enough to review every single test item I've used this year. I try to be careful myself about identifying biased items, and I'm getting pretty good at it, but Ms. Fleming helped me spot several items, particularly at the start of the year, that might have been biased against African American children. I removed or revised all those items.

"What I think is going on in George's case, Mrs. Johnson, is the instruction he's received in the past. I think George is a very bright child, but I know your family transferred to our district this year from another state. I really fear that where George went to school in the past, he may not have been provided with the building-block skills he needs for my class.

"What I'd like to do, if you're willing, is to set up a conference either here at school or in your home, if that's more convenient, to discuss the particular skills George is having difficulty with. I'm confident we can work out an approach, with your assistance, that will help George acquire the skills he needs."

▶ *Now, how would you respond to Mrs. Johnson?*

Some of the newer forms of assessment you'll be reading about in later chapters, particularly performance assessment (in Chapter 8) and portfolio assessment (in Chapter 9), because teachers are less familiar with those types of assessment, contain serious potential for assessment bias. To illustrate, most performance assessments call for students to respond to a fairly elaborate task of some sort (such as researching a social issue and presenting an oral report to the class). Because these tasks sometimes require students to draw heavily on their own experiences, it is imperative to select tasks that present the cherished "level playing field" to all students. You'd certainly not wish to use a performance assessment that gave an up-front advantage to students from more affluent families.

Then there's the problem of how to evaluate students' responses to performance assessments or how to judge the student-generated products in students' portfolios. All too often I have seen teachers evaluate students' responses on the basis of whether those responses displayed "good thinking ability." What those teachers were doing, unfortunately, was creating their own, off-the-cuff version of a group intelligence test—an assessment approach now generally repudiated. Students' responses to performance and portfolio assessments are too often judged on the basis of factors that are more background dependent than instructionally promotable. Assessment bias applies to *all* forms of testing, not merely paper-and-pencil tests.

If you want to expunge bias from your own assessments, try to review *every* item in *every* assessment from the perspective of whether there is anything present in the item that might *offend* or *unfairly penalize* any of your students. If you ever find such potential bias in any of your items, then without delay patch them up or plow them under.

You'll probably never be able to remove *all* bias from your classroom assessments. Biased content has a nasty habit of slipping past even the most bias-conscious classroom teacher. But if you show me 100 teachers who are seriously sensitized to the possibility of assessment bias in their own tests and 100 teachers who've not thought much about assessment bias, there's no doubt in my mind regarding which 100 teachers will create less biased assessments. My doubt-free judgment, of course, might be biased!

Assessing Students with Disabilities and English Language Learners

Assessment bias can blossom in often unforeseen ways when teachers attempt to assess two distinctive categories of children—namely, *students with disabilities* and *English language learners.* In the past, because these two groups of students often received the bulk of their instruction from educational specialists rather than regular classroom teachers, many teachers gave scant attention to the testing of such students. However, largely due to the enactment of two far-reaching federal laws, today's classroom teachers need to understand, at the very least, some fundamentals about how to assess children with disabilities as well as English language learners. We'll briefly consider potential assessment bias as it relates to both of these types of students.

Children with Disabilities and Federal Law

Many teachers, when they hear the phrase "children with disabilities" immediately think of children who, because they are mentally retarded, are euphemistically regarded as *special education* students. Such perceptions are way off the mark. Actually, only about 10 percent of children with disabilities are mentally retarded. Fully two-thirds of children with disabilities either have specific learning disabilities—almost 80% of which arise from students' problems with reading—or impairments in a child's speech or language. There are 13 categories of disability set forth in federal law, including such less-frequent disabilities as autism (2% of children with disabilities), emotional disturbance (8%), and hearing impairments (1%).

Federal law, you see, has triggered substantially reconceptualized views about how to teach and to test students with disabilities. The Education for All Handicapped Children Act (Public Law 94-142) was enacted in 1975 because of (1) a growing recognition of the need to properly educate children who had disabilities and (2) a series of judicial rulings requiring states to provide a suitable education for students with disabilities if those states were providing one for students without disabilities. Usually referred to simply as "P.L. 94-142," this influential law supplied federal funding to states, but only if those states appropriately educated children with disabilities.

Public Law 94-142 also installed the use of an *individualized education program,* or **IEP,** for a student with disabilities. An IEP is the federally prescribed document developed by parents, teachers, and specialized services providers (such as an audiologist) describing how a particular child with disabilities should be educated. An IEP represents a per-child plan that spells out annual goals for the child, indicates how the student's attainment of those goals will be determined, specifies whatever related services are needed by the child, and sets forth any adjustments or substitutions in the assessments to be used with the child. The architects of P.L. 94-142 believed it would encourage many students with disabilities to be educated, to the extent possible, in regular classrooms.

In 1997, P.L. 94-142 was reauthorized and, at the same time, labeled the Individuals with Disabilities Act (IDEA). That reauthorization called for states and districts to identify curricular expectations for special education students that were as consonant as possible with the curricular expectations that had been established *for all other students.* Under IDEA, all states and districts were required to include students with disabilities in their assessment programs—and to publicly report those test results. However, because IDEA of 1997 contained few negative consequences for noncompliance, most of the nation's educators simply failed to comply.

The special education landscape, however, was significantly altered on January 8, 2002, when President George W. Bush affixed his signature to the No Child Left Behind Act. Unlike IDEA of 1997, NCLB possessed significantly increased penalties for noncompliance. The act intends to improve the achievement levels of *all* students—including children with disabilities—and to do so in a way that such improvement will be *demonstrated* on state-chosen tests linked to each state's curricular aims. Students' test scores must improve on a regular basis over a dozen years in order to reflect substantially improved student learning. Even though

NCLB allows states some flexibility in deciding how many more students must earn "proficient or higher" scores each year on that state's NCLB tests, if a school fails to make adequate yearly progress (AYP) based on a state's 12-year improvement schedule, then the school is soon placed on a sanction-laden improvement track.

Importantly, NCLB requires adequate yearly progress not only for students overall but also for subgroups reflecting race/ethnicity, the economically disadvantaged, students with limited English proficiency, and *students with disabilities*. Accordingly, if there are sufficient numbers of any of those subgroups in a school, and *one* of those subgroups fails to score high enough to make that subgroup's AYP targets, then the whole school will have flopped on AYP. Obviously, the assessed performances of students with disabilities became far more significant to a school's educators than was the case prior to the enactment of NCLB.

In 2004, IDEA was reauthorized once again. At that juncture, however, there was already another significant federal statute on the books dealing with the assessment of students with disabilities—namely, NCLB. Federal lawmakers attempted to shape the reauthorized IDEA so it would be as consistent as possible with the assessment provisions of NCLB that had been enacted two years earlier. Even so, there continue to be important procedural differences between IDEA and NCLB, even though one finds few fundamental contradictions between those two laws. Remember that when P.L. 94-142 first trotted onto the scene, one of its most influential contributions was the IEP. Many teachers came to understand that an individualized education program was supposed to be just what it said it was—an *individualized* program for a particular student with disabilities. Thus, the push of IDEA has historically been directed toward an *individualized* approach to instruction and an *individualized* approach to assessing what a student has learned.

Instead of the more student-tailored approach embodied in IDEA, the accountability strategy embodied in NCLB is a far more *group-based* (and *subgroup-based*) approach than the kid-by-kid orientation of IDEA. I thought that a key congressional committee put it well when it observed, "IDEA and NCLB work in concert to ensure that students with disabilities are included in assessment and accountability systems. While IDEA focuses on the needs of the individual child, NCLB focuses on ensuring improved academic achievement for *all* students."[1]

By all odds, the most important thing teachers need to understand about the instruction and assessment of students with disabilities is that the education of all but a *very* small group of those children must be aimed at precisely *the same curricular targets* as the curricular targets teachers have for all other students. Both NCLB and IDEA require the *same* content standards for *all* children—with no exceptions! However, for students with the most severe cognitive disabilities it is possible to use different definitions of achievement. Thus, this small group of students can use modified ways to display their performance related to the same content standards. These modifications take the form of **alternate assessments**. According to NCLB, such alternate assessments are to be used with only that super-small percent of children who suffer from the most severe cognitive disabilities. In other words, whereas the academic content standards must stay the same for all students, it is the academic achievement standards (performance levels) that can differ substantively for children who have the most severe cognitive disabilities.

Because IEPs are central to the assessment of many children with disabilities, I want to deal with the widespread misperception that IEPs are written documents allowing the parents and teachers of children with disabilities to do some serious bar-lowering, but to do so behind closed doors. Many general education teachers know almost nothing about the IEP process. To those teachers, IEPs are born in clandestine meetings in which biased individuals simply soften expectations so that children with disabilities need not pursue the curricular aims identical to those sought for all other children. Perhaps such perceptions were warranted in earlier years, but IEP regulations have been seriously modified in recent years. If those who create today's IEPs deliberately aim at anything less than the same content standards being pursued by all students, then such IEPs violate some big-stick federal statutes.

Accommodations   The most prominent procedure to minimize assessment bias for students with disabilities is to employ *assessment accommodations.* An accommodation is a procedure or practice that permits students with disabilities to have an equitable access to instruction and assessment. The mission of an assessment accommodation is to eliminate or reduce the inference-distorting effects of a student's disabilities. It is not the purpose of accommodations to lower the aspirations educators have for students with disabilities. Typically, but not always, the accommodations provided to a student in an assessment setting are similar to the ones used during instruction for that student.

Although accommodations smack of fairness by providing students with opportunities to circumvent their disabilities, there's a critical limitation on just how much fairness-induction can be provided. Here's the rub: An assessment accommodation must not fundamentally alter the nature of the skills or knowledge being assessed. I can illustrate with respect to the skill of reading. Teachers clearly want children—whether those children have disabilities or not—to learn to read. A teacher, however, can't simply look at a student and tell whether that student can read. That's because the ability to read is a *covert* skill. To determine a child's reading ability, teachers need to have a student engage in an *overt* act, such as silently reading a brief short story, then saying aloud—or in writing—what the story was about. A teacher can, based on the child's *assessed* overt performance, arrive at an inference about the child's reading skills.

However, what if a teacher proposed to use an accommodation for a child with disabilities that called for a short story to be read aloud to the child? This would surely be a meaningful accommodation, and I suppose the child would enjoy hearing a read-aloud story. But suppose the child were then given a written or oral test about the content of the short story. Do you think the child's overt responses to that test would allow a teacher to arrive at a valid inference about the child's reading skills? Of course it wouldn't. Teachers who devise assessment accommodations for children with disabilities must be vigilant so they don't distort the essential nature of the skills or knowledge being measured.

A cracking good analysis of the accommodations needed for the instruction and assessment of students with disabilities was published in 2005 by the Council of Chief State School Officers (CCSSO). If you wish to delve more deeply into the

Figure 4.1 ■ Typical Accommodations Categories

■ **Presentation Accommodations**—Allow students to access information in ways that do not require them to visually read standard print. These alternate modes of access are auditory, multi-sensory, tactile, and visual.

■ **Response Accommodations**—Allow students to complete activities, assignments, and assessments in different ways or to solve or organize problems using some type of assistive device or organizer.

■ **Setting Accommodations**—Change the location in which a test or assignment is given or the conditions of the assessment setting.

■ **Timing and Scheduling Accommodations**—Increase the allowable length of time to complete an assessment or assignment and perhaps change the way the time is organized.

Source: Sandra J. Thompson et al., *Accommodations Manual: How to Select, Administer, and Evaluate Use of Accommodations for Instruction and Assessment of Students with Disabilities,* 2nd ed. (Washington, DC: Council of Chief State School Officers, August 2005), p. 14.

accommodations arena, I recommend that manual highly. I've cited the CCSSO manual in the Additional Stuff at the close of this chapter (see Thompson et al., 2005). In that manual, there is a breakdown of the four common categories of accommodations typically considered for either assessment or instruction. I've supplied those four categories in Figure 4.1. The manual itself provides a host of specific examples of accommodations in each of the four categories presented in Figure 4.1.

Authors of the CCSSO *Accommodations Manual* provide a convincing argument that students themselves should be involved, whenever practical, in the selection of their own accommodations. It is pointed out that if students are involved in the selection of their own accommodations, it is more likely that those accommodations will be used subsequently, especially when students reach adolescence and desire greater independence.

English Language Learners

And what about students whose first language is not English? In other words, how should classroom teachers assess such students? First off, we need to do a bit of term-defining, because there are a number of descriptive labels for such youngsters being used these days. *English language learners (ELL)* represent a diverse, fast-growing student population in the United States and Canada. Included in the ELL group are (1) students whose first language is not English and know little, if any, English; (2) students who are beginning to learn English but could benefit from school instruction; and (3) students who are proficient in English but need additional assistance in academic or social contexts. English language learners also include language minority students (also called "linguistic minority" students) who use a language besides English in the home. The federal government often uses the term *limited English proficient (LEP)* to describe ELL students. Currently, most people, because they believe it more politically correct, describe those students as "English language learners," but it is equally accurate to employ the governmentally favored descriptor of "limited English proficient." I'll be using the ELL and LEP labels interchangeably.

Federal and state laws, if subjected to sufficient political pressure, are capable of being altered almost anytime. As I was wrapping up the writing of this fifth edition of *Classroom Assessment,* two significant assessment provisions of NCLB spelled out the federally required testing of ELL students. But, as noted previously, the provisions of this law might change.

I indicated earlier that NCLB is the current reauthorization of a landmark federal 1965 law, the Elementary and Secondary Education Act (ESEA). Sometime around 2007 or 2008, another reauthorization of ESEA (or, if you prefer, NCLB) is slated to take place. Given the considerable intensity with which certain provisions of NCLB have been assailed and defended, it seems likely that there may well be substantial changes in the next version of ESEA. So, if you are interested in the assessment requirements of the law insofar as ELL students are concerned, be sure to be attentive to any such alterations. Until any changes take place, however, two NCLB requirements spell out the kinds of assessments to be used with language-minority students.

First, there is the requirement to determine the degree to which certain subgroups of students—specifically those subgroups identified in NCLB—are making adequate yearly progress. One of these groups consists of "students with limited English proficiency." If there are sufficient numbers of LEP students in a school (or in a district) to yield "statistically reliable information," then a designated proportion of those students must have earned proficient-or-above scores on a state's NCLB tests. If enough students don't earn those scores, a school (or district) will be regarded as having failed to make its NCLB-stipulated AYP targets.

Interestingly, because federal officials have allowed states some latitude in deciding on the minimum numbers of students (in a subgroup) needed in order to provide "statistically reliable information," there is considerable variation from state to state in these subgroup minimum numbers. You will easily recognize that if a state sets its minimum numbers fairly high, then fewer schools and districts are going to be regarded as having failed AYP. This is because low-performing students in a particular subgroup need not be counted in AYP calculations if there are too few students (that is, below state-set minima) in a particular subgroup. Conversely, a state whose subgroup-minima have been set fairly low will find more of its schools or districts flopping on AYP because of one or more subgroup's shortcomings.

Although the NCLB tests administered to ELL students are typically written in English, students who are counted in these AYP subgroup analyses are only those who have attended U.S. schools for three or more consecutive years. In other words, to satisfy the subgroup-analyses required by NCLB, language-minority students must take the very same tests that all other students take, but are counted for AYP purposes only after having attended U.S. schools for three years in a row. (On a case-by-case individual basis, NCLB allows for a state's academic assessments to be written in another language if this would yield more accurate information about a student's achievement.)

But NCLB contains another assessment requirement related to LEP students. The law calls for states to employ separate "academic assessments of English language proficiency" so that, on an annual basis, such tests can measure LEP students' skills in "oral language, reading, and writing." Because most states did not have such tests on hand (or, if they did, those tests usually measured beginning students' social English skills rather than the now required tests of students' academic English skills), there has been substantial test-development activity underway in individual states or, frequently, in test-development consortia from several participating states.

The technical quality of these tests to assess students' English language proficiency, of course, will be the chief determinant regarding whether valid inferences can be made regarding ELL students' mastery of English. Clearly, considerable attention must be given to evaluating the caliber of this emerging collection of assessment instruments.

Lest you think that the assessment of ELL students, once it is addressed seriously because of NCLB requirements, is going to be easy to pull off, Jamal Abedi, one of the nation's leading authorities on the assessment of ELL students has recently reminded us of a half-dozen issues that must be addressed if NCLB is going to accomplish for LEP students what that law's architects had intended (Abedi, 2004). He points to the following concerns:

1. *Inconsistency in LEP classification across and within states.* A variety of different classification criteria are used to identify LEP students among states and even within districts and schools in a state, thus affecting the accuracy of AYP reporting for LEP students.
2. *Sparse LEP populations.* In a large number of states and districts there are too few LEP students to permit meaningful analyses, thus distorting state and federal policy decisions in such settings.
3. *Subgroup instability.* Because a student's LEP status is not stable over time, a school's LEP population represents a moving, potentially unattainable, target. To illustrate, if a given LEP student's mastery of English has improved sufficiently, that student is moved out of the LEP group only to be replaced by a new student whose English proficiency is apt to be substantially lower. Therefore, even with superlative instruction, there is little chance of improving the AYP status of the LEP subgroup from year to year.
4. *Technical quality of AYP-determining assessment tools.* Because studies have shown that assessment instruments constructed for native English speakers have lower reliability and validity when used with LEP populations, results of such tests are likely to be misinterpreted when employed with ELL students.

5. *Lower baseline scores*. Because schools with large numbers of LEP students are likely to have lower baseline scores and thus may have improvement targets that will be unrealistically challenging, such schools may have difficulty in attaining state-set increments in students' achievement levels.

6. *LEP cut-scores*. Unlike the previous version of ESEA in which a student's weaker performance in one subject area could be compensated for by a higher performance in another subject (referred to as a *compensatory* model), NCLB requires use of a *conjunctive* model in which students' performances in all assessed subject areas must be acceptable. Because students' performances in mathematics are apt to be less dependent on language prowess than their performances in reading/language arts where language demands are higher, this renders the AYP expectations for schools with large LEP populations more challenging than those imposed on schools with fewer LEP students.

Even with all these issues that must be considered when assessing students in the accountability structure of NCLB, Abedi believes the isolation of subgroup performances is "a step in the right direction." He argues that state and federal officials appear to be addressing many of these issues at this time. Abedi believes it necessary to resolve these problems if genuine fairness is to be attained in the assessment-based accountability focused on ELL students. And this quest means there needs to be some sensible judgments made by teachers. It is decisively unsmart to force a child who speaks and reads only Spanish to take an English language test about mathematics, then conclude the child can't do math because the child's test score is low.

The issue of whether teachers should try to make available versions of their tests in non-English languages is, unfortunately, often decided on totally practical grounds. In many settings, teachers may find a dozen or more first languages spoken by their students. In some urban settings, more than 100 first languages other than English are found in a district's students. And, if an attempt is made to create an alternate assessment only in the *most* common language a teacher's students possess, how fair is this to those students whose first languages aren't found in sufficient numbers to warrant the creation of a special test in their native language?

Assessment accommodations, in the form of giving language-minority students more time or the use of dictionaries can, depending on students' levels of English mastery, often help deal with the measurement of such students.

It is difficult to attend any conference on educational assessment these days without finding a number of sessions devoted to the measurement of language-minority students or students with disabilities. Clearly, an effort is being made to assess these children in a fashion that is not biased against them. But, just as clearly, the problems of measuring such students with fairness, compassion, and accuracy are nontrivial.

In 2000, the President's Advisory Commission on Educational Excellence for Hispanic Americans issued an insightful report entitled *Testing Hispanic Students in the United States: Technical and Policy Issues*. The commission's observations regarding the effect of high-stakes testing on Hispanic students are, in almost all instances, applicable to other language-minority students whose first language is not English. Here are the commission's views:

> But in the current rush to implement world-class standards supported by systems of accountability in the nation's public schools, state education leaders have compromised the educational future of Hispanic students by making high-stakes decisions based on inaccurate and inadequate testing information. Hundreds of thousands of Hispanic students, many lacking functional fluency in English, are assessed with a myriad of tests entirely in English and, oftentimes, only in English. The resulting data is used to determine high-stakes decisions, such as for student promotion or retention, or high school graduation—but rarely for the purposes of true accountability. When it comes to holding schools accountable for the academic achievement of our students, states allow Hispanic youngsters to become invisible inside the very system charged with educating them. (The President's Advisory Commission, 2000)

The commission offered 18 recommendations for the assessment of Hispanic students, almost all of which apply with equal force to any student whose native-born language is not English. Several of those recommendations will illustrate the kinds of significant departures from current assessment practices in the United States that must be seriously considered.

> ■ Translated tests should not be used. There is very little likelihood that the new translated test will have the same technical properties as the original, and there is a substantial likelihood that the translated test will not work. The practice of translating tests and of using their scores for making decisions about individuals should stop.
> ■ Tests that purport to have equivalent test versions in English and Spanish need to show empirical evidence that, in fact, there is equivalence. Similarly, research is urgently needed on whether bilingual, Hispanic children in the United States can be validly and fairly compared on Spanish/English tests that relied on monolingual samples to generate monolingual norms in English and Spanish.
> ■ The use of interpreters should be discouraged, if not proscribed. Interpreters are basically poor substitutes for what should be provided to Hispanic students: culturally knowledgeable, linguistically competent testers from their own communities. (The President's Advisory Commission, 2000)

Regulations for NCLB currently allow a state's math and reading tests to be given to LEP students for three years in their native languages, and a fourth or fifth year on a case-by-case basis. Educators who work with LEP students agree the assessment requirements of NCLB and, in particular, the obligatory disaggregation of English language learners' test scores, have brought unprecedented attention to those students. Nonetheless, substantial disagreement exists among those educators whether this attention has, overall, had a beneficial or harmful effect on the education of LEP students (*Education Week*, March 1, 2006).

Clearly, the accurate assessment of students whose first language is not English will continue to pose a nontrivial problem for the nation's teachers. To provide equivalent tests in English and *all* other first languages spoken by students represents an essentially impossible task. The policy issue now being hotly contested in the United States is whether to create equivalent tests for the most numerous of our schools' language-minority students.

What Do Classroom Teachers Really Need to Know about Absence-of-Bias?

Classroom teachers need to know that assessment bias exists. Assessment bias in educational tests is probably less prevalent than it was a decade or two ago because most measurement specialists, after having been sensitized to the presence of assessment bias, now strive to eliminate such biases. However, for the kinds of teacher-developed assessment procedures seen in typical classrooms, systematic attention to bias eradication is much less common.

All classroom teachers *routinely* need to use absence-of-bias as one of the three evaluative criteria by which they judge their own assessments and those educational assessments developed by others. For instance, if you are ever called on to review the quality of a high-stakes test such as a district-developed or district-adopted examination whose results will have a meaningful impact on students' lives, be sure that suitable absence-of-bias procedures, both judgmental and empirical, were employed during the examination's development.

But what about your own tests? How much effort should you devote to making sure your tests don't offend or unfairly penalize any of your students because of personal characteristics such as ethnicity or gender? My answer is that you really do need to devote attention to absence-of-bias for *all* of your classroom assessment procedures. For the least significant of your assessment procedures, I suggest you simply heighten your consciousness about bias eradication as you generate the test items or, having done so, as you review the completed test.

For more important examinations, try to enlist the assistance of a colleague to review your assessment instruments. If possible, attempt to secure the help of colleagues from the same subgroups as those represented in your students. For instance, if many of your students are Hispanics (and you aren't), then try to get a Hispanic colleague to look over your test's items to see if there are any that might offend or unfairly penalize Hispanic students. When you enlist a colleague to help you review your tests for potential bias, try to carry out a mini-version of the bias review panel procedures described in the chapter. Briefly describe to your coworkers how you define assessment bias, give them a succinct orientation to the review task, and structure their reviews with absence-of-bias questions such as those seen earlier in the chapter.

Most importantly, if you personally realize how repugnant all forms of assessment bias are, and how it can distort certain students' performances even if the

but what does this have to do with Teaching?

Decades ago I was asked to serve as an expert witness in a federal court case taking place in Florida. It was known as the *Debra P.* versus *Turlington* case, because Ralph Turlington was the Florida Commissioner of Education and Debra P. was one of nine African American children who were about to be denied high school diplomas because they had not passed a state-administered basic skills test. A class-action lawsuit had been brought against Florida to stop this test-based denial of diplomas.

When I was invited to serve as a witness for the state, I was initially pleased. After all, to be an "expert" witness in a federal court case sounded like a form of instant tenure. So, my first inclination was to agree to serve as a witness. But then I learned that Florida's high school graduation test was having a substantial disparate impact on the state's African American children, far more of whom were going to be denied diplomas than their White counterparts. I pondered whether I wanted to support an assessment program that would surely penalize more minority than majority children.

So, before making up my mind about becoming a witness in the *Debra P.* case, I consulted a number of my African American friends at UCLA and in the Los Angeles Unified School District. "Should I," I asked, "take part in the support of a test that denies diplomas to so many African American youngsters?"

Well, *without exception*, my African American friends urged me to accept the Florida assignment. The essence of their argument was simple. What was going on in Florida, they claimed, was the awarding of "counterfeit" diplomas to African American children. If so many African American youngsters were actually failing the state's basic skills test, then it was most likely those children did not possess the necessary basic skills. Yet, even without those basic skills, many of Florida's African American children had *previously* been given high school diplomas that allowed them to graduate *without* the skills they needed. My friends made it clear. As one put it, "Get your tail down to Tallahassee and support any test that shows many African American children are being instructionally shortchanged. You can't fix something if you don't know it's broken."

And that's where bias detection comes in. If teachers can eliminate bias from their own assessments, then any gaps in performance levels of minority and majority students can be attributed to instruction, not shortcomings in a test. Achievement gaps, properly identified, can then be ameliorated instructionally. If there's no recognition of a bona fide gap, then there's little reason for instructional alterations.

(As a postscript, the *Debra P.* case turned out to be an important precedent-setter. It was ruled that a state *can* deny a high school diploma on the basis of a basic skills test, but if the test covers content that students have not had an opportunity to learn, then this violates a student's—that is, a U.S. citizen's—constitutionally guaranteed property rights. I liked the ruling a lot.)

assessment bias was inadvertently introduced by the test's developer, you'll be far more likely to eliminate assessment bias in your own tests. In education, as in any other field, assessment bias should definitely be *absent*.

The presence of two federal laws, NCLB and IDEA, oblige today's teachers to rethink the ways they should test students with disabilities and ELL students. With few exceptions, children with disabilities are to be assessed (and instructed) in relation to the same curricular goals as all other children. This can often be accomplished through the use of accommodations—that is, alterations in presentations, responses, settings, and timing/scheduling. Assessment accommodations, however, must never alter the fundamental nature of the skill or knowledge being assessed. Assessment accommodations can also be used to reduce potential bias associated with the testing of ELL students. Given the enormous number of first-languages other than English now found in the nation's schools, financial limitations tend to prevent the development of suitable assessments for many language-minority students.

■ Chapter Summary

This chapter on absence-of-bias was, quite naturally, focused on how educators make bias absent. Assessment bias was described as any element in an assessment procedure that offends or unfairly penalizes students because of personal characteristics, such as their gender and ethnicity. Assessment bias, when present, was seen to distort certain students' performances on educational tests, hence reduce the validity of score-based inferences about those students. The two chief contributors to assessment bias were identified as offensiveness and unfair penalization. The essential features of both of these factors were considered. It was contended that an examination having a disparate impact on a particular subgroup was not necessarily biased, although such a differential impact certainly would warrant further scrutiny of the examination's content to discern if assessment bias was present. In many instances, disparate impact from an examination simply indicates that certain groups of students have previously received inadequate instruction.

Two procedures for identifying biased segments of educational assessment devices were described. A *judgmental* approach relies on the considered opinions of properly oriented bias reviewers. Judgmental approaches to bias detection can be formally employed with high-stakes tests or less formally used by classroom teachers. An *empirical* approach that relies chiefly on differential item functioning can also be used, although its application requires large numbers of students. It was recommended classroom teachers be vigilant in the identification of bias, whether in their own tests or in the tests of others. For detecting bias in their own tests, classroom teachers were urged to adopt a judgmental review strategy consonant with the importance of the assessment procedures involved.

Issues associated with the assessment of ELL students or students with disabilities were identified near the chapter's conclusion. In many cases, assessment accommodations can yield more valid inferences about students with disabilities or who have less conversance with English. In other instances, alternate assessments need to be developed. Neither of these assessment modifications, however, is completely satisfactory in coping with this important assessment problem. Absence-of-bias, from a fairness perspective, currently appears to be much more difficult to attain in the case of students with disabilities and ELL students.

 ## Self-Check

For this set of self-check exercises, you are to review five test items, then decide whether you think there are elements in each item that are biased and, if so, why. Supply your response in your own words. If your response is *no* (that is, if you don't think there's bias present), you can respond with any form of that negative word you wish. Following the initial five items, you'll find five short-answer items to which you should also respond.

1. Here's a reading comprehension item for openers:

   In certain Christian religions, there are gradients of sinful acts. For example, in the Roman Catholic Church, a *venial* sin need not be confessed, whereas a *mortal* sin must be confessed.

   Based on the context clues contained in the reading selection above, which of the following statements is most accurate?
   a. For Catholics, there is no difference in the gravity of mortal or venial sins.
   b. For Catholics, a mortal sin is more serious than a venial sin.
   c. For Catholics, a venial sin is more serious than a mortal sin.
   d. Priests are required to forgive mortal sins that are confessed.
   Do you believe this item to be biased? If so, why?

   _____

   _____

2. Here's a mathematics item for you to review:

   Heinrich Homborg collects World War II mementos. His original collection of official swastikas numbered 49. Recently, he sold 12 of his swastikas to another collector. How many swastikas does Heinrich have left? (Show your work.)

   Number of swastikas remaining: _____

   Do you believe this item to be biased? If so, why?

   _____

   _____

3. And now for a language arts item:

    In which of the following three statements are all pronouns used properly?
    a. I truly enjoyed his telling of the joke.
    b. We watched him going to the cafe.
    c. We listened to them singing the song.

    Do you believe this item to be biased? If so, why?

    _____

    _____

4. Next, here's an item designed to measure students' composition skills.

    Write a short essay of at least 500 words on the topic *Soccer in the United States*. Be sure to engage in prewriting activities, draft an initial response, and revise your draft. You have 60 minutes to complete this task.

    Do you believe this item to be biased?

    _____

    _____

5. For the last potentially biased item, let's swing back to mathematics for a moment.

    Ramon Ruiz is sorting out beans. He has four piles based on different groups of beans. He thinks he has made a mistake in adding up how many beans are in each pile. Pick the addition that is in error.
    a. 20 beans plus 32 beans = 52 beans
    b. 43 beans plus 18 beans = 61 beans
    c. 38 beans plus 39 beans = 76 beans

    Do you believe this item to be biased?

    _____

    _____

6. What is a persuasive argument that if an educational test has a disparate impact, it need not be biased?

    _____

    _____

7. What is one very practical impediment to a classroom teacher's use of *empirical* methods to excise biased items from a teacher-developed test?

    _____

    _____

8. Which of the two factors that were identified in the chapter as contributing to the bias of assessment procedures—namely, offensiveness and unfair penalization—do you consider to be more difficult to detect? Why?

_____

_____

9. Why is it inappropriate for an assessment accommodation to fundamentally alter the nature of the skill or knowledge being measured?

_____

_____

10. What appears to be the most significant obstacle to creating assessments for all ELL students using the first-language of those students?

_____

_____

? | Pondertime

1. If you were asked to support a high school graduation test you knew would result in more minority than majority youngsters being denied a diploma, could you do it? If so, under what circumstances?

2. Only in the past decade or so have we seen measurement specialists and commercial test developers become really attentive to assessment bias. Why do you think it took so long for people to become exercised about this form of bias?

3. Which, if either, of the two approaches to bias detection discussed in the chapter (judgmental and empirical) do you think yields the most compelling evidence of assessment bias? Why?

4. Have you ever taken a test that you believed was biased? If you did, what features of the test do you think were biased?

5. What is your view about how much effort a classroom teacher should devote to bias detection and bias elimination?

6. What kind of overall educational assessment strategy can you think of that might make the testing of students with disabilities more fair? How about LEP students?

7. Can bias in educational assessment devices be totally eliminated? Why or why not?

Self-Check Key

Remembering that the detection of bias, at least for these exercises, is a judgmental game, and that your answers may not coincide perfectly with mine, here's what I think about the first five items.

1. I think this item is biased in favor of Catholics and, conversely, biased against non-Catholics. Catholics who already had been taught about a difference between mortal and venial sins would clearly have an advantage over non-Catholics or Catholics who'd forgotten such a distinction. Incidentally, if you messed up on this item, I am told it is barely a venial sin.

2. This fairly simple subtraction problem is surely apt to offend a number of students, such as those children whose family members were killed in World War II as a consequence of Nazi actions in Germany. In particular, many Jewish students would (should) be upset by such an insensitive choice of swastikas as commodities for a subtraction problem.

3. I don't think this item is biased, even though it might be tough for many students to answer correctly. Difficulty does not equal bias. Oh yes, the item is based on my personal hang-up involving modifiers of gerunds. The correct answer is **a.**

4. This composition task clearly appears to be biased against those students who don't know that much about soccer, and particularly those who know little of soccer in the United States. The item unfairly penalizes such students and thus is almost certainly biased.

5. This item is apt to offend Hispanics because it appears that a Hispanic (Ramon Ruiz) is portrayed as a bean counter, and beans have often been used as part of ethnic slurs against Hispanics. Moreover, the item implies that counting beans is, for a Hispanic, a reasonable activity. The item, in my view, is definitely insensitive and biased.

6. I think the best argument to be mounted regarding this issue is that a test that results in disparate impact may be completely unbiased, yet could be detecting instructional inadequacies for those who perform poorly.

7. The most compelling reason classroom teachers shouldn't mess around with empirical bias-detection techniques is there are too few students to yield reliable estimates about differentially functioning items.

8. This is a judgment call, but I think unfair penalization is tougher to spot. Although there are exceptions, offensiveness needs to be fairly blatant if many folks are truly apt to be offended. As a consequence, it's usually rather easy to identify. It's often more difficult to identify content that will unfairly disadvantage particular groups unless you understand the culture of those groups awfully well.

9. By fundamentally changing the nature of the variable (such as a skill or body of knowledge) being assessed, it is then impossible for educators to arrive at valid inferences regarding a student's status with respect to the original variable under consideration.

10. To me, a monster impediment to churning out suitable tests (in students' first-languages) for all ELL students would be the truly staggering costs associated with such an enormous test-development undertaking.

Endnote

1. U.S. Congressional Committee on Education and the Workforce. (2005, February 17). *IDEA Guide to Frequently Asked Questions* (p. 10). Washington, DC: Author.

■ Additional Stuff

Abedi, Jamal. (2004). "The No Child Left Behind Act and English Language Learners: Assessment and Accountability Issues." *Educational Researcher, 33*, no. 1: 4–14.

American Educational Research Association. (1999). *Standards for Educational and Psychological Testing.* Washington, DC: Author.

Gay, Geneva. (2003/2004). "The Importance of Multicultural Education." *Educational Leadership, 61*, no. 4 (December/January): 30–35.

Goodlad, John. (2003/2004). "Teaching What We Hold Sacred." *Educational Leadership, 61*, no. 4 (December/January): 18–21.

Hoover, H. D. (2003). "Some Common Misconceptions about Tests and Testing." *Educational Measurement: Issues and Practice, 22*, no. 1 (Spring): 5–14.

Kozol, Jonathan. (2005). "Confections of Apartheid: A Stick-and-Carrot Pedagogy for the Children of Our Inner-City Poor." *Phi Delta Kappan, 87*, no. 4 (December): 264–275.

McNeil, Linda M. (2000). "Creating New Inequalities: Contradictions of Reform." *Phi Delta Kappan, 81*, no. 10 (June): 728–734.

The President's Advisory Commission on Educational Excellence for Hispanic Americans. (2000). *Testing Hispanic Students in the United States: Technical and Policy Issues* (May Report). Washington, DC: Author.

Ramirez, Al, and Dick Carpenter. (2005). "Challenging Assumptions About the Achievement Gap." *Phi Delta Kappan, 86*, no. 8 (April): 599–603.

Singham, Mano. (2003). "The Achievement Gap: Myths and Reality." *Phi Delta Kappan, 84*, no. 8 (April): 586–591.

Sireci, Stephen G. (2005). "Unlabeling the Disabled: A Perspective on Flagging Scores From Accommodated Test Administrations." *Educational Researcher, 34*, no. 1 (January/February): 3–12.

Thompson, Sandra J. et al. (2005, August). *Accommodations Manual: How to Select, Administer, and Evaluate Use of Accommodations for Instruction and Assessment of Students with Disabilities* (2nd ed.). Washington, DC: Council of Chief State School Officers.

Zwick, Rebecca. (2002). "Is the SAT a 'Wealth Test'?" *Phi Delta Kappan, 84*, no. 4 (December): 307–311.

■ Cyber Stuff

- *Advance Project* is a "democracy and justice action group" whose staff works with communities in pursuit of a fair and just multiracial democracy in America. This group's staff of attorneys, communication specialists, and policy experts collaborates with community organizations whose activities are consonant with the Advance Project's mission. An organization such as this could be a potent ally in settings where it appears that biased high-stakes tests are being employed. www. advanceproject.org

- *The Civil Rights Project at Harvard University* was founded in 1996 by Christopher Edley Jr. of the Harvard Law School and Gary Orfield of the Harvard Graduate School of Education. Many of the activities of this project, as displayed on the group's website, deal with educational assessment issues. www.civilrightsproject. harvard.edu

- *The National Center for Fair and Open Testing (FairTest)* is an advocacy organization that works toward ending abuse, misuse, and defects of standardized testing. A goal of FairTest is to ensure that the evaluation of students is fair, open, and educationally sound. This website describes the full range of FairTest activities. One such activity is the Assessment Reform Network, an online discussion group whose participants are generally committed to FairTest's goals. The site also lists information about K–12 testing in the United States and publications that are available from this organization. www.fairtest.org

To access chapter objectives, practice tests, weblinks, and flashcards, visit the companion website at **www.ablongman.com/popham5e.**

Companion
Website

Where the classroom comes to life!

MyLabSchool is a collection of online tools for your success in this course, your licensure exams, and your teaching career. Discover where the classroom comes to life by visiting **www.mylabschool.com** to access the following resources:

- Video clips from real classrooms
- An archive of real-life cases
- Help with your research papers using Research Navigator™
- Career Center with resources for:
    - Praxis exams and licensure preparation
    - Professional portfolio development
    - Job search and interview techniques
    - Lesson planning with state standard correlations

chapter 5

Deciding What to Assess and How to Assess It

N ow that you've struck up at least a nodding acquaintance with three criteria that can be used to evaluate tests, it's time to focus on what sorts of things a classroom teacher should be assessing in the first place. Because almost all classroom assessment procedures can accurately be described as teacher-made tests, in this chapter you'll learn how to answer two whopper questions about the tests that you'll be making. The two whopper questions, suitably highlighted in uppercase type, are presented below:

1. WHAT SORTS OF THINGS SHOULD A CLASSROOM TEACHER TRY TO ASSESS?
2. HAVING DECIDED ON WHAT TO ASSESS, HOW SHOULD A CLASSROOM TEACHER GO ABOUT ASSESSING IT?

Let's tackle the first of these two questions—that is, the what-to-assess question. Having given you some ways to answer it, we'll then figure out how to respond to the second, how-to-assess-it question.

■ What to Assess

Far too many teachers simply stumble into an assessment pattern without giving serious consideration to why they're assessing what they're assessing. Typically, teachers test students in order to dispense grades in a manner that somehow resembles the levels of academic performances students have displayed. Students who score well on the teacher's tests are given good grades; low-scoring students get the other kind. Traditionally, the need to dole out grades to students has been the chief factor spurring teachers to assess their students.

Yet, as suggested in Chapter 1, there are a number of other significant reasons these days that teachers construct and use assessment instruments. For example, results of classroom assessments may be employed to identify certain students' areas of deficiency so the teacher can more effectively target additional instruction at those content or skill areas where there's the greatest need. Another important function of classroom assessment is to help teachers, *prior* to the design of an instructional sequence, understand more clearly what their end-of-instruction targets really are. This clarification occurs because properly constructed assessment procedures can illuminate the nature of instructional targets for teachers.

Decision-Driven Assessment

Teachers use tests to get information about their students. As we've already seen, teachers typically make score-based inferences about their students' status with respect to whatever curricular aims are being represented by the tests. Based on these inferences, teachers then make decisions. Sometimes the decisions are as straightforward as whether to give Sue Smith an A or a B. Sometimes the decisions are more difficult, such as how to modify an instructional unit based on students' performances on an end-of-unit exam. But, whatever the decisions are, classroom assessment should be unequivocally focused on the *action options* teachers have at their disposal. The information garnered from assessing students is then used to help a teacher make the specific decision that's at issue. Because the nature of the decision to be serviced by the test results will usually influence the kind of assessment approach the teacher selects, it is important to clarify, *prior to the creation of a test*, just what decision or decisions will be influenced by students' test performances.

I realize it may seem silly to you, or at least somewhat unnecessary, to identify *in advance* what decisions are linked to your classroom assessments, but it really does make a difference in determining what you should assess. For instance, suppose the key decision riding on a set of test results is how to structure a series of remedial instructional activities for those students who performed poorly during a teaching unit about a higher-order thinking skill. In this sort of situation, the teacher would definitely need some fine-grained diagnostic information about the *en route* skills or knowledge each student did or didn't possess. Thus, instead of designing a test so it merely assessed students' mastery of the overall thinking skill being taught, there would also need to be a sufficient number of items assessing students' mastery of each key *en route* skill. Based on the diagnostic data derived from the test, a sensible set of remedial instructional activities could then be designed for the low performers.

If, on the other hand, the key decision linked to test results is a simple determination of whether the teacher's instruction was sufficiently effective, a pretest-posttest assessment of more global (and less diagnostic) outcomes would suffice. It's also appropriate, by the way, when judging the effectiveness of a teacher's instruction, that separate assessments should be used containing items intended to assess students' *attitudes* about what was being taught, not merely the knowledge and/or skills being addressed. I'll show you how to measure your students' attitudes in Chapter 10.

In short, the decisions to be serviced by the assessment results should always influence the nature of classroom assessment. Teachers should, therefore, routinely consider the decision(s) at issue prior to creating a classroom assessment device.

A fairly easy way to decide if a test's results will really influence a classroom teacher's decision is to imagine the test results turn out in two opposite ways—for example, a set of excellent student test performances versus a set of inferior student test performances. If the teacher would be apt to make a *different* decision based on those disparate sets of performances, then the teacher truly has a test that can help inform decisions. If the teacher's decision would be pretty much the same, no matter what the test results were, there's a strong likelihood the assessment procedure is more ritual than genuine help for the teacher.

The Role of Instructional Objectives

Most classroom assessment takes place after an instructional sequence has been completed. There are exceptions, of course, such as diagnostic preassessment or the pretesting a teacher might use as part of a pretest-posttest evaluation of the teacher's instructional effectiveness. Yet, most testing in the classroom occurs at the close of instruction. And, because much classroom instruction is intended to help students achieve specified instructional objectives (curricular aims), it is quite reasonable to think that if teachers consider the content of their instructional objectives, those teachers can more readily answer the what-to-assess question. What teachers should assess will, in most instances, stem directly from the teacher's instructional objectives because it will be those objectives that influence what the teacher will be teaching and, in all probability, what the students will be learning.

Consideration of your instructional objectives, therefore, is one action you can take to help get a fix on what you should assess. The more clearly you state your objectives, the more useful they will be to you in answering the what-to-assess question. In the 1960s and 1970s, there was widespread advocacy of *behavioral objectives*—that is, educational objectives stated in terms of the postinstruction behavior of learners. The push for behavioral objectives was fueled, at least in part, by dissatisfaction with the traditional form of general and ambiguous instructional objectives often used by educators. An example of such general objectives would be the following: "At the end of the course, students will understand the true function of our federal government." My favorite gunky instructional objective of that era was one I ran across in a state-level language arts syllabus: "The student will learn to relish literature." After that time, I kept on the lookout for an objective such as "The student will mayonnaise mathematics." I haven't encountered one—yet.

Still, in their attempt to move from unclear general objectives toward superclear behavioral objectives, the proponents of behavioral objectives (and I was right in there proponing up a storm) made a serious mistake. We failed to realize if we encouraged teachers to use instructional objectives that were *too* specific, the result would be an abundance of small-scope behavioral objectives. The resulting piles of hyperspecific instructional objectives would so overwhelm teachers that those overwhelmed teachers would end up paying attention to no objectives at all.

If you are currently a classroom teacher, you know you can't realistically keep track of whether your students are achieving hundreds of curricular aims. If you are preparing to be a classroom teacher, you'll soon discover that dozens and dozens of curricular aims will overwhelm you. The trick in conceptualizing curricular aims that help rather than hinder is to frame those aims broadly enough so you can sensibly organize instruction around them while making sure that the aims are still measurable. The degree of *measurability* is clearly a key in the way you should state your objectives. The broader the objective is, while still measurable, the more useful the objective will be because you can be guided by an intellectually manageable set of curricular intentions. If you can conceptualize your curricular aims so that one broad, measurable aim subsumes a bevy of lesser, smaller-scope objectives, you'll have a curricular aim that will guide your instruction more effectively and, at the same time, will be a big help in deciding what to assess.

In language arts instruction, for example, when teachers set out to have their students become good writers, a curricular aim focused on the students' ability to generate an original composition is an objective that, although still measurable (by simply having students churn out an original essay), encompasses a number of smaller-scope objectives such as the students' ability to employ appropriate syntax, word choice, and proper spelling.

Decision Time

On-Demand Assessment

Dolly Davis is a fourth-grade teacher who has set up her social studies activities on a mastery learning basis. Students are allowed to work through most of their social studies assignments at their own speed. Much of the social studies program in Dolly's class is based on reading assignments, so students can move at their own pace. When students believe they are ready to demonstrate mastery of the social studies skills and knowledge Dolly has described in written documents she distributes early in the school year, students set up an oral assessment. Dolly then spends 10 to 15 minutes presenting a series of short-answer items students must answer orally. So students do not discover from previously assessed students what the items on the assessment are, Dolly selects items at random from a pool of nearly 50 items for each of the four major social studies assessments during the year.

Although most students seem to appreciate Dolly's willingness to let them be assessed when they're ready, several students have complained that they "got a harder test" than some of their classmates. The dissatisfied students have encouraged Dolly to retain her mastery learning model, but to assess all students at the same time.

Dolly is deciding whether to maintain her on-call oral assessments or to revert to her former practice of written examinations administered to the entire class at the same time.

 If you were Dolly, what would your decision be?

Here's an example of two small-scope curricular aims in language arts:

- When presented with reading passages containing unfamiliar words, students can employ context clues to infer the unfamiliar words' meanings.
- The student will be able to write sentences in which verbs agree in number with relevant nouns and pronouns.

Now let's look at a broad-scope language arts curricular aim that subsumes these small-scope objectives plus a load of similar small-scope objectives:

- After reading an age-appropriate nonfiction essay, the student will be able to compose two paragraphs, the first of which summarizes the essay's central message and the second of which provides the student's personal reaction to the essay's message.

Strive to come up with a half dozen or so truly salient, broad, yet measurable, curricular aims for your own classroom. Too many small-scope, hyperspecific objectives will be of scant value to you because, if you're at all normal, you'll soon disregard an overwhelming array of superspecific instructional targets. On the other hand, a small number of intellectually manageable, broad, yet measurable, curricular aims will not only prove helpful to you instructionally but will also help you answer the what-to-assess question. Simply put, you need to create assessments to help you determine whether your students have, as you hoped, achieved your instructional objectives.

Cognitive, Affective, and Psychomotor Assessment

In thinking about what to assess, classroom teachers can often be helped by considering potential assessment targets according to whether they are chiefly focused on cognitive, affective, or psychomotor targets. *Cognitive assessment* targets are those that deal with a student's intellectual operations—for instance, when the student displays acquired knowledge or demonstrates a thinking skill such as decision making or problem solving. *Affective assessment* targets are those that deal with a student's attitudes, interests, and values, such as the student's self-esteem, risk-taking tendencies, or attitudes toward learning. *Psychomotor assessment* targets are those dealing with a student's large-muscle or small-muscle skills. Examples of psychomotor assessments that take place in schools would include tests of the student's keyboarding skills in a computer class or the student's prowess in shooting a basketball in gym class.

The distinction among cognitive, affective, and psychomotor educational outcomes was first introduced in 1956 when Benjamin Bloom and his colleagues (Bloom et al., 1956) proposed a classification system for educational objectives organized around those three categories. While recognizing there are usually admixtures of all three domains of behavior in most things that teachers ask students to do on tests, the 1956 *Taxonomy of Educational Objectives* made it clear there is typically a dominant kind of student behavior sought when teachers devised educational objectives for their students. For example, if a student is completing an essay examination in a social studies class, the student may be using a pencil to write (*psychomotor*) the essays and may be feeling remarkably confident (*affective*) about the emerging quality of the essay, but the chief domain of behavior involved is *cognitive* because it is the student's intellectual analysis of the test's items and the student's intellectual organization of a response that mostly account for what the student's essay contains. Bloom's cognitive taxonomy included six levels of students' intellectual activity—ranging from the lowest level, *knowledge*, all the way up to the highest level, *evaluation*.

Standards-Based Classroom Assessment

Whether you are an elementary teacher who has instructional responsibility for a number of subject areas, or a secondary teacher who has instructional responsibility for one or two subject areas, you should be concerned that your instruction and your assessment address appropriate content. Fortunately, in the last decade or so, various national organizations have attempted to isolate the most important content to teach in their respective subject areas. These content-delineation efforts can prove quite helpful to teachers who are trying to "teach the right things." These national content-delineation efforts are part of the 1990s *educational standards movement*.

First off, let's define what an educational *standard* actually is. Unfortunately, you'll find that different educators use the term all too loosely and often incorrectly. Actually, there are two types of educational standards you need to know about:

- A *content standard* describes the knowledge or skills that educators want students to learn. (The NCLB Act refers to these as "academic content standards" and requires each state to adopt "challenging" ones.)
- A *performance standard* identifies the desired level of proficiency at which educators want a content standard mastered. (The NCLB Act refers to these as "student academic achievement standards" and also wants states to set "challenging" ones.)

It should be apparent that although we might refer to both of the above as "standards," they are very different creatures. Just as cowboys in a western movie might loosely refer to "cattle," those cowpokes know that boy-cattle and girl-cattle perform decisively different functions. It's the same story today when educators utter the many-meaning word *standards*. An academic content standard (a curricular aim) is patently different than an academic achievement standard (a performance level). To refer to them both as "standards" can cause a cattle-car full of confusion!

From a classroom teacher's perspective, the most useful kind of standards, without question, will be content standards because those standards set forth what the standards identifiers regard as the most important content for children to learn. Years ago, when I was a high school teacher, we had a district "curriculum guide" and a state "scope and sequence" manual, both of which attempted to identify the most important knowledge and skills that students should learn in each subject area. To be honest, those documents weren't all that wonderful. My fellow teachers and I found those curriculum materials to be vague, ambiguous, and altogether unhelpful.

During the 1990s, however, there were major attempts on the part of national organizations, led by the National Council of Teachers of Mathematics (NCTM) 1989 publication of *Curriculum and Evaluation Standards for School Mathematics*. In that publication, NCTM made a major effort to reconceptualize how mathematics should be taught by identifying a set of important new content standards. Those content standards defined the chief aim of mathematics education as the promotion of students' mathematical power—that is, students' ability to use mathematical thinking and understanding to solve problems and communicate the results of those solutions mathematically.

Soon thereafter, other national subject-matter associations began to bring forth their own sets of content standards and, in some instances, performance standards as well. I have had a chance to review many of these standards documents. Most of them are very impressive. All of the standards documents represent the efforts of top-flight subject-area specialists who devoted enormous time to circumscribing the knowledge and skills that students should learn.

I think it would be great if *you* spent some time reviewing these standards documents to identify what you might be teaching (and, therefore, testing). But I do *not* believe you should meekly succumb to the curricular preferences expressed in those standards collections. The reason for my warning is straightforward. These standards documents were produced by subject-matter *specialists*. And subject-matter specialists really adore their subject matters. Subject-matter specialists would like to see students master almost *everything* in their field.

Subject specialists usually approach their standards-identification tasks not from the perspective of a busy classroom teacher, but from the perch of a content devoteé. Content devoteés and classroom teachers, just like steers and cows, are different members of the cattle crowd. If teachers tried to teach students to do *all* the things set forth in the 1990s standards documents, there'd be no time left for food, sleep, or movies! So, what I recommend you do is *consult* the national standards document(s) relevant to your own teaching responsibilities, then see which of the content standards you have time to address. Without question, you'll get some wonderful ideas from the standards documents. But select your own content standards judiciously; don't try to stuff the whole wad of standards into your students' skulls. That wad won't fit.

Your State's NCLB-Sanctioned Content Standards

By now, each state has arrived at a set of officially approved content standards. Those content standards must function as the framework for a state's NCLB tests. Some of the collections of content standard are pretty good. Some are not. More often than we'd prefer, there are too many curricular aims laid out in those officially approved sets of state-sanctioned content standards. Moreover, in many states there is a fair amount of descriptive imprecision regarding what is actually meant by certain content standards. Finally, the *grain size* (that is, the breadth of many states' contest standards) varies all over the lot—sometimes in the same state where we might encounter a set of language arts content standards formulated at a large grain size, yet find a companion set of mathematics content standards (prepared, almost always, by a different group of curriculum specialists) conceptualized at very small grain sizes.

Conceding all these problems associated with many states' content standards, teachers nonetheless need to consider the curricular applicability of their state's content standards. This is especially true if a teacher is working at grade levels or subject fields in which the teacher's students are on the receiving end of the state's annual NCLB tests. If that's the case, and the state's NCLB tests are ostensibly based on the state's official content standards, then, prior to deciding on what to measure in the teacher's classroom tests, those official content standards should clearly be consulted.

All of the state-determined tests, as required by the NCLB Act, are to "be aligned with the State's challenging academic content and student achievement standards." Let's take a closer look at a couple of the words in the foregoing quotation that I lifted directly from the law.

First, the use of the term *challenging* makes it clear the federal architects of this law were looking for states to aim for really worthwhile curricular aims ("challenging content standards") and also really demanding levels of performance ("student achievement standards") for those curricular aims. The NCLB Act attempts to get state-level decision-makers to adopt genuinely high-level educational aspirations.

Second, the law says a state's NCLB tests should be *aligned* with those high-level curricular targets. Let's look briefly at the term *alignment*. In the field of education, *alignment* is the only 9-letter word that seems to function as a 4-letter word. This is because many people play fairly fast and loose with a term that, by its nature, seems to evoke fast-and-loose play. *Alignment* refers to the degree to which there is a meaningful agreement between two or more of the following: curriculum, instruction, and assessment. What the NCLB Act is calling for, of course, is the agreement of a state's NCLB tests with a state's (hopefully "challenging") content standards. To the extent that such a *curriculum-assessment* alignment has been achieved, you'd have to be a ninny not to recognize that it is sensible to also align your classroom curricula and assessments with whatever state content standards are being assessed by your state's NCLB tests.

A major difficulty with the concept of alignment, unfortunately, is it is decidedly *squishy*. What constitutes alignment in one educator's eyes may be seen as nonalignment by another educator. And there are often loads of self-interested "seeing alignment where none exists." To illustrate, state officials in recent years have often attempted to adopt nationally standardized achievement tests that are "in alignment" with their state's content standards. The measurement companies who peddle those national tests have often conducted "studies" demonstrating there is substantial alignment between a state's content standards and what their test measures. However, in most of these self-serving endeavors, the test publishers (for obvious reasons) employed remarkably relaxed requirements when determining whether their tests were aligned with a state's curriculum.

So, whenever you hear someone touting the alignment between instruction and curriculum and assessment, try to dig a bit deeper so you can see whether the alignment being described is based on rigorous or relaxed ways of determining agreement levels.

But what does a teacher do to align classroom tests with important accountability exams such as a state's NCLB tests? This constitutes a nontrivial quandary for most teachers, and it turns out to depend—almost totally—on the quality of the accountability exams. If your state's NCLB exams are capable of detecting instructional quality, then you should make sure your classroom assessments mesh with what's assessed on those NLCB tests. If your state's NCLB tests, on the other hand, are *not* capable of detecting instructional quality, then you need to pay less heed to what's assessed by those tests. If you continue reading until you arrive at this book's final chapter, you'll learn how to distinguish between state-level NCLB tests that are grubby versus those that glisten. (See, once more I am enticing you to read on, and on, and on.)

Of Standards and Emperors

Then a small voice called out from the crowd, "But the emperor's not wearing new standards at all; he's wearing old objectives!" According to a classic but uncorroborated fairy tale, a ruler can be persuaded to parade around in the buff if he's made to believe he's wearing wonderful but invisible garments. The moral of "The Emperor's New Clothes" fable, of course, is that a ruler is not apt to redress his state of undress unless someone informs him that he's naked as a jaybird.

Standards, of course, is a warmth-inducing word. Although perhaps not in the same league with *motherhood, democracy,* and *babies,* I suspect that *standards* ranks right up there with *oatmeal, honor,* and *excellence.* It's really tough not to groove on *standards,* especially if those standards are *high.* Everyone wants students to reach high standards. And, because high standards are so intrinsically praiseworthy, if teachers pursue such standards, then teachers can sleep tranquilly at night. Teachers are clearly questing after that which, like the Holy Grail, warrants such questing.

If by the expression *content standards* we refer to the knowledge and skills we want our students to achieve as a consequence of education, how is a content standard different from an instructional objective? The answer (all emperors and emperors-in-training take heed) is that there really is *no* difference between instructional objectives and content standards. Both phrases describe the educational intentions—that is, the curricular aims—we have for our students.

One reason that content standards are much more appealing to almost everyone than instructional objectives, as noted earlier, is that *content standards* is a warmth-inducing phrase; *instructional objectives* is not. What right-minded politician or educational policymaker would not leap with enthusiasm to be "in solid support of high content standards!" It's far less exciting for someone to applaud instructional objectives as well as the NCLB Act's focus on both content and performance standards.

So, for both of these reasons, I foresee continued widespread support for the identification and promotion of defensible content standards. As I listen, however, to today's enthusiastic endorsements of content standards and their pivotal role in educational improvement, I find myself doing a bit of mental transformation, so I guess I'm still covertly thinking about instructional objectives. (I don't tell anyone, of course. One needs to be regarded as up-to-date. And, for the next decade or two—until we revert to educational objectives—I'll be right there, along with other educators, pounding away on the content-standards drum!)

NAEP Frameworks

The National Assessment of Educational Progress (NAEP) is a congressionally mandated project of the U.S. Department of Education. It assesses U.S. students' knowledge and skills in geography, reading, writing, mathematics, science, U.S. history, the arts, civics, and other academic subjects. Since 1969, NAEP has periodically surveyed the achievement of students at ages 9, 13, and 17 and, since the 1980s, in grades 4, 8, and 12. As originally conceptualized, NAEP was intended to measure U.S. students' levels of academic achievement over time.

The National Assessment Governing Board (NAGB) was created by Congress in 1988 to formulate policy for NAEP. Among its responsibilities is the development of assessment objectives for NAEP through a national consensus approach. Although NAGB strives to avoid the perception that its objectives for various academic subjects at grades 4, 8, and 12 constitute a national curriculum, the assessment frameworks produced under NAGB's aegis are typically first-rate curricular documents, hence represent another source teachers might wish to consult as they attempt to decide what to assess.

The NAEP frameworks can be downloaded from the NAGB website listed at the chapter's close. Although never intended to serve as a one-size-fits-all set of assessable objectives for an entire nation, the NAEP assessment/curricular frameworks typically reflect thoughtful analyses regarding what ought to be assessed (taught) at three key grade levels.

As part of the NCLB Act, all states must participate in the biennial administration of NAEP reading and mathematics tests to representative samples of students in grades 4 and 8. The NAEP results are reported as the numbers of students who score on each of the following four categories: *advanced, proficient, basic,* or *below basic.* I need to remind you that most states will report the percentages of students who score in those categories *on the state's own NCLB tests.* Accordingly, how do you think it will look to the public if on the state's own test, 60 percent of the students score at proficient-or-above but, on NAEP, only 20 percent of the state's students earned proficient-or-above scores? That's right, it will look genuinely fishy!

So, because it is likely a state's NAEP scores will function as an external check of the state's achievement, don't be surprised if a state's teachers are urged to give meaningful attention to what's supposed to be measured on the NAEP examinations. For teachers, especially those in elementary and middle schools, to become familiar with the NAEP curricular frameworks, at least in reading and math, is not a dim-witted idea.

Assessment Blueprints

Some teachers find it helpful, especially when constructing major examinations, to develop what's called an *assessment blueprint* or a *test blueprint*. These blueprints are essentially two-way tables in which one dimension represents the content standards (or curricular aims) the teacher wants to assess, while the other dimension represents the levels of cognitive functioning being sought. For instance, the example below from a teacher's assessment blueprint will illustrate how these sorts of organizational schemes work by dividing each curricular aim's items into (1) knowledge (low-level recall of information) and (2) cognitive levels higher than mere recall.

	Number of Items	
	Cognitive Level	
Curricular Aim	*Knowledge*	*Above Knowledge*
1	3	1
2	1	4
3	2	2
etc.	etc.	

Assessment blueprints can help teachers identify content standards or curricular aims not being measured with sufficient items or with sufficient items at an appropriate level of **cognitive demand.**

Collar a Colleague

Too many classroom teachers carry out their professional chores in isolation. If you're trying to figure out what to assess in your own classroom, one straightforward scheme for tackling the task is to seek the counsel of a colleague, particularly one who teaches the same sort of class and/or grade level you teach.

Always keeping in mind that what you assess should be governed by the decisions to be influenced by your students' assessment results, simply solicit the advice of a respected colleague regarding what sorts of things you should be assessing in your class. If you're uncomfortable about making such a request, simply read (with feeling) the following scripted question: "If you were I, what would you assess?" I admit the phrasing of the question isn't all that exotic, but it will get the job done. What you're looking for is some sensible advice from a nonpartisan co-worker.

If you've already devoted a chunk of thought to the what-to-assess question, you might simply ask your colleague to review your ideas so you can discern whether your planned assessment targets seem reasonable to another teacher. A second pair of eyes can frequently prove useful in deciding whether you've really staked out a defensible set of emphases for your planned classroom assessments.

What-to-Assess Considerations

In review, then, we've looked at several factors that can help classroom teachers in deciding what they should measure in their classroom assessment procedures. From the discussion of those points, seven possible ways of addressing the what-to-assess question can be derived:

1. Focus all class assessment procedures on clearly explicated decision options.
2. A small number of significant curricular aims can provide a useful framework for deciding what to assess.
3. An analysis of whether assessments should focus on cognitive, affective, or psychomotor behavior (and, if cognitive, at what cognitive-demand level) can prove helpful.
4. A review of relevant collections of content standards prepared by national subject-matter organizations (such as NCTM in mathematics) can help a teacher identify key knowledge and skills to be pursued.
5. A consideration of the NAEP assessment frameworks can present a useful view of what curricular aims to assess in a number of curriculum fields.
6. Advice from a colleague about what to assess can prove beneficial.
7. A serious analysis of the way your state's approved content standards are assessed by its NCLB exams (or similar accountability tests) so you can plan your classroom assessments based on that analysis.

■ How to Assess It

Let's assume you've decided what you're going to measure in your classroom assessments. Now the task turns to how you're going to assess it. In the remainder of the chapter, we'll look at several choices to consider when deciding how to answer the how-to-assess-it question. More specifically, we'll be dealing with the following choices:

1. Whether to adopt a norm-referenced or a criterion-referenced assessment approach
2. Whether to emphasize selected-response or constructed-response assessment schemes
3. What kind of item type(s) to select from such alternatives as multiple-choice, short-answer, or performance tests

Norm-Referenced versus Criterion-Referenced Interpretations

There are two rather distinctive, yet widely used, assessment strategies available to educators these days: *norm-referenced measurement* and *criterion-referenced measurement.* The most fundamental difference between these two approaches to educational assessment is the nature of the interpretation that's used to make sense out of students' test performances.

With *norm-referenced* measurement, educators interpret a student's performance in relation to the performances of students who have previously taken the same examination. This previous group of test takers is referred to as the *norm group.* Thus, when educators try to make sense out of a student's tests score by "referencing" the score back to the norm group's performances, it is apparent why these sorts of interpretations are characterized as norm referenced.

To illustrate, when a teacher asserts a student "scored at the 90th percentile on a scholastic aptitude test," the teacher means the student's test performance has exceeded the performance of 90% of students in the test's norm group. In education, norm-referenced interpretations are most frequently encountered when reporting students' results on academic aptitude tests, such as the SAT, or on widely used standardized achievement tests, such as the Iowa Tests of Basic Skills, the Metropolitan Achievement Tests, or the California Achievement Tests. In short, norm-referenced interpretations are *relative* interpretations of students' performances because such interpretations focus on how a given student's performance stacks up in relation to the previous performances of other students.

In contrast, a *criterion-referenced* interpretation is an *absolute* interpretation because it hinges on the extent to which the criterion (that is, curricular aim) represented by the test is actually mastered by the student. Once the nature of an assessed curricular aim is properly described, the student's test performance can be interpreted according to the degree to which the curricular aim has been mastered. For instance, instead of a norm-referenced interpretation such as the student "scored better than 85% of the students in the norm group," a criterion-referenced interpretation might be the student "mastered 85% of the test's content and can be inferred, therefore, to have mastered 85% of the curricular aim's skills and/or knowledge represented by the test." Note that a criterion-referenced interpretation doesn't depend at all on how other students performed on the test. The focus is on the curricular aim represented by the test.

As you can see, the meaningfulness of criterion-referenced interpretations is directly linked to the clarity with which the assessed curricular aim is delineated. Clearly described curricular aims can yield crisp, understandable criterion-referenced interpretations. Ambiguously defined curricular aims are certain to yield fuzzy criterion-referenced interpretations of little utility.

Although loads of educators refer to "criterion-referenced tests" and "norm-referenced tests," there are, technically, no such creatures. Rather, there are criterion- and norm-referenced *interpretations* of students' test performances. For example, educators in a school district might have built a test to yield criterion-referenced interpretations, used the test for several years and, in the process, gathered substantial data regarding the performances of district students. As a consequence, the district's educators could build normative tables permitting norm-referenced interpretations of the test which, although born to provide criterion-referenced inferences, can still permit meaningful norm-referenced interpretations.

Because most of the assessment-influenced decisions faced by classroom teachers are benefited by the teacher's understanding of what it is students can and cannot do, not merely their relative standing in relationship to one another, classroom teachers will generally want to arrive at criterion-referenced rather than norm-referenced interpretations. A teacher's instructional choices, for example, are better serviced by evidence about particular students' skills and knowledge than by evidence about how those students compare with one another.

About the only instance in which classroom teachers will need to employ norm-referenced interpretations occurs when there are fixed-quota settings—that is, when there are insufficient slots for all of the teacher's students to be assigned to a given educational experience. For example, suppose there were five students to be chosen for a special outside-of-class enrichment program in mathematics, and the teacher had been directed by the school principal to choose the "best" mathematics students for the program. In such a situation, because *best* is, by definition, a relative descriptor, norm-referenced interpretations would be warranted. A teacher might build a test to spread students out according to their mathematics skills so the top students could be identified. Barring those rare situations, however, most classroom teachers would be better off using tests yielding criterion-referenced interpretations. Criterion-referenced interpretations provide a far more lucid idea of what it is students can and can't do. Teachers need such clarity if they're going to make solid instructional decisions.

Later, in Chapter 12, you'll be considering standardized achievement tests, assessment devices usually built to provide norm-referenced interpretations. At that time, the appropriate and inappropriate uses of test results from such commercially distributed assessment instruments will be identified. For most *classroom assessment*, however, the measurement strategy should almost always be criterion referenced rather than norm referenced.

Selected Responses and Constructed Responses

Assuming a classroom teacher has come up with a reasonable answer to the what-to-assess question, an important point in determining how to assess it arises when the teacher must choose between assessment strategies that elicit *selected responses or constructed responses* from students. If you think for a moment about the way educators assess students' educational status, you'll realize there are really only two kinds of responses students can make. Students *select* their responses from alternatives we present to them—for example, when we give students multiple-choice tests and their responses must be selected from each item's available options. Other examples of selected-response assessment procedures are binary-choice items such as those found in true-false tests where, for each item, students must select either a true or a false answer.

In contrast to selected-response sorts of tests, students *construct* all kinds of responses. In an English class, for instance, students construct original essays. In a woodshop class, students construct end tables. In a speech class, students construct five-minute oral speeches. In a drama class, students construct their responses while they present a one-act play. In a homemaking class, students construct soufflés and upside-down cakes. Constructed-response tests lead either to student *products,* such as the end tables and soufflés, or *behaviors,* such as the speeches and the one-act plays. When the students' constructed responses take the form of tangible product, classroom teachers have the luxury of judging the quality of the product at their leisure. For instance, once students create an original essay, the teacher can take this product home on the weekend and, while relaxing in the jacuzzi, either grade or immerse each essay.

When students' constructed responses are in the form of behavior, however, such as when students are asked in a physical education class to run a mile in less than 12 minutes, the teacher must somehow make a record of the behavior or else it disappears. The record might be created by the teacher's use of written records or be captured electronically via an audio or video recording. For example, when students in a speech class give a series of impromptu speeches, the teacher typically fills out some sort of evaluation form for each speech. Similarly, physical education teachers use their stopwatches to note how much time it takes for students to run a mile, then note the elapsed time in a record book.

It used to be thought, although selected-response tests were difficult to create, they were easy to score. Similarly, it was once believed constructed-response tests were just the opposite—simple to create but tough to score. These days, however, educators have become more sophisticated about constructed-response tests and are employing many more types of constructed-response assessment procedures than only essay tests or short-answer tests. It is generally conceded that both selected-response and constructed-response tests require considerable care when being created. It is still true, however, that the scoring of selected-response tests is substantially easier than the scoring of constructed-response tests.

If, as a classroom teacher, you're really choosing between these two assessment schemes, you need to focus less on the ease of scoring than on the nature of the score-based inference you wish to make. Some score-based inferences simply shriek out for selected-response assessment schemes. For instance, if you want to make inferences about how many historical facts your students know, a selected-response procedure will not only fill the bill, but will be simple to score. Other score-based inferences you might wish to make really require students to display complex behavior, not merely choose among options. If, for example, you want to make inferences about how well students can compose sonnets, then selected-

Parent Talk

Suppose that Ms. Collins, a parent of one of your students, has cornered you after school and asked for a few minutes of your time. She wants to know what all the talk about "new, challenging standards" really means. She's read an article about educational standards in the local newspaper, and she wonders whether the "new" standards are really new. Her question to you is, "Why is there all this fuss about educational standards these days when it seems that teachers in this school are still teaching pretty much what they've always taught and testing what they've always tested?"

 If I were you, here's how I'd respond to Ms. Collins:

"I really understand your concern about educational standards, Ms. Collins. They've certainly been receiving plenty of attention from educators during recent years. But, regrettably, there's still a fair amount of confusion about standards, even among educators.

"Actually, there are two kinds of educational standards that you and I need to consider. A *content standard* simply identifies the skills and knowledge we want students to acquire in school. For example, your daughter has recently been improving her composition skills quite dramatically. She can now write narrative and persuasive essays that are quite wonderful. An example of a content standard would be *written communication skills.*

"A *performance standard,* on the other hand, indicates *how well* a content standard should be mastered. We score students' essays on a four-point scale, and the school's teachers have agreed that a student should achieve at least a three in written communication to be considered satisfactory.

"What we now call *content standards,* we used to describe as goals, objectives, or outcomes. What we now call *performance standards,* we used to describe as passing levels or cut scores. So some of the descriptive labels may be new, but the central idea of trying to teach children important skills and knowledge—this hasn't really changed very much.

"What is new, at least to me, is a much greater concern about the *defensibility* of our content and performance standards. All across the nation, educators are being urged to adopt more challenging standards—standards that demand more of our children. This has been taking place in our school, as well. So if you look more closely at what we're teaching and testing here, I think you'll see important differences in the kinds of skills and knowledge we're pursuing—and the levels of excellence we expect of our students."

 Now, how would you respond to Ms. Collins?

response assessment schemes just won't cut it. To see if students can churn out a sonnet, you need to have them construct sonnets. Reliance on a selected-response test in such a situation would be psychometrically silly. It is, as usual, the *test-based inference* the teacher needs to make that should guide the choice between selected-response and constructed-response assessment strategies.

It is always possible, of course, for teachers to rely on both of these two assessment strategies in their classrooms. A given assessment, for instance, might represent a blend of both selected- and constructed-response approaches. As always, the assessment procedure should be employed to help the teacher get a fix on the students' status with respect to an otherwise unobservable variable in which the teacher is interested.

A Profusion of Item Types

Beyond the basic constructed-response versus selected-response distinction just considered, there are numerous types of items available for inclusion in classroom assessment procedures. Certain of these item types have been employed for many, many years. The essay test, for example, has probably been around since Socrates was strutting his instructional stuff. Multiple-choice tests have been with us for more than a century. True-false tests were probably used, at least in oral form, by prehistoric teachers who might have put such true-false toughies to their students as "True or False: Today's dinosaur was a leaf-munching brontosaurus rather than a people-munching tyrannosaurus rex."

During recent years, however, there have been some significant advances in educational measurement procedures so that, for example, many educational measurement specialists now advocate wider use of *portfolio assessment* and *performance assessment*. These significant item types must now be added to the menu of assessment alternatives open to today's classroom teacher. In the next several chapters I'll be describing how to create classroom assessments using all of the major item types now available in the classroom teacher's assessment arsenal.

We're going to start off with the more traditional sorts of selected- and constructed-response types of items because, quite frankly, you're more likely to be familiar with those item types and you'll have less difficulty in learning about how to crank out, for instance, a simply splendid short-answer test item. Thereafter, in separate chapters, we'll be considering portfolios and how they can be used for classroom assessment, as well as performance tests and how they can be employed. After that, we'll deal with the special kinds of item types to be used when you're trying to get a fix on students' affective status.

As a preview, then, in the next few chapters, you'll be encountering the following types of items that can be employed in classroom assessments:

- Binary-choice items (Chapter 6)
- Multiple binary-choice items (Chapter 6)
- Multiple-choice items (Chapter 6)
- Matching items (Chapter 6)
- Short-answer items (Chapter 7)

- Essay items (Chapter 7)
- Observational approaches (Chapter 8)
- Performance tests (Chapter 8)
- Portfolios (Chapter 9)
- Affective assessment procedures (Chapter 10)

As you can see, there are plenty of options open to classroom teachers when it comes to item types. When I was preparing to be a classroom teacher in the 1950s, my professors familiarized me with several different item types (all as traditional as they could be), then encouraged me to employ different types of items "for variety's sake." This, to be honest, was dumb advice. Classroom assessment is not akin to a fashion show where you need to change styles in your examinations simply to maintain students' interest.

When you're choosing among item types, select the one that best allows you to make the test-based inference in which you're interested and the decision linked to it. Sometimes it won't make much difference which type of item you choose. I suspect in many instances it really isn't the case that a batch of multiple-choice items is vastly superior to a set of matching items. In other cases, however, there will be substantial differences in the suitability of differing item types. To make your own choice, simply ask yourself the question, Will my students' responses to this type of item allow me to reach a defensible inference I must make to arrive at the educational decision facing me?

As we consider various types of items in the next five chapters, you'll become more conversant with the particulars of each item type, and thus more skilled in identifying their utility to you in your own classroom assessments.

■ What Do Classroom Teachers Really Need to Know about What to Assess and How to Assess It?

What is the main message of this chapter for classroom teachers who must decide what to assess and how to assess it? The answer is rather straightforward. All you need to do is to think seriously about both questions. Any experienced teacher will, if pressed, confess that *instructional inertia* plays a key role in what usually goes on in the teacher's classroom. Classroom teachers find it far easier to engage in activities this year that they engaged in last year simply because it takes less effort to employ "same-old, same-old" instructional procedures than to install new instructional procedures. There's also *assessment inertia* inclining teachers to rely on whatever assessment schemes they've previously utilized. It's so much simpler to massage last year's true-false exams than to whip out a brand new performance test.

In recognition of these all-too-human tendencies to adopt the path of least resistance, it becomes more important to try to "get it right the first time" or, putting it in more pedantic parlance, to "eschew egregiously inferior initial assessment conceptualizations." In other words, the more up-front thought teachers give to answering the what-to-assess and how-to-assess-it questions, the more likely they'll be to avoid the kind of serious assessment errors that, because of practical pressures, may plague them for years.

but what does this have to do with Teaching?

As a first-year teacher, I had only a foggy idea of what stuff I should be teaching. Oh, of course, there was a state curriculum syllabus setting forth a seemingly endless array of knowledge and skills that students such as mine might possess. But, as was true with most of my colleagues, I found the syllabus altogether overwhelming.

So, when a new teacher is curricularly overwhelmed, the teacher gravitates toward whatever content is addressed in textbooks. And that's just what I did. Along with courses in high school English, speech, and U.S. government, I also had to teach a course in geography. Having never taken a college course in geography, and knowing barely more than the four major directions on a compass, I thanked heaven each night for the bright red geography text that allowed me to appear geographically suave. Had it not been for that comforting red textbook, I surely would have perished pedagogically before I learned the difference between the equator and a Mercator map projection.

In short, my first year's curricular choices were often made almost unthinkingly. I simply scrambled to fill my lesson plans with something resembling relevant content. But, during my *second* year of teaching, I had a solid basis for my curricular choices—namely, I had taught about those things the previous year!

It should be apparent to you that if teachers carry out a consummately classy instructional act, yet focus on the wrong curricular content, this would be a genuine waste. Yet, many beginning teachers (like me) don't devote sufficient thought to what they need to teach and, therefore, what they need to assess. And even seasoned teachers often can't provide a solid rationale for what they're teaching.

The impact of the NCLB Act on most teachers' instruction—and classroom assessment—has been considerable. That's why you really need to find out how *your* state has implemented the accountability provisions of this federal law. If your state's leaders have installed suitable NCLB tests, you'll be in a good position to key off those tests and supply your students with equally sensible classroom tests and on-target instruction. If your state's NCLB tests are inappropriate, however, you'll find yourself in the midst of an insoluble testing-teaching puzzle.

This chapter's focus on what to test and how to test it should help you recognize that you should be *assessing* the most important skills, knowledge, and affect you want your students to acquire. And this recognition, of course, should help you realize you should make sure you're *teaching* your students such stuff.

Unless, of course, you're using a red textbook. If so, forget everything I've just said.

Because of the current impact of the NCLB Act on you and your fellow teachers, you need to understand the nature of the standardized tests your state's leaders have chosen to satisfy this law's requirements. Do not assume, without careful consideration, those tests are going to help you do a better teaching job. Nor should you assume your state's NCLB tests will have an adverse impact on what goes on in the state's classrooms. You definitely need to find out whether the state's NCLB tests are winners or losers.

■ Chapter Summary

Two major questions guided the content of this chapter—namely, what should a classroom teacher assess and, having answered this question, how should it be assessed? It was contended that both of these decisions must be primarily influenced by the decisions the teacher hopes to illuminate by gathering assessment data from students.

In determining what to assess, it was suggested that a teacher's curricular aims play a prominent role in the teacher's choice of assessment emphases. In particular, broad-scope measurable objectives were recommended as helpful vehicles for identifying potential assessment targets. The three domains of student outcomes contained in Bloom's *Taxonomies of Educational Objectives* were also suggested as a helpful framework to decide whether there are instructional and assessment overemphases on cognitive outcomes. Three other recommended considerations when teachers set out to answer the what-to-assess question were (1) the content standards recommended by national organizations, (2) the NAEP assessment framework, (3) the views of colleagues, and (4) a state's official content standards—especially those designated for NCLB assessment.

When addressing the how-to-assess-it question, the chapter dealt with three topics. First, a distinction was drawn between norm-referenced and criterion-referenced assessment approaches. It was suggested that the bulk of a classroom teacher's assessment needs will be better served by criterion-referenced rather than norm-referenced interpretations because criterion-referenced interpretations tend to provide teachers with a clearer picture of what it is students can or can't do. A discussion of selected-response and constructed-response test options was concluded with a listing of the numerous types of assessment items classroom teachers have at their disposal. It was recommended, because descriptions of how these various types of test items should be constructed will be provided in the book's next five chapters, the reader hold off on deciding which item types for which decisions until those five chapters have been read.

Self-Check

We'll start off this chapter's self-check exercises with several binary-choice items about *grain size*. Look over the following five curricular aims, then decide whether each is *small scope (S S)* or *broad scope (B S)*. I assure you that, at least for the moment, you should regard the initials *B S* as *only* indicative of a broad scope curricular aim—nothing else.

1. Students will be able to select, from four options, the correct answer to any double-digit multiplication problem. (S S or B S?)

2. At the end of the Australasia unit, students will write, without prompting, 10 new facts learned about the geography of Australia or New Zealand. (S S or B S?)

3. When presented with descriptions of educational research situations requiring statistical analyses, students will be able to choose the appropriate analytic technique from any of the 40 statistical procedures treated during the statistics course. (S S or B S?)

4. The student will correctly spell aloud any 10 of the words the teacher identifies from the 50-word "spelling terrors" test. (S S or B S?)

5. The student will be able to write an original essay suitably synthesizing any three related but dissimilar newspaper articles on the same general topic. (S S or B S?)

6. What is the key difference between "academic content standards" and "academic achievement standards"?

   _____

   _____

7. Supply at least two examples of constructed-response test tasks and at least two examples of selected-response test tasks.

   _____

   _____

8. What is the critical difference between norm-referenced and criterion-referenced approaches to educational measurement?

   _____

   _____

 # Pondertime

1. It was argued in the chapter that most classroom assessment tasks call for criterion-referenced approaches to measurement. Do you agree? Why or why not?

2. Why should/shouldn't classroom teachers simply teach toward the content standards isolated by national groups? If teachers don't, are they unpatriotic?

3. If you discovered that your state's NCLB tests (a) attempt to measure too many content standards, (b) are based on badly defined content standards, and (3) don't supply teachers with per-standard results, how do you think it would influence your classroom assessments? How about your classroom instruction?

4. Suppose you were asked to give your best answer to the question, How should a classroom teacher decide what to assess? How would you respond?

5. Suppose you were asked to give your best answer to the question, How should a classroom teacher decide to assess whatever has been determined to be assessed? How would you respond?

Self-Check Key

The answers for the first five self-check exercises should have been these: 1: S S, 2: S S, 3: B S, 4: S S (although, as the number of words on the list gets longer, the curricular aim becomes broader in its scope), 5: B S.

6. Your answer should have approximated the distinction drawn between the two standards that was provided on page 106.

7. You might have supplied examples such as these:

Constructed-response test tasks: Compose a sonnet; give an impromptu speech; create a watercolor; or produce and direct a major motion picture.

Selected-response test tasks: Choose from multiple-choice options; select true or false for each statement; from three choices select the most (or least) plausible solution for the problem presented; or select from three major motion pictures the film most likely to get universal "thumbs up" from film critics.

8. At bottom, norm-referenced assessment approaches require interpretations of test scores based on the student's performance relative to performances of other students. In contrast, criterion-referenced assessment approaches require interpretations of test scores according to the degree of a clearly described curricular aim the student has mastered.

■ Additional Stuff

Bloom, B. S., et al. (1956). *Taxonomy of Educational Objectives: Handbook I: Cognitive Domain.* New York: David McKay.

Kame'enui, Edward J., Lynn Fuchs, David J. Francis, Roland Good III, Rollando E. O'Connor, Deborah C. Simmons, Gerald Tindal, and Joseph K. Torgesen. (2006). "The Adequacy of Tools for Assessing Reading Competence: A Framework and Review." *Educational Researcher, 35,* no. 4 (May): 3–11.

McMillan, James H. (2004). *Classroom Assessment: Principles and Practice for Effective Instruction* (3rd ed.) Boston: Allyn and Bacon.

Pellegrino, James W., Naomi Chudowsky, and Robert Glaser (Eds.). (2001). *Knowing What Students Know: The Science and Design of Educational Assessment.* National Research Council, Division of Behavioral and Social Sciences and Education, Center for Education, Board on Testing and Assessment, Washington, DC: National Academy Press.

■ Nonprint Stuff

Association for Supervision and Curriculum Development. *Curriculum Mapping: Charting the Course for Content* (Entire Series! Videotapes, Stock #499049G20). Alexandria, VA: Author.

Kohn, Alfie. (2000). *Beyond the Standards Movement: Defending Quality Education in an Age of Test Scores* (Videotape VBTS-BSTO). Port Chester, NY: National Professional Resources.

Northwest Regional Educational Laboratory. *Assessing Reading Proficiency* (Videotape #NREL-6). Los Angeles: IOX Assessment Associates.

Northwest Regional Educational Laboratory. *Assessing Mathematical Power* (Videotape #NREL-11). Los Angeles: IOX Assessment Associates.

Northwest Regional Educational Laboratory. *Assessment in the Science Classroom* (Videotape #NREL-12). Los Angeles: IOX Assessment Associates.

Popham, W. James. *Norm- and Criterion-Referenced Testing: What Assessment-Literate Educators Should Know* (Videotape #ETVT-15). Los Angeles: IOX Assessment Associates.

Popham, W. James. *Assessing Young Children: A Guide for Educators and Parents* (Videotape #ETVT-17). Los Angeles: IOX Assessment Associates.

Popham, W. James. *Assessing Mathematics Learning* (Videotape #STVT-26). Los Angeles: IOX Assessment Associates.

■ Cyber Stuff

■ *Achieve, Inc.* is an independent, nonprofit organization founded in 1996 by governors and corporate CEOs who were committed to the view that high-level content standards, rigorous tests to assess those standards, and performance-based accountability could promote excellence in the nation's schools. Links to federal agencies, state agencies, educational organizations, and other resources are available. www.achieve.org

■ *The Mid-continent Regional Educational Laboratory (McREL)* is a private, nonprofit organization located in Aurora, Colorado. Established in 1966, this regional laboratory has taken a major leadership role in the analysis of how educators can most effectively employ content and performance standards. This website lists a variety of McREL publications, often authored or coauthored by former staffer Robert J. Marzano, dealing with standards-relevant topics. A searchable database regarding standards and benchmarks is also available. www.mcrel.org

■ *The National Assessment Governing Board (NAGB)* is an independent, bipartisan group established by the U.S. Congress in 1988 to set policy for, and oversee the activities of, the National Assessment of Educational Progress (NAEP), frequently referred to as "The Nation's Report Card." This website, as would be expected, provides considerable information about current and past NAEP endeavors. The website contains a modest set of links to other sites, mostly governmental, but is dominantly focused on NAGB policies and NAEP activities. Because more widespread administration of NAEP is now required by the NCLB Act, substantially increased use of this website is likely. www.nagb.org

■ *National Association for the Education of Young Children (NAEYC)*, founded in 1926, has a membership of more than 100,000—most of whom are early childhood educators. The association's website contains a rich array of resources dealing with the education of young children, such as NAEYC position statements dealing with guidelines for appropriate curriculum and assessment of children, ages 3 through 8. www.naeyc.org

■ *The OECD Programme for International Student Assessment (PISA)* is a multination student testing project in reading, mathematics, and science. Conducted under the auspices of the Organization for Economic Co-operation and Development, the first survey was carried out in 2000 with 265,000 students from 32 countries. This website describes the project's activities, and also lists the assessment domains measured. www.pisa.oecd.org

To access chapter objectives, practice tests, weblinks, and flashcards, visit the companion website at **www.ablongman.com/popham5e.**

MyLabSchool is a collection of online tools for your success in this course, your licensure exams, and your teaching career. Discover where the classroom comes to life by visiting **www.mylabschool.com** to access the following resources:

■ Video clips from real classrooms

■ An archive of real-life cases

■ Help with your research papers using Research Navigator™

■ Career Center with resources for:
    Praxis exams and licensure preparation
    Professional portfolio development
    Job search and interview techniques
    Lesson planning with state standard correlations

6

Selected-
Response Tests

I n this and the following four chapters, you will learn how to construct almost a dozen different kinds of test items you might wish to use for your own classroom assessments. As suggested in the preceding chapter, you really need to choose item types that mesh properly with the inferences you want to make about students—and to be sure those inferences are directly linked to the educational decisions you need to make. Just as the child who's convinced that vanilla is ice cream's only flavor won't benefit from a 36-flavor ice cream emporium, the more item types you know about, the more appropriate your selection of item types will be. In this chapter and the next four, you'll be learning about blackberry-ripple exams and mocha-mango assessment devices.

Let me level with you regarding what you can really expect after wading through the exhilarating exposition about item construction contained in the next five chapters. Unless you're a remarkably quick study, you'll probably finish the chapters and *not* be instantly transformed into a consummately skilled test constructor. It takes more than reading a set of fairly brief chapters to turn someone into a capable item developer. But just as the journey of a thousand miles begins with a single toe wiggle, you'll have initiated a tentative trot toward the Test Construction Hall of Fame. You'll have learned the essentials of how to construct the most common kinds of classroom assessments.

What you'll need after you complete the five test-construction chapters is tons of practice in churning out classroom assessment devices. And, if you remain in teaching for a while, such practice opportunities will surely come your way. Ideally, you'll be able to get some feedback about the quality of your classroom assessment procedures from a supervisor or colleague who is clearheaded and/or conversant with educational measurement. If a competent cohort critiques your test-construction efforts, you'll profit by being able to make needed modifications in how you create your classroom assessment instruments.

■ Ten (Divided by Two) Item-Writing Commandments

As you can discern from this chapter's title, it's going to describe how to construct selected-response kinds of test items. You'll learn how to create four different varieties of selected-response test items—namely, binary-choice items, multiple binary-choice items, multiple-choice items, and matching items. All four of these selected-response kinds of items can be used effectively by teachers to derive defensible inferences about students' cognitive status—that is, the knowledge and skills teachers typically try to promote in their students.

But no matter whether you're developing selected-response or constructed-response kinds of test items, there are several general guidelines that, if adhered to, will lead to better assessment procedures. And, because the original Ten Commandments were stated in fairly stern "Thou shall not" form and have proved successful in shaping many folks' behavior, I shall now dish out five general item-writing commandments structured along the same lines. If followed, these commandments won't get you into heaven, but they will make your assessment schemes slightly more divine. All five commandments are presented in the box below. (I had requested the use of stone tablets, but the publisher instantly dismissed such whimsy.) A subsequent discussion of each commandment will help you understand how to adhere to the five item-writing mandates being discussed. It will help if you refer to each of the following item-writing commandments before reading the discussion of that commandment.

Five General Item-Writing Commandments

1. Thou shall not provide opaque directions to students regarding how to respond to your assessment instruments.
2. Thou shall not employ ambiguous statements in your assessment items.
3. Thou shall not provide students with unintentional clues regarding appropriate responses.
4. Thou shall not employ complex syntax in your assessment items.
5. Thou shall not use vocabulary that is more advanced than required.

Opaque Directions

The first item-writing commandment deals with a topic most teachers haven't thought seriously about—the directions for their classroom tests. Teachers who have been laboring to create a collection of test items typically know the innards of those items very well. Thus, because of the teacher's intimate knowledge not only of the items but also how students are supposed to deal with those items, it is often the case that only sketchy directions are provided to students regarding how to respond to a test's items. Yet, of course, unclear test-taking directions can result in confused test takers. And the responses of confused test takers don't lead to very accurate inferences about those test takers.

Flawed test directions are particularly problematic when students are being introduced to forms of assessment with which they're not very familiar, such as the performance tests I'll be describing in Chapter 8 or the multiple binary-choice tests to be discussed later in this chapter. It is useful to create directions for students early in the game when you're developing an assessment instrument. When generated as a last-minute afterthought, test directions typically turn out to be tawdry.

Ambiguous Statements

The second item-writing commandment deals with ambiguity. In all kinds of classroom assessments, ambiguous writing is to be avoided. If your students aren't really sure about what you mean in the tasks you present to them, the students are apt to misinterpret what you're saying and, as a consequence, come up with incorrect responses even though they might really know how to respond correctly. For example, sentences in which pronouns are used can frequently be unclear about the individual or individuals to whom the pronoun refers. Suppose, in a true-false test item, you asked your students to indicate whether the following statement was true or false: "Leaders of developing nations have tended to distrust leaders of developed nations due to their imperialistic tendencies." Because it is ambiguous regarding whether the pronoun *their* refers to the "leaders of developing nations" or to the "leaders of developed nations," and because the truth or falsity of the statement depends on the pronoun's referent, students are likely to be confused.

Because you will typically be writing your own assessment items, *you* will know what you mean. At least you ought to. However, try to slide yourself, at least figuratively, into the shoes of your students. Reread your assessment items from the perspective of the students, and modify any statements apt to be even a mite ambiguous to those less well-informed students.

Unintended Clues

The third of our item-writing commandments calls for you to *intentionally* avoid something *unintentional*. Well, nobody said that commandment following was going to be easy! What this commandment is trying to sensitize you to is the tendency of test-development novices to inadvertently provide clues to students about appropriate responses. As a consequence, students come up with correct responses even if they don't possess the knowledge or skill being assessed.

For example, inexperienced item writers often tend to make the correct answer to multiple-choice items twice as long as the incorrect answers. Even clucko students will opt for the lengthy response; they get so many more words for their choice. As another example of how inexperienced item writers unintentionally dispense clues, absolute qualifiers such as *never* and *always* are sometimes used for the false items in a true-false test. Because even uninformed students know there are few absolutes in this world, they gleefully (and often unthinkingly) indicate such items are false. One of the most blatant examples of unintended clue giving occurs when writers of multiple-choice test items initiate those items with incomplete statements such as "The bird in the story was an . . ." then offer answer options in which only the correct answer begins with a vowel. For instance, even though you never read the story referred to in the previous incomplete statement, if you encountered the following four response options, I bet you'd know the correct answer: A. Falcon, B. Hawk, C. Robin, D. Owl. The article *an* gives the game away.

Unintended clues are seen more frequently with selected-response items than constructed-response items, but even in supplying background information to students for complicated constructed-response items, the teacher must be wary of unintentionally pointing truly unknowledgeable students down the correct-response trail.

Complex Syntax

Complex syntax, although it sounds like an exotic surcharge on cigarettes and alcohol, is often encountered in the assessment items of neophyte item writers. Even though some teachers may regard themselves as Steinbecks-in-hiding, an assessment instrument is no setting in which to wax eloquent. This fourth item-writing commandment directs you to avoid complicated sentence constructions and, instead, use very simple sentences. Although esteemed writers such as Thomas Harding and James Joyce are known for their convoluted and clause-laden writing styles, I'll wager they would have been mediocre item writers. Too many clauses, except at Christmas-time, mess up test items. (For readers needing a clue regarding the previous sentence's cryptic meaning, think of a red-garbed guy who brings presents.)

Difficult Vocabulary

Our fifth and final item-writing commandment is fairly straightforward. It indicates that when writing educational assessment items, *you should eschew obfuscative verbiage.* In other words, in almost *any* other words, use vocabulary suitable for the students who'll be taking your tests. Assessment time is not the occasion for you to trot out your best collection of polysyllabic terms or to secure a series of thesaurus-induced thrills. The more advanced the vocabulary level is in your assessment devices, the more likely you'll fail to get a good fix on your students' true status. They will have been laid low by the overblown vocabulary. In the case of the terminology to be used in classroom assessment instruments, simple wins.

In review, you've now seen five item-writing commandments that apply to any kind of classroom assessment device you develop. They certainly apply to tests containing selected-response items. And that's what we'll be looking at in the rest of the chapter. More specifically, you'll be encountering a series of item-writing guidelines to follow when constructing particular kinds of selected-response items. The guidelines are based either on empirical research evidence or on decades of teachers' experience in using such items. If you opt to use any of the item types to be described here in your own classroom tests, try to follow the guidelines for that kind of item. Your tests will typically turn out to be better than if you hadn't.

■ Binary-Choice Items

A *binary-choice item* gives students only two options from which to select. The most common form of binary-choice item is the *true-false item.* Educators have been using true-false tests probably as far back as Socrates. (True or False: Plato was a type of serving-dish used by Greeks for special meals.) Other variations of binary-choice items would be those in which students must choose between yes-no, right-wrong, correct-incorrect, fact-opinion, and so on.

The virtue of binary-choice items is they are typically so terse that students can respond to many items in a short time. Therefore, it is possible to cover a large amount of content in a brief assessment session. The greatest weakness of binary-choice items is that, because there are only two options, students have a 50-50 chance of guessing the correct answer even if they don't have the foggiest idea of what's correct. If a large number of binary-choice items are used, however, this weakness tends to evaporate. After all, although students might guess their way correctly through a few binary-choice items, they would need to be extraordinarily lucky to guess their way correctly through 30 such items.

Here are five item-writing guidelines for binary-choice items. A brief discussion of each guideline is provided in the following paragraphs.

Item-Writing Guidelines for Binary-Choice Items

1. Phrase items so that a superficial analysis by the student suggests a wrong answer.
2. Rarely use negative statements, and never use double negatives.
3. Include only one concept in each statement.
4. Have an approximately equal number of items representing the two categories being tested.
5. Keep item length similar for both categories being tested.

Phrasing Items to Elicit Thoughtfulness

Typically, binary items are quite brief, but brevity need not reflect simplistic choices for students. In order to get the most payoff from binary-choice items, you'll want to phrase items so students who approach the items superficially will answer them incorrectly. Thus, if you were creating the items for a true-false test, you would construct statements for your items that were not blatantly true or blatantly false. Blatancy in items rarely leads to accurate inferences about students. Beyond blatancy avoidance, however, you should phrase at least some of the items so if students approach them unthinkingly, they'll choose false for a true statement and vice versa. What you're trying to do is to get students to *think* about your test items and, thereby, give you a better idea about how much good thinking they can do.

Minimizing Negatives

With binary-choice items, many students have a really difficult time responding to negatively phrased items. For instance, suppose in a true-false test you were asked to decide about the truth or falsity of the following statement: "The League of Nations was not formed immediately after the conclusion of World War II." What the item is looking for as a correct answer to this statement is *true*, because the League of Nations was in existence prior to World War II. Yet, the existence of the *not* in the item really will confuse some students. They'll be apt to answer *false* even if they know the League of Nations was functioning before World War II commenced.

Because I've churned out my share of true-false items over the years, I know all too well how tempting it is to simply insert a *not* into an otherwise true statement. But don't yield to the temptation. Only rarely succumb to the lure of the nagging negative in binary-choice items. Items containing double negatives or triple negatives (if you could contrive one) are obviously to be avoided.

Avoiding Double-Concept Items

The third guideline for binary-choice items directs you to focus on only a single concept in each item. If you were creating a statement for a right-wrong test, and had an item in which half of the statement was clearly right and the other half was clearly wrong, you make it mighty difficult for students to respond correctly. The presence of two concepts in a single item, even if both are right or both are wrong, tends to confuse students and, as a consequence, yields test results apt to produce inaccurate inferences about those students.

Balancing Response Categories

If you're devising a binary-choice test, try to keep an approximately equal number of items representing the two response categories. For example, if it's a true-false test, make sure you have somewhat similar proportions of true and false statements. It's not necessary to have exactly the same number of true and false items. The proportion of true and false items, however, should be roughly the same. This fourth guideline is quite easy to follow if you simply keep it in mind when creating your binary-choice items.

Maintaining Item-Length Similarity

The fifth guideline is similar to the fourth because it encourages you to structure your items so there are no give-away clues associated with item length. If your two response categories are *accurate* and *inaccurate,* make sure the length of the accurate statements is approximately the same as the length of the inaccurate statements. When creating true-false tests, there is a tendency to toss in qualifying clauses for the true statements so those statements, properly qualified, are truly true— but also long! As a result, there's a systematic pattern wherein long statements are true and short statements are false. As soon as students catch on to this pattern, they can answer items correctly without even referring to an item's contents.

In review, we've considered five item-writing guidelines for binary-choice items. If you'll follow those guidelines and keep your wits about you when creating binary-choice items, you'll often find this type of test will prove useful in the classroom. And that's true, not false.

■ Multiple Binary-Choice Items

A *multiple binary-choice item* is one in which a cluster of items is presented to students, requiring a binary response to *each* of the items in the cluster. Typically, but not always, the items are related to an initial statement or set of statements. Multiple binary-choice items are formatted so they look like traditional multiple-choice tests. In a multiple-choice test, the student must choose one answer from several options, but in the multiple binary-choice test the student must make a response for each statement in the cluster. Figure 6.1 is an example of a multiple binary-choice item.

David Frisbie (1992) has reviewed the available research regarding such items and has concluded that multiple binary-choice items are (1) highly efficient for gathering student achievement data, (2) more reliable than other selected-

Figure 6.1 ■ An Illustrative Multiple True-False Item

• • • Suppose that a dozen of your students completed a 10-item multiple-choice test and earned the following number of correct scores:

5, 6, 7, 7, 7, 7, 8, 8, 8, 8, 9, 10

9. The median for your students' scores is 7.5.   (True)
10. The mode for the set of scores is 8.0.   (False)
11. The range of the students' scores is 5.0.   (True)
12. The median is different than the mean.   (False)

response items, (3) able to measure the same skills and abilities as multiple-choice items dealing with comparable content, (4) a bit more difficult for students than multiple-choice tests, and (5) perceived by students to be more difficult but more efficient than multiple-choice items. Frisbie believes when teachers construct multiple binary-choice items, they must be attentive to all of the usual considerations in writing regular binary-choice items. However, he suggests the following two additional guidelines.

Item-Writing Guidelines for Multiple Binary-Choice Items

1. Separate item clusters vividly from one another.
2. Make certain that each item meshes well with the cluster's stimulus material.

Separating Clusters

Because many students are familiar with traditional multiple-choice items, and because each of those items is numbered, there is some danger students may become confused by the absence of numbers where such numbers are ordinarily found. Thus, be sure to use some kind of formatting system to make it clear a new cluster is commencing. In the illustrative item seen in Figure 6.1, notice that three dots (• • •) have been used to signify the beginning of a new cluster of items. You can use asterisks, lines, boxes, or some similar way of alerting students to the beginning of a new cluster.

Coordinating Items with Their Stem

In multiple-choice items, the first part of the item—the part preceding the response options—is called the *stem*. For multiple binary-choice items, we refer to the first part of the item cluster as the cluster's stem or stimulus material. The second item-writing guideline for this item type suggests you make sure all items in a cluster are, in fact, linked in a meaningful way to the cluster's stem. If they're not, then you might as well use individual binary-choice items rather than multiple binary-choice items.

There's another compelling reason you should consider adding multiple binary-choice items to your classroom assessment repertoire. Unlike traditional binary-choice items, for which it's likely students will need to rely on *memorized* information, that's rarely the case with multiple binary-choice items. It is rare, that is, *if* the stimulus materials contain content that's not been encountered previously by students. In other words, if the stem for a subset of multiple binary-choice items contains material that's new to the student, and if each binary-choice item depends directly on the previously unencountered content, it's dead certain the student will need to function above mere recalled knowledge, the lowest level of Bloom's cognitive taxonomy. So, if you make certain your stimulus material for multiple-binary-choice items contains new content, those items will surely be more intellectually demanding than the run-of-the-memory true-false item.

In review, we've considered an item type that's not widely used but has some special virtues. The major advantage of multiple binary-choice items is students can respond to two or three such items in the time it takes them to respond to a single multiple-choice item. Other things being equal, the more items students respond to, the more reliably we can gauge their abilities.

I must confess to a mild bias toward this often overlooked item type because for over 20 years I used such tests as the final examinations in an introductory educational measurement course I taught in the UCLA Graduate School of Education. I'd give my students 20 one- or two-paragraph descriptions of previously unencountered educational measurement situations, then follow up each description with five binary-choice items. In all, then, I ended up with a 100-item final exam that really seemed to sort out those students who knew their stuff from those who didn't. The five items in each cluster were simply statements to which students were to respond *accurate* or *inaccurate*. I could just as appropriately have asked for *true* or *false* responses, but I tried to add a touch of suave to my exams. After all, I was teaching in a *Graduate* School of Education. (In retrospect, my decision seems somewhat silly.) Nonetheless, I had pretty good luck with my 100-item final exams. I used a 50-item version for my midterm exams, and they worked well too. For certain kinds of purposes, I think you'll find multiple binary-choice items will prove useful.

■ Multiple-Choice Items

For a number of decades, the **multiple-choice test item** has dominated achievement testing in the United States and many other nations. Multiple-choice items can be used to measure a student's possession of knowledge or a student's ability to engage in higher levels of thinking. A strength of multiple-choice items is they can contain several answers differing in their *relative* correctness. Thus, the student can be called on to make subtle distinctions among answer options, several of which may be somewhat correct. A weakness of multiple-choice items, as is the case with all selected-response items, is that students need only *recognize* a correct answer. They need not *generate* a correct answer. Although a fair amount of criticism has been heaped on multiple-choice items, particularly in recent years, properly constructed multiple-choice items can tap a rich variety of student skills and knowledge, so can be a useful tool for classroom assessment.

The first part of a multiple-choice item, as noted earlier, is referred to as the item's *stem*. The potential answer options are described as *item alternatives*. Incorrect alternatives are typically referred to as the item's *distractors.* Two common ways of creating multiple-choice items are to use an item stem that is either a direct question or an incomplete statement. With younger students, the direct-question approach is preferable. Using either direct-question stems or incomplete-statement stems, a multiple-choice item can ask students to select either a correct answer or, instead, to select a best answer.

In Figure 6.2 there are examples of a direct-question item requesting a best-answer response and an incomplete-statement item requesting a correct-answer response.

Let's turn now to a consideration of item-writing guidelines for multiple-choice items. Because of the widespread use of multiple-choice items over the past half-century, there are quite a few experience-sired suggestions regarding how to create such items. Below, you'll find five of the more frequently cited recommendations for constructing multiple-choice items.

Item-Writing Guidelines for Multiple-Choice Items

1. The stem should consist of a self-contained question or problem.
2. Avoid negatively stated stems.
3. Do not let the length of alternatives supply unintended clues.
4. Randomly assign correct answers to alternative positions.
5. Never use "all-of-the-above" alternatives, but do use "none-of-the-above" alternatives to increase item difficulty.

Stem Stuffing

A properly constructed stem for a multiple-choice item will present a clearly described task to the student so the student can then get to work on figuring out which of the item's options is best (if it's a best-answer item) or correct (if it's a correct-answer item). A poorly constructed stem for a multiple-choice item will force the student to read one or more of the alternatives in order to figure out what the item is getting at. In general, therefore, it's preferable to load as much of the item's content as possible into the stem. Lengthy stems and terse alternatives are, as a rule, much better than skimpy stems and long alternatives. You might try reading the stems of your multiple-choice items without any of the alternatives to see if the stems (either direct questions or incomplete statements) make sense all by themselves.

Figure 6.2 ■ Illustrative Multiple-Choice Items

Direct-Question Form (best-answer version)

Which of the following modes of composition would be most effective in explaining to someone how a bill becomes a law in this nation?
   A. Narrative
 * B. Expository
   C. Persuasive
   D. Descriptive

Incomplete-Statement Form (correct-answer version)

Mickey Mouse's nephews are named
   A. Huey, Dewey, and Louie.
   B. Mutt and Jeff.
   C. Larry, Moe, and Curly.
 * D. Morty and Ferdie.

Knocking Negatively Stated Stems

It has been alleged, particularly by overly cautious individuals, that "one robin does not spring make." Without debating the causal relationship between seasonal shifts and feathered flyers, in multiple-choice item writing we could say with confidence that "one negative in an item stem does not confusion unmake." Negatives are strange commodities. A single *not,* tossed casually into a test item, can make students crazy. Besides, because *not* is such a tiny word, and might be overlooked by students, a number of students (who didn't see the *not*) may be trying to ferret out the best alternative for a positively stated stem that, in reality, is negative.

For example, let's say you wanted to do a bit of probing of your students' knowledge of U.S. geography and phrased the stem of a multiple-choice item such as this: "Which one of the following cities is located in a state west of the Mississippi River?" If your alternatives were: A. San Diego, B. Pittsburgh, C. Boston, and D. Atlanta, students would have little difficulty in knowing how to respond. Let's say, however, that you decided to add a dollop of difficulty by using the same alternatives but tossing in a *not.* Now your item's stem might read something like this: "Which one of the following cities is not located in a state east of the Mississippi River?" For this version of the item, the student who failed to spot the *not* (this, in psychometric circles, is known as not-spotting) would be in big trouble.

By the way, note in both stems, the student was asked to identify which *one* of the following answers was correct. If you leave the *one* out, a student might have interpreted the question to mean there were two or more cities being sought.

If there is a compelling reason for using a negative in the stem of a multiple-choice item, be sure to highlight the negative with italics, boldface type, or underscoring so that students who are not natural not-spotters will have a fair chance to answer the item correctly.

Attending to Alternative Length

Novice item writers often fail to realize the length of a multiple-choice item's alternatives can give away what the correct answer is. Let's say choices A, B, and C say blah, blah, blah, but choice D says blah, blah, blah, blah, blah, and blah. The crafty student will be inclined to opt for choice D not simply because one gets many more blahs for one's selection, but because the student will figure out the teacher has given so much attention to choice D that there must be something special about it.

Thus, when you're whipping up your alternatives for multiple-choice items, try either to keep all the alternatives about the same length or, if this isn't possible, to have at least two alternatives be of approximately equal length. For instance, if you were using four-alternative items, you might have two fairly short alternatives and two fairly long alternatives. What you want to avoid, of course, is having the correct alternative be one length (either short or long) while the distractors are all another length.

Incidentally, the number of alternatives is really up to you. Most frequently, we see multiple-choice items with four or five alternatives. Because students can guess correct answers more readily with fewer alternatives, three alternatives are not seen all that often except with younger students. Having more than five alternatives puts a pretty heavy reading load on the student. I've usually employed four alternatives on my own multiple-choice tests, but in a few instances, the nature of the test's content has led me to use three or five alternatives.

Assigning Correct Answer Positions

A fourth guideline for writing multiple-choice items is to make sure you scatter your correct answers among your alternatives so students don't "guess their way to high scores" simply by figuring out your favorite correct answer spot is, for instance, choice D or perhaps choice C. Many novice item writers are reluctant to put the correct answer in the choice-A position because they believe it gives away the correct answer too early. Yet, the choice-A position deserves its share of correct answers too. Absence-of-bias should also apply to answer-choice options.

As a rule of thumb, if you have four-alternative items, try to assign roughly 25% of your correct answers to each of the four positions. It may be necessary to do some last-minute shifting of answer positions in order to achieve what is essentially a random assignment of correct answers to the available positions. But always do a last-minute check on your multiple-choice tests to see you haven't accidentally overbooked your correct answers too heavily in a particular answer-choice position.

Dealing with "of-the-above" Alternatives

Sometimes a beginning item writer who's trying to come up with four (or five) reasonable alternatives will toss in a none-of-the-above or an all-of-the-above alternative simply as a "filler" alternative. But both of these options must be considered more carefully.

The fifth guideline for this item type says quite clearly you should never use the all-of-the-above alternative. Here's the reason why. Let's say you're using a five-option type of multiple-choice item and you want to set up the item so the fifth option (choice E), "all of the above," would be correct. This indicates the first four answers, choices A through D, would all have to be correct. The problem with such an item is that even a student who only knows two of the first four alternatives are correct will be able to select the all-of-the-above response because if any two responses are correct, choice E is the only possible best answer. Even worse, some students will read only the first alternative, see that it is correct, mark choice A on their response sheet, and move on to the next test item without going over the full array of alternatives for the item. For either of these reasons, you should never use an all-of-the-above alternative in your multiple-choice items.

What about the none-of-the above alternative? The guideline indicates it should be used when you wish to increase an item's difficulty. You should do so only when the presence of the none-of-the-above alternative will help you make the kind of test-based inference you want to make. To illustrate, let's say you wanted to find out how well your students could perform basic mathematical

Decision Time

Multiple-Guess Test Items?

For all six years that he has taught, Leroy Larson has worked with fifth-graders. Although Leroy enjoys all content areas, he takes special pride in his reading instruction because he believes his students enter the sixth grade with dramatically improved comprehension capabilities. Leroy spends little time trying to promote his students' isolated reading skills but, instead, places great emphasis on having students "construct their own meanings" from what they have read.

All of Leroy's reading tests consist exclusively of four-option, multiple-choice items. As Leroy puts it, "I can put together a heavy-duty multiple-choice item when I put my mind to it." Because he has put his mind to it many times during the past six years, Leroy is quite satisfied that his reading tests are as good as his reading instruction.

At the most recent open house night at his school, however, a group of five parents registered genuine unhappiness with the exclusive multiple-choice makeup of Leroy's reading tests. The parents had obviously been comparing notes prior to the open house, and Mrs. Jenkins (the mother of one of Leroy's fifth-graders) acted as their spokesperson. In brief, Mrs. Jenkins argued that multiple-choice tests permitted even weak students to "guess their way to good scores." "After all," Mrs. Jenkins pointed out, "do you want to produce good readers or good guessers?"

Surprised and somewhat shaken by this incident, Leroy has been rethinking his approach to reading assessment. He concludes he can (1) stick with his tests as they are, (2) add some short-answer or essay items to his tests, or (3) replace all of his multiple-choice items with open-ended items. As he considers these options, he realizes that he has given himself a multiple-choice decision!

 If you were Leroy, what would your decision be?

operations such as multiplying and dividing. Moreover, you want to be confident your students can really perform the computations either "in their heads," by using scratch paper, or by employing a hand-held calculator. Now, if you use only four-alternative multiple-choice items, there's a real likelihood certain students won't be able to perform the actual mathematical operations, but may be able to select by estimation the answer that is most reasonable. After all, *one* of the four options *has* to be correct. Yet, simply by adding the none-of-the-above option (as a fourth or fifth alternative), students can't be sure the correct answer is silently sitting there among the item's alternatives. To determine whether the correct answer is *really* one of the alternatives for the item, students will be obliged to perform the required mathematical operation and come up with the actual answer. In essence, when the none-of-the-above option is added, the task presented to the student more closely approximates the task the teacher is interested in. A student's chance of guessing the correct answer to a multiple-choice item is markedly less likely when a none-of-the-above option shows up in the item.

Here's a little wrinkle on this guideline you might find useful. Be a bit careful about using a none-of-the-above option for a *best-answer* multiple-choice. Care is warranted because there are wily students waiting out there who'll parade a series of answers for you they regard as better than the one option you think is a winner. If you can cope with such carping, there's no problem. If you have a low carping-coping threshold, however, avoid none-of-the-above options for most—if not all—of your best-answer items.

In review, we've taken a cursory look at five guidelines for the creation of multiple-choice items. There are other more subtle suggestions for creating such items, but if you combine these guidelines with the five general item-writing commandments discussed earlier in the chapter, you'll have a good set of ground rules for devising decent multiple-choice items. As with all of the item types I've been describing, there's no substitute for oodles of practice in item writing followed by collegial or supervisorial reviews of your item-writing efforts. It is said that Rome wasn't built in a day. Similarly, in order to become a capable constructor of multiple-choice items, you'll probably need to develop more than one such test—or even two.

■ Matching Items

A *matching item* consists of two parallel lists of words or phrases requiring the student to match entries on one list with appropriate entries on the second list. Entries in the list for which a match is sought are referred to as **premises**. Entries in the list from which selections are made are referred to as **responses**. Usually, students are directed to match entries from the two lists according to a specific kind of association described in the test directions. Figure 6.3 is an example of a matching item.

Notice in Figure 6.3's illustrative matching item that both lists are *homogeneous*. All of the entries in the column at the left (the premises) are U.S. military conflicts and all of the entries in the column at the right (the responses) are names of U.S. presidents. Homogeneity is an important attribute of properly constructed matching items.

An advantage of matching items is that their compact form takes up little space on a printed page, thus making it easy to tap a good deal of information efficiently. Matching items can also be easily scored by simply holding a correct-answer template next to the list of premises where students are to supply their selections from the list of responses. A disadvantage of matching items is, as with binary-choice items, they sometimes encourage students' memorization of low-level factual information that, in at least some instances, is of debatable utility. The illustrative matching item is a case in point. Although it's relatively easy to create matching items such as this, is it really important to know which U.S. chief executive was in office when a military conflict was concluded? That's the kind of issue you'll be facing when you decide what kinds of items to include in your classroom assessments.

Typically, matching items are used as *part* of a teacher's assessment instruments. It's pretty difficult to imagine a major classroom examination consisting exclusively of matching items. Matching items don't work well when teachers are trying to assess relatively distinctive ideas, because matching items require pools of related entries to insert into the matching format.

Let's consider a half-dozen guidelines you should think about when creating matching items for your classroom assessment instruments. The guidelines are presented here.

Item-Writing Guidelines for Matching Items

1. Employ homogeneous lists.
2. Use relatively brief lists, placing the shorter words or phrases at the right.
3. Employ more responses than premises.
4. Order the responses logically.
5. Describe the basis for matching and the number of times responses may be used.
6. Place all premises and responses for an item on a single page.

Employing Homogeneous Entries

As noted earlier, each list in a matching item should consist of homogeneous entries. If you really can't create a homogeneous set of premises and a homogeneous set of responses, you shouldn't be mucking about with matching items.

Going for Relative Brevity

From the student's perspective, it's much easier to respond to matching items if the entries on both lists are relatively few in number. About 10 or so premises should be the upper limit for most matching items. The problem with longer lists is that

Figure 6.3 ■ An Illustrative Matching Item

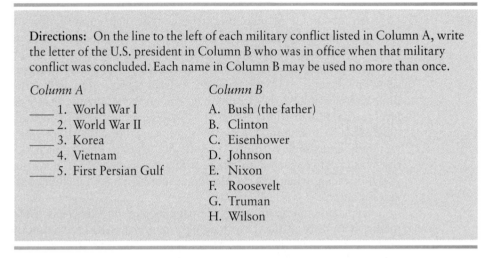

Directions: On the line to the left of each military conflict listed in Column A, write the letter of the U.S. president in Column B who was in office when that military conflict was concluded. Each name in Column B may be used no more than once.

Column A

_____ 1. World War I
_____ 2. World War II
_____ 3. Korea
_____ 4. Vietnam
_____ 5. First Persian Gulf

Column B

A. Bush (the father)
B. Clinton
C. Eisenhower
D. Johnson
E. Nixon
F. Roosevelt
G. Truman
H. Wilson

students spend so much time trying to isolate the appropriate response for a given premise, they may forget what they're attempting to find. Very lengthy sets of premises or responses are almost certain to cause at least some students difficulty in responding because they'll lose track of what's being sought. It would be far better to take a lengthy matching item with 24 premises and split it into three 8-premise matching items.

In addition, to cut down on the reading requirements of matching items, be sure to place the list of shorter words or phrases at the right. In other words, make the briefer entries the responses. In this way, when students are scanning the response lists for a matching entry, they'll not be obliged to read too many lengthy phrases or sentences.

Loading Up on Responses

A third guideline for the construction of matching items is to make sure there are at least a few extra responses. Otherwise, if the number of premises and responses are identical, the student who knows, say, 80% of the matches to the premises may be able to figure out the remaining matches by a process of elimination. A few extra responses reduce this likelihood substantially. Besides, these sorts of responses are inexpensive.

Ordering Responses

So you'll not provide unintended clues to students regarding which responses go with which premises, it's a good idea in matching items to order the responses in some sort of logical fashion—for example, alphabetical or chronological sequence. Notice in the illustrative matching item in Figure 6.3, the names of the U.S. presidents are listed alphabetically.

Describing the Task for Students

The fifth guideline for the construction of matching items suggests the directions for an item always make explicit the basis on which the matches are to be made and, at the same time, the number of times a response can be used. The more clearly students understand how they're supposed to respond, the more accurately they'll respond, and the more validly you'll be able to make score-based inferences about your students.

Parent Talk

Assume that you've been using a fair number of multiple-choice items in your classroom examinations. Benito's parents, Mr. and Mrs. Olmedo, have set up a 15-minute conference with you during a Back-to-Classroom Night to talk about Benito's progress.

When they arrive, they soon get around to the topic in which they are most interested—namely, your multiple-choice test items. As Mr. Olmedo puts it, "We want our son to learn to use his mind, not his memory. Although my wife and I have little experience with multiple-choice tests because almost all of our school exams were of an essay nature, we believe multiple-choice tests measure only what Benito has memorized. He has a good memory, as you've probably found out, but we want more for him. Why are you using such low-level test items?"

 If I were you, here's how I'd respond to Mr. Olmedo's question:

"I appreciate your coming in to talk about Benito's education and, in particular, the way he is being assessed. And I also realize that recently there has been a good deal of criticism of multiple-choice test items. More often than not, such criticism is altogether appropriate. In far too many cases, because multiple-choice items are easy to score, they're used to assess just about everything. And, all too often, those kinds of items do indeed ask students to do little more than display their memorization skills.

"But this doesn't need to be the case. Multiple-choice items, if they are carefully developed, can assess a wide variety of truly higher-order thinking skills. In our school, all teachers have taken part in a series of staff-development workshop sessions in which every teacher learned how to create *challenging* multiple-choice items that require students to display much more than memory. (At this point, I'd whip out a few examples of demanding multiple-choice items used in my own tests, then go through them, from stem to alternatives, showing Mr. and Mrs. Olmedo what I meant. If I *didn't* have any examples of such items from my tests, I'd think seriously about the legitimacy of Benito's parents' criticism.)

"So, although there's nothing wrong with Benito's acquiring more memorized information, and a small number of my multiple-choice items actually do test for such knowledge, the vast majority of the multiple-choice items that Benito will take in my class call for him to employ that fine mind of his.

"That's what you two want. That's what I want."

 Now, how would you respond to Mr. and Mrs. Olmedo's concerns?

Formatting Items to Avoid Page Flipping

The final guideline for this item type suggests that you make sure all premises and responses for a matching item are on a single page. Not only does this eliminate the necessity for massive, potentially disruptive page turning by students, but it will also decrease the likelihood students will overlook correct answers merely because they were on the "other" page.

In review, matching items, if employed judiciously, can efficiently assess your students' knowledge. The need to employ homogeneous lists of related content tends to diminish the applicability of this type of selected-response item. Nonetheless, if you are dealing with content that can be addressed satisfactorily by such an approach, you'll find matching items a useful member of your repertoire of item types.

■ What Do Classroom Teachers Really Need to Know about Selected-Response Tests?

If you engage in any meaningful amount of assessment in your own classroom, it's quite likely you'll find that selected-response items will be useful. Selected-response items can typically be used to ascertain students' mastery of larger domains of content than is the case with constructed-response kinds of test items. Although it's often thought selected-response items must, of necessity, measure only lower-order kinds of cognitive capabilities, inventive teachers can create selected-response options to elicit very high levels of cognitive skills from students.

As for the four types of items treated in the chapter, you really need to understand enough about each kind to help you decide whether one or more of those item types would be useful for a classroom assessment task you have in mind. If you do decide to use binary-choice, multiple binary-choice, multiple-choice, or matching items in your own tests, then you'll find the sets of item-writing guidelines for each item type will come in handy.

Yet, in honesty, even if you adhere to the chapter's five general item-writing commandments and the set of guidelines for a particular type of item, you'll still need practice in constructing selected-response items such as those considered here. As was suggested several times in the chapter, it is exceedingly helpful if you can find someone with measurement moxie, or at least an analytic mind, to review your test-development efforts. It's difficult in any realm to improve if you don't get feedback about the adequacy of your efforts. That's surely true with classroom assessment. Try to entice a colleague or supervisor to look over your selected-response test items to see what needs to be strengthened. However, even without piles of practice, if you adhere to the item-writing guidelines provided in the chapter, your selected-response tests won't be all that shabby.

The most important thing to learn from this chapter is that there are four useful *selected*-response procedures for drawing valid inferences about your students' status. The more assessment options you have at your disposal, the more appropriately you'll be able to assess those student variables in which you're interested.

but what does this have to do with
Teaching?

In this chapter, and the four following it, not only will you become acquainted with varied types of test items but you will learn how to construct them properly. Why, you might ask, does a classroom teacher need to possess such a resplendent repertoire of item types? After all, if a student knows that Abraham Lincoln was assassinated while attending a play, the student could satisfactorily display such knowledge in a variety of ways. A good old true-false item or a nifty multiple-choice item would surely do the necessary assessing.

Well, that's quite true. But what you need to recall, *from a teaching perspective*, is that students ought to master the skills and knowledge they're being taught so thoroughly they can display such mastery in a good many ways, not just one. A cognitive skill that's been learned *well* by a student will be a cognitive skill that can be displayed in all sorts of ways, whether via selected-response items or constructed-response items.

And this is why, when you *teach* children, you really need to be promoting their generalizable mastery of whatever's being taught. Consistent with such a push for generalizable mastery, you will typically want to employ varied assessment approaches. If you gravitate toward only one or two item types (that is, if you become "Multiple-Choice Molly" or "True-False Teddy"), then your students will tend to learn things only in a way that meshes with your favored item type.

Eons ago, when I was preparing to be a teacher, my teacher education professors advised me to employ different kinds of items "for variety's sake." Well, classroom teachers aren't putting on a fashion show. Variety for its own sake is psychometrically stupid. But variety of assessment approaches as a deliberate way of promoting and measuring students' *generalizable mastery* of what's been taught—this is psychometrically suave.

■ Chapter Summary

The chapter was initiated with a presentation of five item-writing commandments that pertain to both constructed-response and selected-response items. The five admonitions directed teachers to avoid unclear directions, ambiguous statements, unintentional clues, complex syntax, and hypersophisticated vocabulary.

In turn, then, consideration was given to the four most common kinds of selected-response test items—namely, binary-choice items, multiple binary-choice items, multiple-choice items, and matching items. For each of these four item types, after a brief description of the item type and its strengths and weaknesses, a set of item-writing guidelines was presented. These four sets of guidelines were presented on pages 130, 132, 134, and 139. Each guideline was briefly discussed. Readers were encouraged to consider the four item types when deciding on an answer to the how-to-assess-it question.

Self-Check

For this chapter's self-check exercises, you'll be asked to evaluate a series of selected-response items. The items deal with content about assessment that was addressed in earlier sections of this book. Therefore, you should regard this chapter's self-check as an instructionally reinforcing experience. Specifically, you'll be asked to evaluate a series of selected-response items. In considering each item, think back to the five general item-writing commandments that apply to all the items you'll write. In addition, recall the specific item-writing guidelines associated with the type of item you're being asked to evaluate. To evaluate these *selected-*response items, you'll be asked to supply *constructed* (short-answer) responses. This requirement will either increase your item-writing flexibility or initiate a bit of assessment schizophrenia.

1. Here are two binary-choice items. In the lined spaces below the items, please evaluate the quality of the two items. Be sure to note any particular item-writing deficits you discern.

    Directions: For each of the following statements, indicate whether the statement is right (R) or wrong (W).

    R or W ____ (1) The most important attribute of validity evidence is content coverage, whereas the most important attribute of reliability evidence is consistency of results.

    R or W ____ (2) Absence-of-bias determinations are not best made only by judgmental procedures.

    Your Evaluation: _____

    _____

2. Now look over the following two multiple-choice items and make an evaluation of their intrinsic virtues. Evaluate them below.

    Directions: Choose the best answer from the alternatives for each of the following items.

    (1) Which of the following kinds of validity evidence, when analyzed carefully, is the most comprehensive descriptor for supportive information regarding the validity of test-based inferences?
       a. Content-related evidence of validity
       b. Predictive criterion-related evidence of validity
       c. Concurrent criterion-related evidence of validity
       d. Construct-related evidence of validity

    (2) If you were a classroom teacher who wished to improve your students' higher-order thinking skills, in which of the following taxonomic domains should you be most interested?
       a. The cognitive domain
       b. The affective domain

  c. The psychomotor domain
  d. None of the domains given above

Your Evaluation: _____

_____

3. Here's a multiple binary-choice item for you to consider. See what you think of it, then evaluate it in the lined spaces below.

>   **Directions:** For *each* statement in the cluster of statements, indicate whether the statement is true (T) or false (F).
>
>   ****In an elaborate effort to ascertain the reliability of a new high-stakes test developed in their district, central-office administrators have calculated the following types of reliability evidence based on a tryout of the test with 2,400 students:
>
>   *   Internal consistency r = .82
>   *   Test-retest r = .78
>   *   Standard error of measurement = 4.3
>
>   ____ (1) The three types of reliability evidence calculated by the central-office staff are essentially interchangeable.
>   ____ (2) The minor difference between the stability and internal consistency coefficients constitutes no cause for alarm.
>   ____ (3) The test-retest r should never be smaller than an internal consistency reliability coefficient.
>   ____ (4) The standard error of measurement is derived chiefly from the test's reliability indices.

Your Evaluation: _____

_____

4. Let's close out this practice scrutiny of selected-response items with a quick look at the following matching item that grabs its content from this very chapter. Evaluate it in the lined spaces below.

>   **Directions:** Choose the best match between the item types in List X and the strengths/weaknesses in List Y.
>
> | *List X* | *List Y* |
> |---|---|
> | ____ (1) matching | a. Can efficiently cover much informational content |
> | ____ (2) binary choice | |
> | ____ (3) multiple binary choice | b. Can measure students' higher-order cognitive skills if properly constructed |
> | ____ (4) multiple choice | c. Often encourages low-level recall of information |
> | | d. Assesses what students can recognize rather than create |

Your Evaluation: _____

_____

Pondertime

1. If you were asked to take part in a mini-debate about the respective virtues of selected-response items versus constructed-response items, what do you think would be your major points if you were supporting the use of selected-response test items?

2. During your lifetime you've probably completed all, or most all, of the item types described in the chapter. Which type was your most favorite and which type was your least favorite? Why?

3. Why do you think that multiple-choice tests have been so widely used in nationally standardized norm-referenced achievement tests during the past half-century?

4. Do you think classroom teachers can become truly effective writers of selected-response test items? If so, how?

5. If you had to build your classroom assessments exclusively using selected-response test items, which item types would you prefer to use? Why?

Self-Check Key

1. The first of the two items violated the third item-writing guideline for binary-choice items: Don't include two concepts in one statement. A student may not be able to keep separate the part of the item dealing with validity evidence from the part that deals with reliability evidence. Incidentally, although the segment of the item dealing with reliability is accurate, the segment about validity is off the mark because not all validity evidence is content related.

   The second of the two items violates Guideline 2: Avoid negative statements. Because the descriptive phrase being used is *absence-of-bias,* the item already has a negative notion built into it. By the time the student reads the *not* and the *only,* full-bodied confusion is apt to have flowered.

2. The first multiple-choice item isn't all that bad. There don't seem to be any major deficits in the item (the correct answer to which is choice d).

   The second multiple-choice isn't all that bad either, except choice d (a version of "none of the above") is pretty much of a throw-away choice. It would be better to have only three alternatives or to split the cognitive domain based on whether the cognitive behavior deals with the lowest level of cognition (knowledge) or higher than the lowest level of cognition (all other kinds of cognitive behavior). The correct answer, of course, is choice a.

3. Although it's surely possible to improve the phrasing of items such as these, in general, this multiple binary-choice item looks fairly acceptable in that it has violated neither the guidelines for multiple binary-choice items nor the guidelines for more conventional binary-choice items. The correct answers, by the way, are (1) F, (2) T, (3) F, and (4) T.

4. This is a genuinely cruddy item. There are almost more mistakes in the item than the words used to create it. First off, the directions are too sloppy and violate Guideline 5 for matching items by giving neither the basis for matching nor the number of times responses can be used. In addition, there are identical numbers of premises and responses, a violation of Guideline 3. The response list isn't homogeneous (Guideline 1) because it contains advantages *and* disadvantages. Guideline 2 also is violated because the shorter phrases are at the left rather than the right. About the only good thing you can say about the item is that it all fits on a single page. Regarding the correct answers—who knows?

■ Additional Stuff

Anderson, Lorin W. (2003). *Classroom Assessment: Enhancing the Quality of Teacher Decision Making*. Mahwah, NJ: Lawrence Erlbaum.

Briggs, Derek C., Alicia C. Alonzo, Cheryl Schwab, and Mark Wilson. (2006). "Diagnostic Assessment with Ordered Multiple-Choice Items." *Educational Assessment, 11*, no. 1: 33–64.

Downing, Steven M., and Thomas M. Haladyna (Eds.). (2006). *Handbook of Test Development*. Mahwah, NJ: Lawrence Erlbaum.

Frisbie, David A. (1992). "The Multiple True-False Format: A Status Review." *Educational Measurement: Issues and Practice, 11*, no. 4 (Winter): 21–26.

Haladyna, Thomas M., Steven M. Downing, and Michael C. Rodriguez. (2002). "A Review of Multiple-Choice Item-Writing Guidelines for Classroom Assessment." *Applied Measurement in Education, 15*, no. 3: 309–334.

McMillan, James H. (2004). *Classroom Assessment: Principles and Practice for Effective Instruction* (3rd ed.). Boston: Allyn and Bacon.

Nitko, A. J. (2004). *Educational Assessment of Students* (4th ed.). Upper Saddle River, NJ: Prentice-Hall/Merrill Education.

Popham, W. James. (2003). *Test Better, Teach Better: The Instructional Role of Assessment*. Alexandria, VA: Association for Supervision and Curriculum Development.

■ Nonprint Stuff

Northwest Regional Educational Laboratory. *Paper-and-Pencil Test Development* (Videotape #NREL-4). Los Angeles: IOX Assessment Associates.

Popham, W. James. *Creating Challenging Classroom Tests: When Students SELECT Their Answers* (Videotape #ETVT-23). Los Angeles: IOX Assessment Associates.

Stiggins, Richard J. *Common Sense Paper and Pencil Assessments* (Videotape). Portland, OR: Assessment Training Institute.

■ Cyber Stuff

■ *WestEd* was established in 1995 by the consolidation of two western regional educational laboratories. WestEd is a nonprofit agency specializing in educational research, development, and service. One of this agency's chief activities deals with assessment, standards, and accountability. The website contains a substantial number of assessment-related resources. For example, it lists Improving Classroom Assessment: A Toolkit for Professional Developers. The toolkit contains numerous staff-development activities related to assessment as well as many samples of both selected-response and constructed-response assessments. The site also has its own search engine that can be used to locate desired materials. www.wested.org

To access chapter objectives, practice tests, weblinks, and flashcards, visit the companion website at **www.ablongman.com/popham5e.**

MyLabSchool is a collection of online tools for your success in this course, your licensure exams, and your teaching career. Discover where the classroom comes to life by visiting **www.mylabschool.com** to access the following resources:

■ Video clips from real classrooms

■ An archive of real-life cases

■ Help with your research papers using Research Navigator™

■ Career Center with resources for:

    Praxis exams and licensure preparation

    Professional portfolio development

    Job search and interview techniques

    Lesson planning with state standard correlations

chapter 7

Constructed-Response Tests

You're going to learn about constructed-response tests in this chapter. To be really truthful, you're going to learn about only two kinds of *paper-and-pencil* constructed-response items—namely, short-answer items and essay items (including students' written compositions). Although I suspect you already know that "you can't tell a book by its cover," now you've discovered that a chapter's title doesn't always describe its contents accurately. Fortunately, as far as I know, there are no state or federal "truth-in-chapter-entitling" laws.

You might be wondering why your ordinarily honest, never-fib author has descended to this act of blatant mislabeling. Actually, it's just to keep your reading chores more manageable. In an earlier chapter, you learned that student-constructed responses can be obtained from a wide variety of item types. In this chapter, we'll be looking at two rather traditional forms of constructed-response items, both of them paper-and-pencil in nature. In the next chapter, the focus will be on *performance tests,* such as those that arise when we ask students to make oral presentations or supply comprehensive demonstrations of skills in class. After that, in Chapter 9, we'll be dealing with portfolio assessment and how portfolios are used for assessment purposes.

Actually, all three chapters could be lumped under the single description of *performance assessment* or *constructed-response measurement* because any time you assess your students by asking them to respond in other than a selected-response manner, the students are *constructing;* that is, they are *performing.* It's just that if I'd loaded all of this performance assessment stuff in a single chapter, you'd have thought you were experiencing a month-long TV mini-series. The self-check exercises would have been as long as a short novel, and you'd have been pondering the pondertime questions for years. Yes, it was my inherent kindness and concern for your well-being that led me to disregard accuracy when entitling this chapter.

The major payoff of all constructed-response items is they elicit student responses more closely approximating the kinds of behavior students must display in

149

real life. After students leave school, for example, their demands of daily living almost never require them to choose responses from four nicely arranged alternatives. And when was the last time, in normal conversation, you were obliged to render a flock of true-false judgments about a set of statements? Yet, you may well be asked to make a brief oral presentation to your fellow teachers or to a parent group, or you may be asked to write a brief report for the school newspaper about your students' field trip to City Hall. Constructed-response tasks unquestionably coincide more closely with nonacademic tasks than do selected-response tasks.

As a practical matter, if the nature of a selected-response task is sufficiently close to what might be garnered from a constructed-response item, then you may wish to consider a selected-response assessment tactic to be a reasonable surrogate for a constructed-response assessment tactic. Selected-response tests are clearly much more efficient to score. And, because almost all teachers I know are busy folks, time-saving procedures are not to be scoffed at. Yet, there will be situations when you'll want to make inferences about your students' status when selected-response tests just won't fill the bill. For instance, if you wish to know what kind of a cursive writer Jamal is, then you'll have to let Jamal write cursively. A true-false test about *i* dotting and *t* crossing just doesn't cut it.

■ Short-Answer Items

The first kind of constructed-response item we'll look at is the ***short-answer item.*** Short-answer items call for students to supply a word, a phrase, or a sentence in response to either a direct question or an incomplete statement. If an item asks students to come up with a fairly lengthy response, it would be considered an essay item, not a short-answer item. If the item asks students to supply only a single word, then it's a *really* short-answer item.

Short-answer items are suitable for assessing relatively simple kinds of learning outcomes such as those focused on students' acquisition of knowledge. If crafted carefully, however, short-answer items can measure substantially more challenging kinds of learning outcomes. The major advantage of short-answer items is that students need to *produce* a correct answer, not merely recognize it from a set of selected-response options. The level of partial knowledge that might allow a student to respond correctly to a choose-the-best-response item won't be sufficient when the student is required to produce a correct answer to a short-answer item.

The major drawback with short-answer items, as is true with all constructed-response items, is that students' responses are difficult to score. The longer the responses sought, the tougher it is to score them accurately. And inaccurate scoring, as we saw in Chapter 2, leads to reduced reliability—which, in turn, reduces the validity of the test-based inferences we make about students—which, in turn, reduces the quality of the decisions we base on those inferences. Educational measurement is much like the rest of life—it's simply loaded with trade-offs. When classroom teachers choose constructed-response tests, they must be willing to trade some scoring accuracy (the kind of accuracy that comes with selected-response approaches) for greater congruence between constructed-response assessment strategies and the kinds of student behaviors about which inferences are to be made.

Here, you will find five straightforward item-writing guidelines for short-answer items. Please look them over, then I'll briefly amplify each guideline and describe how it works.

Item-Writing Guidelines for Short-Answer Items

1. Usually employ direct questions rather than incomplete statements, particularly for young students.
2. Structure the item so that a response should be concise.
3. Place blanks in the margin for direct questions or near the end of incomplete statements.
4. For incomplete statements, use only one or, at most, two blanks.
5. Make sure blanks for all items are equal in length.

Using Direct Questions Rather than Incomplete Statements

For young children, the direct question is a far more familiar format than the incomplete statement. Accordingly, such students will be less confused if direct questions are employed. Another reason short-answer items should employ a direct-question format is that the use of direct questions typically forces the item writer to phrase the item so less ambiguity is present. With incomplete-statements formats, there's often too much temptation simply to delete words or phrases from statements the teacher finds in textbooks. To make sure there isn't more than one correct answer to a short-answer item, it is often helpful if the item writer first decides on the correct answer, then builds a question or incomplete statement designed to elicit a *unique* correct response from knowledgeable students.

Nurturing Concise Responses

Responses to short-answer items, as might be inferred from what they're called, should be *short*. Thus, no matter whether you're eliciting responses that are words, symbols, phrases, or numbers, try to structure the item so a brief response is clearly sought. Suppose you conjured up an incomplete statement item such as this: "An animal that walks on two feet is _____." There are all sorts of answers a student might legitimately make to such an item. Moreover, some of those responses could be fairly lengthy. Now note how a slight restructuring of the item constrains the student: "An animal that walks on two feet is technically classified as _____." By the addition of the phrase "technically classified as," the item writer has restricted the appropriate responses to only one—namely, "biped." If your short-answer items are trying to elicit students' phrases or sentences, you may wish to place word limits on each, or at least indicate in the test's directions that only a *short* one-sentence response is allowable for each item.

Always try to put yourself, mentally, inside the heads of your students and try to anticipate how they are apt to interpret an item. What this second guideline suggests is that you massage an item until it truly lives up to its name—that is, until it becomes a *bona fide* short-answer item.

Positioning Blanks

If you're using direct questions in your short-answer items, place the students' response areas for all items near the right-hand margin of the page, immediately after the item's questions. By doing so, you'll have all of a student's responses nicely lined up for scoring. If you're using incomplete statements, try to place the blank near the end of the statement, not near its beginning. A blank positioned too early in a sentence tends to perplex the students. For instance, notice how this too-early blank can lead to confusion: "The _____ is the governmental body which, based on the United States Constitution, must ratify all U.S. treaties with foreign nations." It would be better to use a direct question or to phrase the item as follows: "The governmental body which, based on the United States Constitution, must ratify all U.S. treaties with foreign nations is the _____."

Limiting Blanks

For incomplete-statement types of short-answer items, you should use only one or two blanks. Any more blanks and the item is labeled a "swiss-cheese item," or an item with holes galore. Here's a swiss-cheese item to illustrate the confusion that a profusion of blanks can make in what is otherwise a decent short-answer item: "After a series of major conflicts with natural disasters, in the year _____, the explorers _____ and _____, accompanied by their _____, discovered _____." The student who could supply correct answers to such a flawed short-answer item should also be regarded as a truly successful explorer.

Inducing Linear Equality

Too often in short-answer items, a beginning item writer will give away the answer by varying the length of the answer blanks so that short lines are used when short answers are correct and long lines are used when lengthier answers are correct. This practice tosses unintended clues to students and so should be avoided. In the interest of linear egalitarianism, not to mention decent item writing, keep all blanks for short-answer items equal in length. Be sure, however, the length of the answer spaces provided is sufficient for students' responses—in other words, not so skimpy that students have to cram in their answers in an illegible fashion.

In review, short-answer items are the most simple form of constructed-response items, but they can help teachers measure important skills and knowledge. Because such items seek students' constructed rather than selected responses, they can be employed to tap some genuinely higher-order skills. Although students' responses to short-answer items are more difficult to score than are their answers to selected-response items, the scoring of such items isn't difficult. That's because short-answer items, by definition, should elicit only *short* answers.

■ Essay Items: Development

The essay item is surely the most commonly used form of constructed-response assessment item. Any time teachers ask their students to churn out a paragraph or two on what the students know about Topic X or to compose an original composition describing their "Favorite Day," an *essay item* is being used. Essay items are particularly useful in gauging a student's ability to synthesize, evaluate, and compose. Such items have a wide variety of applications in most teachers' classrooms.

A special form of the essay item is the *writing sample*—when teachers ask students to generate a written composition in an attempt to measure students' composition skills. Because the procedures employed to construct items for such writing

Decision Time

Forests or Trees?

Allison Allen is a brand-new English teacher assigned to work with seventh-grade and eighth-grade students at Dubois Junior High School. Allison has taken part in a state-sponsored summer workshop that emphasizes "writing as a process." Coupled with what she learned while completing her teacher education program, Allison is confident that she can effectively employ techniques such as brainstorming, outlining, early drafts, peer critiquing, and multiple revisions. She assumes that her students will acquire not only competence in their composition capabilities but also confidence about their possession of those capabilities. What Allison's preparation failed to address, however, was how to grade her students' compositions.

Two experienced English teachers at Dubois Junior High have gone out of their way to help Allison get through her first year as a teacher. Mrs. Miller and Ms. Stovall have both been quite helpful during the early weeks of the school year. However, when Allison asked them one day during lunch how she should judge the quality of her students' compositions, two decisively different messages were given.

Ms. Stovall strongly endorsed *holistic* grading of compositions—that is, a general appraisal of each composition as a whole. Although Ms. Stovall bases her holistic grading scheme on a set of explicit criteria, she believes a single "gestalt" grade should be given so that "one's vision of the forest is not obscured by tree-counting."

Arguing with equal vigor, Mrs. Miller urged Allison to adopt *analytic* appraisals of her students' compositions. "By supplying your students with a criterion-by-criterion judgment of their work," she contended, "each student will be able to know precisely what's good and what isn't." (It was evident during the fairly heated interchanges that Mrs. Miller and Ms. Stovall had disagreed about this topic in the past.) Mrs. Miller concluded her remarks by saying, "Forget about that forest-and-trees metaphor, Allison. What we're talking about here is clarity!"

 If you were Allison, how would you decide to judge the quality of your students' compositions?

samples and, thereafter, for scoring students' compositions are so similar to the procedures employed to create and score responses to any kind of essay item, we'll treat writing samples and other kinds of essay items all at one time in this chapter. You'll find it helpful, however, to remember that the requirement to have students generate a writing sample is, in reality, a widely used type of *performance test*. We'll dig more deeply into performance tests in the following chapter.

For assessing certain kinds of complex learning outcomes, the essay item is the hands-down winner. It clearly triumphs when you're trying to see how well students can create original compositions. Yet, there are a fair number of drawbacks associated with essay items, and if you're going to consider using essay items in your own classroom, you ought to know the weaknesses as well as the strengths of this item type.

One difficulty with essay items is they're more difficult to write—at least write properly—than is generally thought. I must confess that as a first-year high school teacher, I sometimes conjured up essay items while walking to school, then slapped them up in the chalkboard so that I created almost instant essay exams. At the time, I thought my essay items were pretty good. Such is the pride of youth and the product of ignorance. I'm glad I have no record of those items. In retrospect, I assume they were pretty putrid. I now know that generating a really good essay item is a tough task—a task not accomplishable while strolling to school. You'll see this is true from the item-writing rules to be presented shortly. It takes time to create a solid essay item. You'll need to find time to construct suitable essay items for your own classroom assessments.

The most serious problem with essay items, however, is the difficulty teachers have in scoring students' responses reliably. Let's say you use a six-item essay test to measure your students' ability to solve certain kinds of problems in social studies. Suppose that, by some stroke of measurement magic, all your students' responses could be transformed into typed manuscript form so you could not tell which response came from which student. Let's say you were asked to score the complete set of responses *twice*. What do you think is the likelihood your two sets of scores would be consistent? Well, experience suggests that most teachers aren't able to produce very reliable results when they score students' essay responses. The task in this instance, of course, is to *increase* the reliability of your scoring efforts so you're not distorting the validity of the score-based inferences you want to make on the basis of your students' responses.

Creating Essay Items

Because the scoring of essay responses (and students' compositions) is such an important topic, you'll soon be getting a separate set of guidelines on how to score responses to such items. The more complex the nature of students' constructed responses become, as you'll see in the next two chapters, the more attention you'll need to lavish on scoring. You can't score responses to items that you haven't written, however, so let's look at the five guidelines for the construction of essay items.

Item-Writing Guidelines for Essay Items

1. Convey to students a clear idea regarding the extensiveness of the response desired.
2. Construct items so the student's task is explicitly described.
3. Provide students with the approximate time to be expended on each item as well as each item's value.
4. Do not employ optional items.
5. Precursively judge an item's quality by composing, mentally or in writing, a possible response.

Communicating the Desired Extensiveness of Students' Responses

It is sometimes thought that if teachers decide to use essay items, students have total freedom of response. On the contrary, teachers can structure essay items so students produce (1) barely more than they would for a short-answer item or, in contrast, (2) extremely lengthy responses. The two types of essay items reflecting this distinction in the desired extensiveness of student's responses are described as restricted-response items and extended-response items.

A *restricted-response item* decisively limits the form and content of students' responses. For example, a restricted-response item in a health education class might ask students the following: "Describe the three most common ways HIV, the AIDS virus, is transmitted. Take no more than 25 words to describe each method of transmission." In this example, the number of HIV transmission methods was specified, as was the maximum length for each transmission method's description.

In contrast, an *extended-response item* provides students with far more latitude in responding. Here's an example of an extended-response item from a social studies class: "Identify the chief factors contributing to the U.S. government's financial deficit during the past two decades. Having identified those factors, decide which factors, if any, have been explicitly addressed by the U.S legislative and/or executive branches of government in the last five years. Finally, critically evaluate the likelihood that any currently proposed remedies will bring about significant reductions in the U.S. national debt." A decent response to such an extended-response item not only should get high marks from the teacher but might also be the springboard for a successful career in politics.

One technique teachers commonly use to limit students' responses is to provide a certain amount of space on the test paper or in their students' response booklets. For instance, the teacher might direct students to "Use no more than two sheets (both sides) in your blue books to respond to each test item." Although the space-limiting ploy is an easy one to implement, it really disadvantages students who write in a large-letter, scrawling fashion. Whereas such large-letter students may only be able to cram a few paragraphs onto a page, those students who write in a small, scrunched-up style may be able to produce a short novella in the same space.

This first guideline asks you to think carefully about whether the inference at issue that you wish to make about your students is best serviced by students' responses to (1) more essay items requiring shorter responses or (2) fewer essay items requiring extensive responses. Having made that decision, then be sure to convey to your students a clear picture of the degree of extensiveness you're looking for in their responses.

Describing Students' Tasks

Students will find it difficult to construct responses to tasks if they don't understand what the tasks are. Moreover, students' responses to badly understood tasks are almost certain to yield flawed inferences by teachers. The most important part of an essay item is, without question, the description of the *assessment task*. It is the assessment task students respond to when they generate essays. Clearly, then, poorly described assessment tasks will yield many off-target responses that, had the student truly understood what was being sought, might have been more appropriate.

There are numerous labels used to represent the assessment task in an essay item. Sometimes it's simply called the *task*, the *charge*, or perhaps the *assignment*. In essay items that are aimed at eliciting student compositions, the assessment task is often referred to as a ***prompt***. No matter how the assessment task is labeled, if you're a teacher who is using essay items, you must make sure the nature of the task is really set forth clearly for your students. Put yourself, at least hypothetically, in the student's seat and see if, with the level of knowledge possessed by most of your students, the nature of the assessment task is really apt to be understood.

To illustrate, if you wrote the following essay item, there's little doubt your students' assessment task would have been badly described: "In 500 words or less, discuss democracy in Latin America." In contrast, notice in the following item how much more clearly the assessment task is set forth: "Describe how the checks and balances provisions in the U.S. Constitution were believed by the Constitution's framers to be a powerful means to preserve democracy (300–500 words)."

Providing Time-Limit and Item-Value Guidance

When teachers create an examination consisting of essay items, they often have an idea regarding which items will take more of the students' time. But students don't know what's in the teacher's head. As a consequence, some students will lavish loads of attention on items the teacher thought warranted only modest effort, yet devote little time to items the teacher thought deserved substantial attention. Similarly, sometimes teachers will want to weight certain items more heavily than others. Again, if students are unaware of which items count most, they may toss loads of rhetoric at the low-value items and have insufficient time to give more than a trifling response to the high-value items.

To avoid these problems, there's quite a straightforward solution—namely, letting students in on the secret. If there are any differences among items in point value or in the time students should spend on them, simply provide this information in the directions or, perhaps parenthetically, at the end of each item. Students will appreciate such clarifications of your expectations.

Avoiding Optionality

It's fairly common practice among teachers who use essay examinations to provide students with a certain number of items, then let each student choose to answer fewer than the number of items presented. For example, the teacher might allow students to "choose any three of the five essay items presented." Students, of course, really groove on such an assessment procedure because they can respond to items for which they're well prepared and avoid those items for which they're inadequately prepared. Yet, other than inducing student glee, this optional-items classroom assessment scheme has little going for it.

When students select different items from a menu of possible items, they are actually responding to different examinations. As a consequence, it is impossible to judge their performances on some kind of common scale. Remember, as a classroom teacher you'll be trying to make better educational decisions about your students by relying on test-based inferences regarding those students. It's tough enough to make a decent test-based interpretation when you have only one test to consider. It's infinitely more difficult to make such interpretations when you are faced with a medley of different tests because you allow your students to engage in a mix-and-match measurement procedure.

In most cases, teachers rely on an optional-items procedure with essay items when they're uncertain about the importance of the content measured by their examinations' items. Such uncertainty gives rise to the use of optional items because the teacher is not clearheaded about the inferences for which the examination's results will be used. If you spell out those inferences crisply, prior to the examination, you will usually find you'll have no need for optional item selection in your essay examinations.

Previewing Students' Responses

After you've constructed an essay item for one of your classroom assessments, there's a quick way to get a preliminary fix on whether the item is a winner or loser. Simply toss yourself, psychologically, into the head of one of your typical students, then anticipate how such a student would respond to the item. If you have time, and are inclined to do so, you could try writing a response that the student might produce to the item. More often than not, because you'll be too busy to conjure up such fictitious responses in written form, you might try to compose a mental response to the item on behalf of the typical student you've selected. An early mental run-through of how a student might respond to an item can often help you identify deficits in the item because, when you put yourself, even hypothetically, on the other side of the teacher's desk, you'll sometimes discover shortcomings in items you otherwise wouldn't have identified. Too many times I've seen teachers give birth to a set of essay questions, send them into battle on examination day, and only then discover that one or more of the items suffers severe genetic deficits. Mental previewing of likely student responses can help you detect such flaws while there's still time for repairs.

In review, we've looked at five guidelines for creating essay items. If you'll remember that all of these charming little collections of item-specific recommendations should be adhered to *in addition to* the five general item-writing commandments set forth in Chapter 6 (see page 126), you'll probably be able to come up with a pretty fair set of essay items. Then, perish the thought, you'll have to score your students' responses to those items. That's what we'll be looking at next.

■ Essay Items: Scoring Students' Responses

If you'll recall what's to come in future chapters (and, of course, recalled knowledge is the *lowest* level of Bloom's cognitive taxonomy), you'll be looking at how to evaluate students' responses to performance assessments in Chapter 8 and how to judge students' portfolios in Chapter 9. In short, you'll be learning much more about how to evaluate your students' performances in constructed-response assessments. Thus, to spread out the load a bit, in this chapter we'll be looking only at how to score students' responses to essay items (including tests of students' composition skills). You'll find that many of the suggestions for scoring students' constructed responses you will encounter in the following two chapters will also be applicable when you're trying to judge your students' essay responses. But just to keep matters simple, let's look now at recommendations for scoring responses to essay items.

Guidelines for Scoring Responses to Essay Items

1. Score responses holistically and/or analytically.
2. Prepare a tentative scoring key in advance of judging students' responses.
3. Make decisions regarding the importance of the mechanics of writing prior to scoring.
4. Score all responses to one item before scoring responses to the next item.
5. Insofar as possible, evaluate responses anonymously.

Choosing an Analytic and/or Holistic Scoring Approach

During the past decade or two, the measurement of students' composition skills by having students generate actual writing samples has become widespread. As a consequence of all this attention to students' compositions, educators have become far more skilled regarding how to evaluate students' written compositions. Fortunately, classroom teachers can use many of the procedures that have been identified and refined while educators scored thousands of students' compositions during statewide assessment extravaganzas. (In Texas, over a million students' essays were scored annually. Even for Texas, pardner, that's a heap of essays.)

A fair number of the lessons learned about scoring students' writing samples apply quite nicely to the scoring of responses to any kind of essay item. One of the most important of the scoring insights picked up from this large-scale scoring of students' compositions is that almost any type of student-constructed response can be scored either *holistically* or *analytically*. That's why the first of the five guidelines suggests you make an early-on decision whether you're going to score your students' responses to essay items using a holistic approach, an analytic approach or, perhaps, using a combination of the two scoring approaches. Let's look at how each of these two scoring strategies works.

A *holistic scoring* strategy, as its name suggests, focuses on the essay response (or written composition) as a whole. At one extreme of scoring rigor, the teacher can, in a fairly unsystematic manner, supply a "general impression" overall grade to each student's response. Or, in a more systematic fashion, the teacher can isolate, in advance of scoring, those *evaluative criteria* that should be attended to in order to arrive at a single, overall score per essay. Generally, a score range of four to six points is used for each response. (Some scoring schemes have a few more points, some a few less.) A teacher, then, after considering whatever factors should be attended to in a given item, will give a score to each student's response. Here is a set of evaluative criteria teachers might use in holistically scoring a student's written composition.

Illustrative Evaluative Criteria to Be Considered When Scoring Students' Essay Responses Holistically

For scoring a composition intended to reflect students' writing prowess:

- Organization
- Communicative Clarity
- Adaptation to Audience
- Word Choice
- Mechanics (spelling, capitalization, punctuation)

And now, here are four evaluative factors a speech teacher might employ in holistically scoring a response to an essay item used in a debate class.

Potential Evaluative Criteria to Be Used When Scoring Students' Essay Responses in a Debate Class

For scoring a response to an essay item dealing with rebuttal preparation:

- Anticipation of Opponent's Positive Points
- Support for One's Own Points Attacked by Opponents
- Isolation of Suitably Compelling Examples
- Preparation of a "Spontaneous" Conclusion

When teachers score students' responses holistically, they do *not* dole out points-per-criterion for a student's response. Rather, the teacher keeps in mind evaluative criteria such as those set forth in the previous two boxes. The speech teacher, for instance, while looking at the student's essay response to a question regarding how someone should engage in effective rebuttal preparation, will not necessarily penalize a student who overlooks one of the four evaluative criteria. The response as a whole may lack one thing, yet otherwise represent a really wonderful response. Evaluative criteria such as those illustrated simply dance around in the teacher's head when the teacher scores students' essay responses holistically.

In contrast, an *analytic scoring* scheme strives to be a fine-grained, specific point-allocation approach. Suppose, for example, instead of using a holistic method of scoring students' compositions, a teacher chose to employ an analytic method of scoring students' compositions. Under those circumstances, a scoring guide such as the example in Figure 7.1 might be used by the teacher. Note, for each evaluative criterion in the guide, the teacher must award 0, 1, or 2 points. The lowest overall score for a student's composition, therefore, would be 0, whereas the highest overall score from a student's composition would be 10 (that is, 2 points times 5 criteria).

The advantage of an analytic scoring system is it can help you identify the specific strengths and weaknesses of your students' performances and, therefore, communicate such diagnoses to students in a pinpointed fashion. The downside of analytic scoring is that a teacher sometimes becomes so attentive to the subpoints

Figure 7.1 ■ An Illustrative Guide for Analytically Scoring a Student's Written Composition

Factor	Unacceptable (0 points)	Satisfactory (1 point)	Outstanding (2 points)
1. Organization	_____	✓	_____
2. Communicative Clarity	_____	_____	✓
3. Audience Adaptation	_____	✓	_____
4. Word Choice	_____	_____	✓
5. Mechanics	_____	✓	_____

Total Score = ___7___

in a scoring system that, almost literally, the forest (overall quality) can't be seen because of a focus on individual trees (the separate scoring criteria). In less metaphoric language, the teacher will miss the communication of the student's response "as a whole" because of excessive attention to a host of individual evaluative criteria.

One middle-of-the-road scoring approach can be seen when teachers initially grade all students' responses holistically, then return for an analytic scoring of only those responses that were judged, overall, to be unsatisfactory. After the analytic scoring of the unsatisfactory responses, the teacher then relays more fine-grained diagnostic information to those students whose unsatisfactory responses were analytically scored. The idea underlying this sort of hybrid approach is the students who are most in need of fine-grained feedback are those who, on the basis of the holistic evaluation, are performing less well.

This initial guideline for scoring students' essay responses applies to the scoring of responses to all kinds of essay items. As always, your decision about whether to opt for holistic or analytic scoring should flow directly from your intended use of the test results. Putting it another way, your choice of scoring approach will depend on the educational decision linked to the test's results. (Is this beginning to sound somewhat familiar?)

Devising a Tentative Scoring Key

No matter what sort of approach you opt for in scoring your students' essay responses, you'll find it will be useful to develop a tentative scoring key for responses to each item *in advance* of actually scoring students' responses. Such tentative scoring schemes are almost certain to be revised on the basis of your scoring of actual student papers, but that's to be anticipated. If you wait until you commence scoring your students' essay responses, there's too much likelihood you'll be unduly influenced by the responses of the first few students whose papers you grade.

If those papers are atypical, the resultant scoring scheme is apt to be unsound. It is far better to think through, at least tentatively, what you really hope students will supply in their responses, then modify the scoring key if unanticipated responses from students suggest that alterations are requisite.

If you don't have a tentative scoring key in place, there's a great likelihood you'll be influenced by such factors as a student's vocabulary or writing style even though, in reality, such variables may be of little importance to you. Advance exploration of the evaluative criteria you intend to employ, either holistically or analytically, is a winning idea when scoring responses to essay items.

Let's take a look at what a tentative scoring key might look like if employed by a teacher in a U.S. History course. The skill being promoted by the teacher is a genuinely high-level one that's reflected in the following curricular aim:

> When presented with a description of a current real-world problem in the United States, the student will be able to (1) cite one or more significant events in American history that are particularly relevant to the presented problem's solution, (2) defend the relevance of the cited events, (3) propose a solution to the presented problem, and (4) use historical parallels from the cited events to support the proposed solution.

As I indicated, this is no rinky-dink low-level cognitive skill. It's way, way up there in its cognitive demands on students. Now, let's suppose our hypothetical history teacher routinely monitors students' progress related to this skill by having students respond to similar problems either orally or in writing. The teacher presents a real-world problem. The students, aloud or in an essay, try to come up with a suitable four-part response.

In Figure 7.2 you'll see an illustrative tentative scoring key for evaluating students' oral or written responses to constructed-response items measuring their mastery of this curricular aim. As you can discern, in this tentative scoring key, greater weight has been given to the fourth subtask—namely, the student's provision of historical parallels to support the student's proposed solution to the real-world problem the teacher proposed. Much less significance was given to the first subtask of citing pertinent historical events. This, remember, is a *tentative* scoring key. Perhaps when the history teacher begins scoring students' responses, it will turn out that the first subtask is far more formidable than the teacher originally thought, and the fourth subtask seems to be handled without much difficulty by students. At that point, based on the way students are actually responding, this hypothetical history teacher surely ought to do a bit of score-point juggling in the tentative scoring key before applying it in final form to the appraisal of students' responses.

Deciding Early about the Importance of Mechanics

Few things influence scorers of students' essay responses as much as the mechanics of writing employed in the response. If the student displays subpar spelling, chaotic capitalization, and poor punctuation, it's pretty tough for a scorer of the student's response to avoid being influenced adversely. In some instances, of course, mechanics of writing certainly do play a meaningful role in scoring stu-

Figure 7.2 ■ An Illustrative Tentative Scoring Key For a High-Level Cognitive Skill in History

Students' Subtasks	Tentative Point Allocation		
	Weak Response	*Acceptable Response*	*Strong Response*
1. Citation of Pertinent Historical Events	0 pts.	5 pts.	10 pts.
2. Defense of the Cited Historical Events	0 pts.	10 pts.	20 pts.
3. Proposed Solution to the Presented Problem	0 pts.	10 pts.	20 pts.
4. Historical Support of Proposed Solution	0 pts.	20 pts.	40 pts.

Total Points Possible = ___90 pts___

dents' performances. For instance, suppose you're scoring students' written responses to a task of writing an application letter for a position as a reporter for a local newspaper. In such an instance, it is clear that mechanics of writing would be pretty important when judging the student's response. But in a chemistry class, perhaps the teacher cares less about such factors when scoring students' essay responses to a problem-solving task. The third guideline simply suggests you make up your mind about this issue early in the process so, if mechanics aren't all that important to you, you don't let your students' writing mechanics subconsciously influence the way you score their responses.

Scoring One Item at a Time

If you're using an essay examination with more than one item, be sure to score all of your students' responses to one item, then score all of their responses to the next item, and so on. Do *not* score all responses of a given student, then go on to the next student's paper. There's too much danger a student's responses to early items will unduly influence your scoring of responses to subsequent items. If you score all responses to item number 1, then move on to the responses to item number 2, you can eliminate this tendency. In addition, the scoring will actually go a bit quicker because you won't need to shift evaluative criteria between items. Adhering to this fourth guideline will invariably lead to more consistent scoring, hence to more accurate response-based inferences about your students. There'll be more paper shuffling than you might prefer, but the increased accuracy of your scoring will be worth it. (Besides, you'll be getting a smidge of psychomotor exercise.)

Parent Talk

The mother of one of your students, Jill Jenkins, was elected to your district's school board two years ago. Accordingly, any time Mrs. Jenkins wants to discuss Jill's education, you are understandably "all ears."

Mrs. Jenkins recently stopped by your classroom to say that three of her fellow board members have been complaining there are too many essay tests being given in the district. The three board members contend that such tests, because they must be scored "subjectively," are neither reliable nor valid.

Because many of the tests you give Jill and her classmates are essay tests, Mrs. Jenkins asks you if the three board members are correct.

 If I were you, here's how I'd respond to Jill's mom. (Oh yes, because Mrs. Jenkins is a board member, I'd simply ooze politeness and professionalism while I responded.)

"Thanks for giving me an opportunity to comment on this issue, Mrs. Jenkins. As you've already guessed, I truly believe in the importance of constructed-response examinations such as essay tests. The real virtue of essay tests is that they call for students to *create* their responses, not merely *recognize* correct answers, as students must with other types of tests such as multiple-choice exams.

"The three school board members are correct when they say it is more difficult to score constructed-response items consistently than it is to score selected-response items consistently. And that's a shortcoming of essay tests. But it's a shortcoming that's more than compensated for by the far greater *authenticity* of the tasks presented to students in almost all constructed-response tests. When Jill writes essays during my major exams, this is much closer to what she'll be doing in later life than choosing the best answer from four options. In real life, people aren't given four-choice options. Rather, they're required to generate a response reflecting their views. Essay tests give Jill and her classmates a chance to do just that.

"Now, let's talk briefly about consistency and validity. Actually, Mrs. Jenkins, it is important for tests to be scored consistently. We refer to the consistency with which a test is scored as its *reliability*. And if a test isn't reliable, then the interpretations about students we make based on test scores aren't likely to be valid. It's a technical point, Mrs. Jenkins, but it isn't a *test* that's valid or invalid, it's a score-based inference about students that may or may not be valid. As your board colleagues pointed out, some essay tests are not scored very reliably. But essay tests *can* be scored reliably and they *can* yield valid inferences about students.

"I hope my reactions have been helpful. I'll be happy to show you some of the actual essay exams I've used with Jill's class. And I'm sure the District Superintendent, Dr. Stanley, can supply you with additional information."

 Now, how would you respond to Mrs. Jenkins?

Striving for Anonymity

Because I've been a teacher, I know all too well how quickly teachers can identify their students' writing styles, particularly those students who have especially distinctive styles, such as the "scrawlers," the "petite letter-size crew," and those who dot their *i*s with half-moons or cross their *t*s with lightning bolts. Yet, insofar as you can, try not to know whose responses you're scoring. One simple way to help in that effort is to ask students to write their names on the reverse side of the last sheet of the examination in the response booklet. Try not to peek at the students' names until you've scored all of the exams.

I used such an approach for three decades of scoring graduate students' essay examinations at UCLA. It worked fairly well. Sometimes I was really surprised because students who had appeared to be knowledgeable during class discussions displayed just the opposite on the exams, while several Silent Sarahs and Quiet Quentins came up with really solid exam performances. I'm sure if I had known whose papers I had been grading, I would have been improperly influenced by my classroom-based perceptions of different students' abilities. I am not suggesting that you shouldn't use students' classroom discussions as part of your evaluation system. Rather, I'm advising you that classroom-based perceptions of students can sometimes cloud your scoring of essay responses. This is one strong reason for you to strive for anonymous scoring.

In review, we've considered five guidelines for scoring students' responses to essay examinations. If your classroom assessment procedures involve any essay items, you'll find these five practical guidelines will go a long way in helping you come up with consistent scores for your students' responses. And consistency, as you learned in Chapter 2, is something that makes psychometricians mildly euphoric.

Now, after you've completed this chapter's usual end-of-chapter stuff, in the next two chapters you'll learn about two less common forms of constructed-response items. You'll learn how to create and score performance assessments and to use students' portfolios in classroom assessments. You'll find what we've been dealing with in this chapter will serve as a useful springboard to the content of the next two chapters.

■ What Do Classroom Teachers Really Need to Know about Constructed-Response Tests?

At the close of a chapter dealing largely with the nuts and bolts of creating and scoring written constructed-response tests, you probably expect to be told you really need to internalize all those nifty little guidelines so, when you spin out your own short-answer and essay items, you'll elicit student responses you can score accurately. Well, that's not a terrible aspiration, but there's really a more important insight you need to walk away with after reading the chapter. That insight, not surprisingly, derives from the central purpose of classroom assessment—namely, to draw accurate inferences about students' status so you can make more appropriate educational decisions. What you really need to know about short-answer items

but what does this have to do with Teaching?

A teacher wants students to learn the stuff that's being taught—to learn it *well*. And one of the best ways to see if students have really acquired a cognitive skill or have truly soaked up scads of knowledge is to have them display what they've learned by *generating* answers to constructed-response tests. A student who has learned something well enough to toss it out from scratch, rather than choosing from presented options, clearly has learned it pretty darn well.

But, as this chapter points out, the creation and scoring of really first-rate constructed-response items, especially anything beyond short-answer items, requires serious effort from a teacher. And if constructed-response items aren't really first-rate, then they are not likely to help a teacher arrive at valid interpretations about students' correct knowledge and/or skills. Decent constructed-response tests take time to create and to score. And that's where this kind of classroom assessment runs smack into a teacher's instructional-planning requirements.

A classroom teacher should typically reserve constructed-response assessments for a modest number of really *significant* instructional outcomes. And, remembering that a teacher's assessments typically exemplify the outcomes the teacher wants most students to master, then it should be clear that when it comes to constructed-response testing, less is surely going to be much, much more.

It's better to get students to master three to five really *high-level* cognitive skills, adroitly assessed by excellent constructed-response tests, than it is to have students master a litany of low-level outcomes. In short, choose your constructed-response targets with care. Those choices will have curricular and instructional implications.

and essay items is that you should use them as part of your classroom assessment procedures if you want to make the sorts of inferences about your students that those students' responses to such items would support.

Putting it another way, if you, as a classroom teacher, want to determine if your students have the skills and/or knowledge that can be best measured by short-answer or essay items, then you need to refresh your memory regarding how to avoid serious item construction or response scoring errors. A review of the guidelines presented on pages 151, 155, and 158 should give you the brushup you need. Don't believe you are obligated to use short-answer or essay items simply because you now know a bit more about how to crank them out. If you're interested in the extensiveness of your students' *knowledge* regarding Topic Z, it may be far more efficient to employ fairly low-level selected-response kinds of items. If, however, you really want to make inferences about your students' abilities to perform the kinds of tasks represented by short-answer and essay items, then the guidelines provided in the chapter should be consulted.

■ Chapter Summary

After a fairly elaborate, guilt-induced apology for the chapter's mislabeling, the chapter started off with a description of short-answer items accompanied by a set of guidelines (page 151) regarding how to write short-answer items. The chapter then took up essay items and indicated that, although students' written compositions constitute a particular kind of essay response, most of the recommendations for constructing essay items and for scoring students' responses were the same, whether measuring students' composition skills or skills in subject areas other than language arts. Guidelines were provided for writing essay items (page 155) and for scoring students' responses to essay items (page 158). The chapter was concluded with the suggestion that much of the content to be treated in the following two chapters, because those chapters also focus on constructed-response assessment schemes, will also relate to the creation and scoring of short-answer and essay items.

Self-Check

This chapter's self-check exercises will start off with a brief set of illustrative short-answer and essay items. Your task is to identify whether any of the chapter's item-writing guidelines have been violated. If so, you are to indicate what the violated guideline was or, if two or more guidelines have been flaunted, which ones those were. If not, indicate that no guidelines have been violated. Because you'll be responding with brief constructed responses, what kind of test items do you suppose you're about to mess with?

Oh yes, if you want to, you might like to engage in a quick review of the item-writing guidelines on pages 151 and 155. It's not necessary, but some people are compulsive when they think their self-worth is going to be under scrutiny.

1. (The following item was written for fifth-graders.) Before the United States became an independent nation, most of the men and women who had come to settle were from which European nation or nations?

    _____ _____ _____

    Any violation(s)?_____

    _____

2. (This item is for high school students.) You have just viewed a videotape containing three widely seen television commercials. What is the one classic propaganda technique present in all three commercials? _____

    Any violation(s)?_____

    _____

3. (This item is for eighth-grade students.) If a friend has asked you to engage in the use of alcohol or _____ , and you wish to decline, you should _____ and _____ without delay.

    Any violation(s)?_____

    _____

4. (This item was written for eleventh-grade English students.) In the space provided below and on the attached sheet, please compose a brief 200-word editorial in favor of the school district's expanded after-school tutorial program. The intended audience for your position statement consists of those people who read the local newspaper's editorial page. Because you have the entire class period to prepare your response, please use the scratch paper provided for a first draft, then revise your draft editorial before copying it on these sheets. The editorial will contribute 40 percent to your six-week's Persuasive Writing grade.

    Any violation(s)?_____

    _____

5. (This item was written for sixth-graders.) Thinking back over the mathematics lesson and homework assignments you had during the past 12 weeks, what conclusions can you draw? Take no more than one page for your response.

    Any violation(s)?_____

    _____

6. For the chapter's final self-check exercise, please read the description of how a fictitious teacher went about scoring an essay examination in a high school class called U.S. Government Service. Then evaluate how well the teacher carried out the scoring.

    "I was using a four-item essay examination on which my students were to spend 10 to 15 minutes per item. Before scoring students' papers, I worked up a tentative analytic scoring guide for each item. I identified two evaluative criteria that *had* to be satisfied in each response in order for it to receive full credit. If a student satisfied a criterion fairly well, the response earned 5 points; if the criterion was satisfied really well, the response earned 10 points. In all, then, with two criteria per item, and 0 to 10 points per criterion, I could give a student 0 points up to 80 points. My scoring keys, which placed no emphasis on a student's use of mechanics, worked so well that I didn't have to revise them.

    "I scored each student's response to all four items at a single sitting, and I found I could usually interpret students' responses more sensibly because, from the student's name on the first page of the response booklet, I could tell whose responses I was grading. The entire scoring operation for the 29 students in my class took somewhat less than 90 minutes."

What is your evaluation of this teacher's scoring procedures?

_____

_____

? Pondertime

1. What do you think has been the *instructional* impact, if any, of the increasingly wide incorporation of student writing samples in the high-stakes educational achievement tests used in numerous states?

2. How would you contrast short-answer items and essay items with respect to their elicited levels of cognitive behavior as set forth in Bloom's taxonomy? Are there differences in the kinds of cognitive demands called for by the two item types? If so, what are they?

3. What do you see as the major weaknesses of short-answer and essay items? What are their major strengths?

4. What would influence you in deciding whether to use selected-response items or the kinds of constructed-response items treated in this chapter?

5. What kinds of student outcomes could not be assessed properly with short-answer items but could be assessed properly with essay items?

Self-Check Key

1. This item really doesn't violate any of the guidelines listed on page 151, but it's a weak item because it violated one of the general-purpose item-writing commandments cited in Chapter 6. The item presents an ambiguous task to students insofar as it asks for a nation (or nations) from which "most" of the settlers came, then provides three blank spaces, thereby indicating that three, not one, response is sought, even though, by definition, there is only one "most." An astute answer from you for this self-check item would have been something along these lines: "No violations, but cruddy nonetheless."

2. This item violates no guidelines and isn't really all that shabby.

3. This item violates a pair of guidelines. It uses too many blanks and the blanks are unequal in length. It would be difficult for students, given the nearly total ambiguity introduced by the initial blank, to know how to respond to the item. It is, in short, a loser item.

4. This item violates none of the chapter's item-writing guidelines for essay items. As you can note, the first three guidelines on page 155 have all been specifically followed in the item. It's a fairly decent prompt for a persuasive writing task.

5. This item violates several of the chapter's guidelines for writing essay items. Although it limits the student's response to one page, there is substantial ambiguity about the nature of the task the teacher wants the students to undertake. Twelve weeks' worth of mathematics can add up (a mathematical operation) to a pretty hefty pile of math. The number of conclusions the student can legitimately draw are myriad. Thus, Guideline 2 is clearly violated because the student doesn't know what to do. Guideline 3 is also violated because there's no indication given regarding time limit or point value for the item. This item needs a good deal of refurbishing.

6. This fictitious teacher adhered to one of the guidelines on page 158 when a tentative analytic scoring key was used dealing with the importance of a student's written mechanics. There were two serious guideline violations, however, insofar as the teacher didn't score items one at a time and also failed to score students' responses anonymously. On balance, therefore, you should have given a "thumbs-down" to this teacher's essay-scoring effort. The two serious violations are too likely to threaten the validity of any score-based inferences the teacher might wish to draw.

■ Additional Stuff

Anderson, Lorin W. (2003). *Classroom Assessment: Enhancing the Quality of Teacher Decision Making*. Mahwah, NJ: Lawrence Erlbaum.

Downing, Steven M., and Thomas M. Haladyna (Eds.). (2006). *Handbook of Test Development*. Mahwah, NJ: Lawrence Erlbaum.

Kulm, Gerald, Linda Dager Wilson, and Richard Kitchen. (2005). "Alignment of Content and Effectiveness of Mathematics Assessment Items." *Educational Assessment, 10*, no. 4: 333–356.

Marzano, Robert J. (2002). "A Comparison of Selected Methods of Scoring Classroom Assessments." *Applied Measurement in Education, 15*, no. 3: 249–268.

Nitko, A. J. (2004). *Educational Assessment of Students* (4th ed.). Upper Saddle River, NJ: Prentice-Hall/Merrill Education.

Popham, W. James. (2003). *Test Better, Teach Better: The Instructional Role of Assessment*. Alexandria, VA: Association for Supervision and Curriculum Development.

Stiggins, Richard J. (2004). *Student-Involved Assessment FOR Learning* (4th ed.). Upper Saddle River, NJ: Prentice-Hall.

■ Nonprint Stuff

Northwest Regional Educational Laboratory. *Writing Assessment: Issues and Answers* (Videotape #NREL-7). Los Angeles: IOX Assessment Associates.

Northwest Regional Educational Laboratory. *Writing Assessment: Training in Analytical Scoring* (Videotape #NREL-8). Los Angeles: IOX Assessment Associates.

Popham, W. James. *Creating Classroom Tests: When Students CONSTRUCT Their Responses* (Videotape #ETVT-24). Los Angeles: IOX Assessment Associates.

■ Cyber Stuff

■ *The Northwest Regional Educational Laboratory (NWREL)* is one of the nation's federally funded regional laboratories. Over the years, NWREL has devoted special attention to projects associated with educational assessment and evaluation. This site identifies a wide variety of educationally relevant content, but provides a formidable description of the laboratory's assessment and evaluation program. That program features numerous strategies for evaluating students' responses to constructed-response tasks, an assessment resource library, and a "Library in the Sky" featuring thousands of links to educational resources on the Internet. A focused search capability is also provided. www.nwrel.org

To access chapter objectives, practice tests, weblinks, and flashcards, visit the companion website at **www.ablongman.com/popham5e.**

MyLabSchool is a collection of online tools for your success in this course, your licensure exams, and your teaching career. Discover where the classroom comes to life by visiting **www.mylabschool.com** to access the following resources:

■ Video clips from real classrooms

■ An archive of real-life cases

■ Help with your research papers using Research Navigator™

■ Career Center with resources for:

   Praxis exams and licensure preparation

   Professional portfolio development

   Job search and interview techniques

   Lesson planning with state standard correlations

8

Performance Assessment

D uring the early 1990s, a good many educational policymakers became enamored with performance assessment. *Performance assessment* is an approach to measuring a student's status based on the way the student completes a specified task. Theoretically, of course, when the student chooses between *true* and *false* for a binary-choice item, the student is completing a task, although an obviously modest one. But the proponents of performance assessment have measurement schemes in mind that are meaningfully different from binary-choice or multiple-choice tests. Indeed, it was a dissatisfaction with traditional paper-and-pencil tests that caused many educators to travel down the performance-testing trail.

■ What Is a Performance Test?

Before digging into what makes performance tests tick and how you might use them in your own classroom, we'd best explore the chief attributes of such an assessment approach. Even though all educational tests, as noted earlier, require students to perform in some way, when most educators talk about performance tests, they are thinking about assessments in which the student is required to construct an original response. More often than not, an examiner (such as the teacher) *observes* the process of construction so that observation of the student's performance and judgment of that performance are required. Over three decades ago, Fitzpatrick and Morrison (1971) observed that "there is no absolute distinction between performance tests and other classes of tests." They pointed out that the distinction between performance assessments and more conventional tests is chiefly the degree to which the examination simulates the criterion situation—that is, the extent to which the examination approximates the kind of student behaviors about which we wish to make inferences.

Suppose, for example, a teacher who had been instructing students in the process of collaborative problem solving wanted to see whether students had acquired this collaborative skill. The *inference* at issue centers on the extent to which each student has mastered the skill. The *educational decision* on the line might be whether particular students need additional instruction or, instead, whether it's time to move on to other curricular aims. The teacher's real interest, then, is in how well students can work with other students to arrive collaboratively at solutions to problems. In Figure 8.1, you will see there are several assessment procedures that could be used to get a fix on a student's collaborative problem-solving skills. Yet, note that the two selected-response assessment options (numbers 1 and 2) don't really ask students to construct anything. For the other three constructed-response assessment options (numbers 3, 4, and 5), however, there are clear differences in the degree to which the task presented to the student coincides with the class of tasks called for by the teacher's curricular aim. Assessment Option 5, for example, is obviously the closest match to the behavior called for in the curricular aim. Yet, Assessment Option 4 is surely more of a "performance test" than is Assessment Option 1.

Figure 8.1 ■ A Set of Assessment Options That Vary in the Degree to Which Student's Task Approximates the Curricularly Targeted Behavior

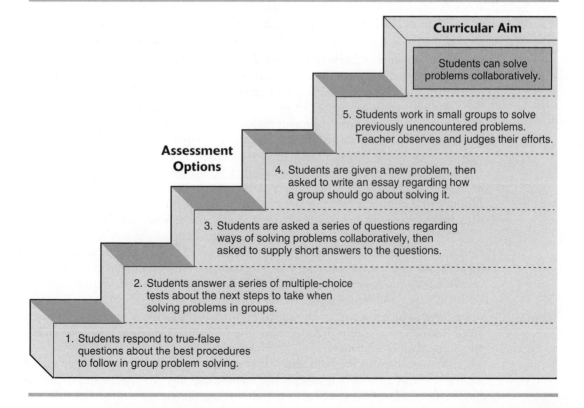

It should be apparent to you, then, that different educators will be using the phrase *performance assessment* to refer to very different kinds of assessment approaches. Many teachers, for example, are willing to consider short-answer and essay tests a form of performance assessment. In other words, those teachers essentially equate performance assessment with any form of constructed-response assessment. Other teachers establish more stringent requirements in order for a measurement procedure to be described as a performance assessment. For example, some performance assessment proponents contend that genuine performance assessments must possess at least three features:

- *Multiple evaluative criteria.* The student's performance must be judged using more than one evaluative criterion. To illustrate, a student's ability to speak Spanish might be appraised on the basis of the student's accent, syntax, and vocabulary.
- *Prespecified quality standards.* Each of the evaluative criteria on which a student's performance is to be judged is clearly explicated in advance of judging the quality of the student's performance.
- *Judgmental appraisal.* Unlike the scoring of selected-response tests in which electronic computers and scanning machines can, once programmed, carry on without the need of humankind, genuine performance assessments depend on human judgments to determine how acceptable a student's performance really is.

Looking back to Figure 8.1, it is clear that if the foregoing three requirements were applied to the five assessment options supplied, Assessment Option 5 would qualify as a performance test, and Assessment Option 4 probably would as well, but the other three assessment options wouldn't qualify under a definition of performance assessment requiring the incorporation of multiple evaluative criteria, prespecified quality standards, and judgmental appraisals.

A good many advocates of performance assessment would prefer that the tasks presented to students represent real-world rather than school-world kinds of problems. Other proponents of performance assessment would be elated simply if more school-world measurement was constructed response rather than selected response in nature. Still other advocates of performance testing want the tasks in performance tests to be genuinely *demanding*—that is, way up the ladder of Bloom's taxonomy. In short, proponents of performance assessment often advocate different approaches to measuring students on the basis of how they perform.

You'll sometimes encounter educators who use other phrases to describe performance assessment. For example, they may use the phrase ***authentic assessment*** (because the assessment tasks more closely coincide with real-life, nonschool tasks) or *alternative assessment* (because such assessments constitute an alternative to traditional, paper-and-pencil tests). In the next chapter, we'll be considering *portfolio assessment,* which is a particular type of performance assessment and should not be considered a synonymous descriptor for the performance-assessment approach to educational measurement.

We now turn to the twin issues that are at the heart of performance assessments: *selecting appropriate tasks* for students and, once the students have tackled those tasks, *judging the adequacy of students' responses.*

■ Identifying Suitable Tasks for Performance Assessment

Performance assessment typically requires students to respond to a small number of more significant tasks rather than respond to a large number of less significant tasks. Thus, rather than answering 50 multiple-choice items on a conventional chemistry examination, students who are being assessed via performance tasks may find themselves asked to perform an actual experiment in their chemistry class, then prepare a written interpretation of the experiment's results and an analytic critique of the procedures they used. From the chemistry teacher's perspective, instead of seeing how students respond to the 50 "mini-tasks" represented in the multiple-choice test, an estimate of each student's status must be derived from a student's response to a single, complex task. Given the significance of each task used in a performance-testing approach to classroom assessment, it is apparent that great care must be taken in the selection of *performance-assessment tasks.* Generally speaking, classroom teachers will either have to (1) generate their own performance test tasks or (2) select performance test tasks from the increasing number of tasks available from educators elsewhere.

Inferences and Tasks

Consistent with the frequently asserted message of this bundle-of-fun book about classroom assessment you are currently reading, the chief determinants of how you assess your students are (1) the inference you want to make about those

Decision Time

Grow, Plants, Grow!

Francine Floden is a third-year biology teacher in Kennedy High School. Because she has been convinced by several of her colleagues that traditional paper-and-pencil examinations fail to capture the richness of the scientific experience, Francine has decided to base almost all of her students' grades on a semester-long performance test. As Francine contemplates her new assessment plan, 90% of the students' grades will stem from the quality of their responses to the performance test's task; 10% of the grades will be linked to classroom participation and a few short true-false quizzes administered throughout the semester.

The task embodied in Francine's performance test requires each student to design and conduct a two-month experiment to study the growth of three identical plants under different conditions, then prepare a formal scientific report describing the experiment. Although most of Francine's students carry out their experiments at home, several students use the shelves at the rear of the classroom for their experimental plants. A number of students vary the amount of light or the kind of light received by the different plants, but most students modify the nutrients given to their plants. After a few weeks of the two-month experimental period, all of Francine's students seem to be satisfactorily underway with their experiments.

Several of the more experienced teachers in the school, however, have expressed their reservations to Francine about what they regard as "overbooking on a single assessment experience." The teachers suggest to Francine that she will be unable to draw defensible inferences about her students' true mastery of biological skills and knowledge based on a single performance test. They urged her to reduce dramatically the grading weight for the performance test so that, instead, additional grade-contributing examinations can be given to the students.

Other colleagues, however, believe Francine's performance-test approach is precisely what is needed in courses such as biology. They recommend she "stay the course" and alter "not one whit" of her new assessment strategy.

 If you were Francine, what would your decision be?

students and (2) the decision that will be based on the inference. For example, suppose you're a history teacher and you've spent a summer at a lakeside cabin meditating about curricular matters (which, in one lazy setting or another, is the public's perception of how most teachers spend their vacations). After three months of heavy curricular thought, you have concluded that what you really want to teach your students is for them to be able to apply historical lessons of the past to the solution of current and future problems that, at least to some extent, parallel the problems of the past. You have decided to abandon your week-long, 1,500-item true-false final examination that your stronger students refer to as a "measurement marathon" and your weaker students refer to by using a rich, if earthy, vocabulary. Instead of true-false items, you are now committed to a performance

Figure 8.2 ■ Relationships among a Teacher's Key Curricular Aim, the Assessment-Based Inference Derivative from the Aim, and the Performance Assessment Task Providing Evidence for the Inference

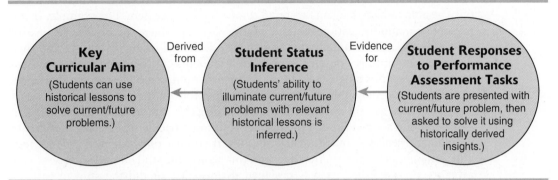

assessment strategy and wish to select tasks for your performance tests to help you infer how well your students can draw on the lessons of the past to illuminate their approach to current and/or future problems.

In Figure 8.2, you will see a graphic depiction of the relationships among (1) a teacher's key curricular aim, (2) the inference that the teacher wishes to draw about each student, and (3) the task for a performance test intended to secure data to support the inference that the teacher wants to make. As you will note, the teacher's curricular aim provides the source for the inference, and the assessment tasks yield the evidence needed for the teacher to arrive at defensible inferences regarding the extent to which students can solve current or future problems using historical lessons. To the degree that students have mastered the curricular aim, the teachers will make a decision about how much more instruction, if any, is needed.

The Generalizability Dilemma

One of the most serious difficulties with performance assessment is, because students respond to fewer tasks than would be the case with conventional paper-and-pencil testing, it is often more difficult to generalize accurately about what skills and knowledge are possessed by the student.

To illustrate, let's say you're trying to get a fix on your students' ability to multiply pairs of double-digit numbers. If, because of your instructional priorities, you can devote only a half hour to assessment purposes, you could require the students to respond to 20 such multiplication problems in the 30 minutes available. (That's probably more problems than you'd need, but I'm trying to draw a vivid contrast for you.) From a student's responses to 20 multiplication problems, you can get a pretty fair idea about what kind of double-digit multiplier the student is. As a consequence of the student's performance on a *reasonable sample* of items representing the curricular aim, you can conclude "Javier really knows how to multiply those sorts of problems," or "Fred really couldn't multiply double-digit multiplication problems if his life depended on it." It is because you have sampled well the kind of student performance (to which you wish to make an inference) that you can confidently make inferences about your students' abilities to solve similar sorts of multiplication problems. With only a 30-minute assessment period available, however, if you moved to a more elaborate kind of performance test, you might only be able to have students respond to one big-bopper item. For example, if you presented a multiplication-focused mathematics problem involving the use of manipulatives, and wanted your students to derive an original solution and then describe it in writing, you'd be lucky if your students could finish the task in a half hour. Based on this single task, how confident would you be in making inferences about your students' abilities to perform comparable multiplication tasks?

And this, as you now see, is the rub with performance testing. Because students respond to fewer tasks, the teacher is put in a trickier spot when it comes to deriving inferences about students' abilities. If you use only one performance test, and a student does well on the test, does this signify the student *really* possesses the category of skills the test was designed to measure, or did the student just get lucky? On the other hand, if a student messes up on a single-performance test, does this signify the student *really* doesn't possess the assessed skill, or was there a feature in this particular performance test that misled the student who, given other tasks, might have performed wonderfully?

As a classroom teacher, you're faced with two horns of a classic measurement dilemma. Although performance tests often measure the kinds of student abilities you'd prefer to assess (because those abilities are in line with really worthwhile curricular aims), the inferences you make about students on the basis of their responses to performance tests must be made with increased caution. As with many dilemmas, there may be no perfect way to hop this one's two horns. But there is, at least, a way of dealing with the dilemma as sensibly as you can. In this instance, the solution strategy is to devote great care to the selection of the tasks embodied in your performance tests. Among the most important considerations in selecting such tasks is to choose tasks that optimize the likelihood of accurately generalizing about your students' capabilities. If you really keep generalizability at the forefront when you select/construct performance-test tasks, you'll be able to make the strongest possible performance-based inferences about your students' capabilities.

Factors to Consider When Evaluating Performance-Test Tasks

We've now looked at what many measurement specialists regard as the most important factor you can consider when judging potential tasks for performance assessments—*generalizability*. Let's look at a list of seven such factors you might wish to consider, whether you select a performance test task from existing tasks or, in contrast, create your own performance test tasks.

Evaluative Criteria for Performance-Test Tasks
- *Generalizability.* Is there a high likelihood the students' performance on the task will generalize to comparable tasks?
- *Authenticity.* Is the task similar to what students might encounter in the real world as opposed to encounter only in school?

- *Multiple foci*. Does the task measure multiple instructional outcomes instead of only one?
- *Teachability*. Is the task one that students can become more proficient in as a consequence of a teacher's instructional efforts?
- *Fairness*. Is the task fair to all students—that is, does the task avoid bias based on such personal characteristics as students' gender, ethnicity, or socioeconomic status?
- *Feasibility*. Is the task realistically implementable in relation to its cost, space, time, and equipment requirements?
- *Scorability*. Is the task likely to elicit student responses that can be reliably and accurately evaluated?

Whether you're developing your own tasks for performance tests or selecting such tasks from an existing collection, you may wish to apply some but not all of the factors listed here. Personally, I would usually try to apply all seven factors, although I can see how one might, on occasion, dump the *authenticity* criterion or the *multiple foci* criterion. In some instances, for example, school tasks rather than real-world tasks might be suitable for the kinds of inferences a teacher wishes to reach, hence the authenticity criterion may not be relevant. And even though it is economically advantageous to measure more than one outcome at one time, particularly considering the time and effort that goes into almost any performance test, there may be instances in which a single educational outcome is sufficiently important so it warrants a solo performance test. More often than not, though, a really good task for a performance test will satisfy all seven of the evaluative criteria presented here.

Performance Tests and Teacher Time

Back in Chapter 1, I promised that if you completed this book with a reasonable degree of attentiveness, you'd become a better teacher. Now I have another promise for you. I promise to be *honest* about the measurement mysteries we're probing together. And this brings me to an important consideration regarding performance testing. In brief, it takes time!

Think for a moment about the time that you, as the teacher, need to give to (1) the selection of suitable tasks, (2) the development of an appropriate scheme for scoring students' responses, and (3) the actual scoring of students' responses. Talk to any teacher who's already used many classroom performance tests and you'll learn it takes a ton of time to use performance assessment.

So what I want to suggest is that there's one additional factor you should throw into your decision making about performance assessment. It is the *significance of the skill* you're using the performance test to assess. Because you'll almost certainly have time for only a handful of such performance tests in your teaching, make sure that every performance test you use is linked to a truly significant skill you're trying to have your students acquire. If performance assessments aren't based on genuinely demanding skills, you'll soon stop using them because, to be truthful, they'll be more trouble than they're worth.

■ Identifying Scoring Criteria

Performance assessments invariably are based on constructed-response measurement procedures in which students generate rather than select their responses. Student-constructed responses must be scored, however, and it's clearly much tougher to score constructed responses than to score selected responses. The scoring of constructed responses centers on the *evaluative criteria* one calls on to determine the adequacy of students' responses. Let's turn our attention now to the evaluative criteria we use to decide whether students' responses to performance tests are splendid or sucko.

A *criterion,* according to *Webster's Dictionary,* is "a standard on which a judgment or decision may be based." In the case of scoring students' responses to a performance test's task, you're clearly trying to make a judgment regarding the adequacy of the student's constructed response. The specific criteria to be used in making that judgment will obviously influence the way you score a student's response. For instance, if you were scoring a student's written composition on the basis of organization, word choice, and communicative clarity, you might arrive at very different scores than if you had scored the composition on the basis of spelling, punctuation, and grammar. The evaluative criteria used when scoring students' responses to performance tests (or their responses to any kind of constructed-response item) really control the whole assessment game.

In passing, having completed five years of Latin in high school and college, I feel compelled to use a word or two of Latin at least on a semi-annual basis. Thus, be aware that the Latin word *criterion* is singular and the Latin word *criteria* is plural. Unfortunately, so many of today's educators mix up these two terms that I don't even become distraught about it anymore. However, now that you know the difference, if you find any of your colleagues erroneously saying "the criteria is" or the "the criterion were," you can display an ever so subtle, yet altogether condescending, smirk.

The scoring procedures for judging students' responses to performance tests are usually referred to these days as *scoring rubrics* or, more simply, **rubrics**. A rubric that's used to score students' responses to a performance assessment has, at minimum, three important features:

- *Evaluative criteria.* These are the factors to be used in determining the quality of a student's response.
- *Descriptions of qualitative differences for the evaluative criteria.* For each evaluative criterion, a description must be supplied so qualitative distinctions in students' responses can be made using the criterion.
- *An indication of whether a holistic or analytic scoring approach is to be used.* The rubric must indicate whether the evaluative criteria are to be applied collectively in the form of *holistic* scoring or on a criterion-by-criterion basis in the form of *analytic* scoring.

The identification of a rubric's evaluative criteria, as might be guessed, is probably the most important task for rubric developers. If you're creating a rubric for a performance test you wish to use in your own classroom, be careful not to come up with a lengthy laundry list of evaluative criteria a student's response should satisfy. Personally, I think when you isolate more than three or four evaluative criteria per rubric, you've identified too many. If you find yourself facing more than a few evaluative criteria, simply *rank each criterion in order of importance,* then chop off those listed lower than three or four.

The next job you'll have is deciding how to *describe in words* what a student's response must be in order to be judged wonderful or woeful. The level of descriptive detail you apply needs to work *for you.* Remember, you're devising a scoring rubric for your own classroom, not a statewide or national test. Keep the aversiveness of the work down by employing brief descriptors of quality differences you can use when teaching and, if you're instructionally astute, your students can use as well.

Finally, you'll need to decide whether you'll make a single, overall judgment about a student's response by considering all of the rubric's evaluative criteria as an amalgam (holistic scoring) or, instead, award the response points on a criterion-by-criterion basis (analytic scoring). The virtue of holistic scoring, of course, is it's quicker to do. The downside of holistic scoring is it fails to communicate to students, especially low-performing students, what their shortcomings are. Clearly, analytic scoring yields a greater likelihood of diagnostically pinpointed scoring and sensitive feedback than does holistic scoring. Some classroom teachers have attempted to garner the best of both worlds by scoring all responses holistically, then analytically rescoring (for feedback purposes) all responses of low-performing students.

Because most performance assessments call for fairly complex responses from students, there will usually be more than one evalautive criterion employed to score students' responses. For each of the evaluative criteria chosen, a numerical scale is typically employed so that for each criterion, a student's response might be assigned a specified number of points—for instance, 0 to 6 points. Usually, these scale points are accompanied by verbal descriptors; sometimes they aren't. For instance, in a 5-point scale, the following descriptors might be used: 5 = Exemplary, 4 = Superior, 3 = Satisfactory, 2 = Weak, 1 = Inadequate. If no verbal descriptors are used for each score point on the scale, a scheme such as the following might be employed:

In some cases, the scoring scale for each criterion is nonnumerical; that is, it consists only of verbal descriptors such as "exemplary," "adequate," and so on. Although such verbal scales can be useful with particular types of performance tests, their disadvantage is that scores from multiple criteria cannot be added together in order to produce a meaningful overall score.

The heart of the intellectual process in isolating suitable evaluative criteria is to get to the essence of what the most significant factors are that distinguish acceptable from unacceptable responses. In this instance, as in many others, less is more. A few truly important criteria are preferable to a ton of trifling criteria. Go for the big ones. If you need help in deciding what criteria to employ in conjunction with a particular performance test, don't be reluctant to ask colleagues to toss in their ideas regarding what *significant* factors to use (for a given performance test) in order to discriminate between super and subpar responses.

In this chapter you'll be presented with scoring rubrics that can serve as useful models for your own construction of such rubrics. In those illustrative scoring rubrics, you'll see that great care has been taken to isolate a small number of instructionally addressable evaluative criteria. The greatest payoff from a well-formed scoring rubric is in its contribution to improved instruction.

■ An Illustrative Performance-Test Task

To give you a better idea about the kinds of tasks that might be used in a performance test and the way you might score a student's responses, let's take a look at an illustrative task for a performance test. The task presented in Figure 8.3 is intended to assess students' mastery of an oral communications skill.

Figure 8.3 ■ Task Description and Sample Tasks for a One-on-One Oral Communication Performance Assessment

An Oral Communication Performance Test

Introduction

There are numerous kinds of speaking tasks students must perform in everyday life, both in school and out of school. This performance assessment focuses on some of these tasks—namely, describing objects, events, and experiences; explaining the steps in a sequence; providing information in an emergency; and persuading someone.

In order to accomplish a speaking task, the speaker must formulate and transmit a message to a listener. This process involves deciding what needs to be said, organizing the message, adapting the message to the listener and situation, choosing language to convey the message and, finally, delivering the message. The effectiveness of the speaker may be rated in terms of how well the speaker meets the requirement of the task.

Sample Tasks

Description Task: Think about your favorite class or extracurricular activity in school. Describe to me everything you can about it so I will know a lot about it. (How about something like a school subject, a club, or a sports program?)

Emergency Task: Imagine you are home alone and you smell smoke. You call the fire department and I answer your call. Talk to me as if you were talking on the telephone. Tell me everything I would need to know to get help to you. (Talk directly to me; begin by saying hello.)

Sequence Task: Think about something you know how to cook. Explain to me, step by step, how to make it. (How about something like popcorn, a sandwich, or scrambled eggs?)

Persuasion Task: Think about one change you would like to see made in your school, such as a change in rules or procedures. Imagine I am the principal of your school. Try to convince me the school should make this change. (How about something like a change in the rules about hall passes or the procedures for enrolling in courses?)

Source: Based on assessment efforts of the Massachusetts Department of Education.

■ Rubrics: The Wretched and the Rapturous

Unfortunately, many educators believe a rubric is a rubric is a rubric. Not so. Rubrics differ dramatically in their instructional worth. I'll now describe two types of rubrics that are sordid and one type that's super.

Task-Specific Rubrics

Some rubrics are created so their evaluative criteria are linked only to the particular task embodied in a specific performance test. These are called *task-specific rubrics*. Such a rubric does little to illuminate instructional decision making because it implies that students' performances on the constructed-response test's specific task are what's important. They're not! What's important is the student's ability to perform well on the *class of tasks* that can be accomplished by using the skill measured in the assessment. If students are taught to shine only on the single task represented in a performance test, but not on the full range of comparable tasks, students lose out. If students learn to become good problem solvers, they'll be able to solve all sorts of problems—not merely the one problem embodied in a particular performance test.

So, to provide helpful instructional illumination—that is, to assist the teacher's instructional decision making—a rubric's evaluative criteria dare not be task specific. Instead, those criteria must be rooted in the skill itself. Let me illustrate by considering an evaluative criterion frequently employed in rubrics used to judge students' written communication skills—namely, the evaluative criterion of *organization*. Presented here is a task-specific evaluative criterion that might be used in a scoring rubric to judge the quality of a student's response to the following task:

> "Compose a brief narrative essay, of 400 to 600 words, describing what happened during yesterday's class session when we were visited by the local firefighters who described a fire-exit escape plan for the home."
>
> **A task-specific evaluative criterion for judging the organization of students' narrative essays:** Superior essays will (1) commence with a recounting of the particular rationale for home fire-escape plans the local firefighters provided, then (2) follow up with a description of the six elements in home-safety plans in the order those elements were presented, and (3) conclude by citing at least three of the life-death safety statistics the firefighters provided at the close of their visit. Departures from these three organizational elements will result in lower evaluations of essays.

Suppose you're a teacher who has generated or been given this task-specific evaluative criterion. How would you organize your instruction? If you really tried to gain instructional guidance from this evaluative criterion, you'd be aiming your instruction directly at a particular task—in this case, a narrative account of the firefighters' visit to your class. You'd have to teach your students to commence their narrative essays with a rationale when, in fact, using a rationale for an introduction might be inappropriate for other sorts of narrative essays. Task-specific evaluative criteria do not help teachers plan instructional sequences that promote their students' abilities to *generalize* the skills they acquire. Task-specific criteria are just what they are touted to be—specific to one task.

During recent years, I've had an opportunity to review a number of rubrics that classroom teachers are trying to employ. From an instructional perspective, most of these rubrics don't pass muster. Many of the rubrics are task specific. Such task-specific rubrics may make it easier to score students' constructed responses. For *scoring* purposes, the more specific evaluative rubrics are, the better. But task-specific rubrics do *not* provide teachers with the kinds of *instructional* insights rubrics should.

Hypergeneral Rubrics

Another variety of scoring rubric that will not help teachers plan their instruction are referred to as *hypergeneral rubrics*. Such a rubric is one in which the evaluative criteria are described in exceedingly general and amorphous terms. The evaluative criteria are so loosely described, in fact, teachers' instructional plans really aren't benefited. For example, using the previous example of a task calling for students to write a narrative essay, a hypergeneral evaluative criterion for organization might resemble the following one:

> **A hypergeneral evaluative criterion for judging the organization of students' narrative essays:** *Superior* essays are those in which the essay's content has been arranged in a genuinely excellent manner, whereas *inferior* essays are those displaying altogether inadequate organization. An *adequate* essay is one representing a lower organizational quality than a superior essay, but a higher organizational quality than an inferior essay.

You may think I'm putting you on when you read the illustrative hypergeneral evaluative criterion just given. But I'm not. I've seen many such hypergeneral scoring rubrics. These rubrics ostensibly clarify how teachers can score students' constructed responses, but really these vague rubrics do little more than loosely redefine such quality descriptors as *superior, proficient,* and *inadequate*. Hypergeneral rubrics often attempt to draw distinctions among students' performances no more clearly than among students' performances in earning grades of A through F. Hypergeneral rubrics provide teachers with no genuine benefits for their instructional planning because such rubrics do not give the teacher meaningfully clarified descriptions of the criteria to be used in evaluating the quality of students' performances.

Skill-Focused Rubrics

Well, because I've now denigrated task-specific rubrics and sneered at hypergeneral rubrics, it's only fair for me to trot out the type of rubric that really can illuminate a teacher's instructional planning. Such scoring guides can be described as *skill-focused rubrics* because they really are conceptualized around the skill that is

(1) being measured by the constructed-response assessment and (2) being pursued instructionally by the teacher. It is my conviction, based on discussions with many teachers who have used a variety of scoring rubrics, that teachers who create a skill-focused scoring rubric prior to their instructional planning will almost always devise a better instructional sequence than will teachers who don't.

For an example of an evaluative criterion you'd encounter in a skill-focused rubric, look over the following illustrative criterion for evaluating the organization of a student's narrative essay:

> **A skill-focused evaluative criterion for judging the organization of students' narrative essays:** Two aspects of organization will be employed in the appraisal of students' narrative essays—namely, *overall structure* and *sequence*. To earn maximum credit, an essay must embody an overall structure containing an introduction, a body, and a conclusion. The content of the body of the essay must be sequenced in a reasonable manner—for instance, in a chronological, logical, or order-of-importance sequence.

Now, when you consider this evaluative criterion from an instructional perspective, you'll realize a teacher could sensibly direct instruction by (1) familiarizing students with the two aspects of the criterion—that is, overall structure and sequence; (2) helping students identify essays in which overall structure and sequence are, or are not, acceptable; and (3) supplying students with gobs of guided and independent practice in writing narrative essays possessing the desired overall structure and sequence. The better students become in being able to employ this double-barreled criterion in their narrative essays, the better those students will be at responding to a task such as the illustrative one we just saw about the local firefighters' visit to the classroom. This skill-focused evaluative criterion for *organization,* in other words, can generalize to a wide variety of narrative-writing tasks, not just an essay about visiting fire-folk.

And even if teachers do not create their own rubrics—for instance, if rubrics are developed by a school district's curriculum or assessment specialists—those teachers who familiarize themselves with skill-focused rubrics in advance of instructional planning will usually plan better instruction than will teachers who aren't familiar with a skill-focused rubric's key features. Skill-focused rubrics make clear what a teacher should emphasize instructionally when the teacher attempts to promote student mastery of the skill being measured.

Let me set out five rubric rules I encourage you to follow if you're creating your own skill-focused scoring rubric—a rubric you must generate *before* you plan your instruction.

> ***Rule 1:*** *Make sure the skill to be assessed is significant.* It takes time and trouble to generate scoring skill-focused rubrics. It also takes time and trouble to score students' responses by using such rubrics. Make sure the skill being promoted instructionally, and scored via the rubric, is worth all this time and trouble. Skills that are scored with skill-focused rubrics should represent demanding accomplishments by students, not trifling ones.

Teachers ought not be ashamed to be assessing their students with only a handful of performance tests, for example. It makes much more sense to measure a modest number of truly important skills properly than to do a shoddy job in measuring a shopping-cart–load of skills.

Rule 2: Make certain all of the rubric's evaluative criteria can be addressed instructionally. This second rule calls for you always to "keep your instructional wits about you" when generating a rubric. Most importantly, you must scrutinize every potential evaluative criterion in a rubric to make sure you can actually teach students to master it.

This doesn't oblige you to adhere to any particular instructional approach. Regardless of whether you are wedded to the virtues of direct instruction, indirect instruction, constructivism, or any other instructional strategy, what you must be certain of is that students can be *taught* to employ appropriately *every* evaluative criterion used in the rubric.

Rule 3: Employ as few evaluative criteria as possible. Because people who start thinking seriously about a skill will often begin to recognize a host of nuances associated with the skill, they sometimes feel compelled to set forth a veritable litany of evaluative criteria. But for instructional purposes, as for most other purposes, less almost always turns out to be more. Try to focus your instructional attention on three or four evaluative criteria; you'll become overwhelmed if you try to promote students' mastery of a dozen evaluative criteria.

Rule 4: Provide a succinct label for each evaluative criterion. The instructional yield of a skill-focused rubric can be increased simply by giving each evaluative criterion a brief explanatory label. For instance, suppose you were trying to improve your students' oral presentation skills. You might employ a skill-focused rubric for oral communication containing four evaluative criteria—namely, *delivery, organization, content,* and *language.* These one-word, easy-to-remember labels will help remind you *and your students* of what's truly important in judging mastery of the skill being assessed.

Rule 5: Match the length of the rubric to your own tolerance for detail. I've spent a fair amount of time worrying about this particular rule because much of my early experience in generating skill-focused rubrics dealt with the creation of lengthy scoring rubrics for high-stakes statewide or districtwide assessments. Such detailed rubrics were intended to constrain scorers so their scores would be in agreement. But I've discovered that many classroom teachers consider fairly long, rather detailed rubrics to be altogether off-putting. Whereas those teachers might be willing to create and/or use a one-page rubric, they would regard a six-page rubric as reprehensible. More recently, therefore, I've been recommending much shorter rubrics—rubrics that never exceed one or two pages.

Of course, not all teachers are put off by very detailed rubrics. Some teachers, in fact, find that abbreviated rubrics just don't do an adequate job for them. Such detail-prone teachers would rather work with rubrics that specifically spell out just what's involved when differentiating between quality levels regarding each evaluative criterion. I've therefore come to the conclusion that rubrics should be built to match the detail preferences of the teachers involved. Teachers who believe in brevity should create brief rubrics, and teachers who believe in detail should create lengthier rubrics. If school districts (or publishers) are supplying rubrics to teachers, I recommend both a short and a long version be provided. Let teachers decide on the level of detail that best meshes with their own tolerance/need for detail.

■ Ratings and Observations

Once you've selected your evaluative criteria, you then need to apply them reliably to the judgment of students' responses. If the nature of the performance test task calls for students to create some sort of *product,* such as a written report of an experiment carried out in a biology class, then at your leisure you can rate the product's quality in relation to the criteria you've identified as important. For example, if you had decided on three criteria to use in evaluating students' reports of biology experiments, and could award from 0 to 4 points for each criterion, then you could leisurely assign from 0 to 12 points for each written report. The more clearly you understand what each criterion is, and what it means to award a different number of points on whatever scale you've selected, the more accurate your scores will be. Performance tests that yield student products are easier to rate because you can rate students' responses when you're in the mood.

It is often the case with performance tests, however, the student's performance takes the form of some kind of *behavior.* With such performance tests, it will usually be necessary for you to observe the behavior as it takes place. To illustrate, suppose that you are an elementary school teacher whose fifth-grade students have been carrying out fairly elaborate social studies projects culminating in 15-minute oral reports to classmates. Unless you have the equipment to videotape your students' oral presentations, you'll have to observe the oral reports and make judgments about the quality of a student's performance as it occurs. As was true when scores were given to student products, in making evaluative judgments about students' behavior, you will apply whatever criteria you've chosen and assign what you consider to be the appropriate number of points on the scales you are using.

For some observations, you'll find it sensible to make instant, on-the-spot quality judgments. For instance, if you are judging students' social studies reports on the basis of (1) content, (2) organization, and (3) presentation, you might make observation-based judgments on each of those three criteria as soon as a report is finished. In other cases, your observations might incorporate a delayed evaluative approach. For instance, let's say that you are working with students in a speech class on the elimination of "filler words and sounds," two of the most prominent of which are starting a sentence with "well" and interjecting frequent "uh"s into a presentation. In the nonevaluative phase of the observation, you could simply count the number of "well"s and "uh"s uttered by a student. Then, at a later time, you could decide on a point allocation for the criterion "avoids filler words and sounds." Putting it another way, systematic observations may be set up so you make immediate or delayed allocations of points for the evaluative criteria you've chosen. If the evaluative criteria involve qualitative factors that must be appraised more judgmentally, then on-the-spot evaluations and point assignments are typically the way to go. If the evaluative criteria involve more quantitative factors, then a "count now and judge later" approach usually works better.

Must All Performance-Based Assessment Be a Big Deal?

If teachers want to make inferences about their students based on nontest sorts of students' performances, is it always necessary to go to a ton of trouble to do so? No, it isn't. There will be frequent occasions, especially for elementary teachers, when teachers will want to use less elaborate ways of getting a fix on students' current skill status. Simple checklists, observation forms, and rating scales are useful additions to a teacher's assessment toolkit. However, if you decide to employ ways to judge your students' work that are less elaborate than rubrics, I need to point out a peril to avoid—a peril that will be addressed in more detail when you get to Chapter 12. Here's the problem.

When teachers try to arrive at an observation-based inference about their students, they sometimes devise checklists or observation forms that focus on the *task* with which a student is wrestling rather than the *skill* that the student's behavior reflects. Remember, as a teacher, your instructional decisions should be influenced by a student's skill mastery, not the student's mastery of the particular task the student is performing. Thus, make sure that any sort of checklist or similar device that you're using to monitor your students' progress is structured around the students' *skill mastery*, not the student's *task mastery*.

If you keep this point in mind, then there's no reason to get carried away when you use your students' performances to arrive at decision-relevant inferences about them. But remember, when you decide to use students' performances as your "data source" in arriving at an inference, it is almost always the case you'll be dealing with students' high-level cognitive *skills*. Although students' acquisition of *knowledge* is important, you'll usually be able to measure your students' knowledge acquisition by using more conventional testing techniques.

■ Sources of Error in Scoring Student Performances

When scoring student performances, there are three common sources of error that can contribute to inaccurate inferences. First, there is the *scoring scale*. Second, there are the *scorers* themselves who may bring a number of bothersome biases to the enterprise. Finally, there are errors in the *scoring procedure*—that is, the process by which the scorers employ the scoring scale.

Scoring-Instrument Flaws

The major defect with most scoring instruments is the lack of descriptive rigor with which the evaluative criteria to be used are described. Given this lack of rigor, ambiguity exists in the interpretations scorers make about what the scoring criteria mean. This typically leads to a set of unreliable ratings. For example, if teachers are to rate students on the extent to which students are "controlling," some teachers may view this as a positive quality and some may view it as a negative quality. Clearly, an inadequately clarified scoring form can lead to all sorts of "noise" in the scores provided by teachers.

Procedural Flaws

Among common problems with scoring students' responses to performance tests, we usually encounter demands on teachers to rate too many qualities. Overwhelmed scorers are scorers rendered ineffectual. Teachers who opt for a large number of evaluative criteria are teachers who have made a decisively inept opt. Care should be taken that no more than three or four evaluative criteria are to be employed in evaluations of students' responses to your performance assessments. Generally speaking, the fewer evaluative criteria used, the better.

but what does this have to do with Teaching?

Teachers are busy people. (This profound recognition will not come as a surprise to anyone who really knows what a teacher's life is like.) But busy people who are apt to survive in their task-buffeted lives will typically try to manage their multiple responsibilities efficiently. Busy people who are teachers, therefore, need to make sure they don't expend their finite reservoir of energy unwisely. And that's where caution needs to be exerted with respect to the use of performance tests. Performance testing, you see, can be so very *seductive*.

Because performance tests are typically focused on measuring a student's mastery of real-world, significant skills, such tests are appealing. If you're an English teacher, for example, wouldn't you rather see whether your students possess composition skills by having them whip out actual "written-from-scratch" compositions rather than having them spot punctuation problems in multiple-choice items? Of course you would. I was, once upon a time, an English teacher. So take my word for it.

But although the allure of performance assessment is considerable, you should never forget that *it takes time*! And the time-consumption requirements of performance testing can readily eat into a teacher's daily 24-hour allotment. It takes time for teachers to come up with defensible tasks for performance tests, to devise suitable rubrics for scoring students' responses, and to actually score those responses. Performance assessment takes time. But, of course, proper performance testing not only helps teachers aim their instruction in the right directions, it also allows students to recognize the skill(s) being promoted.

So, the trick is to select judiciously the cognitive skills you will measure via performance tests. Focus on a small number of truly significant skills. You'll be more likely to maintain your instructional sanity if you employ only a handful of high-level performance tests. Too many performance tests can quickly put a teacher over the edge.

Teachers' Personal-Bias Errors

If you recall Chapter 4's consideration of bias, you'll remember that bias is clearly an undesirable commodity. Teachers, albeit unintentionally, are frequently biased in the way they score students' responses. Several kinds of personal-bias errors are often encountered when teachers score students' constructed responses. The first of these, known as *generosity error,* occurs when a teacher's bias leads to higher ratings than are warranted. Teachers with a proclivity toward generosity errors see good even where no good exists.

At the other extreme, some teachers display *severity errors.* A severity error, of course, is a tendency to underrate the quality of a student's work. When a pupil's product deserves a "good," a teacher suffering from this personal-bias error will award it only an "average" or even a "below average."

Another sort of personal-bias error is known as *central-tendency error.* This describes a tendency for teachers to view everything as being "in the middle of the scale." Very high or very low ratings are avoided by such folks. They prefer the warm fuzziness of the mean or the median. They tend to regard midpoint ratings as inoffensive and therefore dispense midpoint ratings almost thoughtlessly.

A particularly frequent error arises when a teacher's overall impression of a student influences how the teacher rates that student with respect to an individual criterion. This error is known as **halo effect.** If a teacher has a favorable attitude toward a student, that student will receive a host of favorable ratings (deserved or not) on a number of individual criteria. Similarly, if a teacher has an unfavorable attitude toward a student, the student will receive a pile of unfavorable ratings on all sorts of separate criteria.

One way to minimize halo effect, at least a bit, is occasionally to reverse the order of the high and low positions on the scoring scale so the teacher cannot *unthinkingly* toss out a whole string of positives (or negatives). What you really need to do to avoid halo effect when you're scoring students' responses is to remember it's always lurking in the wings. Try to score a student's responses on each criterion using that specific criterion, not a contaminated general impression of the student's ability.

■ What Do Classroom Teachers Really Need to Know about Performance Assessment?

Performance assessment has been around for a long, long while. Yet, in recent years, a growing number of educators have become strong supporters of this form of assessment because it (1) represents an alternative to traditional paper-and-pencil tests and (2) is often more authentic—that is, reflective of tasks people need to perform in the real world. One of the things you need to understand about performance assessment is that it differs from more conventional assessment chiefly in the degree the assessment task matches the skills and/or knowledge about which you wish to make inferences. Because performance tasks often coincide more closely with high-level cognitive skills than do paper-and-pencil tests, more accu-

Parent Talk

The vice president of your school's Parent Advisory Council has asked you to tell him why so many of your school's teachers are now assessing students with performance tests instead of the more traditional paper-and-pencil tests.

 If I were you, here's how I'd respond:

"The reason that most of us are increasingly relying on performance tests these days is that performance tests almost always measure higher-level student skills. With traditional tests, too many of our teachers found they were assessing only the students' abilities to memorize facts.

"In recent years, educators have become far more capable of devising really *demanding* performance tests that require students to display genuinely high-level intellectual skills—skills that are way, way beyond memorization. We've learned how to develop the tests *and* how to score students' responses using carefully developed scoring rules that we refer to as *rubrics*.

"Please stop by my classroom and I'll show you some examples of these demanding performance tests. We're asking more from our students, and we're getting it."

 Now, how would you respond to the vice president of the Parent Advisory Council?

rate inferences can often be derived about students. Another big plus for performance tests is they establish assessment targets that, because such targets often influence the teacher's instruction, have a positive impact on instructional activities.

You need to realize, however, because performance tasks require a fair chunk of time from students, the teacher is often faced with making rather shaky generalizations on the basis of relatively few student performances. It's also important for you to recognize the development of defensible performance tests is difficult cerebral work. It takes rigorous thinking to identify suitable tasks for performance tests, then isolate appropriate evaluative criteria and spell out the scoring scale for each criterion. And, of course, once the test and its associated scoring procedures are in place, you still have to score students' performances, an operation that invariably takes much more time than is required to score a ream of answers to selected-response items.

The chapter's final admonitions regarding the numerous biases teachers bring to the scoring of students' responses to performance tests should serve as a reminder. If you employ performance tests frequently in your classrooms, you'll need to be careful at every step of the process—from the original conception and berthing of a performance test down to the bias-free scoring of students' responses. In Chapter 12, you'll see how performance tests can be used to improve the quality of your instructional procedures.

■ Chapter Summary

Although Chapter 8 dealt specifically with performance assessment, a number of the points made in the chapter apply with equal force to the scoring of any type of constructed-response item such as those used in essay tests or short-answer tests. After defining performance tests as a measurement procedure in which students create original responses to an assessment task, it was pointed out that performance tests differ from more conventional tests primarily in the degree the test situation approximates the real-life situation to which inferences are made.

The identification of suitable tasks for performance assessments was given considerable attention in the chapter because unsuitable tasks will surely lead to unsatisfactory performance assessments. Seven evaluative criteria were supplied for performance test tasks: (1) generalizability, (2) authenticity, (3) multiple foci, (4) teachability, (5) fairness, (6) feasibility, and (7) scorability. Particular emphasis was given to selecting tasks about which defensible inferences could be drawn regarding students' generalized abilities to perform comparable tasks.

The significance of the skill to be assessed via a performance task was stressed. Next, *evaluative criteria* were defined as the factors by which the acceptability of a student's performance is judged. The evaluative criteria constitute the most important features of a *rubric* that's employed to score student responses. The significance of selecting suitable evaluative criteria was emphasized. Once the criteria have been identified, a numerical scoring scale, usually consisting of three to six score points, is devised for each evaluative criterion. The scoring criteria are applied to student performances in the form of ratings for student products or observations for student behaviors.

Distinctions were drawn among *task-specific*, *hypergeneral*, and *skill-focused rubrics*. Deficits in the former two types of rubrics render them inappropriate for supporting a teacher's classroom instructional effort. A skill-focused rubric, however, can markedly enhance a teacher's instruction.

 ## Self-Check

For this chapter's self-check, you'll need to respond to a bit of performance testing yourself. More specifically, you are now asked to generate a scoring guide for a fairly straightforward task requiring students to describe, in a letter to a foreign pen pal, "how a U.S. president is elected." The task is one of several such tasks in which the student is asked to describe an important procedure in U.S. government to a foreign pen pal.

Now, focusing on students at a grade level with which you are familiar, please develop a first-draft scoring guide consisting of one or more evaluative criteria and a scale for each criterion.

Pondertime

1. Do you think the extra effort associated with performance assessment is worth it? Why?

2. What do you personally consider to be the greatest single strength of performance assessment? How about the greatest single weakness?

3. Are there any sorts of topics or instructional objectives for which you think performance assessment most appropriate?

4. What do you think the likelihood is that performance assessment will be widely used by the classroom teachers you know? Why?

5. Do you believe performance assessment is more likely to be used by individual teachers in their classrooms rather than for large-scale, statewide "educational accountability" assessments? Why?

6. Do you prefer *holistic* or *analytic* scoring of students' responses to performance tests? And, pray tell, why?

Self-Check Key

Not knowing what sort of scoring guide you would come up with, it's pretty difficult to provide very specific feedback to help you discern how suitable your scoring guide is. Ideally, you should have (1) identified evaluative criteria, (2) described the criteria, and (3) provided a point scale for each criterion with as much specificity as your energy permitted.

 If you're using this text in connection with a formal class, perhaps you can get a classmate to exchange scoring guides with you for a robust co-critiquing session. If you're married or are engaged in a meaningful relationship, ask your partner to look over your scoring guide and see if that person understands how to score students' responses to the pen pal assignment. If you currently aren't involved in a significant relationship, I do *not* suggest that you try to curry favor with a prospective paramour by calling on that person to mess around with your scoring guide. Instead, try dinner and a movie.

■ Additional Stuff

Andrade, Heidi Goodrich. (2000). "Using Rubrics to Promote Thinking and Learning." *Educational Leadership*, 57, no. 5 (February): 13–18.

Downing, Steven M., and Thomas M. Haladyna (Eds.). (2006). *Handbook of Test Development*. Mahwah, NJ: Lawrence Erlbaum.

Fitzpatrick, R., and E. J. Morrison. (1971). "Performance and Product Evaluation." In E. L. Thorndike (Ed.), *Educational Measurement* (pp. 237–270). Washington, DC: American Council on Education.

McMillan, James H. (2004). *Classroom Assessment: Principles and Practice for Effective Instruction* (3rd ed.). Boston: Allyn and Bacon.

■ Cyber Stuff

■ *The Buros Institute of Mental Measurements,* now located at the University of Nebraska, has for more than 65 years provided assistance to those using commercially published tests. The Institute's *Tests In Print* serves as a comprehensive bibliography for all known commercially published tests. The Buros Institute's *Mental Measurements Yearbook,* the cornerstone of the agency's publishing activities, contains timely and consumer-oriented test reviews. More than a dozen of these periodically revised yearbooks have now been published. This website contains online test reviews as well as links to myriad assessment-related sites. www.unl.edu/buros

■ *Performance Assessment Links in Science (PALS)* is an online resource bank of K–12 performance assessment tasks indexed according to the National Science Education Standards. Developed by SRI International, PALS contains tasks, directions for students, administrative procedures, rubrics, and examples of student work. Rater-training materials are available. Many of the materials and procedures identified on this website are applicable to subject areas other than science. www.pals.sri.com

Companion
Website

To access chapter objectives, practice tests, weblinks, and flashcards, visit the companion website at **www.ablongman.com/popham5e.**

(mylabschool
Where the classroom comes to life!

MyLabSchool is a collection of online tools for your success in this course, your licensure exams, and your teaching career. Discover where the classroom comes to life by visiting **www.mylabschool.com** to access the following resources:

■ Video clips from real classrooms

■ An archive of real-life cases

■ Help with your research papers using Research Navigator™

■ Career Center with resources for:

Praxis exams and licensure preparation

Professional portfolio development

Job search and interview techniques

Lesson planning with state standard correlations

9

Portfolio Assessment

"**A**ssessment should be a part of instruction, not apart from it" is a point of view most proponents of portfolio assessment would enthusiastically endorse. Portfolio assessment, a contemporary entry in the educational measurement derby, has captured the attention of large numbers of educators because it represents a clear alternative to more traditional forms of educational testing.

A *portfolio* is a systematic collection of one's work. In education, portfolios refer to systematic collections of students' work. Although the application of portfolios in education has been a relatively recent phenomenon, portfolios have been widely used in a number of other fields for many years. Portfolios, in fact, constitute the chief method by which certain professionals display their skills and accomplishments. For example, portfolios are traditionally used for that purpose by photographers, artists, journalists, models, architects, and so on. An important feature of portfolios is that they must be updated as a person's achievements and skills grow.

Portfolios have been warmly embraced by those educators who regard traditional assessment with less than enthusiasm. In Table 9.1, for example, a chart presented by Tierney, Carter, and Desai (1991) indicates what those three proponents of portfolios believe are the differences between *portfolio assessment* and assessment based on standardized testing.

■ Classroom Portfolio Assessment versus Large-Scale Portfolio Assessment

Classroom Applications

Most advocates of portfolio assessment believe the real payoffs for such assessment approaches lie in the individual teacher's classroom, because the relationship

Table 9.1 ■ Differences in Assessment Outcomes between Portfolios and Standardized Testing Practices

Portfolio	Testing
Represents the range of reading and writing students are engaged in	Assesses students across a limited range of reading and writing assignments which may not match what students do
Engages students in assessing their progress and/or accomplishments and establishing ongoing learning goals	Mechanically scored or scored by teachers who have little input
Measures each student's achievement while allowing for individual differences between students	Assesses all students on the same dimensions
Represents a collaborative approach to assessment	Assessment process is not collaborative
Has a goal of student self-assessment	Student assessment is not a goal
Addresses improvement, effort, and achievement	Addresses achievement only
Links assessment and teaching to learning	Separates learning, testing, and teaching

Source: Material from *Portfolio Assessment in the Reading-Writing Classroom,* by Robert J. Tierney, Mark A. Carter, and Laura E. Desai, published by Christopher-Gordon Publishers, Inc. © 1991, used with permission of the publisher.

between instruction and assessment will be strengthened as a consequence of students' continuing accumulation of work products in their portfolios. Ideally, teachers who adopt portfolios in their classrooms will make the ongoing collection and appraisal of students' work a central focus of the instructional program rather than a peripheral activity whereby students occasionally gather up their work to convince a teacher's supervisors or students' parents that good things have been going on in class.

Here's a description of how an elementary teacher might use portfolios to assess students' progress in social studies, language arts, and mathematics. The teacher, let's call him Phil Pholio, asks students to keep three portfolios, one in each of those three subject fields. In each portfolio, the students are to place their early and revised work products. The work products are always dated so Mr. Pholio, as well as the students themselves, can see what kinds of differences in quality take place over time. For example, if effective instruction is being provided, there should be discernible improvement in the caliber of students' written compositions, solutions to mathematics problems, and analyses of social issues.

Three or four times per semester, Mr. Pholio holds 15- to 20-minute portfolio conferences with each student about the three different portfolios. The other, non-conferencing students take part in small-group and independent learning activities while the portfolio conferences are conducted. During a conference, the participating student plays an active role in evaluating his or her own work. Toward the close of the school year, students select from their regular portfolios a series of work products that not only represent their best final versions but also indicate how those final products were created. These selections are placed in a display portfolio featured at a spring open-school session designed for parents. Parents who visit the school are urged to take their children's display portfolios home. Mr. Pholio also sends portfolios home to parents who are unable to attend the open-school event.

There are, of course, many other ways to use portfolios effectively in a classroom. Phil Pholio, our phictitious (sic) teacher, employed a fairly common approach, but a variety of alternative procedures could also work quite nicely. The major consideration is that the teacher uses portfolio *assessment* as an integral aspect of the *instructional* process. Because portfolios can be tailored to a specific student's evolving growth, the diagnostic value of portfolios for teachers is immense.

Who Is Evaluating Whom?

Roger Farr, a leader in language arts instruction and assessment, contends that the real payoff from proper portfolio assessment is that students' *self-evaluation* capabilities are enhanced. Thus, during portfolio conferences the teacher encourages students to come up with personal appraisals of their own work. The conference, then, becomes far more than merely an opportunity for the teacher to dispense an "oral report card." On the contrary, students' self-evaluation skills are nurtured not only during portfolio conferences but also throughout the entire school year. For this reason, Farr strongly prefers the use of ***working portfolios*** instead of ***showcase portfolios*** because he believes self-evaluation is nurtured more readily in connection with ongoing reviews of products not intended to impress external viewers.

For self-evaluation purposes, it is particularly useful to be able to compare earlier work with later work. Fortunately, even if a teacher's instruction is downright abysmal, students grow older and, as a consequence of maturation, tend to get better at what they do in school. If a student is required to review three versions of a student's written composition (a first draft, a second draft, and a final draft), self-evaluation can be fostered by encouraging the student to make comparative judgments of the three compositions based on appropriate evaluative criteria. As anyone who has done much writing knows, written efforts tend to get better with time and revision. Contrasts of later versions with earlier versions can prove illuminating from an appraisal perspective and, because students' self-evaluation is so critical to their future growth, from an instructional perspective, as well.

Large-Scale Applications

It is one thing to use portfolios for classroom assessment; it is quite another to use portfolios for large-scale assessment programs. Several states and large school districts have attempted to install portfolios as a central component of a large-scale accountability assessment program—that is, a program in which student performances serve as an indicator of an educational system's effectiveness. To date, the results of efforts to employ portfolios for accountability purposes have not been encouraging.

In large-scale applications of portfolio assessments for accountability purposes, students' portfolios are judged either by the students' regular teachers or by

Decision Time

Does Self-Evaluation Equal Self-Grading?

After a midsummer, schoolwide three-day workshop on the Instructional Payoffs of Classroom Portfolios, the faculty at Rhoda Street Elementary School have agreed to install student portfolios in all classrooms for one or more subject areas. Maria Martinez, an experienced third-grade teacher in the school, has decided to try out portfolios only in mathematics. She admits to her family (but not to her fellow teachers) she's not certain she'll be able to use portfolios properly with her students.

Because she has attempted to follow the guidelines of the National Council of Teachers of Mathematics, Maria stresses mathematical problem solving and the integration of mathematical understanding with content from other disciplines. Accordingly, she asks her students to place in their mathematics portfolios versions of their attempts to solve quantitative problems drawn from other subjects. Maria poses these problems for her third-graders, then requires them to prepare an initial solution strategy and to revise that solution at least twice. Students are directed to put all solutions (dated) in their portfolios.

Six weeks after the start of school, Maria sets up a series of 15-minute portfolio conferences with her students. During the three days on which the portfolio conferences are held, students who are not involved in a conference move through a series of learning stations in other subject areas where they typically engage in a fair amount of peer critiquing of each others' responses to various kinds of practice exercises.

Having learned during the summer workshop that the promotion of students' self-evaluation is critical if students are to get the most from portfolios, Maria devotes the bulk of her 15-minute conferences to students' personal appraisals of their own work. Although Maria offers some of her own appraisals of most students' work, she typically allows the student's self-evaluation to override her own estimates of a student's ability to solve each problem.

Because it will soon be time to give students their 10-week grades, Maria doesn't know whether to base the grades on her own judgments or on students' self-appraisals.

 If you were Maria, what would you decide to do?

---

a cadre of specially trained scorers (often teachers) who carry out the scoring at a central site. The problem with specially trained scorers and central-site scoring is it typically costs much more than can be afforded. Some states, therefore, have opted to have all portfolios scored by students' own teachers who then relay such scores to the state department. The problem with having regular teachers score students' portfolios, however, is that such scoring tends to be too unreliable for use in accountability programs. Not only have teachers usually not been provided with thorough training about how to score portfolios but there is also a tendency for teachers to be biased in favor of their own students. As you can see, the scoring of portfolios in large-scale assessment programs constitutes a nontrivial problem.

One of the most visible of the statewide efforts to use portfolios on every pupil has been a performance assessment program in the state of Vermont. Because substantial national attention has been focused on the Vermont program, and because it has been evaluated independently, many policymakers in other states have drawn on the experiences encountered in the Vermont Portfolio Assessment Program. Unfortunately, independent evaluators of Vermont's statewide efforts to use portfolios found that there was considerable unreliability in the appraisals given to students' work. And, if you harken back to Chapter 2's quick dip into the importance of reliability, it's tough to draw valid inferences about students' achievements if the assessment of those achievements are not made with consistency.

But, of course, this is a book about classroom assessment, not large-scale assessment. (I knew that!) It certainly hasn't been shown definitely that portfolios do *not* have a place in large-scale assessment. What has been shown, however, is there are significant obstacles to be surmounted if portfolio assessment is going to make a meaningful contribution to large-scale educational accountability testing.

■ Key Ingredients in Classroom Portfolio Assessment

Although there are numerous ways to install and sustain portfolios in a classroom, you will find the following seven-step sequence provides a reasonable template for getting underway with portfolio assessment. Taken together, these seven activities capture the key ingredients in classroom-based portfolio assessment.

1. *Make sure your students "own" their portfolios.* In order for portfolios to represent a student's evolving work accurately, and to foster the kind of self-evaluation so crucial if portfolios are to be truly educational, students must perceive portfolios to be collections of their own work and not merely temporary receptacles for products you ultimately grade. You will probably want to introduce the notion of portfolio assessment to your students (assuming portfolio assessment isn't already a schoolwide operation and your students aren't already familiar with the use of portfolios) by explaining the distinctive functions of portfolios in the classroom.
2. *Decide on what kinds of work samples to collect.* Various kinds of work samples can be included in a portfolio. Obviously, such products will vary from subject to subject. In general, a wide variety of work products is preferable to a limited range of work products. Ideally, you and your students can collaboratively determine what goes in the portfolio.
3. *Collect and store work samples.* Students need to collect the designated work samples as they are created, place them in a suitable container (a folder or notebook, for example), then store the container in a file cabinet, storage box, or some suitably safe location. You may need to work individually with your students to help them decide whether particular products should be placed in their portfolios. The actual organization of a portfolio's contents depends, of course, on the nature of the work samples being collected.

4. *Select criteria by which to evaluate portfolio work samples.* Working collaboratively with students, carve out a set of criteria by which you and your students can judge the quality of their portfolio products. Because of the likely diversity of products in different students' portfolios, the identification of evaluative criteria will not be a simple task. Yet, unless at least rudimentary evaluative criteria are isolated, the students will find it difficult to evaluate their own efforts and, thereafter, to strive for improvement. The criteria, once selected, should be described with the same sort of clarity we saw in the previous chapter regarding how to use a rubric's evaluative criteria when judging students' responses to performance test tasks.

5. *Require students to evaluate continually their own portfolio products.* Using the agreed-on evaluative criteria, be sure your students routinely appraise their own work. Students can be directed to evaluate their work products holistically, analytically, or using a combination of both approaches. Such self-evaluation can be made routine by requiring each student to complete brief evaluation slips on 3" × 5" cards on which they identify the major strengths and weaknesses of a given product, then suggest how the product could be improved. Be sure to have your students date such self-evaluation sheets so they can keep track of modifications in their self-evaluation skills. Each completed self-evaluation sheet should be stapled or paper-clipped to the work product being evaluated.

6. *Schedule and conduct portfolio conferences.* Portfolio conferences take time. Yet, these interchange sessions between teachers and students regarding students' work are really pivotal in making sure portfolio assessment fulfills its potential. The conference should not only evaluate your students' work products, but should also help them improve their self-evaluation abilities. Try to hold as many of these conferences as you can. In order to make the conferences time efficient, be sure to have students prepare for the conferences so you can start right in on the topics of most concern to you and the student.

7. *Involve parents in the portfolio assessment process.* Early in the school year, make sure your students' parents understand what the nature of the portfolio assessment process is you've devised for your classroom. Insofar as is practical, encourage your students' parents/guardians periodically to review their children's work samples as well as their children's self-evaluation of those work samples. The more active parents become in reviewing their children's work, the stronger the message will be to the child that the portfolio activity is really worthwhile. If you wish, you may have students select their best work for a showcase portfolio or, instead, simply use the students' working portfolios.

These seven steps reflect only the most important activities teachers might engage in when creating assessment programs in their classrooms. There are obviously all sorts of variations and embellishments possible.

There's one situation in which heavy student involvement in the portfolio process may not make instructional sense. This occurs in the early grades when, in the teacher's judgment, those little tykes are not developmentally ready to take a meaningful hand in a full-blown portfolio self-evaluation extravaganza. Any sort of educational assessment ought to be *developmentally appropriate* for the students who are being assessed. Thus, for students who are in early primary grade levels, a teacher may sensibly decide to employ only *showcase* portfolios to display a child's accomplishments to the child and the child's parents. *Working* portfolios, simply bristling with student-evaluated products, can be left for later. This is, clearly, a teacher's call.

Purposeful Portfolios

There are numerous choice-points you'll encounter if you embark on a portfolio assessment approach in your own classroom. The first one ought to revolve around *purpose*. Why is it that you are contemplating a meaningful prance down the portfolio pathway?

Assessment specialists typically identify three chief purposes for portfolio assessment. The first of these is *documentation of student progress* wherein the major function of the assembled work samples is to provide the student, the teacher, and the student's parents with evidence about the student's growth—or lack of it. These are the *working* portfolios that provide meaningful opportunities for self-evaluation by students.

Pointing out that students' achievement levels ought to influence teachers' instructional decisions, Anderson (2003, p. 44) concludes that "the information should be collected as near to the decision as possible (e.g., final examinations are administered in close proximity to end-of-term grades). However, if decisions are to be based on learning, then a plan for information collection over time must be developed and implemented." The more current any documentation of students' progress is, the more accurate that documentation is apt to be.

A second purpose of portfolios is to provide an opportunity for *showcasing student accomplishments*. Stiggins (2004) describes portfolios that showcase students' best work as *celebration portfolios* and he contends celebration portfolios are especially appropriate for the early grades. In portfolios intended to showcase student accomplishments, students typically select their best work and reflect thoughtfully on its quality.

One midwest teacher I know always makes sure students include the following elements in their showcase portfolios:

- A letter of introduction to portfolio reviewers
- A table of contents
- Identification of the skills or knowledge being demonstrated
- A representative sample of the student's best work
- Dates on all entries
- The evaluative criteria (or rubric) being used
- The student's self-reflection on all entries

The inclusion of student self-reflections about ingredients of portfolios is a pivotal ingredient in showcase portfolios. Some portfolio proponents contend a portfolio's self-evaluation by the student helps the learner to learn better and permits the reader of the portfolio to gain insights about how the learner learns.

A final purpose for portfolios is *evaluation of student status*—that is, the determination of whether students have met previously determined quality levels of performance. McMillan (2004) points out that when portfolios are used for this purpose, there must be greater standardization about what should be included in a portfolio and how the work samples should be appraised. Typically, teachers select the entries for this kind of portfolio and considerable attention is given to scoring so any rubrics employed to score the portfolios will yield consistent results even if different scorers are involved. For portfolios being used to evaluate student status, there is usually less need for self-evaluation of entries—unless such self-evaluations are themselves being evaluated by others.

Well, we've peeked at three purposes underlying portfolio assessment. Can one portfolio perform all three functions? My answer is a somewhat shaky *yes*. But if you were to ask me whether one portfolio can perform all three functions *well*, you'd get a rock-solid *no*. The three functions, though somewhat rather related—like second cousins—are fundamentally different.

That's why your very first decision if you're going to install portfolios in your classroom is to decide on the *primary purpose* of the portfolios. You can then determine what the portfolios should look like and how students should prepare them.

Scripture tells us that "no man can serve two masters." (The authors of that scriptural advice, clearly insensitive to gender equality, were not implying that females are more capable of double-master serving.) Similarly, one kind of portfolio cannot blithely satisfy multiple functions. Some classroom teachers rush into portfolio assessment because they've heard about all of the enthralling things that portfolios can do. But one kind of portfolio cannot fulfill all three functions. Pick your top-priority purpose, then build your portfolio assessment to satisfy this purpose.

Work-Sample Selection

For a teacher just joining the portfolio party, another key decision hinges on the identification of the work samples to be put into the portfolios. All too often, teachers who are novices at portfolio assessment will fail to think divergently enough about the kinds of entries that should constitute a portfolio's chief contents. In Table 9.2 you'll find some examples for mathematics and language arts suggesting the considerable range of work samples that might be included.

But divergency is not necessarily a virtue when it comes to the determination of a portfolio's contents. You shouldn't search for varied kinds of work samples simply for the sake of variety. What's important is the particular kinds of work samples to be included in the portfolio will allow you to derive valid inferences about the skills and/or knowledge you're trying to have your students master. It's far better to include a few kinds of *inference-illuminating* work samples than to include a galaxy of work samples, many of which do not contribute to your inferences about students' knowledge or skills.

Table 9.2 ■ Illustrative Entries for Mathematics and Language Arts Portfolios

Mathematics[1]	Language Arts[2]
A solution to an open-ended question done as homework	Projects, surveys, reports, and units from reading and writing
A mathematical autobiography	Favorite poems, songs, letters, and comments
Papers that show the student's correction or errors or misconceptions	Interesting thoughts to remember
A photo or sketch made by the student of a student's work with manipulatives or with mathematical models of multidimensional figures	Finished samples that illustrate wide writing: persuasive, letters, poetry, information, stories
A letter from the student to the reader of the portfolio, explaining each item	Examples of writing across the curriculum: reports, journals, literature logs
A report of a group project, with comments about the individual's contribution	Literature extensions: scripts for drama, visual arts, written forms, webs, charts, time lines, murals
Work from another subject area that relates to mathematics, such as an analysis of data collected and presented in a graph for social studies	Student record of books read and attempted
	Audiotape of reading
A problem made up by the student	Writing responses to literacy components: plot, setting, point of view, character development, links to life, theme, literary links and criticism
Artwork done by the student, such as string designs, coordinate pictures, and scale drawings or maps	Writing that illustrates critical thinking about reading
Draft, revised, and final versions of student work on a complex mathematical problem, including writing, diagrams, graphs, charts	Notes from individual reading and writing conference
A description by the teacher of a student activity that displayed understanding of a mathematical concept or relation	Items that are evidence of development of style: organization, voice, sense of audience, choice of words, clarity
	Writing that shows growth in usage of traits: growing ability in self-correction, punctuation, spelling, grammar, appropriate form, and legibility
	Samples in which ideas are modified from first draft to final product
	Unedited first drafts
	Revised first drafts
	Evidence of effort: improvement noted on pieces, completed assignments

Sources: [1]Reprinted with permission from *Mathematics Assessment: Myths, Models, Good Questions, and Practical Suggestions,* by Jean Kerr Stenmark, p. 37, copyright © 1991 by the National Council of Teachers of Mathematics, Reston, VA.

[2]Tierney, R. J., Carter, M. A., & Desai, L. E. (1991). *Portfolio Assessment in the Reading-Writing Classroom.* Norwood, MA: Christopher-Gordon Publishers, pp. 72–74. Used with permission of the publisher.

Appraising Portfolios

As indicated earlier in the chapter, students' portfolios are almost always evaluated by the use of a scoring rubric. The most important ingredients of such a rubric are its evaluative criteria—that is, the factors to be used in determining the quality of a particular student's portfolio. If there's any sort of student self-evaluation to be done, and such self-evaluation is almost always desirable, then it is imperative students have access to, and thoroughly understand, the rubric that will be used to evaluate their portfolios.

I realize we've already spent some time dealing with rubrics and evaluative criteria, especially in Chapter 8's treatment of performance assessment. But I'm going to ask you, as a favor (note how inordinately polite I'm being), to wait until you get through with Chapter 12's description of Instructionally Illuminating Assessment to form your final views on portfolio rubrics. In that chapter, you'll see how rubrics can be deliberately designed so they increase the likelihood of successful instruction. Chapter 12's treatment of rubrics is highly pertinent to the type of rubrics you ought to employ if you use portfolio assessment in your own classroom. In short, before becoming concretely close-minded (and that's somewhat solid) about what your portfolio rubrics ought to look like, hold off a bit until you've wrapped up Chapter 12. Please!

If, however, your ability to delay gratification is nonexistent, here's a quick-and-dirty way to appraise any sort of portfolio assessments you might install in your classroom. Simply ask yourself whether your students' portfolios have substantially increased the accuracy of the inferences you make regarding your students' skills and knowledge. If your answer is *yes*, then portfolio assessment is a winner for you. If your answer is *no*, then pitch those portfolios without delay—or guilt. But wait! If your answer resembles "I'm not sure," then you really need to think this issue through rigorously. Classroom assessment is supposed to contribute to more valid inferences from which better instructional decisions can be made. If your portfolio assessment program isn't *clearly* doing those things, you may need to make some serious changes in that program.

■ The Pros and Cons of Portfolio Assessment

You must keep in mind is that portfolio assessment's greatest strength is that it can be tailored to the individual student's needs, interests, and abilities. Yet, portfolio assessment suffers from the drawback faced by all constructed-response measurement. Students' constructed responses are genuinely difficult to evaluate, particularly when those responses vary from student to student.

As we saw with Vermont's Portfolio Assessment Program, it is quite difficult to come up with consistent evaluations of different students' portfolios. Sometimes the scoring guides devised for use in evaluating portfolios are so terse and so general as to be almost useless. They're akin to Rorschach inkblots in which different scorers see in the scoring guide what they want to see. In contrast, some scoring guides are so detailed and complicated that they simply overwhelm scorers. It is

but what does this have to do with Teaching?

Portfolio assessment almost always *transforms* a teacher's approach to instruction. A nifty little selected-response test, or even a lengthy constructed-response exam, can usually be tossed into a teacher's usual instructional program without significantly altering how the teacher goes about teaching. But that's not so with portfolio assessment. Once a teacher hops aboard the portfolio bus, there's a long and serious ride in the offing.

Portfolio assessment, if it's properly focused on helping children improve by being able to evaluate their own work samples, becomes a continuing and *central* component of a teacher's instructional program. Work samples have to be chosen, scoring rubrics need to be developed, and students need to be taught how to use those rubrics to monitor the evolving quality of their efforts. Portfolio assessment, therefore, truly dominates most instructional programs in which it is employed.

The first thing you need to do, therefore, is decide whether the knowledge and skills you are trying to have your students master (and especially the skills) lend themselves to portfolio assessment. Will there be student work samples that, because they permit you to make inferences about your students' skill mastery, could provide the continuing focus for portfolio assessment?

Some content lends itself delightfully to portfolio assessment. Some doesn't. During my first year as a high school teacher, I taught two English courses and a speech class. Because my English courses focused on the promotion of students' composition skills, I think that a portfolio assessment might have worked well in either English course. My students and I could monitor their improvements in being able to write.

But I don't think I would have been able to use portfolios effectively in my speech class. At that time, television itself had just arrived on the West Coast, and videotaping was unknown. Accordingly, my speech students and I wouldn't have had anything to toss in their portfolios.

The first big question you need to ask yourself when it comes to portfolio assessment is quite simple: Is this powerful but time-consuming form of assessment right for what I'm trying to teach?

difficult to devise scoring guides that embody just the right level of specificity. Generally speaking, most teachers are so busy they don't have time to create elaborate scoring schemes. Accordingly, many teachers (and students) find themselves judging portfolios using fairly loose evaluative criteria. Such criteria tend to be interpreted differently by different people.

Another problem with portfolio assessment is it takes time—loads of time—to carry out properly. Even if you're very efficient in reviewing your students' portfolios, you'll still have to devote many hours both in class (during portfolio conferences) and outside of class (if you also want to review your students' portfolios by yourself). Proponents of portfolios are convinced the quality of portfolio assessment is worth the time such assessment takes. You at least need to be prepared for the required investment of time if you decide to undertake portfolio assessment. And teachers will definitely need to receive sufficient training to learn how to carry out portfolio assessment well. Any teachers who set out to do portfolio assessment by simply stuffing student stuff into folders built for stuff stuffing will end up wasting their time and their students' time. Meaningful staff development is a must if portfolio assessment is to work well.

On the plus side, however, most teachers who have used portfolios agree portfolio assessment provides a way of documenting and evaluating growth happening in a classroom in ways standardized or written tests cannot. Portfolios have the potential to create authentic portraits of what students learn. I agree with Stiggins (2004) when he points out for portfolios to merge effectively with instruction, they must have a story to tell. Fortunately, this story can be made compatible with improved student learning.

Most of the teachers I've talked with who use portfolio assessments are primarily enamored with two payoffs. They believe that the *self-evaluation* it fosters in students is truly important in guiding students' learning over time. They also think the *personal ownership* students experience regarding their own work, and the progress they experience, makes the benefits of portfolio assessment outweigh its costs.

■ What Do Classroom Teachers Really Need to Know about Portfolio Assessment?

As noted at the beginning to this four-chapter excursion into item types, the more familiar you are with different kinds of test items, the more likely you will be to select an item type that best provides you with the information you need in order to draw suitable inferences about your students. Until recently, portfolios haven't been viewed as a viable assessment option by many teachers. These days, however, portfolio assessment clearly is a legitimate weapon in a teacher's assessment arsenal.

You need to realize, if portfolio assessment is going to constitute a helpful adjunct to your instructional program, portfolios will have to become a central, not tangential, part of what goes on in your classroom. The primary premise in portfolio assessment is that a particularized collection of a student's *evolving* work will allow both the student and you to determine the student's progress. You can't gauge the student's evolving progress if you don't have frequent evidence of the student's efforts.

It would be educationally unwise to select portfolio assessment as a one-time measurement approach to deal with a short-term instructional objective. Rather, it makes more sense to select some goal of interest, such as the student's ability to write original compositions, then monitor this aspect of the student's learning throughout the entire school year. It is also important for you to realize that although portfolio assessment may prove highly valuable for classroom instruction and measurement purposes, at this juncture there is insufficient evidence it can be used appropriately for large-scale assessment.

A number of portfolio assessment specialists believe the most important dividend from portfolio assessment is the increased abilities of students to evaluate their own work. If this becomes one of your goals in a portfolio assessment approach,

Parent Talk

Suppose that Mr. and Mrs. Holmgren, parents of your student, Harry, stopped by your classroom during a back-to-school night to examine their son's portfolio. After spending almost 30 minutes going through the portfolio and skimming the portfolios of several other students, they speak to you—not with hostility, but with genuine confusion. Mrs. Holmgren sums up their concerns nicely with the following comments: "When we stopped by Mr. Bray's classroom earlier this evening to see how our daughter, Elissa, is doing, we encountered a series of extremely impressive portfolios. Elissa's was outstanding. To be honest, Harry's portfolio is a lot less polished. It seems that he's included everything he's done in your class, rough drafts as well as final products. Why is there this difference?"

 If I were you, here's how I'd respond to Harry's parents:

"It's really good that you two could take the time to see how Harry and Elissa are doing. And I can understand why you're perplexed by the differences in Elissa's and Harry's portfolios. You see, there are *different* kinds of student portfolios, and different portfolios serve different purposes.

"In Mr. Bray's class, and I know this because we often exchange portfolio tips with one another, students prepare what are called *showcase* portfolios. In such portfolios, students pick their very best work to show Mr. Bray and their parents what they've learned. I think Mr. Bray actually sent his students' showcase portfolios home about a month ago so you could see how well Elissa is doing. For Mr. Bray and his students, the portfolios are collections of best work that, in a very real sense, celebrate students' achievements.

"In my class, however, students create *working* portfolios in which the real emphasis is on getting students to make progress and to evaluate this progress *on their own*. When you reviewed Harry's portfolio, did you see how each entry is dated and how he had prepared a brief self-reflection of each entry? I'm more interested in Harry's seeing the improvement he makes than in anyone seeing polished final products. You, too, can see the striking progress he's made over the course of this school year.

"I'm not suggesting that my kind of portfolio is better than Mr. Bray's. Both have a role to play. Those roles, as I'm sure you'll see, are quite different."

 Now, how would you respond to Mr. and Mrs. Holmgren?

you must be certain to nurture such self-evaluation growth deliberately via portfolios instead of simply using portfolios as convenient collections of work samples.

The seven key ingredients in portfolio assessment that were identified in the chapter represent only one way of installing this kind of assessment strategy. Variations of those seven suggested procedures are not only possible, but to be encouraged. The big thing to keep in mind is that portfolio assessment offers your students and you a way to particularize your evaluation of each student's growth over time. And, speaking of time, it's only appropriate to remind you it takes substantially more time to use a portfolio assessment approach properly than to score a zillion true-false tests. If you opt to try portfolio assessment, you'll have to see whether, *in your own instructional situation*, it yields sufficient educational benefits to be worth the investment you'll surely need to make in it.

■ Chapter Summary

After defining portfolios as systematic collections of students' work, contrasts were drawn between portfolio assessment and more conventional standardized testing. It was suggested that portfolio assessment was far more appropriate for an individual teacher's classroom assessment than for large-scale accountability assessments.

An emphasis on self-assessment was suggested as being highly appropriate for portfolio assessment, particularly in view of the way portfolios can be tailored to an *individual* student's evolving progress. Seven steps were then suggested as key ingredients for classroom teachers to install and sustain portfolio assessment in their classroom: (1) establish student ownership, (2) decide on what work samples to collect, (3) collect and score work samples, (4) select evaluative criteria, (5) require continual student self-evaluations, (6) schedule and conduct portfolio conferences, and (7) involve parents in the portfolio assessment process.

Three different functions of portfolio assessment were identified—namely, documentation of student progress, showcasing student accomplishments, and evaluation of student status. Teachers were urged to select a primary purpose for portfolio assessment.

The chapter was concluded with an identification of plusses and minuses of portfolio assessment. It was emphasized that portfolio assessment represents an important measurement strategy now available to today's classroom teachers.

 ## Self-Check

The self-check for this chapter will be somewhat different because it has been stressed that teachers who install portfolio assessment systems in their own classes will undoubtedly devise procedures to mesh with their own subject-matter emphases and the abilities and interests of the students they teach. Nonetheless, to give you a bit of practice in using the seven key ingredients of classroom performance assessments presented in the chapter, you'll be reading a pair of scenarios about fictitious teachers who are installing and operating portfolio assessment programs in their mythical classrooms. Your task, as a compliant self-checker, is to read each scenario, then decide if one or more of the seven key ingredients are missing or have been violated. If you want to review the seven ingredients before you tackle these two self-check exercises, there are no prohibitions to your returning to pages 199 through 201.

Scenario One

Having decided to adopt a portfolio assessment approach for the composition segment of her junior high school English classes, Maria Flores introduces her students to the new assessment scheme by asking a commercial-artist friend of hers to speak to each class. The artist brings his own portfolio and shows students how the portfolio allows prospective clients to judge his work. Ms. Flores tells her students that her friend's portfolio is called a "showcase portfolio" and that students will be preparing both a showcase portfolio to periodically involve their parents in reviewing work products, as well as a "working portfolio" to keep track of *all* of their composition drafts and final products. Ms. Flores and her friend emphasize that both kinds of portfolios must be owned by the students, not the teacher.

Because all of their drafts and final versions are to be collected, students simply place copies of all such products in folders and, when finished, in a designated file drawer. Early in the academic year, Ms. Flores works with each of her classes to decide collaboratively on the criteria to be used on judging the composition efforts for a given class. Although there are slight differences in the criteria decided on for each class, the criteria for all of her classes are fairly similar.

Ms. Flores makes sure to review all students' portfolios at least once a month. Typically, she devotes one preparation period a day to a different class's portfolios. Because the portfolios are readily available in a file cabinet in her classroom, Ms. Flores finds it convenient and time efficient to evaluate students' progress in this manner. She provides a brief (dated) "teacher's evaluation" for students to consider when they work with their own portfolios.

At least twice every term, Ms. Flores selects what she considers to be the students' best finished works from their working portfolios. She places such work products in a showcase portfolio. Students are directed to take these showcase portfolios home to let their families see what kinds of compositions they have been creating. Parents are enthusiastic about this practice. A number of parents have told the school principal Ms. Flores's "take-home" portfolio system is the way they would like to see other aspects of their children's performances evaluated.

Now, please critique Ms. Flores's efforts in relation to the seven key ingredients of portfolio assessment supplied in the chapter.

Scenario Two

A third-grade teacher, Gary Gately, has just completed a summer staff-development workshop on portfolio assessment. He and a number of the teachers at his school have decided to try out performance assessment in at least limited parts of their instructional and assessment programs. Gary has also decided to use portfolios with his students' mathematics work.

He introduces students to the activity by stressing the importance of their personal ownership of the portfolios and the significance of their own evaluations of the kinds of mathematics work they put in their portfolios. Gary suggests to the class that students include only problem-solution mathematics work in their portfolios. Thus, all drill work and simple computational work is not to be put in the portfolios. The students discuss this suggestion and readily agree.

Gary works with students for two full days to decide on the evaluative criteria they, and he, will use to evaluate the mathematics work in the portfolios. They decide that the major criteria will be (1) selection of proper solution strategies, (2) accurate completion of selected solution procedures, and (3) arrival at the correct solution to the problem.

Students routinely collect their work and place it for safekeeping in specially marked cardboard boxes that Gary has placed on the "Portfolio Shelf." Every two months, Gary holds an individual portfolio conference with each student during which he supplies the student with a "teacher's appraisal" of the portfolio's work.

It is clear to Gary that his students' ability to solve mathematics problems has improved substantially. Although it took students several weeks to get used to the process, they now seem to thoroughly enjoy Gary's version of portfolio assessment in mathematics.

Conjure up a critique of Mr. Gately's approach to portfolio assessment.

Pondertime

1. What do you personally believe is the most important strength of portfolio assessment? What about the most important weakness of this form of assessment?

2. Three purposes of portfolio assessment were described in the chapter: documentation of student progress, showcasing student accomplishments, and evaluation of student status. Which of these three purposes do you believe to be most meritorious? And, of course, why?

3. What subjects, if any, do not lend themselves to some form of portfolio assessment?

4. If it is true that portfolios need to be personalized for particular students, is it possible to devise one-size-fits-all criteria for evaluating classroom portfolio work products? Why or why not?

5. How can the substantial time demands of portfolio assessment be effectively addressed by classroom teachers?

Self-Check Key

Scenario One

Ms. Flores's approach to portfolio assessment had much to commend it. Indeed, if the approach is really working, she probably shouldn't tinker with it. There were, however, two ingredients Ms. Flores overlooked that some proponents of portfolio assessment consider important. First, she didn't push students very hard in the direction of self-evaluation. Second, she didn't hold any one-on-one portfolio conferences. During such conferences, of course, Ms. Flores could nurture students' self-evaluation skills. For a first try at performance assessment, however, our fictitious Ms. Flores did a rather nifty job.

Scenario Two

Gary missed out on only two of the chapter's seven key ingredients. He didn't involve parents in the process and, although he made some early noise about promoting self-evaluation on the part of the students, he really didn't push students' self-evaluation during the portfolio conferences or apart from those conferences.

■ Additional Stuff

Anderson, Lorin W. (2003). *Classroom Assessment: Enhancing the Quality of Teacher Decision Making.* Mahwah, NJ: Lawrence Erlbaum.

McMillan, James H. (2004). *Classroom Assessment: Principles and Practice for Effective Instruction* (3rd ed.). Boston: Allyn and Bacon.

Niguidula, David. (2005). "Documenting Learning with Digital Portfolios." *Educational Leadership, 63,* no. 3 (November): 44–47.

Sadler, Philip M., and Eddie Good. (2006). "The Impact of Self- and Peer-Grading on Student Learning," *Educational Assessment, 11,* no. 1: 1–32.

Stiggins, Richard J. (2004). *Student-Involved Classroom Assessment FOR Learning* (4th ed.). Upper Saddle River, NJ: Prentice-Hall.

Tierney, Robert J., Mark A. Carter, and Laura E. Desai. (1991). *Portfolio Assessment in the Reading-Writing Classroom.* Norwood, MA: Christopher-Gordon.

■ Nonprint Stuff

Association for Supervision and Curriculum Development. *Portfolios: A Guide for Students and Teachers* (Four Audiotapes, Stock #299219G20). Alexandria, VA: Author.

Northwest Regional Educational Laboratory. *Using Portfolios in Assessment and Instruction* (Videotape #NREL-13). Los Angeles: IOX Assessment Associates.

Northwest Regional Educational Laboratory. *Putting Portfolio Stories to Work* (Videotape #NREL-15). Los Angeles: IOX Assessment Associates.

Wiggins, Grant, and Richard J. Stiggins. "Tape 2—Portfolios" (Videotape #614226Z35) in *Redesigning Assessment Series*. Alexandria, VA: Association for Supervision and Curriculum Development.

■ Cyber Stuff

■ *Edutopia* is a project of the George Lucas Educational Foundation and, along with a monthly magazine, the group makes available a website often presenting innovative uses of classroom educational assessments such as portfolio assessments and performance assessments. Although a recent arrival for websites featuring assessment-related topics, this site contains a delightful mix of theoretically sound and eminently practical ideas about assessment. www.edutopia.org

To access chapter objectives, practice tests, weblinks, and flashcards, visit the companion website at **www.ablongman.com/popham5e.**

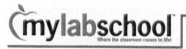

MyLabSchool is a collection of online tools for your success in this course, your licensure exams, and your teaching career. Discover where the classroom comes to life by visiting **www.mylabschool.com** to access the following resources:

■ Video clips from real classrooms

■ An archive of real-life cases

■ Help with your research papers using Research Navigator™

■ Career Center with resources for:

Praxis exams and licensure preparation

Professional portfolio development

Job search and interview techniques

Lesson planning with state standard correlations

10

Affective Assessment

A ffective variables, most educators concede, are important. Students' attitudes toward learning, for example, play a major role in how much learning those students subsequently pursue. The values students have regarding truthfulness and integrity shape their daily conduct. And students' self-esteem, of course, influences almost everything they do. There's little doubt that the affective status of students should concern all educators.

In truth, however, few classroom teachers give explicit attention to influencing their students' attitudes and values. Even fewer classroom teachers actually try to assess the affective status of their students. Certainly, a teacher may observe a student's sour demeanor and conclude he's "out of sorts" or she's "a mite depressed," but how many times have you heard about a teacher who tried to gather *systematic* evidence regarding students' attitudes and interests? Unfortunately, systematic assessment of affect is pretty uncommon.

This chapter will address the issue of affective assessment by providing you with general insights regarding the assessment of students' attitudes, interests, and values. Thereafter, the chapter will give you some practical, step-by-step procedures for gauging students' status regarding a number of educationally important affective variables.

■ Why Assess Affect?

One question you might be asking yourself is, Why assess attitudes at all? Many teachers, particularly those who teach older students, believe that their only educational mission is to increase students' knowledge and skills. Affect, such teachers believe, simply doesn't fall into their proper sphere of influence. However, students who learn to do mathematics like magicians yet abhor mathematics certainly aren't apt to apply the mathematics they've learned. Students who can compose outstanding essays but believe they are "really rotten writers" won't spend much time volitionally churning out essays.

The Importance of Affect

I'd like to get my own bias regarding this issue out on the table so you don't think I'm trying to subliminally influence you. I personally regard affective variables as far more significant than cognitive variables. How many times, for example, have you seen people who weren't all that intellectually "gifted" still succeed because they were highly motivated and hard working? Conversely, how many times have you seen truly able people simply veer away from challenges because they did not consider themselves worthy? Day in and day out, we see the enormous impact people's affective status has on them. Affect is every bit as important as cognitive ability.

Have you ever seen a group of kindergarten students troop off to school loaded with enthusiasm and gumption, only to encounter those same students a few years later and see that a fair number were disenchanted with school and down on themselves? Well, I have. And what's going on with such children is surely taking place in the affective realm. When most kindergartners start school, they are enthused about school and themselves. However, after failing to be successful for a year or two, many of those formerly upbeat children carry around decisively lowered self-concepts. They've tried and been found wanting. Such negative attitudes about self and school will typically influence all of a child's subsequent education. Yet, because few teachers try to assess their students' affective status, most teachers don't know what their students' attitudes, interests, and values really are. This situation, I believe, needs to change.

Spurring Affectively Focused Instruction

Even if there were no such thing as externally imposed "educational accountability" whereby students' performances on high-stakes tests serve as indicators of educational effectiveness, what's on achievement tests would still influence the stuff teachers teach. When I was a high school teacher, I knew what kinds of items I had on my final exams. (That is, I knew in the second year of teaching, after I'd whipped out my first-year final exams only minutes before my students needed to take those exams.) Because I wanted my students to do well on my final exams, I made reasonably sure I spent at least some instructional time on the content covered by the final examinations.

It's the same with affective assessment. Let's say you've installed a fairly straightforward pretest-posttest evaluation design to assess any meaningful changes in your students' responses to an affective inventory regarding how much they are interested in the subject(s) you're teaching. Your recognition that there will be a formal pretest-posttest assessment of students' subject-matter interest

Decision Time

Where Went Wonder?

Lance Larson has decided to try to get an accurate reading of his kindergarten students' attitudes toward school. Although he has worked with kindergartners for the past four years, only recently has Lance become convinced of the importance of student affect.

Because he is dealing with very young children, most of whom can't read when they arrive at Mission Elementary School, Lance uses an orally administered, anonymously completed inventory for which he reads a question to the students and they are to respond by circling either a smiling face or a frowning face. Students respond to one question, and then another, after Lance tells them to "Answer by the bird," "Answer by the star," and so on.

At the end of the first week of school, students' responses to Lance's inventory indicated they really liked school. In fact, 100% of the children responded that they couldn't wait to find out what new things they would learn at school each day. However, three months later, a readministration of the inventory showed students' attitudes toward school seemed to have taken a nosedive. Well over half of his kindergartners indicated they no longer looked forward to coming to school. Almost 75%, in fact, indicated they were often bored in class. Lance was alarmed.

 If you were Lance, what would you decide to do?

will, as surely as school buses run late, influence you to provide instruction so your students will, in fact, become more positive about the subject(s) you're teaching.

In other words, the presence of affective postinstruction measurement will incline you to include affectively focused activities in your instruction. In a sense, you're saying to yourself—and anyone else you care to have understand your instructional planning—affective outcomes are important enough for you to formally assess. You can be assured that what's important enough to be assessed, even if it's measured in your classroom and nowhere else in the world, is likely to influence your instruction. As I confessed earlier, I think affectively focused instruction deals with the kinds of outcomes that are some of the most important we teach.

It has been said *we measure what we treasure*. Well, if we really think affective outcomes are worth promoting, we darn well ought to measure them.

Monitoring Students' Status

In addition to serving as an end-of-instruction target, affective assessment devices, if administered regularly, help teachers determine if modifications in their instructional program are warranted. For example, let's say you're a physics teacher and you want to get a fix on how enthused your students are about continuing their study of physics in college. Ideally, you'd like a fair number of your students to get fairly ecstatic over the raptures of future physics coursework. Suppose each month you employed a brief self-report attitudinal inventory focused on the likelihood of students' pursuing future physics instruction. For illustrative purposes, let's assume in September, 60% of your students registered an interest in taking college physics courses and in October, 65% indicated interest. In November, however, interest in future physics courses nosedived so only 25% of your students signified any interest in college physics. This is a clear message to you that something went on in late October or early November to really turn off your budding Nobel Laureates. A review of your instructional program during that period and some serious effort on your part to generate more interest in postsecondary physics would seem to be warranted. As you can see, periodic monitoring of your students' affective status can assist you in seeing what sorts of shifts in your instructional program might be needed.

In review, there are a number of reasons classroom teachers should devote at least a segment of their assessment program to the measurement of students' affect. If you don't believe your students' attitudes, interests, and values are important, of course, you'll not agree with the views I've expressed. But if you do think student affect is significant, you'll want to learn what kinds of affective variables to assess and how to assess them. That's coming up shortly.

■ The Other Side of the Argument

Before turning to the nuts and bolts of affective assessment, I need to point out that a good many citizens do not share my view regarding the importance of affective assessment and instruction. Particularly in the past few years we have seen the emergence of a vocal group of individuals who have taken strong positions against schools' offering anything other than traditional academic (cognitive) education. Usually representing religious or conservative constituencies, these critics have argued it is the job of the family and church to promote values in children, and any attempt by the schools to systematically modify students' attitudes or values should cease.

I agree with these critics that if any attention to affective outcomes is to be given, it must be focused only on those affective consequences that would be close to universally approved. For example, I regard the promotion of students' positive attitudes toward learning as an affective aspiration almost everyone would support. Similarly, I can't really imagine there are too many people who wouldn't want the schools to nurture students' self-esteem. Yet, I would hate to see educators dabbling with any controversial attitudes or values—that is, those a vast majority of parents wouldn't want their children to possess.

If you decide to devote some of your classroom assessment/instruction time to affective targets, you'll clearly need to consider carefully the legitimacy of the targets you select. And even if you do so, you should recognize there will be some people who may disapprove of such affective education regardless of the care with which you select your affective curricular aims.

■ Which Affective Variables Should Be Assessed?

A Closer Look at Affect

Before discussing the sorts of variables that you, as a classroom teacher, might wish to assess, let's spend just a moment looking at the nature of *affect* itself. The reason such affective variables as students' attitudes, interests, and values are important to us is that those variables typically influence students' future behavior. If you think about this for a bit, you'll realize we don't really care very much, in the abstract, whether students' attitudes toward learning are positive. The reason we want to promote positive attitudes toward learning is because students who have positive attitudes toward learning today will be inclined to pursue learning in the future.

The affective status of students lets us see how students are predisposed to behave subsequently. If we find that students believe healthy bodies are important, those students will be predisposed to maintain their own bodily health in the future. If we find that students have positive attitudes toward persons from other ethnic groups, then in the future such students will be predisposed to behave appropriately toward persons from other ethnic groups. As seen in Figure 10.1, current affective status predicts future behavior.

Do attitudes predict future behavior perfectly? Of course not. But suppose there are 100 third-graders who display very negative attitudes toward violence as a way of settling disputes, and there are 100 third-graders who believe violence is an altogether suitable way of resolving disputes. Probabilistically, in the future there are likely to be fewer violent dispute-resolution behaviors from the first 100 third-graders than from the second. Affective assessment, therefore, allows teachers to get a far-better-than-chance fix on the behavioral dispositions of their students. That's why affective assessment is so important.

As you know, schools have historically focused on cognitive variables. And that's probably the way it's always going to be. Thus, if you are interested in giving some attention to affect in your own classroom, you'll need to select your affective foci judiciously. That's what we'll deal with next. We'll look at attitudes first, then consider interests and values.

Figure 10.1 ■ The Relationship between Current Affect and Future Behavior Wherein an Individual's Affective Status Predicts That Individual's Future Behavior

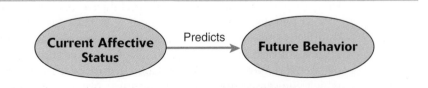

Potential Attitudinal Targets

There are all sorts of possible attitudinal foci for a teacher's instruction. Here are a few of the attitudes most commonly endorsed by teachers as reasonable attitudinal targets:

- *Positive attitudes toward learning.* Students should regard the act of learning positively. Students who are positive today about learning will tend to be tomorrow's learners.
- *Positive attitudes toward self.* Self-esteem is the attitude on which most people's personal worlds turn. Although children's self-esteem is probably influenced more by parents and nonschool events than by teachers, what happens in the classroom can have a significant impact on children's self-esteem.
- *Positive attitudes toward self as a learner.* Self-esteem as a learner is an affective variable over which educators have substantial influence. If students believe they are capable of learning, they will tend to learn.
- *Appropriate attitudes toward those who differ from us.* The more tolerant and accepting students are toward members of other ethnic, gender, national, racial, or religious groups, the more likely those students will behave properly toward such individuals in the future.

There are numerous other subject-specific kinds of attitudes teachers will want to foster. For example, many teachers who deal with language arts will want to enhance students' heightened confidence as writers—that is, students' more positive attitudes toward their own composition capabilities. Science teachers will want to foster students' curiosity. Health education teachers will wish to promote students' accurate perceptions of their vulnerability to health risks such as sexually transmitted diseases. Depending on your own instructional responsibilities, you'll discover there are usually several attitudinal assessment contenders you'll want to consider.

Potential Interest Targets

Students' interests represent another set of potential targets. Clearly, if you're a high school chemistry teacher, you'd like at least some of your students to develop an interest in chemistry. Similarly, teachers of U.S. government would prefer that their students become interested in governmental affairs rather than regard such topics as repugnant. Here, then, are a few illustrations of the kinds of interest targets teachers might consider for possible assessment:

- *Subject-related interests.* Students should regard the subject matter taught (for example, mathematics) as more interesting at the end of instruction than they did when instruction began. At the very least, students should be no less interested in the subject being taught as a consequence of instruction.
- *Interest in reading.* Because of the enormous impact students' reading prowess has on their subsequent lives, we'd like students to be interested in reading and, indeed, enjoy it. Children who read because of their interest will—almost whether they want to or not—become good readers.

- *Interest in emerging technology.* As the world becomes increasingly dependent on technological advances, students who are interested in these sorts of technological improvements are more apt to learn about computers and, as a consequence, be able to utilize such technological tools.

To get a fix on possible interest-focused affective targets that might be suitable for assessment in your particular teaching situation, simply give a good, hard think to the things you'd like to see your students, as a consequence of what goes on in your classroom, become more interested in. It's just that straightforward.

Potential Value Targets

There are all sorts of values to which people subscribe that the schools should have nothing to do with. Most educators agree that political values and religious values, for example, should not be dealt with instructionally in the schools. Whether students turn out to be liberals or conservatives is really none of a teacher's business. And, historically, there's been a long tradition of separating church and state. Teachers, therefore, certainly shouldn't be advocating acceptance of particular religions or rejection of others. Well, then, what sorts of values are sufficiently meritorious and noncontroversial so they could serve as the targets for classroom attention? Here are a few to consider:

- *Honesty.* Students should learn to value honesty in their dealing with others.
- *Integrity.* Students should firmly adhere to their own code of values—for example, moral or artistic values.

- *Justice*. Students should subscribe to the view that all citizens should be the recipients of equal justice from governmental law enforcement agencies.
- *Freedom*. Students should believe that democratic nations must provide the maximum level of freedom to their citizens.

Although these kinds of values may seem to be little more than lofty, flag-waving endorsements of goodness, you may still wish to consider them and similar values for potential effective assessment in your own classroom. If there really are significant values you would like your students to embrace, and those values fall properly in the sphere of what schools should be about, then the possibility of including such values in a classroom assessment program may have real appeal for you.

Don't try to assess too many affective variables. You'd be surprised how quickly you can become overwhelmed with the time required to gather such data, and the time needed to make sense of the data you collect. This is another "less is more" setting in which you should try to get a fix on only a few of the affective dimensions you regard as most important for your students.

■ How Should Affect Be Assessed in Classrooms?

The assessment of affect can be carried out at varying levels of complexity and sophistication. To illustrate, in psychological experiments designed to get a fix on children's honesty, researchers have utilized trained accomplices who contrive elaborate situations where a child can or cannot cheat, then the researchers observe the child's behavior through one-way mirrors in order to draw inferences about the child's tendencies to be honest or dishonest in situations where the attractiveness of the temptations vary. I know few teachers who have the time or inclination to engage in very elaborate assessment of their students' affective status, although I suspect those teachers would know how to use one-way mirrors advantageously.

As a practical matter, the classroom assessment of student affect must be relatively easy to pull off, or it simply isn't going to happen. Teachers are too busy to carry out the galaxy of responsibilities they already face each day. Accordingly, in this chapter I'm only going to set out for you a single, readily accomplishable procedure to assess your students' attitudes and values. If you wish to consider more elaborate and time-demanding ways of measuring your students' affect, there are several excellent volumes cited in the Additional Stuff section at the end of the chapter. The books by Anderson and Bourke (2000) and by Webb and others (1981) are particularly thought provoking.

■ Self-Report Assessment

You can get a decent fix on students' affective status by asking them to complete *self-report inventories.* If you set up the assessment situation so students can respond in a truly anonymous fashion, the data derived from self-report instruments can really be useful to you. Just as importantly, the use of straightforward self-report devices won't be so onerous you become disenchanted with such measurement. Anderson and Bourke (2000) provide a compelling argument in favor of self-report affective measurement by educators.

Likert Inventories

Because of its ready applicability to a variety of affective assessment targets, the approach to attitudinal measurement introduced many years ago by Rensis Likert (1903–1981) is the most widely used. You've probably responded to *Likert inventories* many times in your life. They consist of a series of statements to which you register your agreement or disagreement. For example, you are given a statement such as "Reading this book about classroom assessment represents one of the finest professional experiences of my career." You then choose from a set of options to decide whether you agree or disagree with the statement. The usual options, at least for adults, are *strongly agree, agree, uncertain, disagree,* and *strongly disagree.* (I am altogether confident you would have opted for the *strongly agree* response regarding the previous illustrative statement about this book's impact on your professional life.)

Clearly, depending on the age of the students you're teaching, you'll need to make adjustments in the statements used and in the number and/or phrasing of the response options. For example, with very young children you might need to use brief statements containing very simple words. You might even have to read the statements aloud. Older students might be able to handle the five-choice agreement scale just described, but for younger students you'll most likely want to drop down to three response options (for instance, *agree, don't know,* and *disagree*) or even two response options (perhaps *yes* and *no*). You'll be the best judge of the language level to be used with the students you teach. In general, err in the direction of less-demanding rather than more-demanding language. Incidentally, you could probably win a few faculty-lounge trivia contests by quizzing your colleagues about Likert's first name. Face it, Rensis is not a widely used moniker!

Building a Likert Inventory

Let's look, then, at a simple series of steps you should follow to create a Likert inventory for your own classroom:

1. *Choose the affective variable you want to assess.* Decide what attitude, interest, or value you want to assess, then try to get as clearheaded as you can about what the affective variable truly means. Make certain that the affective variable is *educationally* significant.
2. *Generate a series of favorable and unfavorable statements regarding the affective variable.* For example, if you were interested in students' attitudes regarding reading, you might construct a positive statements such as "I like to read on my own when I have free time" or negative statements such as "People who read for fun are stupid." Try to generate a few more statements than you ultimately plan to use. For students in secondary schools, a 10-item

Likert inventory takes little time to complete. For students at lower grades, you'd probably want to use fewer items, perhaps 5 or 6. Try to construct an approximately equal number of positive and negative statements.

3. *Get several people to classify each statement as positive or negative.* Corral a few colleagues or family members to look at your generated statements and classify each statement as positive or negative. Toss out any statement that isn't *unanimously* classified as positive or negative.

4. *Decide on the number and phrasing of the response options for each statement.* The original Likert inventory had the following five options: SD = Strongly Disagree, D = Disagree, NS = Not Sure, A = Agree, and SA = Strongly Agree. As noted, younger children should employ fewer and, possibly, more simple options. (It is not mandatory to include an "uncertain" or "not sure" option, thereby *forcing* the respondent to register a preference one way or the other, but I usually toss in such an option in my own affective inventories. It seems so much more humane!)

5. *Prepare the self-report inventory, giving students directions regarding how to respond and stipulating that the inventory must be completed anonymously.* If students haven't previously completed such inventories, they'll need clear directions. It is helpful to include an illustration or two of how students might respond. Sample statements about generally known topics, such as foods or movies, work well for such illustrations.

6. *Administer the inventory either to your own students or, if possible (as a try-out), to other students.* If another teacher is willing, try out your inventory with students similar to your own. Based on the responses of those students, you can then improve the inventory before giving it to your own students. If you must use your own students, you can still improve the inventory for use later in the year with the same students or, perhaps, next year with another set of students.

7. *Score the inventories.* Assign points for each student's response to each item based on the *direction* of the statement. For instance, if you are using five response options, you would give five points to *strongly agree* responses to positive statements and also five points to *strongly disagree* responses to negative statements. Thus, for a 10-item inventory the scores could range from 10 to 50. Try to set up your scoring scheme so the higher the score, the more appropriate students' affective status will be.

8. *Identify and eliminate statements that fail to function in accord with the other statements.* If you know how to compute correlation coefficients, simply compute the correlation between students' responses to each item (1, 2, 3, 4, or 5, for example) and their total scores on the inventory (10 to 50). Eliminate those statements whose correlations to the total score are not statistically significant. (This is referred to as "Likert's criterion of internal consistency.") If you don't know how to compute correlation coefficients, simply "eye-ball" students' responses and try to detect statements to which students are responding differently than to the rest of the statements. Dump those statements. (This is referred to as "Likert's criterion of internal consistency for people who don't know diddly about computing correlations.") Then rescore the inventories without the rejected items.

It's really just this simple to bang out a Likert inventory for your own purposes. For each affective variable of interest, you need a different inventory (or at least a different set of items). You can certainly measure several affective variables with different sets of items on the same inventory. The more experience you accumulate in creating Likert inventories, the easier it gets. After a short while, you'll really become quite skilled in whipping out such affective assessment devices.

If you're really under time pressure, and I know of few teachers who aren't, you can even skip some of the eight steps I just listed. For instance, you don't really need to get other people to classify your statements as positive or negative (Step 3) if you don't have the time to do so. And although you'd like to have a formal try-out of the inventory (Step 6), you may not have time to do it. What I'm really trying to suggest is that if you're faced with a choice between (a) skipping some desirable procedural steps and *using* an affective inventory or (b) *not using* an affective inventory because you don't have time to carry out all the recommended procedural steps—do some step skipping!

The essence of this sort of measurement, of course, boils down to the way students who complete the inventory respond to a collection of negative and positive statements. This being so, then the statements in any affective inventory must be created with considerable care. To illustrate, note in the second of the eight steps in the Likert inventory-building model, a series of positive and negative statements must be created. As you can see, a statement must be positive enough (or, in contrast, negative enough) so it doesn't get thrown out during Step 3 because the people helping you can't tell whether the statement is truly positive or negative. Yet, the statement dare not be *too* positive or *too* negative so no student will ever agree (or disagree) with it. Take a look at the two statements about school given below, then decide which statement would elicit a greater *range* of agreement in students' responses:

- *Every day in every way, school is always the most enjoyable part of my day.*
  (Strongly Agree, Agree, Not Sure, Disagree, Strongly Agree)

- *Even though I occasionally find school disagreeable, most of the time I enjoy it.*
  (Strongly Agree, Agree, Not Sure, Disagree, Strongly Agree)

The initial statement is so "goody-goody" that few students are apt to agree with it. In contrast, the second statement has sufficient qualifiers ("occasionally" and "most of the time") so there will most likely be students who will agree with it and also students who will disagree with it. You need to be certain your inventory's statements are constructed so they are neither *too* positive nor *too* negative.

Even though Likert inventories have been around for more than three-quarters of a century (Likert, 1932), I rarely recommend a traditional Likert inventory these days to assess students' affect. As you now see, a Likert inventory is focused on a single affective variable. Thus, Likert inventories require a substantial amount of inventory-development energy from the teacher, and I find most teachers are interested in several, rather than only one, affective variable. Accordingly, I use teachers to employ assessment devices that can simultaneously get at several affective variables, not just one. Let me describe how to build the kind of affective inventory I think will have the most utility for you in your own classroom. As you will see, the assessment strategy being used in this procedure is essentially the same as the one used in a traditional Likert inventory.

Multifocus Affective Inventories

A *multifocus affective inventory* is an assessment device that attempts to collect information about a number of students' affective dispositions. Such inventories must, therefore, reduce the number of statements (items) dealing with a particular affective variable. So, whereas a traditional Likert inventory could devote 10 to 20 items to a single affective dimension, a multifocus affective inventory could contain items measuring only five or six affective dimensions, but assess each one of those with just a few items.

The trade-off is obvious. Will two items dealing with, for example, a student's "interest in science" yield inferences as accurate as a 10-item inventory devoted only to that same affective dimension? Of course not. The key question, however, is the following: Does a teacher really *require* 10 items on an inventory in order to arrive at a sufficiently valid inference regarding a classroom full of students' interest in history? I don't think so.

Remember, all educational measurement devices are much less precise than typically thought by educators and noneducators alike. Affective assessment is no exception. This issue boils down to the following question: If you're trying to get a fix on the affective status of an entire class of students, what's the minimum number of items (statements) you'll be willing to rely on? Having dealt with this issue in my own classes more than a few times, for me the answer turns out to be *two*. That's right; I think I can garner sufficient insights from my students' responses to two affect-related items—one stated positively and one stated negatively—to come up with a defensible inference about my students' affect.

If you regard two items per affective focus as being too skimpy, then you might bump that number up to four items per affective focus. By doing so, of course, this will either (1) reduce the number of affective dimensions you can address in an inventory or (2) make your inventory so long that students, having seen the numerous upcoming responses they must supply, will often race rapidly through such a lengthy inventory and, thereby, reduce the thoughtfulness of their responses to all of the items. You'll get a better idea about how to create a multifocus affective inventory if I supply you with, as I did for Likert inventories, a step-by-step construction procedure—along with an illustrative inventory of this type.

Building a Multifocus Affective Inventory

Here, then, is a five-step process for creating multifocus affective inventories suitable for classroom use.

1. *Select the affective variables to measure.* In recognition that you will be devoting only a small number of items to each affective variable you choose, you'll need to identify the educationally significant attitudes, interests, or values about which you will ask students to respond.

2. *Determine how many items to allocate to each affective variable.* You must include an equal number of positive *and* negative statements for each affective variable you choose. For openers, start with a minimum of two items per variable. Then, if you decide you need to add more items per variable, increase the number of items in multiples of two. For instance, with two items per affective variable, you would use one positively phrased statement and one negatively phrased statement. For four items per affective variable, you would use two positive statements and two negative statements. In a given affective inventory, incidentally, there is no need to devote an identical number of items to each affective variable being assessed. So you might attempt to measure several variables with two items per variable, but allocate four items to other variables being measured in the same inventory. The choice regarding numbers of items you'll need hinges on your judgment regarding the minimum number of items necessary to yield reasonably accurate inferences about a student group's affective status with respect to a particular affective variable.

3. *Create a series of positive and negative statements related to each affective variable.* The statements in a multifocus affective inventory are similar to those used in Likert inventories. Yet, because you are attempting to gauge your students' affective dispositions with only a few items, even greater care should be taken to craft the statements so they are apt to elicit differential responses from students. All of these statements (items) should be scattered randomly throughout the inventory—that is, not placed in any sort of identifiable groups related to a particular affective dimension.

4. *Determine the number and phrasing of students' response options.* Identical to Step 4 for creating Likert inventories, at this point you need to determine whether you'll use three, four, or five response options for students to register agreement/disagreement with the inventory's statements. You'll also need to decide whether you're using the traditional Likert responses (such as "strongly agree") or some sort of alternative responses (such as "true for me").

5. *Create clear directions for the inventory and an appropriate presentation format.* Directions for affective inventories should be given more attention than is usually allotted by those who develop typical classroom achievement tests. Students are often unfamiliar with these sorts of affective assessment devices and, therefore, need to understand what they're being asked to do. Be certain to include (a) lucid directions about how to respond; (b) at least one sample item; (c) a request for students to supply anonymous, honest responses; and (d) a reminder there are no right or wrong answers to the inventory's items.

Please refer to the illustrative multifocus affective inventory presented in Figure 10.2. This inventory was developed for use with students in grades 4 through 6 and was intended to allow teachers to get a fix on students' sentiments regarding three subject areas (science, mathematics, and social studies) as well as three important skills students need to acquire (reading, writing, and making oral presentations). In addition, the inventory seeks students' responses about school in general. In all, then, the 14-item inventory in Figure 10.2 tries to tap seven affective variables by using two items per variable.

Spend just a few moments looking at the items in the Figure 10.2 inventory. Note, for instance, each positively phrased statement regarding a particular variable is balanced by a counterpart statement that's phrased negatively. To illustrate, Statement 5 is a negative statement about giving oral reports, but Statement 11 is a

Figure 10.2 ■ An Illustrative Multifocus Affective Inventory for Students in Grades 4–6

SCHOOL AND ME

Directions: Please indicate how much the statements in this inventory are true for you. Some of the statements are positive and some are negative. Decide whether each statement is true *for you*. There are no right or wrong answers, so answer honestly. Do not write your name on the inventory. Only make X marks.

Here is a sample:

	Response (one per statement)		
	Very true for me.	**Not true for me.**	**I'm not sure.**
I like to go to the movies.	☒	☐	☐

When you are finished, a student will collect your inventory and place it and all other completed inventories in a sealed envelope that will be taken by the student directly to the principal's office. Thank you for your help.

	Response (one per statement)		
Statements	**Very true for me.**	**Not true for me.**	**I'm not sure.**
1. In general, I like school a lot.	☐	☐	☐
2. I like to learn about scientific things.	☐	☐	☐
3. I can write good reports and stories.	☐	☐	☐
4. I don't like to read.	☐	☐	☐
5. I don't like to speak in front of the class.	☐	☐	☐
6. I think that doing mathematics is fun.	☐	☐	☐
7. I like when we learn about social studies.	☐	☐	☐
8. I don't want to grow up to be a scientist.	☐	☐	☐
9. I really don't like to write very much.	☐	☐	☐
10. I like to read books when I have the time.	☐	☐	☐
11. I usually enjoy speaking in front of other students.	☐	☐	☐
12. I don't like to do mathematics problems.	☐	☐	☐
13. When we do social studies in school, I don't like it.	☐	☐	☐
14. Overall, I don't enjoy school very much.	☐	☐	☐

positive statement regarding that same skill. Note also the two statements for each variable need *not* be mirror-image contradictions such as "I like school" versus "I don't like school."

Multifocus affective inventories are scored in the same way Likert inventories are scored: Points are awarded for students' agreement with positive statements and also for students' disagreement with negative statements. So, for example, if there were five agreement options available ranging from strong agreement to strong disagreement in an inventory using only two items per affected variable, you would assign a maximum of five points per item and a minimum of one point per item. Thus, focusing on a pair of items dealing with, for instance, students' interest in science, the scores on this two-item pair could range from a high of 10 to a low of 2.

Perhaps you are uncomfortable about arriving at inferences for an entire class of students based on only two items. But the purpose of this sort of assessment is to give *you* insights regarding your students' affect. If the inference you come up with based on only a pair of items is way out of whack with your own best judgment about your students' affective learnings, then treat the two-item data with a slug of suspicion. *You* are always the decision-maker in your class. I promise you that insights based even on two-item inventories—administered to a whole group of students—will often prove useful to you.

The Importance of Genuine Anonymity

In order for you to draw accurate inferences about your students' affective status based on their responses to self-report inventories, it is clearly necessary for students to *respond truthfully* to your affective inventories. Unfortunately, many students tend to provide what are referred as **socially desirable responses** to affective self-report devices. In other words, many students are inclined to respond in the way they think you want them to respond. Students are particularly apt to provide socially desirable responses if they believe the teacher can trace their responses. Consequently, to increase the likelihood that students will respond honestly to your affective inventories, it is imperative you not only make all students' responses anonymous but you also employ as many procedures as possible so most students regard their responses as truly untraceable.

Among the more simple but effective **anonymity-enhancement procedures** you might want to consider are these:

1. *Directions.* Make sure the directions for your affective inventories stress the importance of honest answers and that students are not to put their names on their inventories.
2. *Response restrictions.* Set up your inventories so the *only* form of student response is to be check marks, circling of preferred answers, and so on. Prohibit students from writing any words whatsoever on their inventories. Because students believe the teacher may figure out who supplied which inventory by recognizing students' handwriting, don't permit any handwriting whatsoever on affective inventories.

3. *Collection.* Install a procedure whereby students deposit their completed inventories in a collection box, or have a student (not one thought to be your "pet" student) collect the completed inventories. Announce *before* students start to fill out the inventories that one of these collection methods will be employed.

As you can see, you must try to make sure your students really don't think there's any way to trace their responses back to them. Even under those circumstances, this doesn't ensure that students will respond truthfully. However, well-conceived anonymity-enhancement techniques increase the odds students will respond honestly.

When to Assess Affect

When should classroom teachers assess their students' affective status? Well, for openers, it seems important to set up at least a preinstruction and a postinstruction measure of students' attitudes, interests, and/or values. Thus, for elementary

Parent Talk

"You're messing with my child's head," was the first comment you heard from Mrs. Jillian, Paul's mother, when she telephoned you at school during your after-school planning period. Mrs. Jillian then continued by saying she had heard from Paul that you were getting students to fill out "attitude tests" that try to find out "whether kids have the right attitudes." Mrs. Jillian concluded by asking, "How dare you delve in Paul's value and attitudes! Isn't this something his dad and I should be influencing?"

▶ *If I were you, here's how I'd respond to Mrs. Jillian:*

"I agree completely with you, Mrs. Jillian, about whose right it is to influence Paul's values and attitudes. That responsibility is yours and Mr. Jillian's. But I have a hunch you may not have a clear picture of what I'm trying to do in Paul's class. Let me explain.

"As you may know, children at Paul's age often become disinterested in certain subjects, especially mathematics and science. What I've been trying to do is determine ways I can help improve or sustain my students' interest in science and mathematics. I've been administering *anonymous* attitude inventories related to math and science on a pretest and posttest basis—that is, in the fall and in the spring. But I'm using the results of those anonymous inventories not to influence the attitudes or values of Paul or any other child. What I'm trying to do is figure out how my own teaching can engender more interest, from the entire class, in science and mathematics.

"I would *never* try to influence a value or attitude that falls within your family's purview. But I'm sure you'd like Paul, and the other students in his class, to regard science and mathematics positively, not negatively. Whether the children eventually pursue careers related to science or mathematics will, of course, be up to them and their families."

▶ *Now, how would you respond to Mrs. Jillian?*

teachers teaching students in self-contained classrooms, an affective assessment at the start of the school year and, again, at its close will allow teachers to discern any meaningful changes in students' affect. Ideally, however, teachers can engage in occasional "affective dip sticking" to monitor students' affect. For example, every couple of months, a teacher might measure students' self-esteem as learners as well as their attitudes regarding learning. If these occasional assessments suggest inappropriate affective changes are occurring, the teacher may wish to modify affect-related aspects of the instructional program.

In the next section of the chapter, you'll discover that you can often *sample* your students' affective status rather than measure all students' affective status. Thus, some of the suggested affective dip sticking might be carried out only with a portion of your students.

■ What Kind of Inferences Are at Stake in Affective Assessment?

When teachers use cognitively oriented tests, they typically make inferences about individual students. If, for instance, Harvey Haley earns a high score on a mathematics test, the teacher makes an inference about Harvey's possession of certain mathematics skills and knowledge. Teachers need to make inferences about individual students in order to make decisions about how to provide suitable instruction for those students.

Teachers also aggregate students' individual scores on achievement tests to arrive at group-focused inferences. For instance, if most students in a history class performed poorly on a start-of-the-term achievement pretest, yet most students topped a comparable posttest administered near the term's conclusion, the teacher would conclude that the students, as a group, had learned substantially more about history.

It's different with affect. Whereas cognitive tests (and, in most cases, psychomotor tests) are measures of students' *optimum performance,* affective inventories strive to measure students' *typical performance.* Remembering that when students complete most affective devices, those results don't count toward the students' grade, so self-report assessment offers students a wonderful opportunity to distort their responses. Thus, there's a strong likelihood that at least some students won't respond honestly. As a consequence, inferences about the affective status of *individual* students (based on a student's responses to an affective inventory) are risky.

Besides, instructional decisions about individual students based on affective assessment devices are rare. If Harry Helms knows history well, but happens to hate it, few teachers would give Harry a low grade in history based on his disdain for "dead folks' foolishness."

In contrast, however, teachers often make instructional decisions about what goes on in class based on aggregated affective data. Assuming that there will be a small number of students who supply inaccurate responses, it is still reasonable to assume that the total collectivity of students' responses will permit meaningful *group-focused inferences.* And that's the kind of inferences you should be making

but what does this have to do with
Teaching?

I know very few teachers who don't believe, at some level, that student affect is important. Most teachers realize that if students learn to detest schooling, it's unlikely those students will wind up near the top of any academic sweepstakes. Most chemistry teachers want their students to groove on chemistry. Most math teachers want their students to get mildly ecstatic over the relationships nestled in the theorem tumbled onto by Pythagoras some 2,500 years ago. Yet, although most teachers recognize that students' interests, attitudes, and values are important, few teachers deliberately strive to promote appropriate affect in their students.

One of the reasons for this neglect of affect is that students' affective dispositions often get lost in the curricular roads today's teachers must travel. There is so much knowledge and so many skills that society wants today's students to master. And the current accountability pressures for teachers to boost students' test scores have made it even less likely teachers will have time to promote positive student affect. It's easy to see how affect gets overlooked, even by teachers who recognize its importance. And that's where affective assessment arrives to save the day. Even if a teacher uses only one self-report inventory, at the start of a term and at its conclusion, the *presence* of this assessment instrument will almost certainly incline the teacher to think about the degree to which any classroom activities are being directed toward the promotion of appropriate affective outcomes.

Affective assessment instruments, even a five-item Likert inventory, will sensitize the teacher to affect's importance. And such sensitized teachers will typically devote at least *some* effort to the promotion of the kinds of student attitudes, interests, and values that—even more than the cognitive content we cram into their cute little heads—will influence their lives.

when you use affective assessment instruments. Because I've already pointed out that affective inventories must be administered anonymously, you've surely recognized that getting a fix on a particular student's affective status is literally impossible. Anonymity is, after all, anonymity.

However, there's another good reason for arriving at only group-focused affective inferences. Even if you were to use all sorts of anonymity-enhancement procedures when you administer any affective inventory, some students will *still* not respond honestly. Certain students will be fearful of offending you in any way, even cloaked by anonymity, and thus will respond more positively than they would if they were being completely truthful. Interestingly, however, there also some students who will use their anonymity cloaks as an opportunity to "get even" with you for your real or imagined shortcomings. Such students will then toss more negativity your way than they really feel. Will these too-positive or too-negative responses cancel each other out perfectly? Of course not. But they will do at least some cancelling out and, as a consequence, should allow you to put greater confidence in your students' *average* response as a reflection of the entire group's affective status.

Affective assessment devices are simply too crude to permit individual-focused inferences. In aggregate, however, you ought to be able to make some very solid judgments about how your students, as a group, are affectively disposed. This is why, in some cases, you can collect affective data from only, say, half your class yet still make a fairly accurate inference about the group based on responses from the sample. Sample-based, en route affective assessment of your students, especially as a way of coming up with dip-stick inferences about those students, really works quite well.

■ What Do Classroom Teachers Really Need to Know about Affective Assessment?

The most important thing you need to know about affective assessment is that if you don't measure your students' affective status in a systematic fashion, you're far less likely to emphasize affect instructionally. Moreover, without systematic affective assessment, you're not apt to have a very decent fix on the affective consequences, possibly unintentional, that you're having on your students.

If you do decide to engage in some affective measurement in your own classes, you'll be much better off if you rely on fairly straightforward self-report instruments (Likert inventories or multifocus affective inventories) rather than trying to employ some exotic affective measurement strategies that are both time consuming and, at the same time, yield inferences of arguable validity. You also need to know affective assessment devices are too imprecise to allow you to make inferences about individual students. Group-focused inferences are as far as you should go in the affective realm.

There's one other thing teachers ought to recognize about the assessment of affect—namely, that most teachers do not possess even a foggy notion about how to promote affect *instructionally*. If teachers actually decide to measure important student affect, they'll typically need some solid professional-development support to learn how to alter students' attitudes, values, and interests. There are a number of instructional techniques for doing so, but most teachers are unaware of those affective-focused instructional procedures.

■ Chapter Summary

The chapter was initiated by your congenial author's unabashed endorsement of the instructional importance of affect and, as a consequence, the importance of assessing students' affective status. It was suggested that the use of affective assessment in classrooms would incline teachers to address affective goals instructionally. It was also argued that if teachers monitor their students' affective status, instructional modifications can be made whenever inappropriate or insufficient affective shifts in students are occurring. Affective variables were described as important predictors of individuals' future behaviors because people's affective status reveals their behavioral dispositions. It was also pointed out, however, that there are vocal groups whose members oppose instructional attention to affect.

Regarding the kinds of affective variables to assess in one's classroom, a series of potential attitudinal, interest, and value foci were presented. Teachers were urged to select only a few, highly meaningful affective variables rather than so many as to induce affective overwhelm.

Self-report assessment procedures were recommended as the most practical way to gather affective data in classrooms. Likert inventories were suggested as a data-gathering device for assessing affective variables. An eight-step procedure for developing Likert inventories was described. Multifocus affective inventories were recommended over Likert inventories on the practical ground that Likert inventories assess only a single affective dimension. Teachers are, it was argued, usually interested in more than one affective variable. A five-step process for constructing multifocus affective inventories was described. Anonymity was identified as an indispensable component of appropriate affective assessment. Several anonymity-enhancement procedures were described. It was also suggested that affective assessments be made prior to and at the conclusion of instruction as well as in the form of occasional affective dip sticking.

Finally, the nature of affective inferences was explored. It was argued the imprecision of affective assessment devices should require teachers to make group-focused inferences rather than inferences about individual students.

 ## Self-Check

For this chapter's self-check exercises, you'll be presented with descriptions of fictitious teachers engaged in some form of affective assessment. Based on what you've read in the chapter (which should be *every single word and punctuation mark*), critique the actions of the teachers described in the following scenarios.

Scenario One

Molly Muggins, having read a chapter such as the one you've just about finished, has jumped into affective assessment with both feet. She measures her third-grade students' attitudes toward reading, writing, mathematics, science, and social studies every month. Molly's students are asked to complete the following sentence for each of the five subjects: My current opinion of (*name of subject*) is:

_____

The monthly affective assessment takes only about 10 minutes. Molly has identified certain students who have particularly negative reactions toward particular subject areas. She intends to work individually with these students in an attempt to foster more positive attitudes.

What do you think of Molly's affective assessment efforts?

Scenario Two

Having decided to employ a Likert inventory for his affective assessments, Alex Allen, an English teacher, decided to focus on his students' confidence as writers. He then authored 10 positive statements such as "When I have to write something, I know I can," and 10 negative statements such as "If I'm called on to do a written report, I really panic." Alex mixed up the order of the 20 statements, then asked three other English teachers to classify each statement as positive or negative. Because three supposedly negative statements and two supposedly positive statements were classified differently by his three co-workers, Alex tossed out those five statements.

He decided to use a five-point response scale—namely, *strongly agree, agree, uncertain, disagree,* and *strongly disagree.* Alex then developed directions for his inventory, which he entitled *You and Composition.* The directions explained the response procedures and made it clear there were no right or wrong answers. The directions also indicated students were to respond anonymously and to deposit their completed inventories in a specially provided collection box. Because he had mixed up the 15 remaining statements (8 positive and 7 negative), he made sure his scoring key coincided with the proper positive and negative statements.

One of the other English teachers in his school offered Alex the opportunity to try out his under-developed affective assessment instrument to see how it worked. Alex jumped at the chance and administered the inventory to 31 of the other teacher's students. In looking over the results, Alex identified 2 negative and 3 positive statements that didn't seem to function like the rest of the statements. Accordingly, he dumped those statements and ended up with a 10-item Likert inventory he intends to use with his class both before he gets into a major unit on composition and, a month later, when the unit has been completed.

What do you think of Alex's efforts to create a Likert inventory?

Scenario Three

Carl Klevins, a woodshop instructor, is immensely interested in affect. Because fewer and fewer students are signing up for his woodshop classes, Carl strives to promote subject-approaching tendencies on the part of his students. "I want my students, boys and girls alike, to become truly enthralled with the feel of sawdust in their pockets and the sound of other students using the woodshop's lathe." Carl spends at least five minutes per week jotting down in his notebook the behaviors that indicate to him certain students are responding positively to woodshop activities.

What do you think of Carl's way of getting a fix on his students' attitudes?

? Pondertime

1. Some citizens are adamantly opposed to having the schools engage in any kind of systematic effort to influence students' attitudes or values. What do you suppose might be the reasons for their resistance to affective instruction and, most probably, to affective assessment as well?

2. Suppose you are an elementary teacher and you've decided to use a multi-focus affective inventory on a pretest-posttest basis for that school year. Assuming that you will measure each affective variable you assess with either two items or four items, and you want to assess only a half-dozen affective variables, what variables would you choose to include in your inventory?

3. Throughout the chapter, a strong preference for self-report assessment devices was registered in contrast to more elaborate exotic assessment schemes. Do you agree with that position? Why or why not?

4. Can you think of procedures, other than those cited in the chapter, to enhance students' perceptions that their responses are truly anonymous?

5. Although the chapter suggested that group-focused inferences should be made from affective assessment devices, can you think of any defensible ways that teachers could get a decent fix on an individual student's attitudes and values? If so, how?

Self-Check Key

Scenario One

Molly messed up on a monthly basis. By requiring students to write out their responses, anonymity was blown. It's not even clear that students weren't supposed to put their names on their responses. In addition, Molly appears to be making individually focused inferences about how much certain subjects are liked. At best, even if she cleaned up her measurement act, Molly should only draw group-focused inferences. Molly's affective assessment efforts were simply not stellar.

Scenario Two

Alex was pretty much on target the whole way through. Indeed, he so compliantly adhered to the eight steps suggested on pages 222 to 223 for creating Likert inventories, you might conclude he had read the chapter.

Scenario Three

There are some teachers who can make extremely insightful judgments about students' unobservable affective status based on certain observable acts of students. Unfortunately, there are probably just as many teachers who are likely to make the wrong inferences about students' affect based on their observed behaviors. One of the more vexing difficulties to be coped with when using observation-based assessments of affect is that people often see what they want to see in a given situation. Teachers are no different. Thus, although we're glad to see Carl's attentiveness to affect, his assessment approach leaves a load to be desired.

■ Additional Stuff

Anderson, Lorin W., and Sid F. Bourke. (2000). *Assessing Affective Characteristics in the Schools* (2nd ed.). Mahwah, NJ: Lawrence Erlbaum.

Apter, Terri. (2006). "Resolving the Confidence Crisis." *Educational Leadership, 63*, no. 7 (April): 42–46.

Brookhart, Susan M., Janet M. Walsh, and Wayne A. Zientarski. (2006). "The Dynamics of Motivation and Effort for Classroom Assessments in Middle School Science and Social Studies." *Applied Measurement in Education, 19*, no. 2: 151–184.

Inlay, Linda. (2003). "Values: The Implicit Curriculum." *Educational Leadership, 60*, no. 6 (March): 69–71.

Likert, R. (1932). "A Technique for the Measurement of Attitudes." *Archives of Psychology, 140*.

McTighe, Jay, and Ken O'Connor. (2005). "Seven Practices for Effective Learning." *Educational Leadership, 63*, no. 3 (November): 10–17.

Webb, Eugene J., Donald T. Campbell, Richard D. Schwartz, Lee Sechreat, and Janet Belew Grove. (1981). *Nonreactive Measures in the Social Sciences* (2nd ed.). Boston: Houghton Mifflin.

■ Nonprint Stuff

Popham, W. James. *Improving Instruction: Start With Student Attitudes* (Videotape #ETVT-19). Los Angeles: IOX Assessment Associates.

Popham, W. James. *Assessing Student Attitudes: A Key to Increasing Achievement* (Videotape #ETVT-20). Los Angeles: IOX Assessment Associates.

To access chapter objectives, practice tests, weblinks, and flashcards, visit the companion website at **www.ablongman.com/popham5e.**

MyLabSchool is a collection of online tools for your success in this course, your licensure exams, and your teaching career. Discover where the classroom comes to life by visiting **www.mylabschool.com** to access the following resources:

- Video clips from real classrooms
- An archive of real-life cases
- Help with your research papers using Research Navigator™
- Career Center with resources for:
    Praxis exams and licensure preparation
    Professional portfolio development
    Job search and interview techniques
    Lesson planning with state standard correlations

11

Improving Teacher-Developed Assessments

I f you've ever visited the manuscript room of the British Museum, you'll recall seeing handwritten manuscripts authored by some of the superstars of English literature. It's a moving experience. Delightfully, the museum presents not only the final versions of famed works by such authors as Milton and Keats but also the early drafts of those works. It is somewhat surprising and genuinely encouraging to learn those giants of literature didn't get it right the first time. They had to cross out words, delete sentences, and substitute phrases. Many of the museum's early drafts are genuinely messy, reflecting all sorts of rethinking on the part of the author. Well, if the titans of English literature had to revise their early drafts, is it at all surprising that teachers usually need to spruce up their classroom assessments?

This chapter is designed to provide you with several procedures by which you can improve the assessment instruments you develop. I can promise you if you use the chapter's recommended procedures, your tests will get better. Yet, they'll probably never make it to the British Museum—unless you carry them in when visiting.

There are two general improvement strategies to be described in this chapter. First, you'll learn about *judgmental item improvement* procedures in which the chief means of sharpening your tests is human judgment—your own and that of others. Second, you'll be considering *empirical item improvement* procedures based on students' responses to your assessment procedures. Ideally, if time permits and your motivation abounds, you can use both forms of test-improvement procedures for your own classroom assessment devices.

But I really need to give you a heads-up regarding the upcoming *empirical* item-repair procedures. What you'll recognize when you get into that section, starting on page 242, is there are *numbers* in it. (There's even a formula or two.) Upon encountering this material, perhaps you'll conclude I've tricked you—lulled you into a sense of nonnumeric complacency for 10 chapters—then blindsided you with a quagmire of quantitative crud. But that's not so. Don't be intimidated by the last half of the chapter's quantitative stuff. It truly constitutes a fairly Mickey-Mouse level of number-nudging. Just take it slow and easy. You'll survive surprisingly well. I promise.

Judgmentally Based Improvement Procedures

Human judgment, although it sometimes gets us in trouble, is a remarkably useful tool. Judgmental approaches to test improvement can be carried out quite systematically or, in contrast, rather informally. Judgmental assessment-improvement strategies differ chiefly according to who is supplying the judgments. There are three sources of test-improvement judgments you should consider—those supplied by (1) yourself, (2) your colleagues, and (3) your students. We'll consider each of these potential judgment sources separately.

Judging Your Own Assessment Instruments

Let's suppose you've created a 70-item combination short-answer and multiple-choice examination for a U.S. government class and, having administered it, you want to improve the examination for your next year's class. We'll assume during item development you did a reasonable amount of in-process sharpening up of the items so they represented what, at the time, was your best effort. Now, however, you have an opportunity to revisit the examination to see if its 70 items are all that marvelous. It's a good thing to do.

Let's consider another kind of assessment. Suppose you have devised what you think are pretty decent directions for your students to follow when preparing portfolios or when responding to tasks in a performance test. Even if you regard those directions as suitable, it's always helpful to review such directions after a time to see if you can now detect shortcomings that, at the time you originally prepared the set of directions, escaped your attention.

As you probably know from other kinds of writing, it is almost always the case that if you return to one of your written efforts after it has had time to "cool off," you're likely to spot deficits that, in the heat of the original writing, weren't apparent to you. However, beyond a fairly casual second look, you'll typically be able to improve your assessment procedures even more if you approach this test-improvement task systematically. To illustrate, you could use specific review criteria when you judge your earlier assessment efforts. If a test item or a set of directions falls short on any criterion, you should obviously do some modifying. Presented here are five review criteria you might wish to consider if you set out systematically to improve your classroom assessment procedures:

- *Adherence to item-specific guidelines and general item-writing commandments.* When you appraise your assessment procedures, it will be useful to review briefly the general item-writing commandments supplied earlier (in

Chapter 6) as well as the particular item-writing guidelines provided for the specific kind of item(s) you've developed. If you now see violations of the principles set forth in either of those two sets of directives, fix the flaws.

- *Contribution to score-based inference.* Recall that the real reason teachers assess students is in order to arrive at score-based inferences about the status of students. Therefore, it will be helpful for you to reconsider each aspect of a previously developed assessment procedure to see whether it does, in fact, really contribute to the kind of inference about your students you wish to draw.
- *Accuracy of content.* There's always the possibility that previously accurate content has now been superseded or contradicted by more recent content. Be sure to see if the content you included earlier in the assessment instrument is still accurate and that your answer key is still correct.
- *Absence of content lacunae.* This review criterion gives me a chance to use one of my favorite words, the plural form of *lacuna* which, incidentally, means a *gap.* Although *gaps* would have done the job in this instance, you'll admit *gaps* look somewhat tawdry when stacked up against *lacunae.* (This, of course, is a norm-referenced contrast.)

  Hindsight is a nifty form of vision. Thus, when you take a second look at the content coverage represented in your assessment instrument, you may discover you originally overlooked some important content. This review criterion is clearly related to an earlier review criterion regarding the assessment's contribution to the score-based inference that you want to make. Any meaningful lacunae in content will obviously reduce the accuracy of your inference.
- *Fairness.* Although you should clearly have tried to eradicate any bias in your assessment instruments when you originally developed them, there's always the chance you overlooked something. Undertake another bias review just to make certain you've been as attentive to bias elimination as you possibly can be.

I can personally attest to a case of bias blindness when I authored a textbook on educational evaluation in the seventies. Recognizing that a number of women at the time were beginning to take offense at authors' use of masculine pronouns when referring to unnamed individuals (for example, "The student lost *his* lunch"), I had assiduously written the textbook so that all my illustrative make-believe people were plural. I never had to use *his* or *her* because I could always use *their.* After churning out the last chapter, I was smugly proud of my pluralization prowess. Yet, having been so attentive to a pronoun issue that might offend some women, I blithely included a cartoon in the book that showed scantily clad females cavorting before male members of a school board. Talk about dumb! If only I'd taken a serious second look at the book before it hit the presses, I might have spotted my insensitive error. As it was, because the cartoon appeared in all copies of the first edition (not the second!), I received more than a few heated, and quite deserved, complaints from readers—both male and female!

I'm not suggesting you fill out an elaborate rating form for each of these five review criteria—with each criterion requiring a numerical rating. Rather, I'm recommending that you seriously think about these five criteria before you tackle any judgmental review of a previously developed assessment instrument.

Collegial Judgments

If you are working with a colleague whose judgment you trust, it's often helpful to ask this person to review your assessment procedures. To get the most mileage out of such a review, you'll probably need to provide your co-worker with at least a brief description of review criteria such as the five previously cited ones—that is, (1) adherence to item-specific guidelines and general item-writing commandments, (2) contribution to score-based inference, (3) accuracy of content, (4) absence of content lacunae, and (5) fairness. You will need to describe to your colleague the key inference(s) you intend to base on the assessment procedure. It will also be useful to your colleague if you identify the decisions that will, thereafter, be influenced by your inferences about students.

I've found that collegial judgments are particularly helpful to teachers who employ many performance tests or who use portfolio assessments. Most of the empirically based improvement procedures you'll be learning about later in the chapter are intended to be used with more traditional sorts of items such as those found in multiple-choice exams. For portfolio assessment and performance tests, judgmental approaches will often prove more useful.

Remember, if *you* are the creator of the portfolio assessment or performance tests you're setting out to improve, you're apt to be biased in their favor. After all, parents usually adore their progeny. What you need is a good, hard, *nonpartisan* review of what you've been up to assessment-wise.

To do a thorough job of helping you review your assessment approaches, of course, your colleague will need to put in some time. In fairness, you'll probably obliged to toss in a *quid pro quo* or two whereby you return the favor by reviewing your colleague's tests (or by resolving a pivotal personal crisis in your colleague's private life). If your school district is large enough, you might also have access to some central-office supervisorial personnel who know something about assessment. Here's a neat opportunity to let them earn their salaries—get them to review your assessment procedures. It is often asserted that another pair of eyes can help improve almost any written document. This doesn't necessarily mean the other pair of eyes see accurately while yours are in need of contact lenses. You should listen to what other reviewers say, but be guided by your own judgments about the virtues of their suggestions.

Student Judgments

When teachers set out to improve assessment procedures, a rich source of data is often overlooked because teachers typically fail to secure advice from their students. Yet, because students have experienced test items in a most meaningful context, more or less as an executionee experiences a firing squad, student judgments can provide useful insights. Student reactions can help you spot shortcomings in

Figure 11.1 ■ An Illustrative Item-Improvement
Questionnaire for Students

Item-Improvement Questionnaire for Students
1. If any of the items seemed confusing, which ones were they?
2. Did any items have more than one correct answer? If so, which ones?
3. Did any items have no correct answers? If so, which ones?
4. Were there words in any items that confused you? If so, which ones?
5. Were the directions for the test, or for particular subsections, unclear? If so, which ones?

particular items and in other features of your assessment procedures such as a test's directions or the time you've allowed for completing the test.

The kinds of data secured from students will vary, depending on the type of assessment procedure being used, but questions such as those on the item-improvement questionnaire in Figure 11.1 can profitably be given to students after they have completed an assessment procedure. Although the illustrative questionnaire in Figure 11.1 is intended for use with a selected-response type of test, only minor revisions would be needed to make it suitable for a constructed-response test, a performance test, or a portfolio assesment system.

It is important to let students finish a test prior to their engaging in such a judgmental exercise. (Note, once more, the possessive pronoun modifying the gerund *engaging*. You are, obviously, reading some grammatically top-drawer stuff here.) If students are asked to *simultaneously* play the roles of test takers and test improvers, they'll probably botch up both tasks. No student should be expected to serve two such functions, at least at the same time.

Simply give students the test as usual, collect their answer sheets or test booklets, and provide them with new, blank test booklets. *Then* distribute a questionnaire, such as the one seen earlier. In other words, ask students to play examinees and item reviewers, but to play these roles consecutively, not simultaneously.

Now, how do you treat students' reactions to test items? Let's say you're a classroom teacher and a few students come up with a violent castigation of one of your favorite items. Do you automatically buckle by scrapping or revising the item? Of course not; teachers are made of sterner stuff. Perhaps the students were miffed about the item because they didn't know how to answer it. One of the best ways for students to escape responsibility for a dismal test performance is to assail the test itself. Teachers should anticipate a certain amount of carping from low-scoring students.

Yet, after allowing for a reasonable degree of complaining, student reactions can sometimes provide useful insights for teachers. A student-castigated item may, indeed, deserve castigation. To overlook students as a source of judgmental test-improvement information, for either selected-response or constructed-response items, would clearly be an error.

To review, then, judgmentally based test-improvement procedures can rely on the judgments supplied by you, your colleagues, or your students. In the final analysis, you will be the decision maker regarding whether to modify your assessment procedures. Nonetheless, it is typically helpful to have others react to your tests.

■ Empirically Based Improvement Procedures

In addition to judgmentally based methods of improving your assessment procedures, there are improvement approaches based on the empirical data students supply when they respond to the assessment instruments you've developed. Let's turn, then, to the use of student-response data in the improvement of assessment procedures. A variety of empirical item-improvement techniques have been well honed over the years. We will consider the more traditional item-analysis procedures first, turning later to a few more recent wrinkles for using student data to improve a teacher's classroom assessments procedures.

Most of the procedures employed to improve classroom assessments on the basis of students' responses to those assessments rely on numbers. And I recognize there are some readers of this book (*you* may be one) who are definitely put off by numbers. I sometimes believe there is a secret cult among teachers and prospective teachers who have taken a "tremble pledge"—that is, a vow to tremble when encountering any numerical value larger than a single digit (a number larger than 9). If you are one of these mathphobics, I beg you to stay calm because the numbers you'll be encountering in this and later chapters will really be Simple-Simon stuff. Tremble not. It'll be pain free. Just work through the easy examples and you'll survive with surprising ease.

Difficulty Indices

One useful index of an item's quality is its *difficulty*. The most commonly employed item-difficulty index, often referred to simply as a *p value,* is calculated as follows:

$$\text{Difficulty } p \; = \; \frac{R}{T}$$

where R = the number of students responding correctly (right) to an item.

T = the total number of students responding to the item.

To illustrate, if 50 students answered an item, and only 37 of them answered it correctly, then the p value representing the item's difficulty would be

$$\text{Difficulty } p \; = \; \frac{37}{50} \; = \; .74$$

It should be clear that such p value can range from 0 to 1.00, with higher p values indicating items that more students answered correctly. For example, a p value of .98 would signify an item answered correctly by almost all students. Similarly, an item with a p value of .15 would be one most students (85%) missed.

The p value of an item should always be viewed in relationship to the student's chance probability of getting the correct response. For example, if a binary-choice item is involved, *on the basis of chance alone* students should be able to answer the item correctly half of the time, and thus the item would have a p value of .50. On a four-option multiple-choice test, a .25 p by chance alone would be expected.

Educators sometimes err by referring to items with high p values (for instance, p values of .80 and above) as "easy" items, while items with low p values (of, say, .20 and below) are described as "difficult" items. Those descriptions may or may not be accurate. Even though we typically refer to an item's p value as its *difficulty* index, the actual difficulty of an item is tied to the instructional program surrounding it. If students are especially well taught, they may perform excellently on a complex item that, by anyone's estimate, is a tough one. Does the resulting p value of .95 indicate the item is easy? No. The item's complicated content has simply been taught effectively. For example, almost all students in a pre-med course for prospective physicians might correctly answer a technical item about the central nervous system that almost all "people off the street" would answer incorrectly. A *p* value of .96 based on the pre-med students' performances would not render the item intrinsically easy.

Item-Discrimination Indices

For tests designed to yield norm-referenced inferences, one of the most powerful indicators of an item's quality is the item discrimination index. In brief, an *item-discrimination index* typically tells us how frequently an item is answered correctly by those who perform well on the total test. Fundamentally, an item-discrimination index reflects the relationship between students' responses for the total test and their responses to a particular test item. One approach to computing an item-discrimination statistic is to calculate a correlation coefficient between students' total test scores and their performance on a particular item.

A *positively discriminating item* indicates an item is answered correctly more often by those who score well on the total test than by those who score poorly on the total test. A *negatively discriminating item* is answered correctly more often by those who score poorly on the total test than by those who score well on the total test. A *nondiscriminating item* is one for which there's no appreciable difference in the correct response proportions of those who score well or poorly on the total test. This set of relationships is summarized in the following chart. (Remember that < and > signify *less than* and *more than*, respectively.)

Type of Item	Proportion of Correct Responses on Total Test
Positive Discriminator	High Scorers > Low Scorers
Negative Discriminator	High Scorers < Low Scorers
Nondiscriminator	High Scorers = Low Scorers

In general, teachers would like to discover that their items are positive discriminators because a positively discriminating item tends to be answered correctly by the most knowledgeable students (those who scored high on the total test) and incorrectly by the least knowledgeable students (those who scored low on the total test). Negatively discriminating items indicate something is awry, because the item tends to be missed more often by the most knowledgeable students and answered correctly more frequently by the least knowledgeable students.

Now, how do you go about computing an item's discrimination index? The following four steps can be employed for the analysis of classroom assessment procedures:

1. *Order the test papers from high to low by total score.* Place the paper having the highest total score on top, and continue with the next highest total score sequentially until the paper with the lowest score is placed on the bottom.
2. *Divide the papers into a high group and a low group, with an equal number of papers in each group.* Split the groups into upper and lower halves. If there is an odd number of papers, simply set aside one of the middle papers

so the number of papers in the high and low groups will be the same. If there are several papers with identical scores at the middle of the distribution, then randomly assign them to the high or low distributions so the number of papers in the two groups is identical. The use of 50% groups has the advantage of providing enough papers to permit reliable estimates of upper and lower group performances.

3. *Calculate a* p *value for each of the high and low groups.* Determine the number of students in the high group who answered the item correctly, then divide this number by the number of students in the high group. This provides you with p_h. Repeat the process for the low group to obtain p_l.

4. *Subtract* p_l *from* p_h *to obtain each item's discrimination index* (D). In essence, then, $D = p_h - p_l$.

Suppose you are in the midst of conducting an item analysis of your midterm examination items. Let's say you split your class of 30 youngsters' papers into two equal upper-half and lower-half papers. All 15 students in the high group answered item 42 correctly, but only 5 of the 15 students in the low group answered it correctly. The item discrimination index for item 42, therefore, would be $1.00 - .33 = .67$.

Parent Talk

Suppose a parent of one of your students called you this morning, before school, to complain about his son's poor performance on your classroom tests. He concludes his grousing by asking you, "Just how sure are you the fault is in Tony and not in your tests!"

▶ *If I were you, here's how I'd respond to the parent:*

"I'm glad you called about your son's test results because I'm sure we both want what's best for Tony, and I want to be sure I'm making the instructional decisions that will be best for him.

"The way I use my classroom tests is to try to arrive at the most accurate conclusion I can about how well my students have mastered the skills and knowledge I'm trying to teach them. It's very important, therefore, the conclusions I reach about students' skill levels are valid. So, every year I devote systematic attention to the improvement of each of my major exams. You'll remember that it was on the last two of these exams that Tony scored so badly.

"What I'd like to do is show you the exams I've been giving my students and the data I use each year to improve those exams. Why don't we set up an after-school or, if necessary, an evening appointment for you and your wife to look over my classroom assessments and the evidence I've been compiling over the years to make sure my tests help me make valid inferences about what Tony and the rest of my students are learning."

▶ *Now, how would you respond to this parent?*

Decision Time

To Catch a Culprit: Teacher or Test

Susan Stevens teaches sixth-grade social studies in Exeter Middle School. During the seven years she has taught at Exeter, Susan has always spent considerable time in developing what she refers to as "creditable classroom assessments." She really has put in more than her share of weekends working to create crackerjack examinations.

This last spring, however, Susan completed an extension course on educational testing. In the course she learned how to compute discrimination analyses of her test items. As a consequence, Susan has been subjecting all of her examinations to such analyses this year.

On one of her examinations containing mostly selected-response items, Susan discovered to her dismay that 4 of the test's 30 items turned out to have negative discriminators. In other words, students who performed well on the total test answered the 4 items incorrectly more often than students who didn't do so well on the total test. To her surprise, all 4 negatively discriminating items dealt with the same topic—that is, relationships among the legislative, judicial, and executive branches of the U.S. government.

Susan's first thought was to chuck the 4 items because they were clearly defective. As she considered the problem, however, another possibility occurred to her. Because all 4 items were based on the same instructional content, perhaps she had confused the stronger students with her explanations.

 If you were Susan and wanted to get to the bottom of this issue so you could decide whether to overhaul the items or the instruction, how would you proceed?

Now, how large should an item's discrimination index be in order for you to consider the item acceptable? Ebel and Frisbie (1991) offer the experience-based guidelines in Table 11.1 for indicating the quality of norm-referenced test items. If you consider their guidelines as approximations, not absolute standards, they'll usually help you decide whether your items are discriminating satisfactorily.

An item's ability to discriminate is highly related to its overall difficulty index. For example, an item answered correctly by all students has a total p value of 1.00. For that item, the p_h and p_l are also 1.00. Thus, the item's discrimination index is zero ($1.00 - 1.00 = 0$). A similar result would ensue for items in which the overall p value was zero—that is, items no student had answered correctly.

With items that have very high or very low p values, it is thus less likely substantial discrimination indices can be obtained. Later in the chapter you will see this situation has prompted proponents of criterion-referenced interpretation of tests (who often hope almost all postinstruction responses from students will be correct) to search for alternative ways to calculate indices of item quality.

Table 11.1 ■ Guidelines for Evaluating the Discriminating Efficiency of Items

Discrimination Index	Item Evaluation
.40 and above	Very good items
.30–.39	Reasonably good items, but possibly subject to improvement
.20–.29	Marginal items, usually needing improvement
.19 and below	Poor items, to be rejected or improved by revision

Source: Ebel and Frisbie (1991).

Distractor Analyses

For a selected-response item that, perhaps on the basis of its p value or its discrimination index, appears to be in need of revision, it is necessary to look deeper. In the case of multiple-choice items, we can gain further insights by carrying out a *distractor analysis* in which we see how the high and low groups are responding to the item's distractors.

Presented in Table 11.2 is the information typically used when conducting a distractor analysis. Note that the asterisk in Table 11.2 indicates that choice B is the correct answer to the item. For the item in the table, the difficulty index *(p)* was .50 and the discrimination index *(D)* was −.33. An inspection of the distractors reveals there appears to be something in alternative D that is enticing the students in the high group to choose it. Indeed, while over half of the high group opted for choice D, not a single student in the low group went for choice D. Alternative D needs to be reviewed carefully.

Also note alternative C is doing nothing at all for the item. No student selected choice C. In addition to reviewing choice D, therefore, choice C might be made a bit more appealing. It is possible, of course, particularly if this is a best-answer type of multiple-choice item, that alternative B, the correct answer, needs

Table 11.2 ■ A Typical Distractor-Analysis Table

Item No. 28	Alternatives				
(p = .50, D = −.33)	*A*	*B**	*C*	*D*	*Omit*
Upper 15 students	2	5	0	8	0
Lower 15 students	4	10	0	0	1

a bit of massaging as well. For multiple-choice items in particular, but also for matching items, a more intensive analysis of student responses to individual distractors can frequently be illuminating. In the same vein, careful scrutiny of students' responses to essay and short-answer items can typically supply useful insights for revision purposes.

■ Item Analysis for Criterion-Referenced Measurement

When teachers use tests intended to yield criterion-referenced interpretations, they typically want most students to score well on those tests after instruction has occurred. In such instances, because postinstruction p values may approach 1.0, traditional item-analysis approaches will often yield low discrimination indices. Accordingly, several alternative approaches to item analysis for criterion-referenced measurement have been devised in recent years.

Two general item-analysis schemes have been employed thus far, depending on the kinds of student groups available. Both of these item-analysis schemes are roughly comparable to the item-discrimination indices used with tests that yield norm-referenced inferences. The first approach involves the administration of the test to *the same group of students* prior to and following instruction. A disadvantage of this approach is the teacher must wait for instruction to be completed before securing the item-analysis data. Another problem is the pretest may be *reactive*, in the sense that its administration sensitizes students to certain items so students' posttest performance is actually a function of the instruction *plus* the pretest's administration.

Using the strategy of testing the same groups of students prior to and after instruction, we can employ an item discrimination index calculated as follows:

$$D_{ppd} = p_{post} - p_{pre}$$

where p_{post} = proportion of students answering the item correctly on posttest.

   p_{pre} = proportion of students answering the item correctly on pretest.

The value of D_{ppd} (discrimination based on the pretest-posttest difference) can range from –1.00 to +1.00, with high positive values indicating an item is sensitive to instruction.

For example, if 41% of the students answered item 27 correctly in the pretest and 84% answered it correctly on the posttest, then item 27's D_{ppd} would be .84 – .41 = .43. A high positive value would indicate the item is sensitive to the instructional program you've provided to your students. Items with low or negative D_{ppd} values would be earmarked for further analysis because such items are not behaving the way one would expect them to behave if instruction were effective. (It is always possible, particularly if many items fail to reflect large posttest-minus-pretest differences, the instruction being provided was not so very wonderful.)

The second approach to item analysis for criterion-referenced measurement is to locate two *different groups of students*, one of which has already been instructed and one of which has not. By comparing the performance on items of instructed and uninstructed students, you can pick up some useful clues regarding item quality. This approach has the advantage of avoiding the delay associated with pretesting and posttesting the same group of students and also of avoiding the possibility of a reactive pretest. Its drawback, however, is that you must rely on human judgment in the selection of the "instructed" and "uninstructed" groups. The two groups should be fairly identical in all other relevant respects (for example, in intellectual ability) but different with respect to whether or not they have been instructed. The isolation of two such groups sounds easier than it usually is. Your best bet would be to prevail on a fellow teacher whose students are studying different topics.

but what does this have to do with Teaching?

Because of the demands on most teachers' time, the typical teacher really doesn't have time to engage in unbridled test-polishing. So, as a practical matter, very few teachers spend *any* time trying to improve their classroom assessments. It is all too understandable.

But there are two approaches to item improvement described in this chapter, one of which, a judgmentally based strategy, doesn't burn up much time at all. It's a judgmental approach to item improvement that represents a realistic item-improvement model for most classroom teachers.

Whereas teachers should understand the basics of how a test can be made better by using empirical data based on students' responses, they'll rarely be inclined to use such data-based strategies for improving items unless a test is thought to be a superimportant one.

During the 29 years that I taught courses in the UCLA Graduate School of Education, the *only* tests that I ever subjected to empirical item-improvement analyses were my midterm and final exams in courses I taught year after year. Oh, to be sure, I applied judgmental improvement techniques to most of my other tests, but the only tests I did a full-throttle, data-based improvement job on were the one or two most important tests for an oft-taught course.

My fear is that the apparent complexity of empirical item-improvement efforts might even dissuade you from routinely employing *judgmental* item-improvement procedures. Don't let it. Even if you *never* use students' data to sharpen your classroom tests, those tests will almost surely still need sharpening. Judgmental approaches will help do the job.

If you use two groups—that is, an instructed group and an uninstructed group—one of the more straightforward item discrimination indices is D_{uigd} (discrimination based on uninstructed versus instructed group differences). This index is calculated as follows:

$$D_{uigd} = p_i - p_u$$

where p_i = proportion of instructed students answering an item correctly.

p_u = proportion of uninstructed students answering an item correctly.

The D_{uigd} index can also range in value from −1.00 to +1.00. To illustrate its computation, if an instructed group of students scored 91% correct on a particular item, while the same item was answered correctly by only 55% of an uninstructed group, then D_{uigd} would be .91 − .55 = .36. Interpretations of D_{uigd} are similar to those used with D_{ppd}.

As suggested earlier, clearly there are advantages associated with using both judgmental and empirical approaches to improving your classroom assessment procedures. Practically speaking, classroom teachers have only so much energy to expend. If you can spare a bit of your allotted energy to spiff up your assessment instruments, you'll usually see meaningful differences in the quality of those instruments.

■ What Do Classroom Teachers Really Need to Know about Improving Their Assessments?

You ought to know that teacher-made tests can be improved as a consequence of judgmental and/or empirical improvement procedures. Judgmental approaches work well with either selected-response or constructed-response kinds of test items. Empirical item improvements have been used chiefly with selected response tests, hence are more readily employed with such test items. You should realize that most of the more widely used indices of item quality, such as discrimination indices, are intended for use with test items in norm-referenced assessment approaches, and may have less applicability to your tests if you employ criterion-referenced measurement strategies. Finally, you must understand because educators have far less experience in using (and improving) performance assessments and portfolio assessments, there isn't really a delightful set of improvement procedures available for those assessment strategies—other than good, solid judgment.

■ Chapter Summary

A focus on two strategies for improving assessment procedures was seen in this chapter. It was suggested that, with adequate time and motivation, teachers could use judgmental and/or empirical methods of improving their assessments.

Judgmentally based improvement procedures were described for use by teachers, teachers' colleagues, and students. Five review criteria for evaluating assessment procedures were presented for use by teachers and their colleagues: (1) adherence to item-specific guidelines and general item-writing commandments, (2) contribution to score-based inferences, (3) accuracy of content, (4) absence of content lacunae, and (5) fairness. A set of possible questions to ask students about test items was also provided.

Two empirical item-improvement indices described in the chapter were p values and item discrimination indices. A step-by-step procedure for determining item discrimination values was described. Designed chiefly for use with norm-referenced measurement, item discrimination indices do not function well when large numbers of students respond correctly (or incorrectly) to the items involved. Distractor analyses have proven highly useful in the improvement of multiple-choice items because the effectiveness of each of an item's alternatives can be studied. Finally, two indices of item quality for criterion-referenced measurement were described. Although roughly comparable to the kind of item discrimination indices widely used with norm-referenced measurement, the two indices for criterion-referenced assessment can be used in settings where many effectively taught students perform well on examinations.

Self-Check

For the first five exercises on this chapter's self-check, see if you can determine whether the item-improvement scheme described is primarily a *judgmental* or an *empirical* item-improvement approach.

1. A mathematics teacher (wouldn't you know?) improves her test items by modifying those items that fail to correlate highly with students' total test scores.

2. At the end of his major examinations, a chemistry teacher requires his students to critique a blank copy of test they just completed in order to identify any confusing items.

3. Because he has learned very difficult or very easy items don't discriminate among students, a sixth-grade teacher discards any test items having p values less than .10 or more than .90.

4. Groups of high school science teachers interested in "alternative assessment in the sciences" regularly exchange newly developed performance tests with one another for purposes of evaluation and to secure test-improvement suggestions. Accompanying each performance test is a set of information indicating how students appraised the test after completing it.

5. An art teacher rejects the idea that his fellow art teachers' appraisals of test items are meritorious, hence scrutinizes all of his criterion-referenced test items using a discrimination index based on pretest-to-posttest differences in p values.

For the last five self-check exercises, you'll be presented with a brief description of a teacher's actions or a set of data from an analysis of a classroom assessment item. Then you'll be asked a parenthetical question. See how well you can answer each parenthesized question.

6. A music teacher has analyzed her History of Music final examination and discovered that for 5 of the 35 short-answer items, the p values were .95 or above.

   (Should this music teacher delete the five items the next time she uses the test?)

7. Here's a distractor analysis for a multiple-choice item in a social studies teacher's geography test:

Item No. 10	Alternatives			
$(p = .50, D = .50)$	A	B	C	D*
Upper 12 students	2	0	1	9
Lower 12 students	1	6	2	3

   (Is there anything present in these data to suggest serious item deficits?)

8. A teacher reports to her principal that almost all of her items she has studied based on the D_{uigd} index have values well in excess of .50.

   (Should the teacher toss these items out?)

9. Now check out this distractor analysis from a multiple-choice item in a physical education instructor's examination on Sports Safety Rules:

Response Options						Item No. 27
A	B*	C	D	F	Omit	$(p = .62, D = .15)$
1	15	1	1	2	0	Top 20 students
2	12	2	1	3	0	Bottom 20 students

   (If the teacher is using the test to select the very best students, is this item acceptable?)

10. Mr. Philips, a health education teacher, analyzes his tests using empirical data from students' performances. He tries to reuse items that have discrimination indices below .20 and p values between .23 and .75. If he gets a negatively discriminating item, he is elated.

   (Is Mr. Philips making sensible decisions?)

Pondertime

1. Why is it difficult to generate discrimination indices for performance assessments consisting of only one or two fairly elaborate tasks?

2. If you found there was a conflict between judgmental and empirical evidence regarding the merits of a particular item, which form of evidence would you be inclined to believe?

3. Why do you suppose relatively few classroom teachers attempt systematically to improve their assessment procedures?

4. Why is it usually true, when teachers review tests they've written earlier, the teachers can often spot deficits not previously discerned?

5. Why is it many teachers who employ criterion-referenced assessment strategies tend to place little emphasis on traditional item discrimination indices?

Self-Check Key

1. Empirical

2. Judgmental

3. Empirical

4. Judgmental

5. Empirical

6. Not necessarily. The students' high performances may simply indicate superb instruction.

7. No, the item is a pretty tough one, but it discriminates well. The distractor analysis suggests the three distractors (Choices A, B, and C) appear to be doing their jobs. It seems to be an okay item.

8. Again, a negative answer wins here. The whopping difference between the performance of instructed versus uninstructed students attests to the teacher's potent instruction.

9. The physical education teacher appears to be using the test in order to make norm-referenced interpretations (selecting "the very best students"). In this case, the discrimination index (.15) is too low.

10. Unfortunately, Mr. Philips is shooting for lower discrimination indices than he should. There's nothing wrong with choosing middle difficulty items, but he should be distressed, not jubilant, when his items discriminate negatively. Such negative discriminators arise when more of the most capable students miss an item while more of the least capable answer it correctly. Unless Mr. Philips is truly perverse, he should be chagrined when such items are encountered in his tests.

■ Additional Stuff

Downing, Steven M., and Thomas M. Haladyna (Eds.). (2006). *Handbook of Test Development*. Mahwah, NJ: Lawrence Erlbaum.

Ebel, R. L., and D. A. Frisbie. (1991). *Essentials of Educational Measurement* (5th ed.). Englewood Cliffs, NJ: Prentice-Hall.

McMillan, James H. (2004). *Classroom Assessment: Principles and Practice for Effective Instruction* (3rd ed.). Boston: Allyn and Bacon.

■ Nonprint Stuff

Northwest Regional Educational Laboratory. *Paper-and-Pencil Test Development* (Videotape #NREL-4). Los Angeles: IOX Assessment Associates.

To access chapter objectives, practice tests, weblinks, and flashcards, visit the companion website at **www.ablongman.com/popham5e.**

MyLabSchool is a collection of online tools for your success in this course, your licensure exams, and your teaching career. Discover where the classroom comes to life by visiting **www.mylabschool.com** to access the following resources:

- Video clips from real classrooms
- An archive of real-life cases
- Help with your research papers using Research Navigator™
- Career Center with resources for:
    Praxis exams and licensure preparation
    Professional portfolio development
    Job search and interview techniques
    Lesson planning with state standard correlations

chapter 12

Instructionally Oriented Assessment

T eachers test a child in order to make better decisions about how to educate the child. At least, they ought to.

In this chapter I will attempt to synthesize much of the content you've encountered in the previous 11 chapters. More specifically, I'm going to describe the following two ways the quality of a teacher's instruction can be markedly improved as a consequence of classroom assessments:

Strategy One: Making instructional decisions in light of assessment results. A teacher makes instructional decisions after assessing students to determine their status regarding the teacher's curricular aims.

Strategy Two: Planning instruction to achieve the curricular aim(s) represented by a test. A teacher deliberately designs instruction to promote students' attainment of the knowledge, skills, and/or affect exemplified by an assessment.

The first of these two assessment-based strategies for improving instruction is fairly well known by teachers—even if it's not all that widely employed. The second assessment-based strategy for improving instruction, on the other hand, is understood by relatively few teachers. It will be the second instructional improvement strategy, therefore, that will receive the greatest attention here. This chapter, in short, deals with *how testing can help teaching*.

■ Instructional Decisions and Assessment Results

If you were to ask a flock of teachers how assessment results might improve the quality of their teaching, a fair number of the teachers would respond that better classroom decisions can ordinarily be made if teachers have a more accurate idea of their students' current learning levels. We considered such decisions way back in Chapter 1. Unfortunately, too many teachers still think the chief role of classroom tests is for the assignment of students' grades. But any teacher who uses tests *dominantly* to determine whether students get high or low grades should receive a solid F in classroom assessment. Surely, classroom tests have helped teachers dispense grades since the Middle Ages. But classroom tests can do so much more than abet the disbursing of grades. If teachers use classroom assessments properly, students' performances on those tests can help teachers make better instructional decisions. Let's see how such assessment-based decision making works.

Assessment, Inferences, and Decisions

Most teachers have a ton of experience with classroom tests. As participants in the testing game, they've often been on the receiving end of assessment when they, themselves, were students. Or, after they finally arrived at the grown-up side of the teacher's desk, they've dispensed numerous tests to their own students. Because of all this testing, many teachers have become so inured to assessment they've actually forgotten the reason teachers test in the first place. Accordingly, let's take a brief look at *why* teachers assess students.

Ordinarily, a teacher assesses a student to determine the student's status with respect to a curricular aim that the teacher wants the student to master. Putting it another way, the teacher wants to know the student's level of learning in relationship to some sort of outcome the teacher intends to promote. Usually, the outcome is *cognitive* in nature—for instance, the student's mastery of a skill or a body of knowledge. The desired outcome could, however, be *affective*—for example, when the teacher attempts to promote particular attitudes or interests. And, of course, in certain subjects, such as the arts or physical education, teachers are concerned with promoting their students' *psychomotor* prowess.

So, whether the intended educational outcome is cognitive, affective, or psychomotor, teachers often need to determine their students' status with respect to that outcome. In Figure 12.1, you'll see an intended instructional outcome represented as a thick-walled circle. I have labeled the circle as a curricular aim because, as you saw in Chapter 5, curricular aims describe skill, knowledge, or affect that teachers intend to have their students acquire. If you prefer, think of the circle in Figure 12.1 as "the stuff the teacher wants to teach."

Figure 12.1 ■ The Cognitive, Affective, or Psychomotor Outcome the Teacher Intends to Promote Instructionally

To give you an idea of the kinds of curricular aims Figure 12.1 is intended to exemplify, here are a few illustrative educational outcomes teachers frequently pursue:

Cognitive

- Students will become skilled in solving age-appropriate mathematical word problems.
- Students will become knowledgeable regarding the key historical events leading to the U.S. Revolutionary War.

Affective

- Students will become more confident in their ability to make oral presentations to their peers.
- Students' enjoyment of volitional reading will increase dramatically.

Psychomotor

- Students will substantially increase the speed and accuracy of their keyboarding skills.
- Students will become more proficient in shooting basketball "jump shots" despite being closely guarded by an opposing player.

If you spend a moment or two reviewing these illustrative instructional outcomes, you'll realize each of these curricular aims is really quite substantial. Consider, for example, the cognitive curricular aim dealing with the student's ability to solve mathematical word problems. We could conjure up an almost unlimited number of such problems, and students would really have to be quantitatively savvy to solve those problems. That's a hefty curricular aim. Similarly, the affective aim dealing with students' confidence in being able to make oral presentations to peers covers a ton of oral-communication terrain, ranging from confidence in giving one-minute impromptu speeches or oral presentations resembling presidential State of the Union addresses. And, when it comes to the psychomotor aim of shooting jump shots while being closely guarded, there are myriad places on the basketball court from which such shots can be launched, and there are at least half a myriad ways a closely guarding opponent can closely guard a jump-shooter.

Putting it simply, almost any really significant curricular aim is so substantial that teachers, as a practical matter, will be unable to determine a student's status by *exhaustively* assessing a student's status with respect to this aim. It would take too long. If students were actually assessed regarding *all* components of teachers' curricular aims, those students would surely be drawing social security checks before they earned their high school diplomas.

As a practical solution, therefore, teachers *represent* curricular aims by *sampling* from those aims. That's really what a classroom assessment ought to be—a representative sample of a curricular aim. In Figure 12.2, you'll see represented the original curricular aim you first bumped into in Figure 12.1, as well as a classroom assessment that can be used to help teachers ascertain a student's status with regard to the curricular aim. Note that Figure 12.2's thick-walled curricular aim is being represented by a thin-walled classroom assessment. Because it's far too time

Figure 12.2 ■ How an Assessment That Samples a Curricular Aim Is Used to Determine a Student's Status with Respect to That Aim

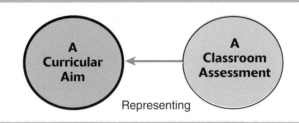

consuming, for example, to test a student's knowledge of *all* the "key historical events leading to the U.S. Revolutionary War," a teacher's classroom test must *sample* this content. The thin-walled, content-sampling classroom test, therefore, only *represents* the curricular aim.

Teachers should never be interested in a student's performance on a classroom test in and of itself. The student's assessment performance should be regarded as a *proxy* for the student's status with respect to the curricular aim represented by the test. It is the student's test performance that allows teachers to draw an *inference* about the student's curricular aim status. This inference is then used by the teacher to make instructional decisions. Such a decision chain is shown in Figure 12.3. It is the assessment-based inference about students' status with respect to the curricular aim that should influence the teacher's decisions about instruction. And this, of course, is why I fussed so much about the *validity* of assessment-based inferences in Chapter 3.

Now, as noted before, many teachers regard tests chiefly as tools by which to determine students' grades. And, of course, there ought to be a relationship between students' grades and the way those students perform on tests. What I'm suggesting, however, is that tests-as-grade-determiners are far less important than tests-as-instruction-determiners.

If teachers want to approach classroom assessment *exclusively* in terms of the contribution students' performances make to improved *instructional* decisions, there will still be plenty of assessment results available to use for grading purposes.

Figure 12.3 ■ The Assessment-Inference-Decision Chain That Should Guide Classroom Teachers

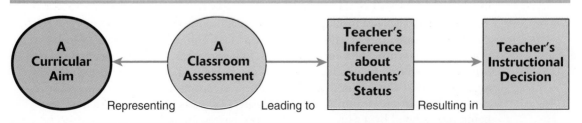

When grading time comes, teachers will still have access to oodles of test results that can influence grades. But the role of test-as-grade-determiners ought to be a decisively secondary role. The foremost function of classroom assessment should be to help teachers make better instructional decisions.

What Kinds of Instructional Decisions Are Abetted by Assessment Results?

If teachers do accept the proposition that students' performances on assessments should inform a teacher's instructional decisions, they'll usually discover there are three major categories of decisions that can be made better if students' assessment performances are considered. Those three kinds of instructional decisions are listed in Table 12.1.

What to Teach?   As seen in Table 12.1, one important kind of instructional decision that's almost certain to be made better on the basis of students' assessment results is what to teach in the first place. Kids come to school in all sorts of sizes, loaded with different amounts of smarts and with dissimilar skills. At any grade level, it is folly to assume this year's crop of students will be a mirror image of last year's crop. And, given such anticipatable crop variation, this year's students will often need to be taught different stuff than last year's students.

One of the best ways for teachers to make a decision about what they should be teaching is to *preassess* students at the very beginning of a school year or school term. A teacher should find out what skills and knowledge students have when they walk through the classroom door. Based on the results of such preassessments, a teacher can then determine what instructional activities are really needed and what instructional activities would be redundant. The teacher can dump any plans for redundant instruction and focus instruction, instead, on curricular aims suitable for *those particular students.*

Table 12.1 ■ Categories of Instructional Decisions Enhanced by a Consideration of Students' Assessment Performances

Decision Category	Typical Assessment Strategy	Decision Options
■ What to teach in the first place?	Preassessment prior to the start of instruction	Whether to provide instruction for specific instructional objectives?
■ How long to keep teaching toward a particular instructional objective?	En route assessments of students' progress	Whether to continue or cease instruction for an objective, either for an individual student or for the whole class?
■ How effective was an instructional sequence?	Comparing students' posttest to pretest performances	Whether to retain, discard, or modify a given instructional sequence the next time it's used?

If teachers fail to preassess their incoming students, teachers' judgments about what instruction is needed are apt to be wrong. Some teachers, of course, can make sensible judgments about their students' entry behavior based on observations of students during the first few days of class. That, too, is a form of preassessment. Not all classroom assessment obliges students to make marks on paper. But, without any *systematic* form of preassessment, many teachers will make mistakes about what they should be teaching.

How Long to Teach?   The second kind of decision that can be beneficially influenced by students' assessment results concerns the duration of instruction. Progress-monitoring assessments—for instance, some sort of mini-test—can be most helpful in arriving at such stop/go decisions.

How long should the teacher continue to teach toward a given instructional objective? In some instances, this decision will be made for a whole class. For example, a planned three-week instructional unit on How a Bill Becomes a Law might be appropriately wrapped up in only two weeks if the students display, on an en route progress-monitoring quiz, they've really mastered the particulars of the bill-to-law sequence.

The teacher's decision to halt instruction on a particular objective might also be made on a student-by-student basis. For instance, suppose an English teacher were promoting her students' abilities to compose paragraphs that not only "glisten" from a communication perspective, but are also "devoid of mechanical muckups." If, via occasional en route assessments during class, the teacher spots individual students who have already mastered this paragraph-composition skill, she may choose to send those students down some sort of enrichment road while keeping the rest of her students on the paragraph path. Progress-monitoring assessments, because they typically provide teachers with better evidence than might be obtained from the teacher's casual observations, will help teachers decide more accurately when to terminate instruction focused on a particular curricular aim.

Some of the very best thinking directed toward the use of assessments for monitoring a student's growth has been carried out for more than a decade by Geoff Masters, Margaret Forster, and their colleagues at the Australian Council for Educational Research (ACER). These Australian researchers employ a *progress map* to describe the nature of students' typical path of learning toward mastery of a curricular aim. Such progress maps, therefore, provide a conceptual structure for monitoring an individual student's growth.

> *An essential feature of a progress map is that it describes developing competence in words and examples. A progress map describes the knowledge, skills and understandings of a learning area in the sequence in which they typically develop and provides examples of the kinds of performances and student work typically observed at particular levels of attainment.* (Masters and Forster, 1996)

A progress map provides an excellent framework for teachers to rely on when attempting to assess their students' movement toward the attainment of a curricular aim. In the United States, during the last half of the twentieth century, the identification of the enabling subskills and knowledge students needed en route to the mastery of a more ultimate curricular aim was generally referred to as a *task analysis*. What the ACER researchers have done is carry out task analyses often ending up in the form of large wall-charts not only describing, for a curricular aim, the knowledge and subskills a student must achieve along the way but also what such progress might look like—in the form of students' actual work samples. Some educators refer to these analyses of what students must achieve "along-the-way" as *learning progressions*.

Because of the substantial energy that must be devoted to the creation of ACER-like progress maps, few teachers (or even few groups of teachers) will have the time to generate progress maps for their own classes. If, however, state departments of education provide well-conceived progress maps to teachers, those maps can become marvelous tools to use in the generation of progress-monitoring assessments.

How Effective Was Instruction?   A third type of assessment-influenced instructional decision deals with the effectiveness of an instructional sequence. Most teachers want to know whether the instructional scheme they devised did, in fact, "work." If the instructional sequence was a winner, then the next time the teacher tackles the curricular aim for which the instruction was devised, essentially the same instructional approach ought to be followed. If, however, there's assessment evidence to indicate the instruction was only so-so or, worse, downright dismal, then major alterations are warranted when this instructional sequence is next implemented.

The most straightforward way for teachers to discover whether their instructional sequences are effective is to rely on comparisons between assessments of students made both prior to and following instruction. Although, from a ritzy research perspective, there may be difficulties associated with simple pretest-to-posttest contrasts, from an in-the-busy-classroom perspective, such contrasts usually help teachers arrive at sensible conclusions about the effectiveness of their instruction.

Suppose, for example, prior to a one-month teaching unit about narrative essays, only 20% of the students could write such essays properly but, at the close of the unit, almost 80% of the students could churn out satisfactory narrative essays. This would be pretty compelling evidence that whatever the teacher was doing instructionally seemed to work. In contrast, if the end-of-unit posttest showed there were *still* only 20% of the students who could write a satisfactory narrative essay, the teacher ought to think seriously about revamping what appears to be a consummately cruddy instructional approach.

Because, in the classroom, *testing time* takes away from *teaching time,* teachers may sometimes want to take advantage of *item sampling,* a time-saving assessment strategy. In an item-sampling approach, a classroom assessment is subdivided into separate parts so that different students can complete different parts of the assessment. For instance, if there were a 20-item pretest that usually took students about 20 minutes to complete, the teacher might split the 20-item test into four 5-item subsections, then have one-fourth of the students in the class complete each of the four subsections. The pretest now requires only 5 minutes of class time instead of 20 minutes. To get a fix on the total class performance, the teacher simply lumps the subpart scores together and computes the average percent-correct score for the entire 20-item test. The average performance of the class, estimated via item sampling, will almost always give teachers a reasonably accurate picture of how the entire class would have scored on the total test if all students had taken all the items. Because students' *posttest* performances are often used for grading purposes, item sampling is less frequently employed at posttest time because each student, to be graded accurately, ordinarily needs to complete all the assessment items. But, for preassessment guidance regarding the status of an entire class, item sampling is a time-saver.

Incidentally, in Chapter 15 you'll learn about a far juicier way to collect meaningful pretest and posttest evidence regarding your students. Can't wait to read about it? I don't blame you. Therefore, get going immediately on the next paragraph.

In review, we've now dealt with several sorts of instructional decisions that can be made more appropriately if teachers have access to students' assessment results. Those decisions involve what to teach, how long to teach it, and whether it was taught effectively. Students' test results, of course, are not the *only* factor teachers should consider when making instructional decisions. But teachers who rely on assessment results to help them make better instructional decisions will, in fact, almost always make better instructional decisions.

■ Planning Instruction to Achieve Assessment-Exemplified Curricular Aims

We now turn to the second of our two assessment-based strategies for improving the quality of classroom instruction. As indicated earlier, it's an improvement strategy with which few teachers are familiar. This second strategy requires a substantial rethinking about the role of educational assessment. Let's get that rethinking underway.

Tests as Instructional Influencers

Historically, teachers have used classroom tests at or near the close of an instructional sequence. And, of course, teachers would like their students to perform well on any end-of-instruction tests. If students are successful on end-of-instruction classroom tests, it usually means that students have learned well and, accordingly, teachers have taught well. More often than not, teachers' classroom tests have been constructed only *after* instruction is over or when instruction is nearing its conclusion (for instance, near the end of a semester, a school year, or a short-duration teaching unit). Obviously, classroom assessments devised *after* instruction is over will have scant impact on what the teacher teaches. The teacher's instruction, or at least the vast majority of it, is a "done deal" by the time the test is constructed.

Classroom assessments, therefore, have typically had little impact on instructional planning. At least this was true until the era of *educational accountability* arrived in the 1970s and 1980s. During that period, legislators in most states enacted a string of laws requiring students to pass basic skills tests in order to receive high school diplomas or, in some cases, to be advanced to higher grade levels. Thus was born what educators have come to call "high-stakes" tests because there were important consequences for the students who were required to take those tests.

There was another sense in which statewide tests became high stakes. In schools where all, or almost all, students passed the tests, a school's teachers and administrators were applauded. But in schools where many students failed the tests, a school's teachers and administrators were blamed. The stakes associated with statewide testing were elevated even more when newspapers began, in the 1980s, to publish annual statewide test scores of all districts and all schools in the state. Each school and district was *ranked* in relation to the state's other schools and districts. There were, of course, numerous winners as well as an equal number of losers.

As noted in Chapter 1, what was being measured by the tests began to influence the nature of what was taught in classrooms. The phrase *measurement-driven instruction* became widely used during the eighties to depict an educational reform strategy in which it was hoped the content of high-stakes tests would have a substantial and positive influence on the content of classroom instruction.

Because of this heightened attention to student performance on important statewide and districtwide tests, we also saw increased attention being given to the evidence of student success on teacher-made *classroom* tests. Many educational administrators and policymakers concluded that if students' performances on statewide tests reflected a school's educational effectiveness, then even at the classroom level, test results could indicate whether good teaching was taking place. Greater and greater emphasis was given to "evidence of effectiveness" in the form of improved student performance on whatever types of classroom tests were being employed. Increasingly, *evidence* of student learning—evidence in the form of student performance on classroom tests—is being used in personnel appraisals of teachers. In many settings, a teacher's competence is currently being determined, at least in part, by how well a teacher's students perform on the teacher's classroom tests.

Given this ever-increasing administrative reliance on student test results as one indicator of a teacher's instructional effectiveness, it was only natural that many teachers tried to address instructionally whatever was to be tested. Tests had

Decision Time

At What Cost Score-Boosting?

The new superintendent in Little Lakes Unified School District was appointed by the district's school board on the basis of her promise to "boost our standardized test scores." Subsequently, Rebecca Rowe, an English teacher in Placid Waters High School, was on the receiving end of a strident spoken message from her principal. "Get those standardized test scores up in language arts or else!" was the last sentence spat out by the principal as she strode out of Rebecca's classroom.

Rebecca does want to see her students learn more, but after consulting the Teacher's Manual for the standardized test used by the district, she is baffled about how to devise more effective instructional plans. The descriptions of what the language arts section of the test measures, Rebecca believes, are far too vague for her purposes.

One of her colleagues points out to Rebecca that in the school counselor's office a teacher can review the actual forms of the standardized test because the same test is given each spring and then stored in each school. The colleague suggests that student familiarity with the content of some actual test items will lead to a bit of "mandated score-boosting."

 If you were Rebecca and were faced with this situation, what would your decision be?

clearly begun to influence teaching. And it was increasingly recognized by teachers not only that the content of their tests *could* influence their teaching but, perhaps, the content of those tests *should* influence their teaching.

If testing should influence teaching, why not construct classroom assessments *prior* to instructional planning? In this way, any planned instructional sequence could mesh more effectively with the content of the test involved. Moreover, why not build classroom assessments with the instructional implications of those assessments deliberately in mind? In other words, why not build a classroom assessment not only before any instructional planning, but in such a way that the assessment would beneficially inform the teacher's instructional planning? Such an approach, as you might have already guessed, is the essence of the second assessment-based strategy to improve instructional quality. A contrast between a more traditional educational approach in which instruction influences assessment and the kind of assessment-influenced instruction being described here can be seen in Figure 12.4.

In a traditional approach to instructional design, an approach in which instruction influences assessment, the teacher (1) is guided by the curriculum that's been adopted by the state and/or district, (2) plans instructional activities to promote the educational objectives set forth in that curriculum, and (3) assesses students. In an assessment-influenced approach to instructional design, also indicated in Figure 12.4, the teacher still (1) starts with the educational objectives set forth in the curriculum, (2) then moves to create assessments based on those goals, and (3) only thereafter plans instructional activities intended to promote students' mastery

Figure 12.4 ■ Traditional Instruction-Influenced Assessment versus Assessment-Influenced Instruction, Both of Which Are Governed by Curricular Considerations

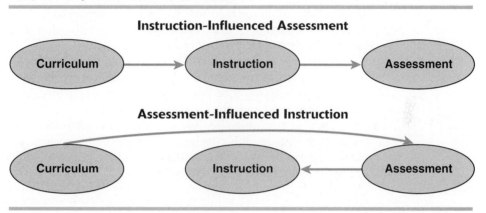

Instruction-Influenced Assessment

Curriculum → Instruction → Assessment

Assessment-Influenced Instruction

Curriculum   Instruction ← Assessment

of the knowledge, skills, and/or attitudes to be assessed. In both approaches, curriculum is the starting point. Curricular aims (whether they're labeled instructional objectives, content standards, benchmarks, or some synonymous descriptor) still govern the entire process. But in the two contrasting approaches, the sequence of instructional planning and assessment development is reversed.

Dividends of Assessment Illumination

Assessment-illuminated instruction rests on the assumption that, in many instances, what is to be assessed *will* influence the teacher's instructional decisions. Consequently, if the assessment can be created prior to the teacher's instructional planning, the resultant clarity provided to the teacher will help the teacher make more appropriate instructional choices.

When teachers develop their classroom assessments *before* instructional plans are made, teachers are meaningfully *clarifying* the curricular aims being pursued. In other words, the assessment serves as the operational definition of whether an instructional objective has been achieved. Such clarity provides far more insight for teachers when, subsequently, they make their instructional plans.

It is important to remember, as indicated earlier, classroom assessments *represent* the knowledge and/or skills being promoted. Teachers should *never* teach toward the classroom test itself. Instead, teachers should teach toward the knowledge, skills, and/or attitudes sampled by the classroom test. But, when teachers construct classroom assessments prior to instructional decision making, those teachers will have a markedly better understanding of what the instructional objectives really are. And, of course, the more clear-headed teachers are about curricular *ends,* the more skillfully such teachers can select suitable instructional *means* to accomplish those ends.

With increased clarity regarding the nature of the curricular aims being promoted, there are all sorts of derivative instructional-planning benefits. Here are a few of the most salient dividends you, as a teacher or teacher-in-preparation, will receive:

- *More accurate task analyses.* Because you'll know more clearly what the terminal results of an instructional sequence are supposed to be, you can better pinpoint the enabling or en route knowledge/skills your students must acquire before mastering what's being taught.
- *More on-target practice activities.* Because you'll know better what kinds of end-of-instruction outcomes are being sought for your students, you can make sure to select guided-practice and independent-practice activities more accurately aligned with the target outcomes.
- *More lucid expositions.* Because you'll understand more clearly what's to be assessed at instruction's conclusion, during the instruction you can provide clearer explanations to your students about the content involved and where the instructional activities are heading.

Instructional planning will benefit from early development of classroom assessments most fundamentally because you will, as a consequence of prior assessment development, better understand what it is hoped that your students will be able to do when instruction has been concluded.

Constructing Assessments with Instruction in Mind

Because the nature of assessment instruments will often influence a teacher's instructional plans, why not *deliberately* construct those assessment instruments so appropriate instructional decisions are more likely? If teachers wish to derive the maximum instructional dividends from their classroom assessments, they must construct their assessment devices with specific attention being given to how students can be *taught* to do whatever that assessment device is measuring. Putting it another way, teachers must constantly be "thinking instructional possibilities" as they create their classroom assessments. Whether it's a selected-response test, a constructed-response test, or a self-report affective inventory, teachers must continually ask themselves, "Can I teach what this assessment instrument represents?"

When classroom assessments are skillfully crafted, with instructional implications in mind, the resulting assessment devices will almost certainly illuminate a teacher's instructional decision making more beneficially than will a classroom assessment device cranked out with little attention given to instruction. This can be seen in Table 12.2, where it is suggested that instructional-planning dividends are most substantial when classroom assessments are created *before* such planning takes place and if those assessments are deliberately generated *with instruction in mind.*

Yet, you might be thinking, it's easier to *say* assessment instruments ought to be created with instructional considerations in mind than it is to actually *create* such instruments. You're right. And that's the topic with which we'll conclude this chapter—namely, how to build instructionally illuminating assessment instruments. In turn, we'll consider how to create instructionally beneficial constructed-response tests (such as essay exams), selected-response tests (such as multiple-choice exams), and affective assessments (such as self-report attitudinal inventories).

Table 12.2 ■ Instructional-Planning Dividends Associated with the Timing of When Classroom Assessments Are Developed

Timing of Classroom Assessment Development	Instructional Planning Dividends
■ Developed at or near the end of instruction	None
■ Developed prior to teaching, but with no special consideration given to instruction	Substantial
■ Developed prior to teaching, with primary consideration given to the assessment's instructional implications	*Really* Substantial

Constructed-Response Assessments

Constructed-response assessments, as we saw in Chapter 7, can range from the most rudimentary "fill-in-the-blank" quizzes all the way to very complex performance tests in which students must create elaborate written and/or oral responses to an intellectually demanding assignment. Stripping away the frills, in each constructed-response test there is a *task* for students to perform and a *scoring scheme* to determine the adequacy of a student's performance.

The less elaborate the students' tasks are, the less elaborate the scoring scheme needs to be. For example, if students are given a test where they are being asked only to fill in the dates when certain historical events occurred (a decidedly dismal chore), there's really no need for a more elaborate scoring approach than "Did students come up with the correct dates?"

For more demanding tasks, however, students' responses are generally evaluated on the basis of a scoring rubric. A rubric, as seen in Chapter 8, has three essential features. It (1) identifies the evaluative criteria to be employed when judging a student's response to the task, (2) describes for each criterion how to judge qualitative differences in students' performances, and (3) indicates whether the evaluative criteria are to be applied holistically or analytically.

Whether a rubric's evaluative criteria are applied holistically or analytically, those criteria are the rubric's most important feature—at least from an instructional perspective. Fundamentally, the evaluative criteria in a rubric identify those factors used to distinguish among differences in the quality of students' responses. Evaluative criteria *that can be addressed instructionally* will guide the teacher's planning so appropriate instruction is more likely to ensue. Evaluative criteria generated without keeping instruction in mind will render effective instruction less likely. Let's spend a moment to explore how a rubric's evaluative criteria can help or hurt a teacher's instructional decision making.

Think back to Figure 12.2, where it was shown a classroom assessment is intended to represent the student's mastery of a curricular aim. (If you don't have keen visual recollective powers, you are hereby granted permission to go back to Figure 12.2 and take a peek.) In reality, almost all significant constructed-response tests are focused on the measurement of students' *skills* rather than their *knowl-*

edge (knowledge usually being more efficiently assessed via selected-response tests). Therefore, a demanding performance test is usually intended to provide the teacher with a valid rubric-based inference about the student's mastery of the skill the performance test samples. If students flop on a performance test, then teachers can pick up some diagnostic insights about the reasons for such failure by using the rubric's evaluative criteria to find out where it was that students went awry.

Selected-Response Assessments

In contrast to constructed-response assessments when rubrics must be employed to evaluate students' performances, selected-response assessments provide options from which students make choices. As indicated in Chapter 6, the most common examples of selected-response tests used by teachers are multiple-choice tests and binary-choice tests. If selected-response tests are to be employed as part of an assessment-illuminated instructional design strategy, then those tests must also be created *prior* to instructional planning, and they must certainly be created with their instructional implications clearly in mind.

Fundamentally, we can distinguish between two kinds of educational objectives that selected-response tests can be used to assess. First, selected-response tests can assess a student's *knowledge*—that is, the student's recollection of memorized information such as facts or dates of significant events. Memorized information resides at the lowest level of Bloom's cognitive taxonomy of educational objectives. For the higher levels of Bloom's taxonomy, the student is required to employ a *skill*—a skill not fundamentally unlike the kinds of skills measured by most constructed-response performance tests. Let's look briefly at how to create selected-response tests to illuminate instructional planning when teachers are trying to promote students' knowledge or skills.

Assessing Knowledge via Selected-Response Tests Knowledge is a good thing. We want our students to know lots of content. But if the *only* thing teachers did was to pour knowledge into students' heads, of course, this would be unacceptable. We want our students to possess not only knowledge but also a host of higher-level cognitive skills. Because selected-response tests can be efficiently employed to measure students' knowledge, such tests are often used for just this purpose. The question is, therefore, How can selected-response assessments of knowledge be constructed so they are instructionally illuminating? The answer is straightforward. To make selected-response assessments of knowledge instructionally illuminating, *the domain of knowledge being sampled by the test must be fully explicated* prior to the test's creation.

Let me use a simple example. If Mrs. Jones, an elementary teacher, is trying to promote her students' ability to remember the correct spelling of the new words systematically introduced by their language arts textbook during the school year, Mrs. Jones needs to list *all* the eligible words at the time she generates her selected-response test of students' spelling abilities. There might, for example, be 500 words on the total list, and the selected-response test itself might contain a sample of only 20 or 25, but Mrs. Jones needs to identify, prior to her instructional planning, the complete domain of knowledge (in this case, the 500 eligible spelling words) that students should learn.

It is the same story for any body of information to be memorized. Whether it's a set of dates of historical events, definitions of vocabulary words, or rules for a complex game, when teachers create their selected-response tests in advance of instruction, they need to set forth exactly what's involved in the total domain of knowledge that's being assessed. Then the assessment itself is easily created by sampling (representatively, if possible) from the domain. The delineation of the full knowledge domain prior to instruction will, of course, enable teachers to plan their instruction more accurately so that attention is given to the content of the entire domain, not merely the content that's actually assessed.

Assessing Skills via Selected-Response Tests   As indicated before, when students are asked to display higher-than-lowest-level cognitive behavior, it is possible to identify criteria that can be used to distinguish between correct and incorrect responses. For example, suppose the teacher is building a test to measure students' abilities to distinguish between reasonable newspaper advertisements versus those advertisements that employ one or more unscrupulous advertising ploys. What the teacher needs to do when developing the test is to list all of the reprehensible advertising ploys, then make sure the test items give students an opportunity to

Parent Talk

Suppose one of your better students, Mary Ruth Green, brings in a note from her parents, expressing concern that your classes seem to be organized to "teach to the test, not educate students." Mr. and Mrs. Green ask you to call them at home so they can, using their speaker phone, both discuss this concern with you.

 If I were you, here's what I'd say on the phone to Mary Ruth's parents:

"Thanks for raising this issue. It's an important concern, and because we all want what's best for Mary Ruth, I'm pleased to be able to explain how we're using tests in my class.

"Actually, I do use tests to influence my instruction. But the tests really only *represent* the skills and knowledge I'm trying to get Mary Ruth and her classmates to learn. I use the tests to help me plan my instruction and to make an interpretation about whether students are mastering what the test represents. In this way, I'll know whether more instruction is needed on particular topics.

"Please be assured, I am definitely not teaching to particular test items. All of the items on my tests, in fact, have never been seen before by the students. But those items do reflect the knowledge and skills my class is supposed to promote.

"You'll also realize that half of Mary Ruth's grade is based on the portfolio assessment system we use. I think the portfolio work samples, when blended with the test results, give me an even better picture of my students' progress."

Now, how would you respond to Mr. and Mrs. Green?

determine whether a given advertisement is reasonable or embodies one of the unscrupulous ploys. There are a good many ways teachers could create selected-response items for such a test. But let's imagine the teacher builds a 10-item exam in which each item first presents an actual advertisement, and is then followed by five choices. For example, an actual advertisement might be followed by the five choices given here:

> The above advertisement (choose the best answer):
> a. uses emotionally charged language.
> b. contains an *ad hominem* argument.
> c. includes deceptive statistics.
> d. invokes unknown authority.
> e. contains none of the four weaknesses listed above.

Notice that in order to answer this kind of item correctly, the student needs to be able to recognize *all* of the unscrupulous advertising ploys because, for any given item, the advertisement provided may be unreasonable, but it might not include one of the ploys given. (The advertising ploys would typically vary with each item.) Yet, because the teacher listed, prior to the test's creation, all the disdainful advertising ploys, not only will the items be easier to construct but the teacher's instructional planning is also apt to be better.

For selected-response assessments requiring students to apply skills, it is important for the teacher to isolate the key factors constituting those skills (much as we saw in the way the evaluative criteria should be spelled out for skill-focused scoring rubrics). The teacher then systematically represents those factors (by formal inclusion or exclusion) in the choices from which students are making their selections for each test item.

Teachers need to make sure that whatever knowledge or skills are required (for students to master a curricular aim) will be clearly identified in advance of item generation, typically via some sort of task analysis, then fully employed in the creation of the assessment's selected-response options. Instructional planning directed toward the promotion of those skills or that knowledge will, then, be more likely to be effective because the skills or knowledge can be directly addressed during the instructional sequence.

Affective Assessments

Finally, we should consider how to make classroom affective assessments helpful when teachers plan their instruction. For me, the chief instructional dividend of formally assessing students' affect is that the very *commitment* to formal affective assessment inclines teachers to give more direct attention to affective instruction than otherwise would have been the case.

To illustrate, let's say Mr. Hovens, a third-grade teacher, decides to promote students' *confidence* in their abilities to use mathematics. Suppose Mr. Hovens develops a 10-item self-report inventory students are to complete anonymously at the beginning and at the end of the school year. Each of the inventory's 10 items asks students to agree or disagree with statements such as "If I'm in a store and I have to figure out how much something costs when it's not marked, I usually can do it." Students respond to each item by circling responses ranging from "very confident" to "not at all confident." Now the very fact Mr. Hovens is going to administer the affective inventory on a pretest and posttest basis will almost certainly sensitize Mr. Hovens to the importance of the affective variable being assessed—and will invariably incline him to devote meaningful instructional attention to such affect.

Also, as with the other kinds of assessments we've been considering, the construction of affective assessments prior to instructional planning will almost certainly lead teachers to more defensible instructional-design decisions. By clarifying what a teacher intends to promote in the affective realm, the teacher really gets a better understanding of the nature of the affective variable being assessed. Such clarity, of course, contributes to better instructional planning.

Assessment *for* Learning

In the past several years, increasing numbers of educators have become excited about the potential instructional dividends of exchanging a three-letter preposition with a two-letter preposition. I know it's difficult to imagine any sort of prepositional trading capable of generalizing even a tiny bit of educational excitement but, trust me, it has.

I'm referring to the notion of assessment *for* learning that's being recommended instead of the more traditional way of thinking about assessment—namely, assessment *of* learning. You see, when most educators have thought about assessment for years and years, those educators regarded assessment chiefly as a way of figuring out how much students had learned. Clearly, the time-honored way of regarding testing was to conceive of it as assessment *of* learning. But, increasingly, we find prominent instructional specialists arguing that if teachers are ever to get the most instructional mileage out of the classroom testing they do, then the way to regard such testing is to view it as a vehicle to enhance instructional effectiveness or, with only a simple preposition-flip, to view it as assessment *for* learning.

Incidentally, assessment *for* learning is not supposed to replace all instances of assessment *of* learning. There are many instances in education when we really do want to find out what kids know and what they don't know. That's assessment *of* learning, and it's not a bad thing. However, there should be many more occasions when we see assessment *for* learning dominating an instructional scene.

There is, happily, a growing body of empirical evidence that when classroom assessments are employed along the lines suggested earlier in this chapter—that is, as catalysts to improve student achievements—then students will also meaningfully improve their scores on externally imposed exams. Two British researchers (Black and Wiliam, 1998), using a comprehensive meta-analysis of previously conducted research, found that students who had been taught using assessment *for* learning were able to achieve in six or seven months what it took other students a full year to achieve. But before getting into some of the ways assessment *for* learning can be installed in a teacher's classroom, let me clarify for you where this feisty little phrase came from in the first place.

Origins of Assessment *for* Learning

In the United States, the expression "assessment *for* learning" is often mistakenly attributed to Richard Stiggins (2002) or to Paul Black and Dylan Wiliam (1998), even though all three of these individuals always deny paternity regarding their fathering of the phrase. Because Wiliam is an able colleague and a good friend, and is associated with the Assessment Reform Group in England where many people think the phrase emerged, I asked Dylan if he would be willing to sleuth the origin of assessment *for* learning. (Sherlock Holmes, after all, was a British bloke.) Dylan agreed, and what he came up with you'll find in the following paragraph.

The earliest use of the phrase "assessment for learning" appears to have been in a paper presented by Mary James (1992) at a New Orleans conference of the Association for Supervision and Curriculum Development. Three years later, the phrase was used by Ruth Sutton of England as the title of a book she wrote (Sutton, 1995). However, the first explicit contrast of assessment *for* learning with assessment *of* learning seems to have occurred in the third edition of a book by Gipps and Stobart (1997) where their first chapter is entitled "Assessment of Learning" and their second chapter is entitled Assessment for Learning." This prepositional distinction was brought to a wider audience two years later by England's Assessment Reform Group in a guide for policymakers (Broadfoot et al., 1999).

So, thanks to Dylan's dogged Sherlocking, we now have an idea where this fine formulation came from. It is apparent that most, if not all, of the early thinking on this issue came to the United States from Great Britain. So, in addition to the debt we owe the Brits for tea, scones, and the Beatles, we now have something in the assessment realm for which we should be grateful.

Essentials of Assessment *for* Learning

Now that you've learned something about the lineage of assessment *for* learning, you should surely be wondering about how a teacher really does it. For openers, teachers should try to incorporate the two assessment-based strategies recommended in this chapter: (1) making instructional decisions in light of assessment results and (2) planning instruction to achieve the curriculum aim(s) represented by a test. But, beyond those two overall strategies, proponents of assessment *for* learning urge that the dividing line between instruction and assessment should become as blurred as can be. Everything students do, or don't do, can serve as a potential source of information about their levels of understanding. Teachers who wish to employ assessment *for* learning in their classrooms must focus in on a manageable, sanity-preserving number of data sources, then base subsequent instructional decisions on students' current understandings.

Leahy and her colleagues (2005) argue that teachers who use assessment *for* learning appear to be most successful when they attempt to implement as many of the following broad strategies as their instructional situations permit:

- Clarifying and sharing learning intentions and criteria for success
- Engineering effective classroom discussions, questions, and learning tasks
- Providing feedback that moves learners forward

- Activating students as the owners of their own learning
- Activating students as instructional resources for one another

Clearly, assessment *for* learning represents a shift in the way most teachers regard educational testing. Testing, in assessment *for* learning, becomes an ally of the teacher and of the teacher's students. This, I submit to you, is a definitely atypical way to think about educational testing.

"Formative Assessment:" A Hijacked Label?

I'll deal briefly with a subtle but potentially important definitional issue today's teachers ought to understand—namely, how best to define the phrase *formative assessment*. Earlier in the book, way back in Chapter 1 as well as only a few paragraphs ago, I referred to the pioneering reviews by Paul Black and Dylan Wiliam indicating that classroom assessments focused on the improvement of instruction frequently led to higher scores by students on external examinations (such as standardized accountability tests). Because this key finding had also been confirmed by other researchers in recent years, a generally accepted notion now exists in the education community that formative assessments can boost students' performances on summative assessments (such as a state's NCLB tests).

Therefore, we now find test publishers hawking all sorts of assessment products using the label "formative assessment." Lorrie Shepard, a leading U.S. assessment expert, has become particularly vexed with what she regards as test vendors' corruption, for marketing purposes, of an otherwise serviceable assessment concept. As Shepard points out:

> The research-based concept of formative assessment, closely grounded in classroom instructional processes, has been taken over (hijacked) by commercial test publishers and used instead to refer to formal testing systems called benchmark or interim assessment systems. (Shepard, 2006)

What is it, then, that makes a test a *formative* one rather than a *summative* one? Unfortunately, a substantial number of educators toss the phrase "formative assessment" around as though it's widely understood by all. Yet, as you can see in the comment from Shepard, many commercial test-development outfits are plastering this label on any assessment-related product that might conceivably sell. You need to recognize that increasing numbers of teachers and administrators have had stuffed in their heads the notion that *the use of formative tests helps raise students' scores on summative tests*. Couple that message with the almost ubiquitous pressure on teachers to boost students' test scores, and you'll see why many educators grasp, in desperation, at the score-boosting promises associated with formative assessment. It's no wonder that commercial test organizations have been so successful in peddling any product carrying a formative-assessment label. You will often encounter tests these days labeled as "interim" assessments or "benchmark" assessments that do not necessarily qualify as formative assessments. Some will qualify; most won't.

What, then, is "formative assessment"? The definition on the next page was hammered out by a number of first-rate assessment specialists. It nicely captures the nature of formative assessment in a way that meshes well with the conception Black and Wiliam (1998) employed in their influential review of classroom assessment literature:

> An assessment is formative to the extent that information from the assessment is used, during the instructional segment in which the assessment occurred, to adjust instruction with the intent of improving the learning of the students assessed.

As you can see, for an assessment to be formative, it needs to provide information so that adjustments are made during the instructional segment in which the assessment was administered, Thus, for example, if you were teaching a three-week unit aimed at promoting students' acquisition of a key skill in science, the results of the formative assessment would need to get back to you in time for you to make instructional adjustments during the unit *while there was still sufficient instructional time left in the unit for those adjustments to do some good.* Formative assessments must result in actual adjustments—either in instruction or in the way students are tying to learn something.

Formative assessment need not be thought of only as paper-and-pencil "tests" or computer-dispensed "tests." Teachers can employ very informal ways, such as question-and-answer activities or classroom discussions, to get a better fix on where students currently are with respect to a curricular aim being sought. But it is imperative that formative assessments are constructed so their "adjustment implications" are as clear as possible. In other words, if you were to devise a brief quiz for your students, and you wanted to use the results of that quiz for purposes of adjusting your instruction (if, based on the results, it appeared you needed to make adjustments), then you should deliberately build the items in the quiz so your students' responses reveal more than merely "they didn't get it." What a really good formative assessment must do is provide insights about what to do next. Clearly, crafting a good formative assessment is not fool's play!

There are two sorts of adjustments that can flow from a formative assessment. First, there are adjustments a teacher can make in instruction—for example, when a teacher discovers from the results of a formative assessment that students need to be instructed more vigorously regarding a subskill the teacher thought the students had already mastered. The teacher, thereupon, would return to the treatment of that subskill and adjust the instruction. A second payoff of formative assessment is that it can help students adjust the tactics they are using in order to attain whatever curricular aim the teacher is promoting.

A number of individuals writing on the topic of classroom assessment have urged teachers to make their students active participants in the learning process, not merely as receptacles but rather as self-directed partners. Indeed, Black and Wiliam (1998) make an eloquent plea for the meaningful involvement of students in classroom assessments, not in a competitive sense, but in the spirit of learning collaboratively and, insofar as possible, under each student's self-direction. But even self-directed learners need to know how they are doing, and that's where formative assessment comes careening onto the scene.

If I were to poll 100 experienced teachers in the United States to find out how many of them really have even a remote idea regarding what formative assessment is, I'd be amazed if 50 of them could come up with a fog-free notion about the nature of formative assessment. But, because I am in a mood to be amazed, let's say that a full 50 of the 100 teachers described formative assessment in a manner more or less consistent with the definition proposed on page 274. I'd then be willing to wager lots of "previously owned" lesson plans that almost all of those knowledgeable 50 teachers would be thinking about formative assessment *exclusively* from a *teacher's* point of view. In other words, the 50 measurement-moxie teachers would believe the role of classroom formative assessment is to produce evidence for teachers so that those teachers could adjust their instruction and, thereby, teach kids better. But such an all-too-common idea about formative assessment really misses the mark. It misses the mark by about 50 percent. That's because roughly half the payoff from classroom formative assessment can, and should, come from involving students actively in the *instructional* use of formal and informal assessment. A continuing mission of such assessment should be to help students make more knowledgeable decisions regarding their current learning tactics. It's tough for a student to relax because, "I've mastered this skill," when a formative assessment supplies inescapable evidence that skill-mastery is simply not there.

If one significant role of formative assessment in the classroom is to help students learn more effectively and more efficiently, then teachers will need to engage in serious rethinking about the role most classroom tests play as students' grade-determiners. Although in U.S. classrooms there currently exists a time-honored tradition of using tests to compare students, it is fundamentally wrong-headed to try to use a test to help students guide their own learning while at the same time using the results of that test to grade or rank those students. Teachers, of course, must give grades. And tests—some tests—will most likely play a part in grade-determination. But the vast majority of classroom tests, the ones intended to help students better manage their own learning, should be nongraded. To differentiate the "learning-focused" tests from the "grading-focused" tests, all a teacher needs to do is inform students in advance by saying something such as "Because of the need for me to supply grades, the upcoming classroom test on Wednesday, unlike our usual ones, will be used for grading purposes." It is imperative not to contaminate the learning dividends derivative from classroom formative assessments by the needless affixing of grades to students' performances on those assessments.

Making classroom assessments a pivotal part of the instructional process will not take place overnight. It will take teachers, and most definitely students, a good long while to accept the idea most classroom tests can function in a way intended to improve learning, not appraise students. Teachers will obviously need to let students know, in advance, which tests are intended for grade-determination. But such tests really should be very few in number. And if we are going to get the most instructional mileage out of our classroom tests, then we need to get cracking right away with this approach. Teachers need to tell their students, "There's a new testing game in our class, and its *only* function is to help you learn better the things you need to learn!" I suspect you can see that if nongraded formative assessments are made a constant component of what takes place in a classroom, and the thrust of all such formative assessment is to help kids learn, a decisively different atmosphere ought to prevail in that classroom. Students can, sans embarrassment, reveal they don't know something. That's because there is a clear commitment on the part of the teacher to help all students learn what they need to, and the heart of this learn-better game is formative assessment. There will be a new zeitgeist present in any classroom dominated by frequent formative testing. It is a zeitgeist to be cherished. (Note the classy use of "zeitgeist" in this book. Clearly the concepts here must be high-level crud!)

The chief point I'm trying to make here is all too simple: Teachers dare not judge books by their covers, students' motivation by their smiles, or assessments by their labels. A test that's called formative might turn out to be a test to revile. Formative assessments, just like summative assessments, can differ considerably in their quality. For instance, if a formative assessment is truly terrific, its results will be made available in a timely manner so instruction, if necessary, can be shaped up in order to better teach the test-takers what they need to learn. Then too, a good formative assessment should supply evidence yielding instructional insights well beyond those that are derivative from a summative test. A nifty formative assessment will permit students to improve their performances over time, especially if those students are helped to internalize the evaluative criteria by which to judge their current and future performances.

So summing up, once classroom teachers develop formal or informal assessment procedures that are patently formative in nature, then there's still the need to make certain those assessments are as effective as they can be. A first-rate formative assessment, happily, will invariably be a measurement device that is, unarguably, an assessment *for* learning.

■ What Do Classroom Teachers Really Need to Know about Instructionally Oriented Assessment?

The view of classroom assessment given in this chapter represents what, for many teachers, is a decisively different way of thinking about assessment. What teachers really need to do in connection with this "different" view of classroom assessment is decide whether they want to employ it. At bottom, instructionally oriented assessment is really quite simple. To implement such an approach, teachers merely need to (1) develop their assessments prior to instructional planning, (2) make certain the content of those assessments can be addressed instructionally, and (3) use relevant along-the-way evidence about students' status when making instructional decisions.

I don't want to suggest the adoption of an instructionally oriented approach to classroom assessment is fools-play. It surely isn't. To adopt this assessment approach, teachers must be consistently clear-headed about how they're going to proceed instructionally. And it's tough to be consistently clearheaded. Time periods during which one can think sloppily are so downright gratifying. But clearheaded planning of classroom assessments that clarify the teacher's instructional aims will bring about what all teachers want—better learning for students.

For most classroom teachers, viewing assessments as bona fide *instructional allies* will require a meaningful reconceptualization of the way they view the relationship between teaching or testing. Tests should not be regarded merely as in-

but what does this have to do with
Teaching?

Everything!

structional afterthoughts. Tests, if they are worth the considerable effort we often put into their creation, really ought to help teachers teach better. There's a meaningful role for assessment *of* learning. But it definitely ought to be a supporting role. Assessment *for* learning ought to get the starring role in this educational drama.

■ Chapter Summary

In this chapter an attempt was made to extol the virtues of instructionally oriented assessment—that is, assessment conceived chiefly as a vehicle to improve the caliber of teachers' instructional decision making. Two ways of enhancing a teacher's instructional efforts were described. First, attention was given to *making instructional decisions in light of assessment results.* This approach, well known to most teachers (although not practiced by many), calls for teachers to make instructional decisions only after ascertaining their students' status with respect to the curricular aims being pursued. Three general kinds of instructional decisions were identified as those likely to benefit from results-influenced decision making—namely, what to teach, how long to keep teaching it, and whether the teaching was effective. Assessment *for* learning is a marvelous exemplification of this strategy.

Second, attention was then given to *planning instruction to achieve the curricular aim(s) represented by a test.* Such an assessment-illuminated instruction calls for classroom assessments to be created before instructional plans are made so greater clarity can be obtained by teachers regarding their instructional intentions. For such assessment-illuminated instructional design to yield optimal benefits, however, classroom assessments must be constructed with instruction clearly in mind. Ways of creating assessments so what they measure is more instructionally addressable were described for constructed-response, selected-response, and affective assessments.

Self-Check

This is a particularly important chapter because it suggests how you can use classroom assessment to do the very thing that most people originally went into teaching to do—namely, teach students well. Because of the chapter's significance, I'm going to ask to tackle two tasks that will require you to enlist the assistance of another person.

First, I want you to describe to someone else, orally and without notes, the overall message of this chapter about instructionally oriented assessment. Ideally, the person you'd choose would be a teacher or a teacher-in-training, but any human being (whose vital signs are still positive) will do. After the person has listened to your scintillating summary, ask this individual to explain it back to you—to see how well you did.

Next, and this is really tough, I'd like you to build a classroom test, constructed response or selected response, that can illuminate instructional *planning*. Then briefly describe how you'd plan successful instruction to promote what the test is measuring. Having done so, again I'd like to you snare an educationally knowledgeable person and have this individual look over your test and your instructional plans to give you some feedback about the likelihood your instruction will promote the cognitive, psychomotor, or affective objective you're hoping to accomplish.

If you choose a performance test, of course, you'll need to whomp up a rubric for scoring students' responses to the performance test's task. Keep the instructional objective modest in scope so this self-check doesn't become a life's endeavor. You still have three chapters to go!

? Pondertime

1. The chapter identified two major strategies—that is, making instructional decisions in light of assessment results and planning instruction to achieve the objective(s) represented by a test—to link assessment and instruction. Which of the two strategies do you prefer? Why?

2. How can teachers teach toward what's measured by a classroom test without teaching directly to the test's items?

3. Why do you think the chapter attempted to dissuade teachers from creating their own progress maps?

4. What are the positives you see that might be associated with assessment *for* learning? How about any negatives?

Self-Check Key

For this chapter's two tasks, you're really going to have to rely on your own judgments about how well you did. Did the person (or persons) you involved seem to know what you'd done? Is that person still speaking to you? (If not, there are numerous other persons available. They're everywhere!)

■ Additional Stuff

Black, Paul, Christine Harrison, Clare Lee, Bethan Marshall, and Dylan Wiliam. (2002). *Working Inside the Black Box: Assessment for Learning in the Classroom.* London: Kings College London.

Black, Paul, Christine Harrison, Clare Lee, Bethan Marshall, and Dylan Wiliam. (2003). *Assessment for Learning: Putting It Into Practice.* New York: Open University Press.

Black, Paul, and Dylan Wiliam. (1998). "Inside the Black Box: Raising Standards through Classroom Assessment." *Phi Delta Kappan, 80,* no. 2: 139–148.

Broadfoot, P. M., R. Daugherty, J. Gardner, C. V. Gipps, W. Harlen, M. James, and G. Stobart. (1999). *Assessment for Learning: Beyond the Black Box*. Cambridge, UK: University of Cambridge School of Education.

Gipps, C. V., and G. Stobart. (1997). *Assessment: A Teacher's Guide to the Issues* (3rd ed.). London, UK: Hodder and Stoughton.

Herman, Joan L., and Eva L. Baker. (2005). "Making Benchmark Testing Work." *Educational Leadership, 63,* no. 3 (November): 48–55.

James, M. (1992). *Assessment for Learning*. Paper presented at the Annual Conference of the Association for Supervision and Curriculum Development (Assembly session on "Critique of Reforms in Assessment Testing in Britain") held in New Orleans, LA. Cambridge, UK: University of Cambridge Institute of Education.

Leahy, Siobhan, C. Lyon, M. Thompson, and D. Wiliam. (2005). "Classroom Assessment—Minute by Minute, Day by Day," *Educational Leadership, 63,* no. 3 (November): 18–24.

Masters, Geoff, and Margaret Forster. (1996). *Progress Maps*. Melbourne, Australia: Australian Council for Educational Research.

Popham, W. James. (2003). *Test Better, Teach Better: The Instructional Role of Assessment*. Alexandria, VA: Association for Supervision and Curriculum Development.

Sadler, Philip M., and Eddie Good. (2006). "The Impact of Self- and Peer-Grading on Student Learning." *Educational Assessment, 11,* no. 1: 1–32.

Shepard, Lorrie. (2005). "Linking Formative Assessment to Scaffolding." *Educational Leadership, 63,* no. 3 (November): 66–71.

Shepard, Lorrie. (2006). *Can Benchmark Assessments Be Formative? Distinguishing Formative Assessment from Formative Program Evaluation*. A presentation during the National Large-Scale Assessment Conference, Council of Chief State School Officers, San Francisco, California.

Stiggins, Richard J. (2002). "Assessment Crisis: The Absence of Assessment for Learning." *Phi Delta Kappan, 83,* no. 10: 758–765.

Stiggins, Richard J. (2004). *Student-Involved Assessment FOR Learning* (4th ed.). Upper Saddle River, NJ: Prentice-Hall.

Stiggins, Rick. (2005). "From Formative Assessment to Assessment FOR Learning: A Path to Success in Standards-Based Schools." *Phi Delta Kappan, 87,* no. 4 (December): 324–328.

Sutton, R. (1995). *Assessment for Learning*. Salford, UK: RS Publications.

Wise, Steven L., and Christine E. DeMars. (2005). "Low Examinee Effort in Low-Stakes Assessment: Problems and Potential Solutions." *Educational Assessment, 10,* no. 1: 1–18.

■ Nonprint Stuff

Association for Supervision and Curriculum Development. (2002). *Using Classroom Assessment to Guide Instruction* (Entire Series Videotape Stock #402286Z59). Alexandria, VA: Author.

Association for Supervision and Curriculum Development. *How to Informally Assess Student Learning* (How to Video No. 22). Alexandria, VA: Author.

Association for Supervision and Curriculum Development. *How to Spiral Questions to Provoke Student Thinking* (How to Video No. 23). Alexandria, VA: Author.

Phi Delta Kappan. (1999). *Imagine! Assessments That Energize Students* (Videotape #IATES). Bloomington, IN: Author.

Popham, W. James. *Improving INSTRUCTION through Classroom Assessment* (Videotape #ETVT-25). Los Angeles: IOX Assessment Associates.

■ Cyber Stuff

■ *King's College London* has a Department of Education and Professional Studies which offers, under the research pages of this website, a number of assessment-related publications (some downloadable) of the King's Assessment For Learning Group. www.kcl.ac.uk/depsta/education

■ *The U.S. Department of Education* hosts an especially comprehensive website, providing visitors with a considerable array of instructional and assessment resources. To illustrate, the site contains a lengthy list of topics such as testing, accountability, and instructional materials. By consulting this list, a site visitor can obtain leads to a variety of instructional materials, many of which are free because they have been created under federal auspices. The website contains a quick-search and full-search capability so that a visitor may obtain leads to many resources regarding instruction-related or assessment-related topics. www.ed.gov

To access chapter objectives, practice tests, weblinks, and flashcards, visit the companion website at **www.ablongman.com/popham5e.**

Companion Website

Where the classroom comes to life!

MyLabSchool is a collection of online tools for your success in this course, your licensure exams, and your teaching career. Discover where the classroom comes to life by visiting **www.mylabschool.com** to access the following resources:

■ Video clips from real classrooms

■ An archive of real-life cases

■ Help with your research papers using Research Navigator™

■ Career Center with resources for:
Praxis exams and licensure preparation
Professional portfolio development
Job search and interview techniques
Lesson planning with state standard correlations

13

Making Sense Out of Standardized Test Scores

C lassroom teachers need to be able to interpret the results not only of their own assessment procedures but also of the various kinds of standardized tests that are frequently administered to students. Teachers need to be able to interpret such test results so they can base classroom instructional decisions on those results and also be able to respond accurately when students' parents raise such questions as, "What does my child's grade-equivalent score of 7.4 really mean?" or "When my child's achievement test results are at the 97th percentile, is that three percentiles from the top or the bottom?"

This chapter focuses on the task of making sense out of students' performances on standardized achievement and aptitude tests. One of the kinds of tests under consideration will be the achievement tests (for instance, in mathematics or reading) developed and distributed by commercial testing companies. Achievement tests are also developed and administered by state departments of education in connection with statewide assessment programs in such subjects as social studies, sciences, mathematics, reading, and writing. These state tests often employ reporting procedures akin to those used with commercially distributed standardized achievement tests.

And, even though I've desperately tried to avoid numbers larger than 9, in this chapter you'll encounter a few that are, indeed, larger. Don't be dismayed. Simply go through the examples, one step at a time, and you'll emerge from the chapter a finer human being. The numbers in this chapter will be easier to deal with than might be thought at first glance.

These days, standardized tests (especially standardized *achievement* tests) are often misused. In Chapter 15 you'll learn why it is altogether klutzy to try to evaluate educators' effectiveness on the basis of students' scores on many such tests. Nonetheless, standardized tests *do* have an important, educationally useful role to play. This chapter focuses on the appropriate uses of standardized tests.

The chapter will be wrapped up with a consideration of two aptitude tests that have a whopping impact on students' lives. You'll be looking at the two examinations that often become determiners to a student's continued education. That's right, we'll be dealing with the two most widely used college entrance exams: the SAT and the ACT.

If you're a current or would-be secondary school teacher, you'll immediately recognize the need for you to know about the SAT and the ACT. After all, many of your students will soon be taking one or both of these tests. But if you're an elementary teacher, or are preparing to be one, you might be thinking, What do college entrance exams have to do with me? Well, all teachers—elementary and secondary—ought to understand at least the most significant facts about these two examinations. Even teachers of primary-grade kids will find parents asking them questions such as, How can we get our child really ready for those in-the-future, important college entrance tests? Every teacher should be familiar with any really significant information associated with the teaching profession. Thus, because most students and their parents will, at some point, want to know more about college entrance exams, I think every single teacher—and even married ones—should know the basic SAT and ACT facts you'll learn about in this chapter.

■ Standardized Tests

A *standardized test* is a test, either designed to yield norm-referenced or criterion-referenced inferences, that is administered, scored, and interpreted in a standard, predetermined manner. Almost all *nationally* standardized tests are distributed by commercial testing firms. Most such firms are for-profit corporations, although there are a few not-for-profit measurement organizations, such as the Educational Testing Service (ETS), that distribute nationally standardized tests. Almost all nationally standardized tests, whether focused on the measurement of students' aptitude or achievement, are chiefly intended to provide norm-referenced interpretations.

Standardized achievement tests have also been developed in a number of states under the auspices of state departments of education. These statewide tests (clearly intended to be administered, scored, and interpreted in a standard, predetermined fashion) have usually been installed to satisfy a legislative mandate aimed at achieving a form of educational accountability. In some instances, important decisions about individual students are made on the basis of a student's test performance. In many states, for example, if a student does not pass a prescribed statewide basic skills examination by the end of high school, the student is not awarded a diploma, even though the student has satisfied all other curricular requirements. In other cases, although no contingencies for individual students depend on how a student performed on a test, results of student tests are publicized by the media on a district-by-district or school-by-school basis. The test results thus serve as an indicator of local educators' effectiveness, at least in the perception of many citizens. These state-sired standardized achievement tests are generally intended to yield

Decision Time

Which Test to Believe

Each spring in the Big Valley Unified School District, students in grades 5, 8, 10, and 12 complete nationally standardized achievement tests in reading and mathematics as well as a nationally standardized test described by its publishers as "a test of the student's cognitive aptitude." Because William White teaches eighth-grade students in his English classes, he is given the task of answering any questions about the test results raised by his eighth-graders' parents.

He is faced with one fairly persistent question from most parents, particularly those parents whose children scored higher on the aptitude test than on the achievement test. For example, Mr. and Mrs. Wilkins (Wanda's parents) put the question like this: "If Wanda scored at the 90th percentile on the aptitude test and only at the 65th percentile on the achievement test, does that mean she's not putting in enough study time? Putting it another way," they continued, "should we really believe the aptitude tests results or the achievement test's results? Which is Wanda's 'true' test performance?"

 If you were William, and had to decide how to answer the questions posed by Wanda's parents, what would your answers be?

criterion-referenced interpretations. Educational aptitude tests are rarely, if ever, developed by state departments of education.

Although standardized tests have traditionally consisted almost exclusively of selected-response items, in recent years the developers of standardized tests have attempted to incorporate an increasing number of constructed-response items in their tests. Standardized tests, because they are intended for widespread use, are developed with far more care (and cost) than is possible in an individual teacher's classroom. Even so, the fundamentals of test development you've learned about in earlier chapters are routinely employed when standardized tests are developed. In other words, the people who create the items for such tests attempt to adhere to the same kinds of item-writing and item-improvement precepts you've learned about. The writers of multiple-choice items for standardized tests worry, just as you should, about inadvertently supplying students with clues that give away the correct answer. The writers of short-answer items for standardized tests try to avoid, just as you should, the inclusion of ambiguous language in their items.

There are, of course, staggering differences in the level of effort associated with the construction of standardized tests and the construction of classroom tests. A commercial testing agency may assign a fleet of item writers and a flock of item editors to a new test-development project, whereas you'll be fortunate if you have a part-time teacher's aide or, possibly, a malleable spouse to proofread your tests to detect typographical errors.

■ Group-Focused Test Interpretation

Although the bulk of this chapter will be devoted to a consideration of score-reporting mechanisms used to describe an individual student's performance, you'll sometimes find you need to describe the performance of your students as a group. To do so, you'll typically compute some index of the group of scores' *central tendency*, such as when you determine the group's **mean** or **median** performance. For example, you might calculate the *mean raw score* or the *median raw score* for your students. A **raw score** is simply the number of items a student answers correctly. The *mean*, as you probably know, is the arithmetic average of a set of scores. For example, the mean of the scores 10, 10, 9, 8, 7, 6, 3, 3, and 2 would be 6.4 (that is, summing the nine scores and then dividing by nine). The *median* is the midpoint of a set of scores. For the nine scores in the previous example, the median would be 7 because this score divides the group into two equal parts. Means and medians are useful ways to describe the point at which the scores in a set of scores are centered.

In addition to describing the central tendency of a set of scores (via the mean and/or median), it is also helpful to describe the *variability* of the scores—that is, how spread out the scores are. One simple measure of the variability of a set of students' scores is the **range**. The range is calculated by simply subtracting the lowest student's score from the highest student's score. To illustrate, suppose the highest test score by students in your class was a 49 correct out of 50 earned by Hortense (she always tops your tests; it is surprising she missed one). Suppose further that the lowest score of 14 correct was, as usual, earned by Ed. The range of scores would be 35—that is, Hortense's 49 minus Ed's 14.

Because only two scores influence the range, it is less frequently used as an index of test score variability than is the **standard deviation.** A standard deviation is a kind of average. More accurately, it's the average difference between the individual scores in group of scores and the mean of that set of scores. The larger the size of the standard deviation, the more spread out are the scores in the **distribution.** (That's a posh term to describe a set of scores.) Presented here is the formula for computing a standard deviation for a set of scores:

$$\text{Standard Deviation (S.D.)} = \sqrt{\frac{\Sigma(X - M)^2}{N}}$$

where: $\Sigma(X - M)^2$ = the sum of the squared raw scores (X) – the mean (M)

N = number of scores in the distribution

Here's a step-by-step description of how you compute a standard deviation using this formula. First, compute the mean of the set of scores. Second, subtract the mean from each score in the distribution. (Roughly half of the resulting values, called *deviation scores,* will have positive values and half will have negative values.) Third, square each of these deviation scores. This will make them all positive. Fourth, add the squared deviation scores together. Fifth, divide the resulting sum by the number of scores in the distribution. Sixth, and last, take the square root of

Figure 13.1 ■ Two Fictitious Sets of Tests Scored with Equal Means but Different Standard Deviations

More Homogenous Scores:

3, 4, 4, 5, 5, 5, 5, 6, 6, 7

Mean = 5.0

$$S.D. = \sqrt{\frac{12}{10}} = 1.1$$

More Heterogeneous Scores:

0, 1, 2, 4, 5, 5, 6, 8, 9, 10

Mean = 5.0

$$S.D. = \sqrt{\frac{102}{10}} = 3.2$$

the results of the division you did in the fifth step. The square root that you get is the standard deviation. Not too tough, right?

To illustrate the point that larger standard deviations represent more spread in a distribution of scores than smaller standard deviations, take a look at the two fictitious sets of scores on a 10-item short-answer test presented in Figure 13.1. Both sets of scores have a mean of 5.0. The distribution of scores at the left is much more homogeneous (less spread out) than the distribution of scores at the right. Note the standard deviation for the more homogeneous scores is only 1.1, whereas the standard deviation of the more heterogeneous scores is 3.2. The larger the standard deviation, therefore, the more distant, on average, will be the distribution's scores from the distribution's mean.

You may have occasions to describe the scores of an entire group of the students you teach. Those descriptions might portray your students' performances on standardized tests or on teacher-made tests. If you get at all comfortable with means and standard deviations, those two indices usually provide a better picture of a score distribution than do the median and range. But if you think means and standard deviations are statistical gibberish, then go for the median (midpoints are easy to identify) and range (ranges require only skill in subtraction). With group-based interpretations out of the way, let's turn now to interpreting individual students scores from the kinds of standardized tests commonly used in education.

■ Individual Student Test Interpretation

Two overriding frameworks are generally used to interpret students' test scores. Test scores are interpreted in *absolute* or *relative* terms. When we interpret a student's test score *absolutely,* we infer from the score what it is that the student can or cannot do. For example, based on a student's performance on test items dealing with mathematics computation skills, we make an inference about the degree to which the student has mastered such computation skills. The teacher may even boil the interpretation down to a dichotomy—namely, whether the student should be classified as having mastered or not having mastered the skill or knowledge being assessed. A mastery versus nonmastery interpretation represents an *absolute* interpretation of a student's test score. Classroom teachers often use this absolute interpretive approaches when creating tests to assess a student's knowledge or skills based on a particular unit of study.

When we interpret a student's test score *relatively,* we infer from the score how the student stacks up against other students who are currently taking the test or have already taken the test. For example, when we say that Johnny's score is "above average" or "below average," we are making a relative test interpretation because we use the average performance of other students to make sense out of Johnny's test score.

As pointed our earlier, this chapter focuses on how teachers and parents can interpret scores on standardized tests. Because almost all standardized test scores require relative interpretations, the three interpretive schemes to be considered in the chapter are all relative score-interpretation schemes. The vast majority of standardized tests, whether achievement tests or aptitude tests, provide relative interpretations. Accordingly, teachers need to be especially knowledgeable about relative score-interpretation schemes.

Percentiles

The first interpretive scheme we'll consider, and by all odds the most commonly used one, is based on *percentiles* or, as they are sometimes called, *percentile ranks.* Percentiles are used most frequently in describing standardized test scores because percentiles are readily understandable to most people.

A percentile compares a student's score with those of other students in a *norm group.* A percentile indicates the percent of students in the norm group that the student outperformed. A percentile of 60, for example, indicates the student performed better than 60% of the students in the norm group.

Let's spend a moment describing what a norm group is. As indicated, a percentile compares a student's score with scores earned by those in a norm group. This comparison with the norm group is based on the performances of a group of individuals who have already been administered a particular examination. For instance, before developers of a new standardized test publish their test, they will administer the test to a large number of students who then become the norm group for the test. Typically, different norm groups of students are assembled for all the grade levels for which percentile interpretations are made.

Figure 13.2 shows a graphic depiction of a set of 3,000 students' scores such as might have been gathered during the norming of a nationally standardized achievement test. Remember, we refer to such students as the norm group. The area under the curved line represents the number of students who earned scores at that point on the baseline. You'll notice, for a typical norm group's performance, most students score in the middle while only a few students earn very high or very low scores.

In fact, *if* the distribution of test scores in the norm group is *perfectly* normal, then, as you see in Figure 13.3, over two-thirds of the scores (represented by the area under the curved line) will be located relatively close to the center of the distribution—that is, plus or minus one standard deviation (S.D.) from the mean.

Figure 13.2 ■ A Typical Norm Group

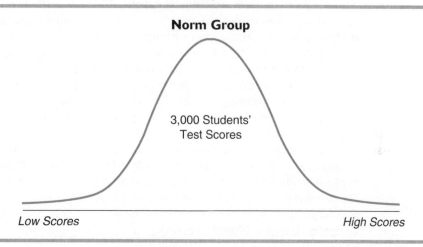

Norm Group

3,000 Students'
Test Scores

Low Scores   *High Scores*

Not all norm groups are national norm groups. Sometimes test publishers, at the request of local school officials, develop local norms. These local norms can be either state norms or school-district norms. Comparisons of students on the basis of local norms is sometimes seen as being more meaningful than are comparisons based on national norms.

In many instances, local norms are different from national norms because the students in a particular locality are not representative of the nation's children as a whole. If there is a difference between local and national norms, then there will be a difference in a student's percentile scores. A student's raw score—that is, the number of test items answered correctly—might be equal to the 50th percentile

Figure 13.3 ■ A Normally Distributed Set of Norm-Group Scores

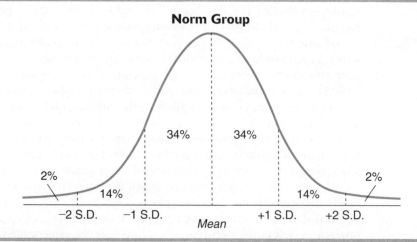

Norm Group

34%   34%

2%   2%
       14%   14%

−2 S.D.   −1 S.D.   +1 S.D.   +2 S.D.
              Mean

based on *national* norms but be equal to the 75th percentile based on *local* norms. This kind of situation would occur if the students in the local group hadn't performed as well as students in the nation at large. National and local norms provide decisively different frameworks for interpreting standardized test results. When reporting test scores to parents, make sure you communicate clearly whether a child's percentiles are based on national or local norms.

It's also true that some norm groups have been more carefully constituted than others. For example, certain national norm groups are more representative of the nation's population than are other national norm groups. There are often large differences in the representativeness of norm groups based on such variables as gender, ethnicity, geographic region, and socioeconomic status of the students in the groups. In addition, many standardized tests are renormed only every 5 to 10 years. It is important to make sure the normative information on which percentiles are based is both representative and current.

Grade-Equivalent Scores

Let's turn from percentiles to look at a *grade equivalent* or, as they're often called, *grade-equivalent scores.* Grade-equivalent scores constitute another effort to provide a relative interpretation of standardized test scores. A *grade equivalent* is an indicator of student test performance based on grade level and months of the school year. The purpose of grade equivalents is to transform scores on standardized tests into an index reflecting a student's grade-level progress in school. A grade-equivalent score is a *developmental* score in the sense that it represents a continuous range of grade levels.

Let's look at a grade-equivalent score of 4.5:

A Grade-Equivalent Score:

Grade → 4.5 ← Month of School Year

The score consists of the grade, a decimal, and a number representing months. The number to the left of the decimal point represents the grade level, in this example, the fourth grade. The number to the right of the decimal point represents the month of the school year, in this example, the fifth month of the school year.

Some test publishers, using statistical schemes, convert raw scores on standardized tests to grade-equivalent scores. These grade-equivalent scores often appear on students' score reports. Grade-equivalent scores are most appropriate for basic skills areas such as reading and mathematics where it can be assumed the degree of instructional emphasis given to the subject is fairly uniform from grade to grade.

The appeal of grade-equivalent scores is they appear to be readily interpretable to both teachers and parents. However, many teachers and parents actually have an incorrect understanding of what grade-equivalent scores signify. To see why these scores are misunderstood, it's necessary to understand a bit about where they come from in the first place.

To determine the grade-equivalent scores to be hooked up with particular raw scores, test developers typically administer the same test to students in several

Figure 13.4 ■ Student Performances at Three Third-Grade Levels

grade levels, then establish a trend line reflecting the raw score increases at each grade level. The test developers then *estimate* at other points along this trend line what the grade equivalent for any raw score would be.

Let's illustrate this important point. In Figure 13.4, you will see the respective performance of students at three grade levels. The same 80-item test has been given to students at all three grade levels: grades 4, 5, and 6. A trend line is then established from the three grades where the test was actually administered. The result of that estimation procedure is seen in Figure 13.5.

Figure 13.5 ■ A Trend Line Used to Estimate Average Performance of Students at Nontested Grades

In order for these estimated grade-equivalent scores to be accurate, several assumptions must be made. First, it must be assumed that the subject area tested is emphasized equally at each grade level. It must also be assumed students' mastery of the tested content increases at a reasonably constant rate at each grade level over an extended period of time. The assumption that the mastery of the test's content increases consistently over time is particularly difficult to support in subject areas other than reading and mathematics. And even in those two bread-and-butter subjects, students' consistent increases in mastery of content are definitely debatable.

The implied precision associated with a grade-equivalent score of 6.2, therefore, is difficult to defend. A 6.2 grade-equivalent score suggests a degree of accuracy that's simply not warranted. An unskilled interpreter of a standardized achievement test results may think a 6.2 grade-equivalent score indicates the student's raw score represents a performance equal to that of a sixth-grade pupil in the second month of the sixth-grade year. Remember, most grade-equivalent scores are created on the basis of estimation, not real test-score data. Because substantial sampling and estimation errors are apt to be present, grade-equivalent scores should always be taken with several grains of salt.

Now you understand grade-equivalent scores to be, at best, rough estimates, let's return to the potential misinterpretations teachers and parents often make regarding grade-equivalent scores. Let's say a third-grade student makes a grade-equivalent score of 5.5 in reading. What does this grade-equivalent score mean? Here's a wrong answer: "The student can do fifth-grade work." Here's a *really* wrong answer: "The student should be promoted to the fifth grade." The right answer, of course, is that the third-grader understands reading skills the test covers about as well as an average fifth-grader does at midyear. A grade-equivalent score should be viewed as the point where a student is along a developmental continuum, not as the grade level in which the student should be placed.

If standardized tests are used in your school district, and if those tests yield grade-equivalent scores, it is important to provide parents with an accurate description of what a grade-equivalent score means. Parents who have not been given an accurate definition of such scores frequently think a high grade-equivalent score means their child is capable of doing work at the grade level specified. Some parents even use high grade-equivalent scores as a basis for arguing their child should be advanced to a higher grade. Because many parents have a misconception of what a grade-equivalent score means, they may have an inflated estimate of their child's level of achievement. The high frequency of parental (and teacher) misinterpretations is the reason some districts have, as a matter of policy, eliminated grade-equivalent scores when reporting standardized test results.

Remember, if a fourth-grade student gets a grade equivalent of 7.5 in mathematics, it is *not* accurate to say the fourth-grader is doing well in seventh-grade mathematics. It is more appropriate to say a grade-equivalent score of 7.5 is an estimate of how an average seventh-grader might have performed *on the fourth-grader's mathematics test*. Obtaining a 7.5 grade-equivalent score doesn't mean the fourth-grader has any of the mathematics skills taught in the fifth, sixth, or seventh grade because those mathematics skills were probably not even measured on the fourth-grade test.

But what happens when grade-equivalent scores are *below* the actual grade level tested? Let's say a fifth-grader earns a mathematics grade-equivalent score of 2.5. It doesn't make much sense to say the fifth-grader is doing fifth-grade mathematics work as well as a second-grader, because second-graders obviously aren't given fifth-grade mathematics work. About the best you can say is that, in mathematics achievement, the fifth-grader appears to be lagging several years behind grade level.

Scale Scores

Let's move, now, to the last of our three score-interpretation schemes: *scale scores*. A scale score constitutes yet another way to give relative meaning to a student's standardized test performances. Scale scores are being employed with increasing frequency these days to report results of national and state-level standardized programs.

Although scale scores are sometimes not used in reporting standardized test results to parents, scale-score reporting systems are often employed in describing group test performances at the state, district, and school levels. Because of the statistical properties of scale scores, they can be used to permit longitudinal tracking of students' progress. Scale scores can also be used to make direct comparisons among classes, schools, or school districts. The statistical advantages of scale scores are considerable. Thus, we see scale-score reporting systems used with more frequency in recent years. As a consequence, you need to become familiar with the main features of scale scores because such scores are likely to be used when you receive reports of your students' performances on standardized tests.

A *scale* used for reporting test scores typically refers to numbers assigned to students on the basis of their test performances. Higher numbers (higher scores) reflect increasing levels of achievement or ability. Thus, such a scale might be composed of a set of raw scores where each additional test item correctly answered yields one more point on the raw-score scale. Raw scores, all by themselves, however, are difficult to interpret. A student's score on a raw-score scale provides no idea of the student's *relative* performance. Therefore, measurement specialists have devised different sorts of scales for test interpretation purposes.

Scale scores are *converted raw scores* that use a new, arbitrarily chosen scale to represent levels of achievement or ability. Shortly, you'll be given some examples to help you understand what is meant by converting scores from one scale to another. In essence, a scale-score system is created by devising a brand-new numerical scale that's often very unlike the original raw-score scale. Students' raw scores are then converted to this brand-new scale so, when score interpretations are to be made, those interpretations rely on the converted scores based on the new scale. Such converted scores are called *scale scores*.

For example, in Figure 13.6, you see a range of raw score points from 0 to 40 for a 40-item test. Below the raw-score scale, you see a new, converted scale ranging from 500 to 900. For a number of reasons, to be described shortly, it is sometimes preferable to use a scale-score reporting scheme rather than a raw-score reporting scheme. Thus, a student who achieved a raw score of 30 items correct might be assigned a scale score of 800, as shown in Figure 13.7.

Figure 13.6 ■ A Raw-Score Scale and a Converted-Score Scale

Raw-Score Scale				
0	10	20	30	40

Converted-Score Scale				
500	600	700	800	900

Figure 13.7 ■ An Illustration of a Raw-Score Conversion to a Scale Score

Raw-Score Scale			✕	
0	10	20	30	40
			↓	

Converted-Score Scale			✕	
500	600	700	800	900

One of the reasons scale scores have become popular in recent years is the necessity to develop several equidifficult forms of the same test. For example, a basic skills test must sometimes be passed before high school diplomas are awarded to students. Those students who initially fail the test are, typically, given other opportunities to pass it. The different forms of the test used for such retake purposes should, for the sake of fairness, represent assessment challenges for students that are equivalent to those represented by the initial form of the test. However, because it is next to impossible to create test forms that are absolutely identical, scale scores can be used to help solve the problem. Scores on two test forms of differing difficulty levels can be statistically adjusted so, when placed on a converted score scale, the new scale scores represent students' performances as if the two test forms had been completely equidifficult.

Most of the more popular types of scale-score systems are based on what statisticians refer to as *item response theory,* or IRT. IRT scale-score reporting systems are distinctively different from raw-score reporting systems because IRT scale-score schemes take into consideration the difficulty and other technical properties of every single item on the test. Thus, some test publishers have produced IRT-based scale scores for their tests ranging from 0 to 1,000 across an entire K–12 grade range. For each grade level, there is a different average scale score. For example, the average scale score for third-graders might be 585 and the average scale score for the tenth-graders might be 714.

These IRT-based scale scores can, when constructed with care, yield useful interpretations if one can reference them back to some notion of relative performance such as percentiles. If average scale scores are provided at different grade levels, this also can aid in the interpretation of scale scores. Without such interpretation crutches regarding a scale score's *relative* meaning, however, scale scores cannot be meaningfully interpreted by either educators or parents.

Mistakes are often made in interpreting scale scores because educators assume all scale scores are somehow similar. For example, when initially administered over 80 years ago, the mean scale score on the verbal section of the Scholastic Assessment Test was 500. This does not signify the mean score on that test today is 500 or that other tests using scale scores will always have mean scores of 500. Scale-score systems can be constructed so the mean score is 50, 75, 600, 700, 1,000, or any number the scale constructor has in mind.

One kind of scale score you may encounter when you work with your students' scores on standardized tests in the *normal curve equivalent.* A normal curve equivalent, usually referred to as an NCE, represents an attempt to use a student's raw score to arrive at a percentile for a raw score as if the distribution of scores on the test had been a perfectly symmetrical, bell-shaped normal curve. So, one of your students might get an NCE score indicating the student was performing at or near the top of a norm group's performance. Sometimes, unfortunately, neither the norm group's performance nor that of subsequent test takers is distributed in a normal fashion, so the meaningfulness of the student's NCE evaporates. Normal curve equivalents were originally created in an attempt to amalgamate students' performances from *different* standardized tests, perhaps none of which yielded normal distributions. As might be suspected, NCEs failed to solve this problem satisfactorily.

A final kind of scale score you should know about is called a *stanine*. Stanines are somewhat like NCEs in the sense that they assume a normal distribution for a set of scores. And this assumption, as you just read, runs counter to reality. But, as you'll soon see, a stanine score is a more gross score, so it can more easily tolerate a score distribution's departure from a normal shape.

A stanine scale divides a score distribution into nine segments that, though equal along the baseline of a set of scores (actually one-half standard deviation in distance), contain differing proportions of the distribution's scores. As you can see in Figure 13.8, the fifth stanine is at the center of a score distribution and contains about 20% of the scores. A ninth stanine score, however, contains only about 4% of the scores.

One advantage of stanines is they are *approximate* scale scores, and their very inexact nature conveys more clearly to everyone that educational measurement is not a superprecise assessment enterprise. As with most hierarchical classification systems, of course, a student may be *almost* at the next higher (or lower) stanine, yet may miss out by only a point or two. Such is the imprecision of measurement, even if you're using a deliberately approximation-engendering scoring system.

Contrasting Common Interpretive Options

We've now considered several types of score interpretation schemes, the most frequently used of these being percentiles, grade-equivalent scores, and scale scores. (Stanines and NCEs tend to be used less frequently.) It's time to review and sum-

Figure 13.8 ■ Stanine Units Represented in Approximate Percentages of the Normal Curve

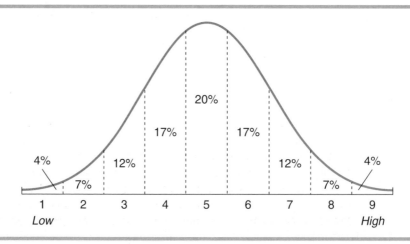

marize what's really important about the three most popular ways of making sense out of standardized test scores.

We first considered percentiles. A *percentile* indicates a student's standing in relationship to that of a norm group. If a student's test score is equal to the 25th percentile, the student's performance exceeds the performances of 25% of the individuals in the norm group. One advantage of percentiles is they're easy to interpret. And, for the most part, people's interpretations of percentiles are accurate. A disadvantage of percentiles is the defensibility of the interpretation is totally dependent on the nature of the normative data on which the percentiles are based. Unrepresentative or out-of-date norm data yield inaccurate percentile interpretations. As pointed out earlier, because percentile interpretations are so widely used, it's imperative for teachers to be knowledgeable about such interpretations.

Percentiles

Advantage: readily interpretable

Disadvantage: dependent on quality of norm group

Next we considered grade-equivalent scores. A *grade equivalent* indicates the nature of a student's test performance in terms of grade levels and months. Thus, a grade equivalent of 3.7 would indicate the student's test score was estimated to be the same as the average performance of a third-grader during the seventh month of the school year. One advantage of grade-equivalent scores is, because they are based on grade levels and months of the school year, they can be readily communicated to parents. A significant disadvantage associated with grade equivalent scores, however, is they're frequently misinterpreted.

Grade Equivalents

Advantage: readily communicable

Disadvantage: often misinterpreted

Finally, scale scores were described. *Scale scores* are interpreted according to a converted numerical scale that allows us to transform raw scores into more statistically useful scale-score units. A student who gets a raw score of 35 correct out of 50 items, for example, might end up with a converted scale score of 620. An advantage of scale scores is they can be used to create statistically adjusted equidifficult test forms. Scale-score schemes based on *item response theory* (IRT) do this by weighting individual test items differently based on an item's difficulty and other technical properties in relation to those same properties for all of a test's items. A disadvantage of scale-score reporting schemes is, with the possible exception of stanines, they're almost impossible to interpret all by themselves. Unless we mentally reference scale scores back to percentiles or average grade-level scale scores, such scores are essentially uninterpretable.

Scale Scores

Advantage: useful in equalizing difficulties of different test forms

Disadvantage: not easily interpretable

It should be clear to you that each of these three score-interpretation schemes has some potential virtues as well as some potential vices. You probably realize, even if you understand the general nature of each of these three interpretation schemes, it may be necessary to secure additional technical information to interpret each reporting scheme with confidence. Such information is usually found in the technical manuals that accompany standardized tests. For example, what was the nature of the norm group on which a test's percentiles were based? What sort of mathematical operations were used in generating a scale-score reporting scheme? Is a score distribution sufficiently normal to warrant the use of NCEs? To interpret a particular standardized test's results sensibly, teachers sometimes need to do a bit of homework themselves regarding the innards of the reporting scheme being used.

The Instructional Yield from Standardized Achievement Tests

Nationally standardized achievement tests, as noted previously, are developed and sold by commercial testing companies. The more tests those companies sell, the more money those companies make. Accordingly, the representatives of commercial testing companies usually suggest that their standardized achievement tests will not only yield valid norm-referenced interpretations about the students who take the tests but will also provide classroom teachers with a galaxy of useful information for instructional decision making. In my experiences, the *instructional* payoffs of standardized achievement tests are more illusory than real. More often than not, claims for the instructional dividends of such achievement tests reflect the zeal of a testing firm's sales force, not the reality of how teachers can actually use the results of standardized tests for instructional purposes.

Are standardized achievement tests better than no tests at all? Of course they are. But will standardized tests provide the instructionally sensible, fine-grained diagnostic data teachers need for accurate decisions? My answer, based on many years of using these tests, is decisively negative.

but what does this have to do with
Teaching?

Depending on the grade levels at which elementary teachers teach, or the subjects secondary teachers teach, many teachers these days find their attention focused on their students' scores on standardized achievement tests. That's because students' scores on such tests are increasingly used as an indicator of educators' instructional success. So, if you're a teacher whose state (or school district) requires that standardized achievement tests be administered at the end of school for a grade level you teach, you can be assured there will be plenty of attention given to your students' standardized test performances. In Chapter 15 you'll learn why this practice is inappropriate when certain types of standardized tests are employed.

But even if you're a teacher whose students are at grade levels or in classes where standardized tests don't play a major role, you need to become familiar with the way teachers and parents should interpret such test performances. And that's because, as a professional, a teacher is supposed to know such things. Parents will sometimes ask you what is meant by a percentile or an NCE. You don't want to blubber forth, "Beats me!"

And, of course, if your students *are* assessed with a standardized achievement test, such as those called for by NCLB, you'll want to be able to interpret what their scores signify, because this information will help you instructionally. Suppose, for example, it is the first week of school and you're reviewing your new fifth-grade students' end-of-year *fourth*-grade test performances. You discover that Martha Childs earned a 94th percentile in mathematics but only a 43rd percentile in reading. This information should give you some insights about how you'll approach Martha instructionally.

And if Billy Jenkins's fourth-grade test scores gave him a seventh stanine in language arts, but a first stanine in math, I suggest you don't have Billy keep track of your students' lunch money.

The better fix you get on your students' relative achievement levels, the more appropriately you can teach them. Proper interpretations of standardized test scores will often help you do so.

■ The SAT and the ACT: Three-Letter, High-Import Exams

Each year, millions of students put their futures on the line when they sit down to take the SAT and ACT exams, the nation's college entrance tests. Because not only students, but also students' parents, are understandably apprehensive about one or both of these college admission tests, teachers at all grade levels are apt to be questioned about the SAT or the ACT. Therefore, in the next few paragraphs I'll be describing the general nature of both exams, how they came into existence, and what

Parent Talk

Suppose that one of your students' parents, Mr. Lopez, visits your classroom during a back-to-school evening and raises a series of questions about his daughter, Concepción. Most prominently, Mr. Lopez is concerned with Concepción's scores on the nationally standardized achievement tests administered each spring in your district. Mr. Lopez is troubled by spring-to-spring changes in Concepción's percentiles. As he says, "For the last three springs, her percentile scores in language arts have been the 74th, the 83rd, and the 71st. What's going on here? Is she learning, then unlearning? What accounts for the differences?"

 If I were you, here's how I'd respond to Mr. Lopez:

"You are certainly wise to look into what appears to be inconsistent measurement on Concepción's standardized achievement tests. But what you need to understand, Mr. Lopez, is that these sorts of tests, even though they are nationally standardized, developed by reputable testing firms, and widely used, are not terrifically precise in how they measure students. Many parents, of course, recognize that their children's test scores are often reported numerically in the form of national percentiles. But this does *not* signify a given child's national percentile is unerringly accurate.

"The kinds of year-to-year shifting you've seen in Concepción's language arts percentiles is quite normal because a given year's test result is not unerringly accurate. Assessment specialists even admit the *anticipated* amount of flip-flop in students' scores when they talk about each test's 'standard error of measurement.' It's something like the sampling errors we hear about for national surveys—you know, 'plus or minus so many percentage points.' Well, measurement error is similar to sampling error. And let me assure you Concepción's scores will, quite predictably, vary from spring to spring.

"What we do see in her language arts performances over the last three years is a consistently high, well above average achievement level. When her performance is compared to that of a representative, nationally normed sample, Concepción is doing very well, indeed."

their scale scores look like. I'll close out this treatment of the two tests with a candid look at the accuracy with which those tests predict a high school student's academic success in college.

The SAT

First administered in 1926, the SAT was initially called the *Scholastic Aptitude Test*, and its function was to assist admissions officials in a group of elite Northeastern universities in determining which applicants should be admitted. The original name of the test really reveals what the test's developers were up to—namely, they wanted their tests to measure the largely in-born academic *aptitudes* of high school students. Because, much later, the idea of a test's measuring innate, genetically determined aptitudes became unappetizing to many educators, the Scholastic Aptitude Test became known only as the SAT. (One wonders if the developers of the SAT took their cues from the purveyors of Kentucky Fried Chicken who, recognizing the public's concern about the health risks of fried foods, morphed their famous label into KFC. It is, of course, difficult to become genuinely negative toward any three-letter label—with the possible exception of the IRS.)

The SAT was originally conceived of as a group-administrable intelligence test designed to compare test-takers according to their inherited verbal, quantitative, and spatial aptitudes. For many years, the SAT functioned in precisely that way, although during the last few decades we have seen less attention given to the *inherited* nature of what's being assessed.

Currently, the SAT is divided into three sections: Critical Reading, Writing, and Mathematics. All SAT items are multiple-choice in nature except for a small number of "grid-in" math items and a 25-minute essay in the Writing section. In all, the SAT takes about three hours for students to complete. Each of the three sections of the SAT uses a scale-score range from 200 to 800. Thus, after the installation of a writing test in 2005, the highest score a student can earn on the SAT is now 2400—that is, a *total* of a student's score on the three separate sections. Although the 2005 addition of an essay-writing task to the SAT attracted substantial media attention, students' essay scores do not contribute excessively to their overall SAT scores—or even to their scores on the Writing section where an essay performance is only worth about 20 percent of the student's score.

The test is still owned by the College Board, the group that originally created the test, but since 1947 the SAT has been developed and administered for the College Board by the Educational Testing Service (ETS). Both organizations are not-for-profit entities. A less demanding version of the test, referred to most often as the PSAT, is administered once each year in October—typically to high school students in their sophomore or junior years. The SAT itself is administered throughout the nation on several preannounced occasions during the year.

The ACT

Although both the SAT and the ACT are typically characterized as *aptitude* exams because they are employed in an effort to predict a high-schooler's subsequent academic performance in college, the ACT's lineage makes it a decisively different kind of "aptitude" test than the SAT. Following World War II, and the subsequent enactment of the G.I. Bill of Rights (a federal law providing college tuition for returning military personnel), many more American men and women wanted to secure a college education. There was, therefore, a substantially increased need for college entrance exams.

At the University of Iowa, a gifted professor named E. F. Lindquist believed the SAT, given its ancestry as an aptitude test designed for students attending elite colleges, was not a suitable exam for many of these post-WWII college applicants. Thus, in 1959 Lindquist and his colleagues established the American College Testing Program as a not-for-profit testing company which, in 1996, changed its official name to ACT.

From the very outset, the ACT was intended to be an unabashed *achievement* test. Architects of the ACT certainly wanted their new test to be predictive of a high school student's academic success in college, but they conceived of their new test chiefly as a measure of a student's "educational development."

The ACT is made up of separate tests in essentially the same four content areas it initially assessed: English, mathematics, reading, and science. An optional writing test is now available in which the student has 30 minutes to write an essay supporting one of two positions presented in a writing "prompt," or a task. As is true with the SAT, the ACT takes about three hours to complete.

Developers of the ACT routinely solicit content suggestions, in each of the content areas tested, from large samples of secondary teachers and curriculum coordinators as well as from college professors in the four core subject areas. Secondary-school educators are asked to identify the skills and content that students in their school or district have an option to learn by the end of their junior year in high school. College professors are asked what skills or knowledge that, having been taught at the secondary-school level, are essential for students to be academically successful during their first year of college. Based on a combination of what's taught in secondary schools and what's considered requisite for first-year success in college, items are then developed for the ACT.

Every ACT item is multiple-choice in nature, and a student gets one point for every correct answer with no subtraction of points (or partial points) for a wrong answer—as is the case in the SAT. Number-correct scores are then converted to a new 1–36 point scale for each of the separate tests from which an overall (composite) score is derived that represents the *average* of the four separate-tests' 1–36 points (unlike the SAT, where scores from its three sections are added together). The optional writing test, equivalent to the SAT's essay test, is scored on the basis of a 2–12 point scale using the judgments of two scorers who can each award 1–6 points to a student's essay.

As with the SAT, there are variations of the ACT available to be used with younger students. EXPLORE is aimed at eighth- and ninth-grade students, and PLAN is available for tenth-graders.

Predictive Accuracy—And Its Implications

Because of the important decisions linked to secondary students' scores on the SAT and the ACT, test-preparations options abound for each test. These test-prep possibilities range from low-cost printed and online Internet materials all the way up to very pricy in-person preparation classes and tutorials. Although there are exceptions, the more money that's spent on a preparation activity for either of these two tests, the more effective such preparation is apt to be. This is a troubling reality, of course, because children from more affluent families have greater access to the most costly preparation options, hence tend to score better than do their less affluent classmates who can't afford high-cost preparation alternatives.

But, as important as it is, lets put test-prep bias aside for a moment. There is one, overridingly important realization all teachers must arrive at regarding the predictive accuracy of the SAT and the ACT. Here it is, all gussied up in italics:

> *Only about 25% of academic success in college is associated*
> *with a high school student's performance on the SAT or ACT.*

To calculate how well a high school student's scores on a college entrance test accurately predict his or her academic success in college, a correlation is computed between high school students' scores on the SAT (or the ACT) and their subsequent college grades—for instance, their first-year college grade-point-averages. With few exceptions, the resulting correlation coefficients turn out to be approximately .50. A predictive coefficient of .50 is statistically significant, hence certainly reflects a *bona fide* relationship between students' scores on college entrance tests and their subsequent college grades.

However, to determine the practical meaningfulness of that relationship, what we must do is *square* the .50 coefficient (.50 × .50 = .25) so it becomes .25. This tells us that 25 percent of students' college grades can be linked to their performances on college admission tests. In other words, fully 75 percent of a student's college grades are due to factors *other* than scores on the SAT or the ACT. Such factors would include a student's motivation, study habits, and other variables over which a student has substantial control.

Now, if you are not a numerical ninny, you'll realize a student's college grades are three times more dependent on nontest factors than they are on test factor, that is, 75 percent (test-unrelated) versus 25 percent (test-related). And yet we find hoards of students who earn only "so-so scores" on the SAT or the ACT simply writing themselves off as "not smart enough" to succeed in college. College success, and success in life, is unarguably dependent on much more than a test score. Unfortunately, because the nation's teachers are often unfamiliar with the predictive *imprecision* of college entrance tests, they don't do enough to dissuade students from prematurely foreclosing their college aspirations.

Over the years, a student's SAT or ACT scores have become, to many educators, and to students themselves, an unalterable definition of one's ability. That's simply not true. And teachers need not only to know it, but to make sure their students (and students' parents) know it too.

The SAT and the ACT help college officials distinguish among applicants in the common fixed-quota setting where there are more applicants for admission to a college than there are openings to that college. But the *general* predictive power of the SAT and the ACT doesn't transform those exams into definitively accurate assessment tools in the case of *any particular* student. Teachers at all levels need to help students recognize what the SAT and the ACT exams can do—and what they can't.

■ What Do Classroom Teachers Really Need to Know about Interpreting Standardized Test Scores?

Because results of standardized tests are almost certain to come into your professional life, at least in some form, you need to have an intuitive understanding of how to interpret those results. The most common ways of describing a set of scores is to provide an index of the score distribution's central tendency (usually the mean or median) and an index of the score distribution's variability (usually the standard deviation or the range). There will probably be instances in which you either have to describe the performances of your students or to understand the descriptions of the performances of other groups of students (such as all students in your school or your district).

To make accurate interpretations of standardized test scores for your own students, and to help parents understand how to make sense of their child's standardized test scores, you need to comprehend the basic meaning of percentiles, grade-equivalent scores, and scale scores. You really ought to know what the major advantage and disadvantage of each of those three score-interpretation schemes is. You'll then be in a position to help parents make sense out of their children's performances on standardized tests.

Two of the more influential tests many students will ever take are the SAT and the ACT, the most widely used college entrance tests. Classroom teachers need to know that, because of their differing lineages, the SAT and the ACT represent somewhat overlapping but fundamentally different assessment strategies. Whereas the SAT's focus is more heavily on assessing students' academic aptitudes, the ACT's focus is on measuring the kinds of skills and knowledge that, having been previously learned, are necessary in college. Although both tests are predictive of a student's college grades, only about 25 percent of students' college grades are associated with students' SAT or ACT scores.

■ Chapter Summary

Standardized tests were defined as assessment instruments administered, scored, and interpreted in a standard, predetermined manner. Standardized tests are used to assess students' achievement and aptitude. Tests of student achievement are developed by large testing companies as well as by state departments of education (usually to satisfy a legislatively imposed educational accountability requirement, such as NCLB). Although most standardized tests feature the use of selected-response items, many developers of such tests attempt to incorporate modest numbers of constructed-response items in their assessment devices.

For describing a distribution of test scores, two indices of central tendency—the mean and the median—were described as well as two indices of variability—the range and the standard deviation.

Several ways of interpreting results of standardized tests were discussed: percentiles, grade-equivalent scores, scale scores, stanines, and normal curve equivalents (NCEs). The nature of each of these interpretation procedures, as well as the strengths and weaknesses of the three most popular interpretation procedures, were described.

The SAT and the ACT are, by far, America's most widely used college entrance tests. Because of its history, the SAT (originally known as the Scholastic Aptitude Test) aims to assess students' academic aptitudes—for example, a student's innate verbal, quantitative, and spatial aptitudes. The ACT attempts to function as an achievement test that, albeit predictive of students' college success, measures high school students' mastery of the skills and knowledge they'll need in college. Although predictive criterion-related validity coefficients of approximately .50 indicate students' SAT and ACT scores are certainly correlated with students' college grades, fully 75 percent of a student's academic success in college is linked to factors *other* than scores on either of these two tests.

Self-Check

It's time for a good, old-fashioned true-false test to sharpen your conversance with all these exotic notions about score interpretations. Give the following true-or-false statements your best shot:

(T or F)   1. Most standardized aptitude tests have been developed by state departments of education to implement legislatively enacted accountability laws.

(T or F)   2. One of the shortcomings of the range as an index of variability is that it is derived from only two raw scores.

(T or F)   3. If a distribution of test scores were particularly heterogeneous, it would have a larger standard deviation than if it were particularly homogeneous.

(T or F)   4. The ACT is, at bottom, an aptitude test, whereas the SAT is fundamentally an achievement test.

(T or F)   5. Locally devised norms based on the performance of local students are almost always lower than nationally devised norms based on the performance of students nationally.

(T or F)   6. Percentiles are the most commonly used way of describing students' performances on standardized tests.

(T or F)   7. Whereas percentiles represent a *relative* scheme for interpreting standardized test results, grade-equivalent scores represent an *absolute* scheme for interpreting standardized test results.

(T or F)   8. Fifty percent of a college student's grades can be linked back to that student's score (in high school) on the SAT or the ACT.

(T or F)   **9.** For grade-equivalent scores to function properly, it is assumed the subject area tested is emphasized about equally at each grade level tested.

(T or F)   **10.** A grade-equivalent score of 6.2 for a fifth-grader indicates the fifth-grader is performing six months and two weeks ahead of expectations.

(T or F)   **11.** Scale scores, although increasingly used to describe results in standardized tests, are difficult to interpret all by themselves.

(T or F)   **12.** Scale-score interpretations of standardized aptitude tests are almost always based on a mean score of 500.

(T or F)   **13.** One advantage of the scale scores derived from item response theory is their use permits the presentation of equidifficult challenges to students when different test forms are used.

(T or F)   **14.** Although grade-equivalent scores are readily communicable, they are often misinterpreted.

(T or F)   **15.** Empirical research shows test-preparation activities associated with getting students ready for the SAT and the ACT are essentially ineffective.

? | Pondertime

1. If you had to use only *one* of the three individual student interpretation schemes treated in the chapter (percentiles, grade-equivalent scores, and scale scores), which one would it be? Why did you make that choice?

2. It is sometimes argued that testing companies and state departments of education adopt scale-score reporting methods simply to make it more difficult for everyday citizens to understand how well students perform. (It's easier for citizens to make sense out of "65% correct" than "an IRT scale score of 420.") Do you think there's any truth in that criticism?

3. There are meaningful geographic differences in the use of the SAT and the ACT as college admissions tests. Why do you suppose that is?

4. If you were trying to explain to a group of parents how to make sense out of percentile, grade equivalents, and scale scores, how would you go about it so that the parents would really grasp the rudiments of these three score-interpretation procedures?

5. Twenty years ago, it was much less difficult to get district educational officials to require their students to participate in the re-norming of standardized tests than it is today. What factors account for that difference? What effect might this situation have on a recently re-normed standardized test?

Self-Check Key

1.	F	4.	F	7.	F	10.	F	13.	T
2.	T	5.	F	8.	F	11.	T	14.	T
3.	T	6.	T	9.	T	12.	F	15.	F

You'll note that there are seven true statements and eight false statements. (Yes, your author also follows the guidelines given in Chapter 6 for binary-choice items.)

Notice the 15 items you just completed deal largely with knowledge. Yet, I'll wager the readers who performed well on this little excursion into knowledge assessment also have a pretty fair general understanding of the content addressed in the chapter. That's the reason many teachers, over the years, have been willing to use selected-response sorts of tests as stand-ins for higher-level constructed-response assessments. I'm not recommending such a practice, because I really believe loftier assessment targets spur loftier instructional approaches. I simply wanted you to see why large numbers of teachers may be inclined to reject many of the "new-fangled" assessment approaches currently being touted. Such teachers tend to believe the old-fashioned selected-response tests allow them to get a sufficiently accurate fix on their students' abilities.

■ Additional Stuff

Boaler, Jo. (2003). "When Learning No Longer Matters: Standardized Testing and the Creation of Inequality." *Phi Delta Kappan, 84*, no. 7 (March): 502–506.

Boe, Erling E., and Sujie Shin. (2005). "Is the United States Really Losing the International Horse Race in Academic Achievement?" *Phi Delta Kappan, 86*, no. 9 (May): 688–695.

Phelps, Richard P. (Ed.). (2005). *Defending Standardized Testing.* Mahwah, NJ: Lawrence Erlbaum.

■ Nonprint Stuff

Association for Supervision and Curriculum Development. *Reporting Student Progress* (Videotape #495249T87). Alexandria, VA: Author.

Northwest Regional Educational Laboratory. *Understanding Standardized Tests* (Videotape #NREL-10). Los Angeles: IOX Assessment Associates.

■ Cyber Stuff

■ *CTB-McGraw-Hill* is one of the nation's leading publishers of standardized achievement tests. This website contains a complete description of the company's tests and services. In addition, visitors to the site will find a first-rate assessment glossary, guidelines for effective assessment, a discussion of test-preparation issues, and a variety of other assessment-related resources. www.ctb.com

■ *Educational Records Bureau (ERB)* is a membership organization composed of more than 1,000 independent and suburban public schools. The ERB publishes achievement (grades 1–12) and aptitude tests (grades 3–12) chiefly for independent schools. Its tests attempt to differentiate among the most able test takers—that is, "those who typically rank above the 80th national percentile on other standardized tests." This website describes ERB products and services. www.erbtest.org

■ *Harcourt Educational Measurement* is one of the three major publishers of standardized achievement tests in the United States. On this website visitors will find not only descriptions of the company's services and products but also a fine glossary of assessment terms, frequently asked questions (FAQs), and a Code of Fair Testing Practices in Education. www.hbem.com

■ *Riverside Publishing* is, along with CTB/McGraw-Hill and Harcourt Educational Measurement, the remaining member of the "big three" publishers of U.S. standardized achievement tests. On this website there are the customary listings of the company's tests and other products as well as a set of assessment-related links to other websites. In addition to an interactive glossary, there is a history of the company that traces its origins to the creation of an intelligence test in 1916. www.riverpub.com

To access chapter objectives, practice tests, weblinks, and flashcards, visit the companion website at **www.ablongman.com/popham5e.**

MyLabSchool is a collection of online tools for your success in this course, your licensure exams, and your teaching career. Discover where the classroom comes to life by visiting **www.mylabschool.com** to access the following resources:

■ Video clips from real classrooms

■ An archive of real-life cases

■ Help with your research papers using Research Navigator™

■ Career Center with resources for:

Praxis exams and licensure preparation

Professional portfolio development

Job search and interview techniques

Lesson planning with state standard correlations

14

Appropriate and Inappropriate Test-Preparation Practices

T his chapter deals with an important assessment-related issue that never really troubled teachers a decade or two ago. Unfortunately, it is a problem today's classroom teachers have to confront seriously. Faced with growing pressures to increase students' scores on achievement tests, pressures that have been ratcheted up dramatically because of the No Child Left Behind Act's accountability requirements, some teachers have responded by engaging in test-preparation practices that are highly questionable. In recent years, for example, a number of reports have been made of teachers and administrators who deliberately coached students with actual copies of a supposedly "secure" examination. There are even reports of educators' erasing students' incorrect answers and substituting correct answers in their place. Teachers caught cheating on high-stakes tests have lost both their teaching licenses and their jobs. Rather than a few isolated instances, such violations of test security are becoming, sadly, quite common.

■ High-Stakes Assessment Arrives

The preoccupation with student test scores as the definitive indicator of educational effectiveness first surfaced in the 1980s. Although attention had been given to the quality of student test performances prior to that decade, it was in the 1980s that attentiveness to student test performance became pervasive. In large measure, the focus on pupils' test scores stemmed from increasing incredulity on the part of citizens that public education was performing properly. Taxpayers, and their elected representatives, registered serious doubts that educational tax dollars were being well spent. Spawned by such doubts, the era of educational accountability became a reality in the 1980s when state after state enacted laws requiring students to be assessed by annually administered achievement tests. Students' performances on such tests were used not only to determine the quality of statewide schooling but also (because of the widespread practice of publishing such test scores in local newspapers) to mirror the effectiveness of individual school districts and schools.

In every sense of the expression, these legislatively mandated achievement tests were *high-stakes tests* because there were significant contingencies associated with the test results. The contingencies were experienced either by the students who took the tests or by the educators who administered the tests. To students, the tests were significant because test scores were often linked to high school graduation or to grade-level promotion. To educators, because of the manner in which test results were publicized by the local media, high test scores were viewed as indicating an effective instructional program and, of course, low test scores were seen to indicate the opposite. Because of these contingencies, teachers and administrators found themselves frequently called on to raise test scores. Candid educators will agree that pressures to boost students' test scores are still widespread.

When President George W. Bush signed the NCLB Act into law on January 8, 2002, high-stakes testing in America became the law of the land. Not surprisingly, a good many educators regarded NCLB-mandated accountability with both fear and loathing. Some protesters came up with a variety of arguments and slogans against such testing. My favorite was "High stakes are for tomatoes!" But protesters notwithstanding, the enactment of NCLB elevated our test-related stakes to previously unforeseen heights.

Discussions with classroom teachers regarding what sorts of test-preparation practices they regard as appropriate and inappropriate have led to one inescapable conclusion: Most teachers have not devoted serious thought to the appropriateness of their test-preparation practices. Given the relatively recent arrival of high-stakes testing in education, it is not surprising that scant attention has been given to the appropriateness of various test-preparation practices. Yet, because no decrease in the pressures on educators to promote higher test scores seems likely, it is apparent teachers need to consider seriously what sorts of test-preparation practices are, indeed, appropriate.

■ Assessment Results as Inference Illuminators

Before addressing topics related to test preparation, it is important to remember the function of educational achievement tests. An educational achievement test is employed in order for us to make a reasonable inference about a student's status

Figure 14.1 ■ The Inference-Illuminating Relationship between a Test and the Curricular Aim It Represents

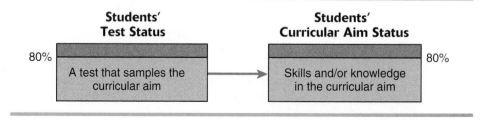

Decision Time

Was It Really Wrong?

Judy Jameson is a tenth-grade history teacher in Grant High School. All tenth-graders are given language arts and mathematics tests that must be passed if the students are to receive a state-sanctioned diploma from the district.

The test administration takes place during a two-day period in the school cafetorium and is supervised by Grant High teachers. During those two days, on three occasions Judy overheard Mr. Pelkins respond to students who raised their hands for clarification. Mr. Pelkins did not merely clarify; he told the student what the correct answer was to the test item. After some subtle inquiries, Judy learned that each of the students that Mr. Pelkins had helped was currently in his tenth-grade general mathematics class.

Judy is now trying to decide whether she should do anything about Mr. Pelkins's conduct and, if so, what?

 If you were Judy, what would your decision be?

with respect to the knowledge and/or skills in the curricular aim the test represents. Ideally, of course, an achievement test will sample the curricular aim representatively so the level of a student's performance on the achievement test will serve as a reasonably accurate reflection of the student's status with respect to the curricular aim. The nature of this relationship is illustrated in Figure 14.1 where it is indicated that a student who answered correctly 80% of the items in an achievement test would be expected to have mastered about 80% of the content in the curricular aim (and its knowledge and/or skills) the test was measuring. The relationship between a student's test performance and the student's mastery of the curricular aim represented by the achievement test, as will be seen later, is a key factor in establishing the appropriateness of test-preparation practices.

■ Two Evaluative Guidelines

Two guidelines can be employed by teachers who wish to ascertain the appropriateness of given test-preparation practices. Taken together, the two guidelines provide teachers with advice regarding the suitability of particular test-preparation activities. Here, then, is the first guideline—the *professional ethics guideline.*

Professional Ethics

No test-preparation practice should violate the ethical norms of the education profession.

This first guideline obliges teachers to avoid any unethical test-preparation practice. Ethical behaviors, of course, are rooted not only in fundamental morality but also in the nature of a particular profession. For example, physicians should be governed by general ethical principles dealing with honesty and respect for other people's property as well as by ethical principles that have evolved specifically for the medical profession. Similarly, teachers should not engage in test-preparation practices that involve violations of general ethical canons dealing with theft, cheating, lying, and so on. In addition, however, teachers must take seriously the ethical obligations arising because teachers have agreed to serve *in loco parentis*. Teachers who serve "in place of the parent" take on an ethical responsibility to serve as models of ethical behavior for children.

When teachers engage in test-preparation practices that, if brought to the public's attention, would discredit the education profession, such practices should be considered professionally unethical. This is because, in the long term, such practices erode public confidence in our schools and, as a result, financial support for the schools. Consequently, this erosion of public support renders the education profession less effective and, as a result, leaves children less properly educated.

Thus, according to the guideline of professional ethics, teachers should not engage in test-preparation practices that involve such behaviors as violating state-imposed security procedures regarding high-stakes tests. A growing number of states have enacted serious and widely promulgated regulations so teachers who breach state test-security procedures will have their credentials revoked. Accordingly, teachers should not engage in test-preparation practices that are unethical because there are potential personal repercussions (for example, loss of credentials)

or professional repercussions (for example, reduced citizen confidence in public schooling). Most importantly, teachers should avoid unethical test-preparation practices because such practices are *wrong*.

Let's look, then, at the second of our two guidelines—the *educational defensibility guideline.*

Educational Defensibility

No test-preparation practice should increase students' test scores without simultaneously increasing students' mastery of the curricular aim tested.

This second standard emphasizes the importance of engaging in instructional practices that are in the educational best interests of students. Teachers should not, for example, artificially increase students' scores on a test while neglecting to increase students' mastery of the knowledge and/or skills that the test is supposed to reflect.

An appropriate test-preparation practice raises not only students' preparation-to-postpreparation performance on a test but also raises students' preparation-to-postpreparation mastery of the curricular aim being tested. This situation is illustrated in Figure 14.2 where you can see that a 20% prepreparation-to-postpreparation jump in students' mastery was seen both on the test and on the curricular aim it represents.

Conversely, an inappropriate test-preparation practice raises students' prepreparation-to-postpreparation performance on the test, but not students' mastery of the curricular aim itself. This situation is illustrated in Figure 14.3 where students' test performances increase, but their curricular aim mastery doesn't.

The result of such inappropriate test-preparation practices is that a deceptive picture of students' achievement is created. The test results no longer serve as an

Figure 14.2 ■ Appropriate Test Preparation Based on the Guideline of Educational Defensibility

Figure 14.3 ■ Inappropriate Test Preparation Based on the Guideline of Educational Defensibility

accurate indicator of students' status with respect to a curricular aim. As a consequence, students who in reality have not mastered a curricular aim's content may fail to receive appropriate instruction regarding such content. The students will have been instructionally shortchanged because inappropriate test-preparation practices led to an inflated estimate of their content mastery. Such test-preparation practices, because they rob students of needed instruction, are educationally indefensible.

■ Five Test-Preparation Practices

We can now turn to a consideration of five common test-preparation practices. These five practices are not exhaustive in the sense that there are no other conceivable test-preparation procedures. The five practices do, however, capture most of the important test-preparation options available to teachers. Some of these involve special instruction rather than regular classroom instruction. *Special instruction* consists of extra preparation sessions, during or outside class, devoted exclusively to the readying of students for tests. In contrast, *regular classroom instruction,* although its focus may be relevant to the content of a test, occurs as part of the teacher's ongoing instructional program. The five test-preparation practices are the following:

1. *Previous-form preparation* provides special instruction and practice based directly on students' use of a previous form of the actual test. For example, if the currently published form of a nationally standardized achievement test is being used on a statewide basis as part of an NCLB accountability system, the teacher gives students guided or independent practice with earlier, no longer published, versions of the same test.
2. *Current-form preparation* provides special instruction and practice based directly on students' use of the form of the test currently being employed. For

example, the teacher gives students guided or independent practice with actual items copied from a currently used state-developed high school graduation test.

3. *Generalized test-taking preparation* provides special instruction covering test-taking skills for dealing with a variety of achievement-test formats. For example, the teacher shows students how to make calculated guesses for certain types of items or how to allocate test-taking time judiciously.

4. *Same-format preparation* provides regular classroom instruction dealing directly with the content covered on the test, but employs only practice items that embody the same format as items actually used on the test. For example, if a mathematics achievement test includes addition problems formatted only in vertical columns, the teacher provides practice with addition problems formatted solely in this manner. Some teachers create "clone" items for same-format preparation activities—such items being almost mirror images of a test's actual items. For many of these "clone" items, the practice items are essentially indistinguishable from the actual items.

5. *Varied-format preparation* provides regular classroom instruction dealing directly with the content covered on the test, but employs practice items representing a variety of test-item formats. For example, if the achievement test uses subtraction problems formatted only in vertical columns, the teacher provides practice with problems formatted in vertical columns, horizontal rows, and in story form.

■ Applying the Two Guidelines

When these five test-preparation practices are scrutinized according to the guidelines of professional ethics and educational defensibility, only two turn out to be appropriate.

Previous-form preparation violates the educational defensibility guideline because students' test scores are apt to be boosted via such special preparation sessions without concomitant rises in students' mastery of the curricular aim being tested. In addition, because in the public's view this kind of test-preparation practice may be seen as an improper instance of coaching students *merely* for test-score gains, it may be viewed by some as professionally unethical. Previous-form preparation, therefore, is inappropriate. (This same judgment would apply to the use of commercial test-preparation materials based chiefly on specially created "parallel" forms of a currently used test.)

Current-form preparation clearly loses out on both guidelines. Not only is it educationally indefensible but such preparation also constitutes an outright example of cheating. Current forms of the test must be stolen or surreptitiously copied in order to be used in such potentially improper score-boosting special sessions. Teachers who are caught readying their students via current-form preparation should, in fact, be caught.

Generalized test-taking preparation turns out to be an appropriate form of test preparation because such special instruction on how to take tests is, characteristically, rather brief and not seriously deflective of a student's ongoing education.

Parent Talk

Mrs. Stern is the mother of Sara, one of your most talented students. Mrs. Stern, it is rumored, will be running for election to your district's school board in the fall. Accordingly, whenever Mrs. Stern raises questions about Sara's education, you always try to be especially responsive. You are no dummy.

When Sara arrived at school this morning, she gave you a brief note from her mother. The note said, "Why is so much time spent in our school, and in your class, 'teaching to the test' this year? Shouldn't our children be learning more than what's on a test?"

 If I were you, here's how I'd respond to Mrs. Stern in person or with a note (if in person, I might reply on bended knee):

"You're right on target to be raising this issue, Mrs. Stern, but I want you to understand an important difference between teaching to the test, in the sense you teach to the students to do well on particular test items, versus teaching to the test, in the sense you teach the students to master the skills and/or knowledge represented by the test.

"What I do in my class is the latter, and that's also what most of my colleagues do. In other words, we teach directly toward the important skills and knowledge that our tests measure. Those are the key kinds of skills and the significant bodies of knowledge that you and I both want Sara to acquire. But the classroom assessments we use only sample a student's mastery of such knowledge or skills.

"So it would be instructionally unwise for us to teach toward particular test items. We want Sara and her classmates to master skills and knowledge so they can apply what they've learned in many settings, not merely on a specific test.

"Putting it simply, we do not teach toward a set of test items, but we do teach toward the skills and knowledge our tests represent."

Now, how would you respond to Mrs. Stern?

More importantly, because such test-taking preparation readies students to cope with a number of different sorts of tests, students will be less apt to be intimidated by a previously unencountered type of test item. In a very real sense, therefore, generalized test-taking preparation sessions allow students' test performances to be more accurately reflective of their true state of knowledge and/or skill. Such preparation, *if not excessively lengthy,* is clearly appropriate.

Same-format preparation, although it may be ethical, is not educationally defensible. If students in their regular classroom instruction are allowed to deal *only* with the explicit item format used on a test, then those students will be far less likely to generalize what they have learned. Test scores may rise, but comparable content mastery is not apt to rise. Although many administrators may, because of powerful pressures to boost scores, endorse this form of test-preparation practice, it should be resisted because it is educationally unsound. The more "clone" items

Table 14.1 ■ Per-Guideline Indicator of the Appropriateness
of Five Test-Preparation Practices

	Guideline Satisfied?	
Test-Preparation Practice	*Professional Ethics*	*Educational Defensibility*
Previous Form	No	No
Current Form	No	No
Generalized Test Taking	Yes	Yes
Same Format	Yes	No
Varied Format	Yes	Yes

there are in a set of practice items, the more inappropriate such test-preparation activities are.

Varied-format preparation, in contrast, satisfies both of our two evaluative guidelines. Students during their regular classroom instruction are given practice not only with content as it is conceptualized on the test but also with content conceptualized in other ways. Rises in test scores will, in general, be accompanied by rises in mastery of the curricular aim being tested because students' generalized mastery of the content is being fostered.

Of the five test-preparation variants, then, only varied-format preparation and generalized test-taking preparation satisfy both evaluative guidelines. This can be seen in Table 14.1.

■ What about "Teaching to the Test"?

If you get into any sort of meaningful discussion of test preparation, it's almost certain that someone will soon use the expression "teaching to the test." This someone should not be you! Here's why.

There are two decisively different meanings people employ when they use the phrase ***teaching to the test***. First, they can mean a teacher is directing instruction toward the knowledge, skills, or affective variables represented by the test. Another way to put this same meaning of "teaching to the test" is teachers are aiming their instruction so that students accomplish the curricular aim sampled by the actual test. This is good instruction. A second meaning of "teaching to the test," however, is that it describes teachers who are directing their instruction specifically toward the actual items on the test itself. This is bad instruction.

So, when someone uses the expression "teaching to the test," we can't tell whether they're talking about something swell or something sordid. Conversations that take place about test preparation in which this double-meaning expression is tossed around mindlessly will, almost certainly, end up being mindless conversations.

As a consequence, I implore you *never to use this ambiguous expression* yourself. Rather, say either "teaching to the test's items" or "teaching to the curricular aim represented by the test." To emphasize the importance of this advice, I have summarized it in the box below:

> **NEVER, NEVER SAY:**
>
> "Teaching to the test"
>
> **SAY:**
>
> "Teaching to the test's items"
>
> (or)
>
> **SAY:**
>
> "Teaching to the curricular aim represented by the test"

If you should momentarily forget my fine advice and find yourself blurting out the foul phrase I've just been castigating, or if you are forced at gunpoint to say it, be sure to quickly follow up by saying which meaning of the expression you intended. By and large, however, you'll be better off if you expunge the phrase completely from your potential utterances.

And if a *friend* uses the phrase, you might gently and supportively seek clarification about which meaning is intended. If an *enemy* uses the phrase, however, I recommend a crisp facial slap on the left or right cheek—depending on either cheek's proximity to you. Enemies deserve little more.

One way of thinking about how teachers ought to prepare their students for important assessments is presented in Figure 14.4. As you can see, a teacher's instruction should be directed toward the body of knowledge and/or skills (it could also be affect) represented by the test, but not toward the specific set of items doing the representing.

And this way of thinking about test preparation brings us to an important point for teachers to understand. You can only direct your instruction toward the knowledge and/or skills represented by a high-stakes test if there is a suitable description of the assessed curricular aim available. Remember from Chapter 12 how important it is for a teacher to understand the nature of the *test-represented* curricular aim? You can't expect a teacher to teach toward a curricular aim if there's no clear description of that aim provided.

Unfortunately, many of the nation's teachers are now experiencing immense pressure to raise their students' scores on high-stakes test that are unaccompanied by instructionally meaningful descriptions of what they measure. And without such descriptions, it is far from surprising many pressured teachers have succumbed to the lure of item-focused teaching.

I've spent a good deal of time reviewing the descriptions of assessed behavior provided by publishers of all the nation's standardized achievement tests, and I can

Figure 14.4 ■ Appropriate and Inappropriate Directions
for a Teacher's Instruction

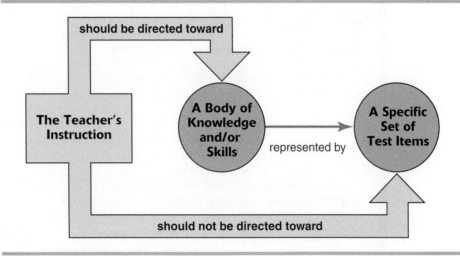

tell you, from a teacher's perspective, the descriptions of these tests' curricular targets are way short of what teachers need. Oh, of course there are some loose descriptions of objectives or content assessed, but those descriptions just aren't sufficient if a teacher is planning day-to-day instruction.

My point is this: If the high-stakes test on which you're asked to boost students' scores is not accompanied by descriptions of what the test's items *represent*, then you should let the world know you're being put in an untenable instructional position. Teachers should not be forced to play the score-boosting game if they are obliged to use rules making it certain the teacher will lose. And there's no way to satisfy this chapter's two test-preparation guidelines if a curricular aim's description (suitable for instructional planning) has not been supplied.

■ What Do Classroom Teachers Really Need to Know about Test-Preparation Practices?

As a classroom teacher, you may find your own test-preparation practices may not coincide perfectly with one of the five practices described. You'll probably discover, if you are preparing your students specifically for some sort of high-stakes test, however, your approach will be reasonably close to one of the five practices treated in the chapter. More important than the five preparation practices, of course, are the two evaluative guidelines. You should review with care your own preparation activities linked to high-stakes tests. The two evaluative guidelines provided here—professional ethics and educational defensibility—will prove useful in such a review.

but what does this have to do with
Teaching?

Today's teachers find themselves in a terrible bind. Their caliber is often being judged on the basis of students' scores on high-stakes tests. And, as a consequence, teachers frequently find themselves pressured by their principals to improve students' scores on the locally anointed high-stakes tests. But many heavily pressured teachers fail to recognize that their principal is often being squeezed just as hard to make sure a school's test scores take a giant jump.

As you'll learn in the next chapter, evaluating a school's staff on the basis of students' scores on certain kinds of standardized tests is fundamentally wrong. Yet that recognition, all by itself, doesn't make the score-boosting pressures on teachers or administrators evaporate.

As a teacher, or a prospective teacher, you really must comprehend the nature of the two test-preparation guidelines offered in the chapter, and you need to understand (from Chapter 15) why it is that some standardized achievement tests measure the socioeconomic makeup of a school's student body—not how well the school's teachers are teaching.

At that point, instead of assuming a school's principal is the "heavy" in this score-boosting frenzy, you need to recognize school principals are, themselves, under enormous pressure to elevate their school's test scores. Accordingly, by the time you wrap up this book, you'll know (1) how to and how not to prepare students for high-stakes tests and (2) what kinds of high-stakes tests give educators—that is, teachers *and* principals—a chance to succeed.

Therefore, why not collaborate *with* your school's principal to explain ways of responding to extant test pressures with test-preparation practices that help, not harm, children. What you need to do, frankly, is put the stuff you've already learned in Chapter 12 (about instructionally oriented assessment) and this chapter (about test preparation) together with what you will learn in Chapter 15. Then, working collaboratively with your school's (also pressured) principal, figure out a strategy to benefit kids.

■ Chapter Summary

This chapter dealt with an important assessment-related issue—namely, how teachers should prepare their students for significant tests. After a recounting of why it is that classroom teachers are under substantial pressure to boost their students' test scores, especially subsequent to the arrival of the NCLB Act, two evaluative guidelines were supplied by which test-preparation practices can be judged. The two guidelines were (1) *professional ethics*, which indicates that no test-preparation practice should violate the ethical norms of the education profession, and (2) *educational defensibility*, which indicates that no test-preparation practice should increase students' test scores without simultaneously increasing students' mastery of the curricular aim tested. Five test-preparation variants were then described:

(1) previous-form preparation, (2) current-form preparation, (3) generalized test-taking preparation, (4) same-format preparation, and (5) varied-format preparation. Having applied the two evaluative guidelines to the five test-preparation practices, it was concluded that the only two practices satisfying both guidelines were generalized test-taking preparation (if brief) and varied-format preparation. Readers were urged to eschew the phrase *teaching to the test*. Readers should also have been urged to eschew the word *eschew*. The chapter was concluded by a discussion of the necessity for the creators of high-stakes tests to supply curricular aim descriptions from which sound instructional decisions can be made.

Self-Check

To see how skillfully you can use the chapter's two guidelines for evaluating teachers' test-preparation practices, you'll now be given five written descriptions of fictitious teachers' test-preparation activities. Your task is to decide, for each description, whether either, neither, or both of the two evaluative guidelines (professional ethics and educational defensibility) have been violated by the preparation activity described. Having done that, decide personally whether you think the preparation activities described were appropriate or inappropriate.

Description One

Mrs. Gordon makes sure she has her sixth-grade students practice in the fall for the nationally standardized achievement tests required in the spring by the district's school board. Fortunately, she has been able to make photocopies of most of the test's pages during the past several years, so she can organize a highly relevant two-week preparation unit wherein students are given actual test items to solve. At the close of the unit, students are supplied with a practice test on which about 60% of the test consists of actual items copied from the nationally standardized commercial test. Mrs. Gordon provides students with an answer key after they have taken the practice test so that they can check their answers.

Any violations? _____ If so, which?_____

What's your opinion of this preparation? _____

_____

Description Two

Mrs. Hillard knows the reading test administered to all state eighth-graders contains a set of six fairly lengthy reading selections, each of which is followed by about 10 multiple-choice items dealing with such topics as (1) the main idea of the selection as a whole or the main idea of its constituent paragraphs, (2) the meaning of selection's technical terms that can be arrived at from contextual clues, and (3) the defensibility of inferential statements linked to the selection.

Mrs. Hillard routinely spends time in her eighth-grade language arts class trying to improve her students' reading comprehension capabilities. She has the students read passages similar to those used in the statewide test, then gives her students a variety of practice tests, including written multiple-choice, true-false, and oral short-answer tests in which, for example, individual students must state what they believe to be the main idea of a specific paragraph in the passage.

Any violations? _____   If so, which?_____

What's your opinion of this preparation? _____

_____

Description Three

Because there is a statewide reading comprehension test that must be passed by all high school students before they receive state-sanctioned diplomas, Mr. Gillette, a tenth-grade English teacher, spends about four weeks of his regular class sessions getting students ready to pass standardized tests. He devotes one week to each of the following topics: (1) time management in examinations, (2) dealing with test-induced anxiety, (3) making calculated guesses, and (4) trying to think like the test's item writers. Mr. Gillette's students seem appreciative of his efforts.

Any violations? _____   If so, which?_____

What's your opinion of this preparation? _____

_____

Description Four

Because she is eager for her students to perform well on their twelfth-grade senior mathematics tests (administered by the state department of education), Mrs. Williamson gives students answer keys for all of the test's selected-response items. When her students take the test in the school auditorium, along with all of the school's other twelfth-graders, she urges them to use the answer keys discreetly and only if necessary.

Any violations? _____   If so, which?_____

What's your opinion of this preparation? _____

_____

Description Five

Mr. Phillips prepares his sixth-grade social studies students to do well on a state-administered social studies examination by having all of his students practice with test items similar to those on the examination. Mr. Phillips tries to replicate the nature of the state examination's items without ever using exactly the same content as it is apt to appear on the examination. He weaves in his test-preparation activities as part of his regular social studies instruction. Most students really don't know they are receiving examination-related preparation.

Any violations? _____   If so, which?_____

What's your opinion of this preparation? _____

_____

? Pondertime

1. Can you think of guidelines, other than the two described in the chapter, to be used in evaluating a classroom teacher's test-preparation practices? If so, what are they?

2. How about test-preparation practices? Can you think of any other sorts of test-preparation guidelines that are meaningfully different from the five described in the chapter? If so, using the chapter's two evaluative guidelines or any new ones you might prefer, how appropriate are such test-preparation practices?

3. How do you think classroom teachers can best be prepared to deal with the test-preparation issue in an appropriate fashion?

4. Do you think the author's rant about the expression, "teaching to the test," was warranted? Why or why not?

Self-Check Key

1. Mrs. Gordon has violated both evaluative guidelines by engaging in what most people regard as downright cheating. Hopefully, you didn't consider this teacher's preparation efforts to be wonderful.

2. Mrs. Hillard is clearly engaged in a version of varied-format preparation. She is violating neither of the two evaluative guidelines. Indeed, because of the likelihood that she is promoting her students' generalized reading comprehension abilities during her regular language arts evaluation, she is engaging in solidly appropriate test preparation.

3. Mr. Gillette's month-long test-preparation marathon was simply too long. Although both of the two evaluative guidelines appear to have been satisfied, the lengthy test-preparation activities really are costing students a full month of English instruction. To be absurd, let's say Mr. Gillette spent his entire, year-long instructional efforts on generalized test-preparation schemes such as described in this chapter. That kind of approach would clearly be depriving students of an English course. In that sense, particularly if parents discovered Mr. Gillette's stu-

dents were learning nothing about English, there would surely be some negative repercussion and, as a consequence, an erosion of confidence in the schools. Thus, the professional ethics guideline might have been violated. But even if neither of the two evaluative guidelines had been violated, Mr. Gillette's month-long test-preparation extravaganza was simply too, too long.

4. Mrs. Williamson is engaged in dishonest test preparation that loses out on both evaluative guidelines. Before you think this is a silly and obvious example, you should know many teachers have been fired and had their teaching licenses revoked because of precisely the kind of behavior depicted in this silly scenario.

5. Mr. Phillips satisfied the professional ethics guidelines but lost out on the educational defensibility guideline. Irrespective of whether his students know they were being prepared, and without regard to the inclusion of the test preparation as part of his regular instruction, Mr. Phillips's students aren't likely to be able to generalize the social studies mastery they'll display on the state examination to other settings in which they'll need to possess such mastery.

■ Additional Stuff

Cannell, J. J. (1989). *How Public Educators Cheat on Standardized Achievement Tests*. Albuquerque, NM: Friends for Education.

Mehrens, W. A., and J. Kaminski. (1989). "Methods for Improving Standardized Tests Scores: Fruitful, Fruitless, or Fraudulent." *Educational Measurement: Issues and Practice*, 8, no. 1: 14–22.

Sacks, Peter. (1999). *Standardized Minds: The High Price of America's Testing Culture and What We Can Do To Change It*. Cambridge, MA: Perseus Books.

■ Nonprint Stuff

Popham, W. James. *Test Preparation: The Wrong Way/Right Way* (Videotape #ETVT-14). Los Angeles: IOX Assessment Associates.

■ Cyber Stuff

■ *Alfie Kohn* is an outspoken critic of the way standardized tests are being currently misused and, as a consequence, how the pressures to raise students' scores on these tests are degrading education. A frequent lecturer on this topic, Kohn has created a website containing a host of references and resources that can be used to oppose the misuse of high-stakes tests. The site is replete with links to the writings of those who share Kohn's views regarding the negative impact of America's preoccupation with test scores. www.AlfieKohn.org

- *Education Week on the Web* (ETS) is the online version of a widely read weekly publication devoted exclusively to educational concerns. Although this online publication deals with a full range of educationally relevant topics, more than a few of its reports focus on assessment, accountability, and evaluation. Because of the perceived "newsworthiness" of stories regarding educators who are coping with assessment-based pressures, frequent visitors to this site are often apt to encounter descriptions of such situations. www.edweek.org

- *The Educational Testing Service* is the world's largest private educational organization. Its website contains a wide range of content related to assessment. Many visitors to the ETS site will be interested in its description of the College Board SAT program because the SAT's widespread use as a college admission examination. The ETS website contains a substantial amount of information dealing with how one can prepare for the SAT. Site visitors will find it interesting to see how a major publisher of educational aptitude tests deals with the issue of test preparation for its own examinations. The site also contains descriptions of 10 major testing programs offered by ETS.www.ets.org

To access chapter objectives, practice tests, weblinks, and flashcards, visit the companion website at **www.ablongman.com/popham5e**.

MyLabSchool is a collection of online tools for your success in this course, your licensure exams, and your teaching career. Discover where the classroom comes to life by visiting **www.mylabschool.com** to access the following resources:

- Video clips from real classrooms
- An archive of real-life cases
- Help with your research papers using Research Navigator™
- Career Center with resources for:
    Praxis exams and licensure preparation
    Professional portfolio development
    Job search and interview techniques
    Lesson planning with state standard correlations

15

Evaluating Teaching and Grading Students

T his chapter is the one right before the glossary and index. If you possess modest powers of inference, and have ever read another book containing a glossary and index, you are likely to conclude that this is the book's last chapter. You are correct. And, if you have reveled in reading the initial 14 chapters of the book, you'll surely greet this last-chapter news with unrestrained sadness. If, on the other hand, you've found Chapters 1 through 14 less than scintillating, your burden will soon be over. In either case, this final chapter will deal with two important uses to which classroom teachers can put the results of assessments—evaluating teaching and grading students.

Most teachers, and prospective teachers, are more interested in how to dispense grades than how to evaluate their teaching. That's understandable. But in this chapter, I've reversed that order. First, you will be reading about how to determine the caliber of your instruction. Then, you'll look into the mysteries and myths associated with student grading. So, if you're dying to dig into grading, be patient for a bit. We'll get there. To toss a bit of authorial honesty your way, I personally regard the evaluation of a teacher's teaching as tons more important than how teachers toss grades at their students.

■ Distinction Drawing

Just so we're all on the identical page of music, let's make certain you and I are employing the same meaning when we use the two terms around which this final chapter is fashioned. In casual conversation, you'll sometimes find educators using the terms *evaluation* and *grading* interchangeably, but these two words really stand for distinctively different education-related activities.

There was a time when educators really didn't distinguish between *evaluation* of students and *grading* of students, but those days have passed. Because program evaluation has now become such a prominent part of educational practice, when most educators encounter the term *evaluation* these days, they think about the evaluation of an educational program, such as a newly installed cooperative learning scheme.

When classroom teachers engage in *evaluation*, those teachers are typically arriving at conclusions about the quality of their own instructional efforts. In this sense, therefore, you should think about evaluation as "program evaluation." Because the program under consideration in most classrooms is the instructional program provided to students by the teacher, then *evaluation* will be used in this chapter to signify the attempt on the part of teachers to determine how well they're doing instructionally. Evaluation, then, can be roughly equated with "teacher evaluation" because when teachers' evaluate their instructional endeavors, they're really evaluating the quality of the instructional program they put together as well as the way they delivered the program. The focus of *evaluation* in this chapter, therefore, is on *teachers*.

In contrast, the focus of *grading* is on *students*. When a teacher grades a student, the teacher is assigning some kind of symbol (we'll discuss several options later), such as a letter grade of A, B, C, D, or F, that signifies "how well the student has done." Although in most classrooms there's surely a relationship between the quality of the teacher's instructional program and the grades students receive, those two notions are really independent. For example, Mrs. Bevins, a third-grade teacher, could evaluate her own language arts program very negatively because her instruction seemed to confuse many students. Nevertheless, Mrs. Bevins would still award grades of A to several students who, despite the confusing language arts instruction, effortlessly seemed to grasp the language arts concepts being considered.

Although I've tried to draw a nice, crisp distinction between *evaluation* as the appraisal of an instructional activity and *grading* as the appraisal of a student's performance, don't be surprised if you encounter colleagues who don't slice their appraisal cake in the same way. Some educators (I think mistakenly) refer to the grading of students as the "evaluation" of students. Other educators (also, in my view, mistakenly) talk about "grading" the quality of instruction. So, prepare yourself for some amount of semantic stumbling when you discuss these concepts with others. Not all educators will agree with me. Fools!

Teachers' judgments about their own instructional effectiveness, as well as their decisions about what grades to assign individual students, can be greatly influenced by assessment results. Both grading and evaluation, of course, can be illuminated by other sources of information. Neither of those two activities should be ruled by test results.

■ Evaluation of Teaching and the Use of Assessment Data

There are two types of evaluation bearing on teachers' appraisals of their instructional efforts. *Formative evaluation* refers to the appraisal of the teacher's instructional program for purposes of improving the program. For example, suppose you're teaching a three-week social studies unit on International Cooperation to a class of fifth-graders for the first time and you want to improve the unit so the next time you offer it, your teaching will be more effective. That's a task for formative evaluation, and students' assessment results will surely help you. Summative evaluation, in contrast, is not improvement focused. *Summative evaluation* refers to appraisals of teachers' competencies in order to make more permanent decisions about those teachers such as (1) continuation of employment or (2) awarding of tenure. When teachers are evaluated summatively, they're almost always evaluated by some type of external evaluator—for example, an administrator or supervisor.

Classroom teachers, therefore, usually do their own formative evaluation because they wish to spruce up their instruction. For summative evaluation, classroom teachers may be called on to supply evidence (such as students' test results) to supervisors who will then use such evidence evaluatively.

The evaluation of a teacher's instructional effectiveness will also be influenced by the presence of a federal law that, for many teachers, will require students' scores on standardized tests to be used for evaluating schools and, by implication, the teachers who teach in those schools. If you find yourself teaching a grade level or in a subject field where No Child Left Behind tests are given annually, you can bet that your students' scores on those tests will figure into any evaluation of your effectiveness.

Thus, if you are "blessed" with a requirement that your students be NCLB assessed, some of the approaches I'll be describing in this chapter can be employed to snare supplementary evidence regarding the quality of your teaching. If your students are not to be NCLB assessed, then the data-gathering procedures treated in the chapter may represent, for you, the dominant kind of student-performance data to be used in the evaluation of your teaching.

A Preinstruction versus Postinstruction Paradigm

Whether for formative evaluation or summative evaluation, the classic pretest-posttest paradigm presented in Figure 15.1 will prove serviceable for gauging instructional impact. If you assess your students prior to teaching them, then assess your students after you've taught them, any difference between their preinstruction and postinstruction performances ought be chiefly attributable to what went on in between—your teaching.

There are certain problems associated with the classic pretest-posttest scheme for discerning instructional impact, of course, but as a general paradigm for figuring out whether your instruction is making any dents in your students, the

Figure 15.1 ■ A Classic Preinstruction versus Postinstruction Paradigm for Determining Instructional Impact approach represented in Figure 15.1 isn't all that bad. One of the difficulties with the pretest-posttest model you need to watch out for is the possibility the pretest will be *reactive;* that is, it will sensitize your students to "what's important" so they behave atypically when taught about what was on the pretest. In other words, the effects measured by the posttest will really be a function of your instruction *plus* the pretest. However, if the posttest results for Topic X truly turn out to be what you want when you use a reactive pretest, then you might decide to toss in a pretest every time you teach Topic X.

Different Students, Different Results

For purposes of summative evaluation, such as when you are being evaluated by school district officials for purposes of continued employment, there's a really difficult problem to consider, and this is the extent to which pretest-to-posttest assessment results for students will be influenced by the caliber of the students you happen to be teaching. If you're teaching a ninth-grade geography class and have been blessed with a group of bright, motivated, and well-informed students, it is certain the pretest-to-posttest gains you obtain will be quite different from the gains you might see if you were teaching a collection of dull, unmotivated students whose conception of geography stops at the boundaries of the schoolyard.

Yet, even though those who would use your students' performance as evidence of your effectiveness must take into consideration the particular students you teach and the education context in which you instruct those students, it would be unreasonable to say teachers should not be evaluated, *at least in part,* by the learning they are able to produce in their students. Thus, in addition to other sources of information regarding your instructional efforts (such as classroom observations), evidence of student growth typically based on a contrast of pretest and posttest performances, should be considered as a reflection of your instructional prowess. It is *imperative,* however, those who use student-assessment data for purposes of summative evaluation do so in the context of the situation in which the teacher teaches—the most important feature of which are the specific students being taught.

For your own formative evaluation purposes, there's somewhat less need to get caught up with the "dissimilar students" problem. After all, you'll know your own students and will be able to judge whether you have a group of fast-thinking wizards whose pretest-to-posttest gains will be astounding or a group of slow-thinking students whose progress will be substantially less electrifying.

To the extent you're using gain scores (that is, posttest-minus-pretest scores), you should be aware of another technical problem likely to get in your way. If your students do *very* well on the pretest, it's more difficult for them to show gains than if they'd scored lower prior to instruction. When students score very high on tests, they tend to "top out" because of what is called a *ceiling effect.* Sometimes, in fact, if your students score really poorly on a pretest, they'll be likely to score higher on the posttest *by chance alone.* (If you want to intimidate your colleagues during faculty meetings, this is called a *regression effect,* wherein extremely low-scoring [or high-scoring] students tend to regress toward the mean when retested. By casually asserting your "students' progress, of course, might be attributable to a regression effect," you'll surely awe a few of your fellow teachers.)

There's another potential way of dealing with the difficulties of a simple pretest-versus-posttest evaluation design, and that's to use different but *equidifficult* tests. The only problem with this solution is it's almost impossible to create two truly equidifficult forms of a test. So, if the form used as a posttest is easier than its pretest counterpart, the teacher's instruction might look terrific, but students' high posttest performances could be caused chiefly by the softer posttest. Or, worse, if the posttest form is tons tougher than the pretest form, then a pretest-to-posttest comparison might suggest that the impact of the teacher's instruction has been to make students "unlearn" what they knew when they took the pretest. No, two test forms, even if they are intended to be equidifficult, won't save the day.

■ An Alternative Data-Gathering Design

There is a simple modification of the classic pretest-posttest design that will work for you if you have a reasonably large class of, say, 25 or more students. It's called the *split-and-switch design,* and here's how it works.

First, you need two forms of the test you're going to use as a pretest and as a posttest. The two forms ought to be *somewhat similar* in degree of difficulty, but need not be equidifficult or all that close to it. Let's call the two forms Test 1 and Test 2.

Second, you *split* your class into two roughly equal *half-class* groups, perhaps by counting half way down your class roster so all students whose last names start with the letters A through L are in Half-Class A, while all students whose last names start with the letters M through Z are in Half-Class B.

Next, you administer one of the two forms to each half-class, but ask students *not* to date their test forms. Ideally, in fact, students should write their names only on the *back* of their completed tests. You should then *code* the two sets of pretests (Test 1 and Test 2) so you can tell they are pretests. You can even use the pretest to help you plan your instruction. But you should not score, or write on, the pretests (on the actual test forms) at this time.

Then you should instruct all of your students for as long as you have allowed for the instruction. Suppose, for example, you were trying to teach your students how to write an effective narrative essay. This might take several months or even a full school year. Let's say, however, you devote one full semester to the teaching of this skill.

At the end of instruction, you then *switch* your two half-classes so if Half-Class A took Test 1 as a pretest, it now takes Test 2 as a posttest. Similarly, if Half-Class B received Test 2 as a pretest, at the end of instruction it will receive Test 1 as a posttest.

You then *code* the posttests so *you* can distinguish them, after consulting the codes, from the pretests. You next *mix* together all the copies of Test 1 (both pretests and posttests). You do the same with Test 2.

Next, you, colleagues, or even parents judge the quality of the mixed-together Test 1s. That is, the tests are subjected to *blind scoring*. The same is then done for the mixed-together Test 2s. *After* all scoring has been done, the codes are consulted so the blind-scored papers are separated into pretests and posttests.

This data-gathering model, one I've called the *split-and-switch design,* provides you with *two* indications of whether your instruction promoted posttest improvement—that is, the pretest-to-posttest changes for Test 1 as well as those for Test 2.

Because the pretest and posttest comparisons are made using the *very same test*, there is clearly no problem caused by differential test difficulty. Moreover, because your students will not have previously seen the posttest they receive, the reactive impact of the pretesting is minimized.

In essence, you have taken two 50 percent samples of your class, at both pretest time and posttest time, to help you determine if students have made the progress you wish. The split-and-switch design, of course, becomes less accurate as class sizes get smaller, but it does help you dodge some of the more troublesome aspects of the simple pretest-versus-posttest data-gathering model. The evidence it provides can be particularly compelling if you secure *nonpartisans* (such as parents) to supply the blind scoring.

The split-and-switch design is depicted graphically in Figure 15.2. If you are not sure yet in how it is supposed to function, please consider the Figure 15.2 diagram until you see what happens when. Note the appropriate comparisons, and there will be *two*, are signified by the colored arrows.

Teachers can use pretest results to guide their instructional decision making. And they can use posttest results to assign grades (remembering to make allowances for test forms of differing difficulties). But, of course, no permanent marks should be made on any tests until after they've been mixed together and blind-scored.

What to Assess

Whether you use your students' assessment results yourself for the formative evaluation of your own teaching or, in contrast, supply those results to others who will use such evidence for summative evaluation, you still have to decide what to assess. Think back, if you can remember that long ago, to Chapter 5's discussion of what to assess. Remember the key factor governing what you should assess in your

Figure 15.2 ■ A Split-and-Switch Data-Gathering Design

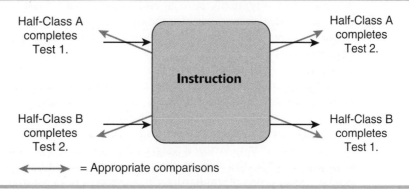

classroom is always the educational decision(s) you need to make. For purposes of formative evaluation, you'll have to think through for yourself what kinds of evidence you'll need in order to tinker with or to fundamentally overhaul your instructional activities. Surely you'll want to know how well your students have learned the most important things they were supposed to learn.

You should also seriously consider the assessment of students' *affect*. Affective assessment is of little utility for decisions about individual students because, as seen in Chapter 10, such measurement is too imprecise for defensible inferences about particular students. However, for judging the effectiveness of your instructional efforts, group-based inferences about students' pretest-to-posttest shifts in affect are useful. The split-and-switch design, incidentally, works wonderfully when affective data are being gathered.

If a classroom teacher is stuck with a small class (tough luck!), so small that a split-and-switch design wouldn't work, then I recommend the straight out pretest-posttest model with all its problems. You can still use blind-scoring of coded pretests and posttests after having mixed them together. And you can also round up one or more nonpartisan scorers. Such pretest-to-posttest evidence is surely way better than none.

In sum, students' assessment results are clearly important when teachers evaluate themselves or when others evaluate teachers. Although there are other important sources of evidence to be used in appraising a teacher's instructional efforts, what happens to students as a consequence of instruction is, unarguably, a significant source of evidence.

■ Evaluating Teaching via Standardized Achievement Tests

There's a widespread belief among parents and educational policymakers that the best way to evaluate the instructional effectiveness of teachers or schools is to use students' performances on standardized achievement tests. Despite the prevalence of this view, however, it is absolutely inappropriate to evaluate instructional quality on the basis of students' results on *certain* kinds of standardized achievement tests. Yet, because many teachers don't understand why students' performances on particular types of standardized tests don't provide an accurate indication of instructional quality, many parents and members of school boards continue to believe that scores on any sort of standardized achievement test provide a good indication of how well teachers have been teaching. Such parents and members of school boards are mistaken.

That's why, in this section of the chapter, I want to explain why students' scores on certain standardized achievement tests should not be used to evaluate teachers—either one at a time or collectively (as would occur when a school's entire faculty, as a group, is evaluated with accountability tests). If you truly understand why it is so wrong-headed to judge the caliber of teachers on the basis of their students' scores on inappropriate standardized tests, then you'll be able to explain to parents and to policymakers why the evaluation of education on the basis of students' scores on inappropriate kinds of standardized achievement tests is a dumb idea.

What's in a Name?

Many teachers think a standardized test is a standardized test. Those teachers are incorrect. In the next section of this chapter you'll discover there are three different species of standardized tests currently being used to evaluate a teacher's instructional efforts. Two of those three types of standardized tests are altogether inappropriate for this function.

A standardized test, as noted earlier, is any examination that's administered and scored in a predetermined, standard manner. And, as you've already seen, there are two major kinds of standardized tests: *aptitude* tests and *achievement* tests. Standardized aptitude tests predict how well students are likely to perform in some subsequent educational setting. The most common examples of these are academic predictor tests such as the SAT and the ACT, both of which attempt to forecast how well high school students will perform in college. But because standardized *achievement* tests scores are what citizens and school board members chiefly rely on when they evaluate a school's effectiveness, we'll be focusing on standardized achievement tests in this chapter. Let's get the three types of standardized achievement tests to be considered out there on the picnic table—so you'll know what's coming. First off, there are traditional, *nationally standardized achievement tests*, some of which have been around for more than three-quarters of a century. Five such tests are currently in use—namely, the California Achievement Tests, the Terra Nova (formerly called the Comprehensive Tests of Basic

Skills), the Iowa Tests of Basic Skills, the Metropolitan Achievement Tests, and the Stanford Achievement Tests.

The second kind of standardized achievement tests being used to evaluate teachers' success these days are *standards-based achievement tests*. These tests are intended to determine students' status with respect to their mastery of important curricular aims—typically referred to as content standards. Standards-based achievement tests are usually state-level tests; that is, most such tests are customized assessments built for particular states by external test-development contractors. More often than not, state-specific standards-based tests have been created to satisfy the requirements of federal accountability legislation such as the NCLB.

However, standards-based achievement tests come in two fundamentally different flavors. One kind of standards-based test is *instructionally insensitive*; that is, the tests are essentially unable to detect either successful or unsuccessful instruction. A second kind of standards-based achievement test is *instructionally sensitive*; that is, these tests are capable of discerning if teachers' instruction is working or not.

We'll now look at all three genres of standardized achievement tests. I'm sure you'll soon see that two of the three types of standardized tests I'll be describing should not be employed to evaluate a teacher's performance.

Nationally Standardized Achievement Tests

The measurement specialists who create nationally standardized achievement tests are psychometric whizbangs. They construct assessment tools that permit someone to make a valid inference about the knowledge and skills a given student possesses in a particular content area. More precisely, this inference is to be *comparative* so student's relative knowledge and skills can be compared with the knowledge and skills possessed by a national sample of students at the same age or grade level. Such relative inferences about a student's status with respect to the mastery of knowledge and skills in a particular subject area can be quite informative to both parents and educators.

Yet, there's an enormous amount of knowledge and a hefty number of skills that children at any grade level are supposed to learn. Not surprisingly, therefore, the substantial amount of content a standardized achievement test is supposed to represent poses genuine difficulties for the developers of such tests. If a test actually covered *all* eligible knowledge and skills, it would be way too long.

Accordingly, standardized achievement tests often need to accomplish their measurement mission with a much smaller collection of test items than might otherwise be employed if testing-time were not an issue. The way out of this assessment bind is for standardized achievement tests to *sample* knowledge and skills. Frequently, such tests try to do their assessment job with only 40 to 50 items in a content area.

As a consequence of (1) carefully sampling the content eligible for assessment and (2) concentrating on items that discriminate optimally among students, developers of nationally standardized achievement tests have produced assessment tools that do a great job of providing relative comparisons of a student's content mastery with the content mastery of students nationwide. Assuming the national norm group is genuinely representative of the nation at large, then educators and parents can make useful inferences about students. But nationally standardized achievement tests should not be used to evaluate the quality of education. That's not what they are supposed to do. Let's consider three significant reasons why it is inappropriate to base inferences about the caliber of instruction on traditional, nationally standardized achievement test scores.

"Alignment" That Isn't Aligned   Companies that build and sell nationally standardized achievement tests are all owned by larger for-profit corporations. Like all for-profit corporations, these companies attempt to produce revenue for their shareholders. Accordingly, these for-profit companies, if they're going to live up to their name, try to make a profit.

Recognizing the substantial pressure to *sell* nationally standardized achievement tests, those who market such tests encounter a difficult dilemma arising from the considerable curricular diversity present in the United States. When different states choose somewhat different curricular aims, these publishers still need to build standardized achievement tests that appear to be properly matched to educators' meaningfully different curricular preferences.

At a very general level, the goals educators pursue in different settings are reasonably similar. For instance, you can be sure all schools will give attention to language arts, mathematics, and so on. But that's at a general level. At the level where it really makes a difference to instruction—in the classroom—there are often significant differences in the curricular aims being sought in different locales. And this presents a problem to those who must sell standardized achievement tests.

Because of the nation's substantial curricular diversity, developers of standardized achievement tests are obliged to create a series of one-size-fits-all assessments. But, as most of us know from attempting to wear one-size-fits-all garments, sometimes one size really doesn't fit all.

The developers of standardized achievement tests do the best job they can in selecting test items likely to measure a content area's knowledge and skills the nation's educators regard as important. But the test developers can't really pull it off. Thus, standardized achievement tests will invariably contain a number of items that do not jibe with what's emphasized instructionally in a particular setting.

If you spend much time with the descriptive materials presented in the literature accompanying standardized achievement tests, you'll find the descriptors for what's tested are almost always quite general. Those descriptors need to be general in order to make the tests acceptable to a nation of educators whose curricular preferences vary. But such general descriptions of what's tested often permit assumptions about teaching-testing alignments that are way off the mark. And such mismatches, recognized or not, will lead to faulty conclusions about the effectiveness of instruction in a given setting if students' scores on standardized achievement tests are used as the indicator of instructional effectiveness. Clearly, it is in the economic best interests of those who publish nationally standardized achievement tests to have educators regard those tests as being aligned with a state's content standards. But, in many instances, the judged alignment between a state's curricular aims and what's measured by a nationally standardized achievement test should be reported as "alignment"—with a heavy emphasis on the quotation marks! The people who judge the alignment between a test and a state's curricular goals, sometimes because of self-interest, tend to see "alignment" even when it's simply not present. And that's the first reason nationally standardized achievement tests should not be used to determine the effectiveness of the educational efforts of a state, a district, a school, or a teacher. There's almost certain to be a significant mismatch between what's taught and what's tested.

A Tendency to Eliminate Important Test Items   A second reason standardized achievement tests should not be used to evaluate instructional quality arises directly from the requirement that these tests permit meaningful comparisons among students on the basis of only a small collection of items. Moreover, to make the comparisons properly, the test's items must yield a substantial degree of *score-spread*—that is, different scores for different students, especially in the test's norm group.

A test item that does the best job in producing score-spread is a test item answered correctly by about half the students. Items answered correctly by 40 to 60 percent of the students do a solid job in dispersing the total scores of test takers. Items answered correctly by very large numbers of students, in contrast, do not make a suitable contribution to spreading out students' test scores. A test item answered correctly by 90 percent of the test takers is, from the perspective of a test's efficiency in providing comparative interpretations, being answered correctly by too many students.

Many items answered correctly by 80 percent or more of the test takers, therefore, usually don't make it past the final cut when a standardized achievement test is first developed, and such items will most likely be jettisoned when the test is revised. As a result, the vast majority of the items on standardized achievement tests are "middle difficulty" items.

In the quest for score-spread on oft-revised nationally standardized achievement tests, items on which students perform well are frequently excluded. *Yet, items on which students perform well often cover the content that, because of its importance, teachers stress.* Thus, the better the job teachers do in teaching important knowledge and skills, the less likely it is there will be items on a traditional standardized achievement test measuring such knowledge and skills. To evaluate teacher's instructional effectiveness by using assessment tools that deliberately avoid important content is foolish.

Causality Confusion   A final reason students' performances on nationally standardized achievement tests should not be used to evaluate educational quality is, at least to me, the most compelling. Students' performances on standardized achievement tests are heavily influenced by three causative factors, only one of which is linked to instructional quality. Thus, asserting that students' low or high test scores are caused by the quality of instruction is illogical.

For you to understand this confounded-causation problem clearly, you need to look at the kinds of test items actually appearing on standardized achievement tests. Remember, students' test scores are based on how well students do on the test's items. To get a really solid idea of what's in standardized tests, you need to spend some time grubbing around with the items themselves.

The three illustrative items I'll present now are mildly massaged versions of actual test items in currently used standardized achievement tests. For security's sake, I've modified the items' content slightly, without altering the essence of what the items are trying to measure. In other words, the cognitive demands of the original items and these slightly altered items are equivalent.

The problem of confounded causation involves three factors that contribute to students' scores on standardized achievement tests: (1) what's taught in school, (2) a student's inherited academic aptitudes, and (3) a student's out-of-school learning. Items on nationally standardized achievement tests measure each of these factors.

Some of the items in nationally standardized achievement tests measure the knowledge or skills students learn in school. In certain subject areas, such as mathematics, children learn in school most of what they know about a subject. Few parents spend much time teaching their children about the intricacies of algebra or how to prove a geometric theorem.

So, if you look over the items in any traditional standardized achievement test, you'll find a fair number of items similar to the mathematics item presented in Figure 15.3, which, as I pointed out earlier, is a mildly modified version of an item appearing in a standardized achievement test intended for third-grade children.

This mathematics item would help teachers arrive at a valid inference about third-graders' abilities to choose number sentences that coincide with verbal representations of subtraction problems. Or, along with other somewhat similar items dealing with addition, multiplication, and division, this item would contribute to a valid inference about a student's ability to choose appropriate number sentences for a variety of basic computation problems presented in verbal form.

However, as you saw in connection with the previously described curriculum-test mismatch problem, there's always a chance the actual items on a standardized achievement test won't match local curriculum emphases. And, based on many educators' familiarity with the content of standardized achievement tests, there are almost always *major* mismatches between what teachers try to teach and what the nationally standardized achievement test actually assesses.

If the items in traditional standardized achievement tests measured only what actually had been taught in school, I wouldn't be at all negative about using these tests to determine educational quality. As you'll soon see, however, other kinds of items are lurking in nationally standardized achievement tests.

Figure 15.3 ■ A Third-Grade Standardized Achievement Test Item in Mathematics

- José had 14 apples. Then he gave away 6. Which of the number sentences below can you use to find out how many apples José has left?

    A. $6 + 14 = \Box$ C. $14 - 6 = \Box$

    B. $14 + 6 = \Box$ D. $\Box - 6 = 14$

I wish I believed all children were born with identical intellectual abilities, but I don't. Some kids were luckier at gene-pool time. Some children, from birth, will find it easier to mess around with mathematics than will others. If children came into the world having inherited identical academic aptitudes, teachers' pedagogical problems would be far more simple.

Recent thinking among many leading educators suggests there are various forms of intelligence, not just one (Gardner, 1994). A child who is born with less aptitude for dealing with quantitative or verbal tasks, therefore, might possess greater "interpersonal" or "intrapersonal" intelligence, but these two abilities are not tested by conventional achievement tests. For the kinds of items most commonly found on nationally standardized achievement tests, children differ in their innate aptitudes, such as their verbal, quantitative, and spatial aptitudes. And some items on nationally standardized achievement tests are linked directly to such *inherited* aptitudes.

Consider, for example, the social studies item in Figure 15.4. This item attempts to measure a sixth-grader's ability to "figure out" what the right answer is. I don't think the item measures what's taught in school. The item measures what students come to school with, not what they learn there.

In Figure 15.4's item, look carefully at the four answer options. Read each option and see if it might be correct. A verbally advantaged student, I contend, can figure out that Choices A, B, and D really would not "conserve natural resources" particularly well; hence, Choice C is the winning option. Verbally adept kids will have a better time with this item than their less verbal classmates.

You'll find many other "native smarts" items in any of today's nationally standardized achievement tests. The items I find particularly galling are the ones that measure a child's inborn spatial aptitude. To illustrate, one math item in a current fourth-grade standardized achievement test presents four letters to students (such as "F, L, R, and B"), then asks, Which letter, "when bent in half," will have two equal parts? The answer, in case you weren't born with adequate spatial aptitude, is the B. But what kind of a silly skill is involved in mental letter-bending? Dumb! Yet, many nationally standardized achievement tests contain items tapping the spatial-visualization aptitudes children obviously inherited via the gene-pool lottery.

Figure 15.4 ■ A Sixth-Grade Standardized Achievement Test Item in Social Studies

- If a person truly wants to conserve natural resources, one good way to do so is to:

  A. leave the radio turned on even if no one is listening to it.
  B. wash tiny loads instead of large loads in an automatic dishwashing machine.
  C. write on both sides of a piece of paper.
  D. discard used magazines in the trash.

But why, you might be thinking, do developers of nationally standardized tests include such items on their tests? The answer is all too simple. These sorts of items, because they are based on nicely spread out innate academic aptitudes not readily modifiable in school, do a wonderful job in spreading out test-takers' scores. The quest for score-spread, coupled with the limitation of having only a few items to use in assessing students, makes such items appealing to those who construct traditional standardized achievement tests.

Yet, items that primarily measure differences in students' inborn academic verbal, quantitative, and spatial obviously do not contribute to valid inferences about "how well children have been taught." Would we like all children to do well on such "inherited aptitudes" items? Of course, we would. But to use such items to arrive at a judgment about a teacher's instructional effectiveness is laughable.

A particularly troubling kind of item on nationally standardized achievement tests chiefly assesses what students have learned outside of school. Unfortunately, you'll find more of these items on standardized achievement tests than you'd suspect. If children come from advantaged families and from stimulus-rich environments, then those children are more apt to succeed on certain items in nationally standardized achievement tests than will other children whose environments don't mesh as well with what the items measure. Hopefully, the item in Figure 15.5 will illustrate what's actually being assessed by a number of the items on standardized achievement tests.

This fourth-grade reading item asks students to tell from context what the meaning of a multiple-meaning word is. I have no problem with this as a skill children should acquire. But I have a big problem with the item itself.

Notice the fourth-grader's task is to figure out how the word *field* is being used in the item's item. And, of course, answer Option C is correct. But please recognize that children whose parents are physicians, attorneys, or journalists do, indeed, have parents who have a field. If a child's parents work in a car wash or as a cashier in a convenience store, the child's parents will rarely, if ever, refer to their *field* of employment. Those parents have *jobs*. Clearly, kids from affluent families in which one or more parents are professionals will be more likely to do well on Figure 15.5's reading item than will kids whose parents are employed in menial jobs. This item is clearly linked to children's socioeconomic status (SES).

Suppose you're a teacher of a school in which most students come from a genuinely low socioeconomic environment. How are your students likely to perform on nationally standardized achievement tests if a substantial number of a test's items actually measure the stimulus-richness of your students' backgrounds? In other words, how will your students do if many of the test's items are SES-linked? That's right, your students are not apt to earn very high scores. Does this mean your school's teachers are doing a poor instructional job? Of course not.

Conversely, let's imagine you're a teacher in an affluent school whose students tend to be the offspring of upper-class, well-educated parents. Each spring, your students' scores on nationally standardized achievement tests are dazzlingly high. Does this mean your school's teachers are doing a superb instructional job? Of course not.

One of the chief reasons children's SES is so highly correlated with standardized test scores is that there are many items on nationally standardized achieve-

Figure 15.5   ■   A Fourth-Grade Reading Item

> My uncle's *field* is computer programming.

- Look at the sentences below. In which sentence does the word *field* mean the same as it does in the boxed sentence above?

    A. The softball pitcher knew how to *field* her position.
    B. They prepared the *field* by spraying and plowing it.
    C. I know the *field* I plan to enter when I finish college.
    D. The doctor used a wall chart to examine my *field* of vision.

ment tests really focused on assessing knowledge and skills learned outside of school. Most of such knowledge and skills are more likely to be learned in higher-level SES settings than in lower-level SES settings.

Again, you might ask, Why would developers of nationally standardized achievement tests place such items on their tests? As usual, the answer is consistent with the dominant measurement mission of those tests—namely, to spread out students' test scores so accurate and fine-grained norm-referenced interpretations can be made. Because there is substantial variation in children's socioeconomic strata, and this variation doesn't evaporate overnight, items reflecting such variation are efficient in producing the much-cherished spread in test scores.

Summing up, then, nationally standardized achievement tests have three attributes that render them inappropriate for evaluating teachers' success. First, there's the likelihood those tests are not aligned, in any rigorous manner, with a state's curricular aims. Second, in a necessary quest for score-spread, there's a tendency for nationally standardized achievement tests to eliminate items covering important, teacher-emphasized content. Finally, because many items on nationally standardized achievement tests are linked to students' SES or to their inherited academic aptitudes, such tests often measure what students bring to school instead of what they are taught in school. The net effect of these three problems is that nationally standardized achievement tests are instructionally insensitive. Let's turn, now, to a second kind of standardized achievement tests.

Standards-Based Tests: Instructionally Insensitive Ones

Standards-based assessment makes scads of sense. This approach to assessment calls for educators to set forth their curricular aims in the form of content standards, then build an assessment device based on those content standards. It follows, then, students' performances on those tests will allow educators to determine which content standards have been mastered by students and which ones haven't. Standards-based tests, at least most of them, were developed for a particular state on a customized basis. Unfortunately, most of these tests have not stimulated the kind of educational improvements promised by their proponents. I will soon show you why most states' standards-based tests are every bit as instructionally insensitive as traditional standardized achievement tests are. Moreover, because many of these instructionally insensitive standardized tests have now been decreed by state officials to be their state's official NCLB tests, and because NCLB demands substantial improvements in students' scores on those tests, I'm sure you recognize that any teachers who work in a state using instructionally insensitive NCLB standards-based tests are in serious jeopardy. How did this seemingly sensible assessment approach go wrong?

I'll be identifying two major shortcomings of *most* of today's standards-based tests. A prominent exception is the array of standards-based *composition tests* that we find throughout the United States. Almost all of these standards-based tests are not only instructionally *sensitive,* but have been deliberately devised to support the instruction students receive about how to write good compositions. However, with that single exception, let's consider two shortcomings of just about all of today's standards-based accountability tests.

A Profusion of Curricular Aims The first problem flows from the enormous number of content standards typically staked out by a state's curriculum specialists. Curriculum specialists are, in every sense of the term, *specialists*. And most specialists adore their fields of specialization. Thus, for instance, when a state-convened panel of 30 mathematics curriculum experts is asked to determine what mathematics content the state's students should master, you can safely predict that those mathematics specialists will want the state's students to learn *everything!* That is, those math mavens will want students to master anything that's even mildly mathematical. Indeed, when considering most state's vast arrays of content standards in mathematics, we begin to grasp the conceptual meaning of infinity!

Although in many states there can be a hundred or more content standards to be mastered by students at a single grade level, sometimes a state's curricular officials may appear to have chosen a much smaller number of content standards— perhaps only a dozen or so fairly broad curricular aims per grade level. However, a closer inspection of those content standards will typically reveal that beneath each of the dozen broad curricular aims, there are numerous "benchmarks" or "indicators." Usually, it is only these more specific descriptions of skills and knowledge that are stated at a level of clarity suitable for the state's teachers to make sense of instructionally. This means there are still far too many curricular aims for teachers to teach in a given school year. Besides that, there are far too many curricular aims to assess students' mastery of them in the hour or so typically available for the administration of any standards-based test.

What the developers of standards-based tests are typically trying to do in this situation is to *sample.* In other words, they design their tests to measure some, but not all, of their state's sprawling collection of content standards. This sampling-based solution means, however, that numerous state-sanctioned content standards will be left unmeasured by a given year's tests. Teachers are thus forced to *guess* about which content standards will actually be measured on a particular year's standards-based accountability tests. Due to the huge number of curricular aims involved, many teachers guess wrong. Students, therefore, frequently fail to receive instruction regarding content standards that *are* assessed by a standards-based test because a teacher's guesswork-based classroom instruction has focused on content standards that *aren't* measured.

In most cases, today's standards-based accountability tests fail to measure the full set of content standards on which they are supposedly based. Moreover, even those content standards that are actually addressed in a standards-based test are usually measured in only a tokenistic manner. This leads to rampant guesswork by teachers each year about what to stress instructionally in their classrooms.

Instructionally Opaque Reporting   Assuming that a state's content standards identify the skills and knowledge to be learned by students, then an instructionally beneficial standards-based accountability test surely ought to provide information regarding *which* standards have been well taught and *which* standards haven't. Otherwise, how can teachers identify the parts of their instruction that should be fixed or instruction that's just fine as it is? But the bulk of today's standards-based accountability tests do not yield standard-by-standard score reports, for districts, schools, or individual students.

What's typically reported is some sort of overall score for each subject area. We often see attempts to provide subcategory reports—for instance, a student's reading subscores dealing with the student's mastery of (1) fictional or (2) nonfictional reading passages. Yet, most standards-based accountability tests currently do not provide teachers, students, or students' parents with the sort of standard-by-standard or benchmark-by-benchmark results that can contribute meaningfully to appropriate *classroom* instructional decisions.

What sense can a teacher make out of a total "mathematics" score, or even a "geometry" subscore? If standards-based accountability tests are going to help teachers do a better instructional job, those tests must supply the kind of information regarding students' status that allows teachers to tell which parts of their instruction were winners and which parts were losers. At the moment, most of the nation's standards-based tests don't do so. The failure to supply teachers with performance results allowing those teachers to improve their classroom instruction is a second shortcoming in most of today's standards-based accountability tests.

What are teachers apt to do after dealing with accountability tests that (1) try to measure too many curricular aims and (2) report results that have limited instructional value? Most teachers simply give up. That is, they give up in their instructional efforts to promote students' mastery of a mystery accountability test with too many targets and dysfunctional reports of students' performances. Sadly, when teachers give up in their efforts to work with instructionally insensitive standards-based accountability tests, then students' socioeconomic status and their inherited academic aptitudes turn out to be the factors that dominantly influence how well students score on those tests. Such standards-based tests will function precisely in the same way traditional standardized achievement tests function. Regrettably, a genre of assessment originally conceived to determine if students had accomplished key curricular aims has morphed into nothing more than a gussied-up assessment tool measuring what students bring to school.

Standards-Based Tests: Instructionally Sensitive Ones

Instructionally sensitive standards-based tests can detect the impact of instruction—good or bad—on students' learning. Accordingly, if a school's teachers engaged in a zealous assault on their students' low reading abilities, and were successful in improving those students' reading skills, this instructional triumph would be clearly identified by the use of an instructionally sensitive standards-based test administered to the school's students.

In recognition of today's relentless pressures on teachers to produce evidence of improved student learning, any sensible teachers will yearn for the effectiveness of their instructional efforts to be accurately appraised with instructionally sensitive tests rather than instructionally insensitive ones. Standards-based tests, if properly designed, can be instructionally sensitive.

For standards-based tests to be instructionally sensitive, those tests must possess three attributes. First, the skills and/or bodies of knowledge being assessed must be sufficiently few so teachers do not become overwhelmed by too many assessment targets. Second, the skills and/or bodies of knowledge being assessed must be sufficiently well described so teachers have a crisp idea of what skills and/or bodies of knowledge their students are supposed to master. Finally, the tests' results must permit teachers to identify whether *each* assessed skill and/or body of knowledge has been mastered by an individual student. If a standards-based test doesn't possess all three of these attributes, that test won't be instructionally sensitive.

A Manageable Number of Targets   If a standards-based test contends it measures 40 curricular aims, most teachers will be unable to focus their instruction on so many targets. An NCLB test, for example, that alleges it measures large numbers of content standards (or benchmarks, etc.) is almost certain to be instructionally insensitive.

Being realistic, there's a limited amount of time that can be used to administer an achievement test to students, especially young students. Thus, it's truly impossible to measure children's mastery of very large numbers of curricular aims. We can't accurately measure a student's mastery of a given curricular aim with only an item or two—even if those items are terrific! Thus, if numerous curricular aims are to be assessed, a test simply cannot measure all of them *well*—or even measure some of them *at all*. What's going to be assessed on each year's accountability tests, therefore, frequently turns into a gigantic lottery—a game of chance in which teachers frequently guess wrong. A state's teachers will unquestionably have trouble in properly focusing their classroom activities if they are obliged to speculate about what's going to be assessed.

Instructionally, it's tough for most teachers to keep too many targets in mind. Intellectually, many teachers can handle six or seven instructional targets. Few teachers can intellectually handle *six or seven dozen* instructional targets. This is a classic instance in which *more* turns out to be *less*. A standards-based accountability test that sets out to measure myriad curricular aims typically provides a truly feckless framework for teachers' instructional decision-making.

Typically, NCLB accountability tests are based on state-approved curricula that often contain an avalanche of content standards (benchmarks). The chief reason NCLB tests try to measure too many curricular aims is usually the nature of the state's curriculum itself. But a state standards-based NCLB test that tries to assess a huge number of curricular targets, by its meek deference to the state's ill-conceived profusion of curricular targets, presents the state's teachers with an unmanageably large set of assessment targets. Such standards-based tests are certain to be instructionally insensitive.

If only modest numbers of curricular aims are going to be assessed via a standards-based accountability test, then it is crucial that those curricular aims be exceptionally important—typically high-level cognitive skills that subsume an array of subskills and/or bodies of en route knowledge. For example, promoting students' composition skills is a significant curricular aim that covers a number of subskills such as being able to organize an essay's content and being able to use appropriate mechanics. High-level skills such as this one can form the basis of a praiseworthy standards-based accountability test. Standards-based accountability tests that try to assess many more than a half-dozen or so curricular aims in any subject area are usually aimed at an unreasonable number of assessment targets. Such standards-based tests will almost certainly be instructionally insensitive.

Lucid Descriptions of Assessment Targets   All of the statewide accountability tests now in use are supposed to assess students' mastery of a state's content standards—that is, the skills and knowledge designated in state-approved curricular aims. But in many states, those content standards are formulated in a rather mushy manner. Many states have made their content standards nothing more than general labels—for instance, "geometry" in math or "inferential comprehension" in reading. Such general designations are intended to describe a flock of small-scope, en route curricular outcomes described to as "benchmarks," "indicators," and so on.

To determine whether a standards-based test's assessment targets are sufficiently well described, we need to focus on the descriptive "grain size" (that is, breadth) teachers will typically need to rely on in order to arrive at their instructional decisions. So, if a state's curricular aims are set forth as collections of rather general content standards that subsume more specific benchmarks, the descriptive level to which we must pay attention is the benchmark level, not the content-standard level. We need to look at curricular aims crafted at a level of generality that meshes with the way teachers think about their instructional activities.

Instructionally sensitive standards-based tests, therefore, should be accompanied by *assessment descriptions* that spell out, in teacher-palatable language, what the nature of a to-be-assessed skill or body of knowledge truly is. Such assessment descriptions, stated as succinctly as possible, let teachers know where they should be aiming their instructional activities. A concise set of clear assessment descriptions, typically containing a sample item or two, constitutes the second required feature of an instructionally sensitive standards-based test.

Instructionally Illuminating Reports   If standards-based tests don't supply teachers with students' test results in a form allowing teachers to determine which segments of their instruction have been effective or ineffective, such tests usually turn out to be instructionally insensitive. Over time, these sorts of tests can't be used by teachers to improve the quality of their instruction. Students won't be taught better because teachers won't know which parts of their instruction require repairs. Accordingly, the third factor by which the instructional sensitivity of standards-based tests should be determined rests on the way a test's results are reported.

When standards-based tests are organized around a manageable number of assessment targets (for instance, six to eight), then the tests' results should be reported so a teacher can determine *which* of the targets were mastered (by the teacher's students) and *which* ones weren't. To provide such per-outcome reporting, a test must usually include a reasonable number of items per curricular aim. The number of items required per curricular aim depends most heavily on the grain size of the curricular aim being assessed.

Ideally, the score-reports from an instructionally sensitive standards-based test will allow classroom teachers to get an acceptably accurate fix on each of their students' status with respect to every curricular aim assessed by the test. Moreover, that "acceptably accurate fix" about each assessed curricular aim will help teachers make better instructional decisions. Thus, to find out if a standards-based test's reporting system is paying off instructionally, it really is necessary to secure reactions from classroom teachers who have been receiving those reports. Teachers will be easily able to tell you if the way students' test results are reported is too general, too detailed, or simply too confusing. Moreover, if students' test reports are pitched at an appropriate level of generality, and are not so detailed as to be off-putting, then those reports can be usefully relayed to students and to students' parents.

Summing up, if standards-based tests are deficit in any *one* of the three attributes just described—(1) a reasonable number of curricular aims to be assessed, (2) suitably described assessment targets, and (3) instructionally useful results— then those tests are apt to be instructionally insensitive. If a test falls short on even one of these attributes, it will almost certainly be instructionally insensitive. Use of instructionally insensitive tests as accountability assessments will unquestionably lower the quality of education a state provides for its students. Accordingly, only instructionally sensitive standards-based tests should be used as high-impact accountability assessments.

■ What's a Teacher to Do?

I've just described an assessment situation that, from the perspective of a classroom teacher, can look pretty bleak. What, if anything, can be done? I suggest a three-pronged attack on the problem. First off, I think *you* need to learn more about the viscera of the three kinds of standardized achievement tests I've just described. Second, I think *you* need to help initiate an effective assessment-literacy campaign so your educational colleagues, parents of children in your school, and relevant educational policymakers understand what the evaluative shortcomings of particular kinds of standardized achievement tests really are. Finally, I think *you* need to obtain a more appropriate form of assessment-based evidence regarding your own instructional effectiveness.

Far too many teachers haven't really studied the items on standardized achievement tests since the time they were, as test-takers themselves, obliged to respond to those items. But the inferences made on the basis of students' test performances rest on nothing more than an aggregated sum of students' item-by-item responses. What teachers need to do is to spend some quality time with standardized achievement tests—scrutinizing the test's items, one at a time, to see what the items are really measuring—and what they aren't.

Most teachers, and almost all parents and school board members, think schools should be rated on the basis of students' scores on standardized achievement tests. Those people need to be educated so they recognize that students' performances on only *certain* kinds of standardized tests should be used to evaluate schools. It is the responsibility of all educators to carry out that educating.

If you try to explain to the public, to parents, or to policymakers why *certain* kinds of standardized test scores will probably provide a misleading picture of educational quality, be sure to indicate you're not running away from the need to be held accountable. No, you must be willing to identify other, more credible evidence of student achievement. Certainly, if your local schools are being evaluated on the basis of instructionally *sensitive* standards-based tests, then you're likely to be in pretty good shape. If, however, you're going to argue against specific sorts of standardized achievement tests as a source of evidence for determining school quality, and you still are willing to be held educationally accountable, then you'll need to ante up some other form of evidence to show the world you really are doing a good educational job.

I recommend you attempt to assess students' mastery of genuinely significant cognitive skills, such as their ability to write effective compositions, their ability to use lessons from history to make cogent analyses of current problems, and their ability to solve high-level mathematical problems. If the skills you choose (1) measure really important cognitive outcomes, (2) are seen by parents and policymakers to be genuinely significant, and (3) can be addressed instructionally by competent teachers, then the assembly of a set of pretest-to-posttest evidence showing substantial student growth in such skills can be truly persuasive. Earlier in this chapter you saw how a split-and-switch design (with blind-scoring of students' responses by nonpartisan raters) can be employed to collect compelling evidence of a teacher's instructional effectiveness. Use of pretest-to-posttest designs to gauge your own instructional success makes much more sense than succumbing to the absurdity of measuring your teaching prowess with the wrong kinds of tests.

Right Task, Wrong Tools

Teachers should definitely be held accountable. The teaching of a nation's children is too important to be left unmonitored. But to evaluate educational quality by using unsound assessment instruments is a subversion of good sense. Although teachers need to produce valid evidence regarding their effectiveness, you've seen that two of the three most important commonly used standardized achievement tests are the wrong tools for this important task.

If inappropriate standardized achievement tests are chosen by a state's officials to satisfy the provisions of the NCLB Act, you can bet that a good many public schools are going to be labeled as failing when, in fact, they are doing a good instructional job. Equally disturbing, many schools will appear to be doing a stellar job based on their students' test scores, but those high scores are chiefly attributable to the composition of the advantaged students who make up such schools' student bodies. In contrast, instructionally *sensitive* standards-based tests are the right kinds of assessments to use when evaluating schools. Teachers should, solo or in collaboration, use whatever influence they can so the proper kinds of standardized achievement tests are used with their students.

■ Assessment-Based Grading

Teachers give grades. One supposes when the original blueprints for "teacher" were drawn, there must have been a mandatory grade-giving component included somewhere. Other than tradition, however, why is it teachers dispense grades to students so regularly?

The answer's fairly simple. A teacher needs to let students know (1) how well they're doing, as when a teacher assigns interim grades on various assignments during the course of the school year; and (2) how well they've done, as when a teacher dishes out end-of-year grades. For teachers to find out how well they've *taught*, as we saw earlier in the chapter, the level of students' achievement must be determined. For students to find out how well they've *learned*, the extent of their achievement must also be determined.

Although, as we shall see, there are other factors to be considered in grading students than simply how well the students performed on classroom assessments, there's little argument that a *major* consideration in the grade a student receives

Decision Time

Should Level-of-Effort Be Rewarded?

Karl Kramer teaches second-graders at Twelfth Street Elementary School. He's been doing so for six years. During the past year, however, Karl has seriously been reconsidering his whole approach to grading. This reconsideration was stimulated by three students who in the past would have been placed in some form of special needs program but now have been included in Karl's second-grade class.

Although the three students, Marie, Floyd, and James, are having difficulty with much of the content treated in class, all three are obviously trying hard to succeed. In fact, if Karl were to grade on effort alone, the three students would probably get the highest grades in class.

In the past, Karl has given no credit for student effort when grades were awarded. Now, however, he finds that he's rethinking that decision.

 If you were Karl, what would you do?

should be the quality of the student's assessment performances. In this final section of the chapter, we'll be briefly looking at different ways those assessment results can be incorporated into students' grades.

Deciding on Grading Criteria and Weighting the Criteria

It is all too common, unfortunately, for teachers to give little serious thought to grading until they are confronted, face to face, with the need to give grades. (As a beginning high school teacher, I believe I decided how to give my initial set of first-semester grades a full 30 seconds before assigning those grades.) A more appropriate approach to grade giving would be to think out—well in advance of the press of grade-giving demands—just what criteria should be used in awarding grades to students and, beyond that, just how much weight should be assigned to each criterion.

It may well be that several of the grading criteria you use will be based on students' assessment performances—but on different types of tests. For instance, final examination results are apt to be weighted more heavily than midterm examination results which, in turn, are likely to be weighted more heavily than results on weekly quizzes. If a portfolio system is employed in the class, substantial weight would be given to the evidence of students' capabilities reflected by the contents of their portfolios. In a similar vein, if students are required to respond to fairly elaborate performance test tasks, then surely the resulting student performances would be deemed more important by the teacher than other, less demanding assessment activities. In short, you'll weight differently the importance of students' performances on various kinds of assessments based on your judgments about the significance of the various assessments. If you, as most teachers, employ some sort of gradebook (paper or electronic) to keep a record of your students' performances, be certain to highlight any sorts of differential weightings of various test results or assessment.

Beyond assessment-based evidence, however, there are other criteria that teachers often employ when dispensing grades. For example, class participation, homework-completion rates, and classroom cooperation are used by some teachers as criteria to be employed in the grading process. What I'm suggesting here is simply that, before you are faced with time-induced pressures to award grades, you should give serious thought to (1) identifying the factors you'll consider when grading and (2) deciding how much those factors will count.

Elementary school teachers, of course, often are concerned about grading considerations of less interest to teachers in middle schools or high schools. For instance, first-grade teachers may think a significant *educational* aim in their classrooms is to have children develop self-control in a social setting. For example, a 7-year-old boy who pounds on male or female classmates during recess would not be behaving in an appropriate manner, nor would a 7-year-old girl who pounds on male or female classmates during recess. (A teacher afflicted with many such students might give serious thought to establishing a "cooperative pounding group.")

Although as students become older, a teacher's grading scheme might be based on typical academic criteria, teachers who work with younger children will often need to describe—and weigh—a much more developmentally appropriate set of factors. The essentials of their grading enterprise are identical to the approach used in later grades. But elementary teachers need to think through what they regard as relevant grading criteria, describe them, then weigh their contribution to a child's grade.

Grade Descriptors

When teachers award grades, there are several options available to them. For final, end-of-term or end-of-year grades, it is necessary to adhere to whatever grade-descriptor system has been adopted by the district. Thus, if the district's policy is to use grades of A, B, C, D, or F, then the district's teachers must use those grades even if, during the course of the year, the teachers employed a different grade-descriptor scheme in class. Although many school districts, or schools within those districts, have grading policies that are quite general, some grading policies are particularly restrictive—setting forth specific limits on the percentages of particular grades that can be awarded by teachers.

Generally speaking, there are three major options available to teachers when they describe how well a student has performed. Teachers can use (1) letter grades, (2) numerical grades, or (3) verbal descriptors. Most of us are familiar with *letter grades* because such grades have been widely used for a long, long time. A grade of A is yummy and a grade of F is sucko. In some districts, teachers are also allowed to add pluses or minuses to letter grades, thus transforming a grading scale that has 5 points (A, B, C, D, or F) to one with 15 points. A grade of F–, we assume, reflects genuinely abysmal rock-bottom performance. A *numerical grading system* is usually organized around some chosen number of points such as 100, 50, or 10. Students are then given a number of points on each classroom assessment so that when students see their grade for the assessment, they realize they have earned, for example, "7 points out of a possible 10." *Verbal descriptors* are used instead of numerical or letter grades when teachers rely exclusively on phrases such as "excellent," "satisfactory," and "needs improvement," The number of such phrases used—that is, the number of possible verbal-descriptor grades that might be employed—is up to the teacher. If verbal-descriptor grades are used throughout an entire district, the choice of verbal descriptors is typically decided by district officials.

One increasingly common form of a verbal-descriptor grade is the *achievement-level* classification system used to describe performance on the National Assessment of Educational Progress (NAEP). When NAEP tests are administered, students' performances are classified as *Advanced, Proficient, Basic,* or *Below Basic.* This four-category achievement-level classification model has become widely used across the United States. Because the NCLB Act calls for states to use at least three of these descriptive labels (that is, *Basic, Proficient,* and *Advanced*), many states have simply adopted the NAEP four-category model. Thus, the use of the NAEP achievement-level labels is clearly a prominent variation of verbal-descriptor grades. A number of districts have tried to devise *standards-based report cards* wherein the quality of each student's mastery of each content standard (curricular aim) is described. In many instances, the level of detail being used in such reporting systems has proven overwhelming to students, their parents, and more than a few teachers.

Grade-Giving Options

Let's look at three common grade-giving approaches. Each of these approaches can be used not only for end-of-term or end-of-year grades but also for grading the assessment performances of students during the school year. In other words, these four grading approaches can be applied whether you are assigning Johnny an end-of-term grade in your science class or a grade on his two-week experiment on Psychological Depression in Earthworms.

You're probably already familiar with the three grading approaches to be described because, when you were a student, you most likely encountered them all:

- *Absolute grading.* When grading *absolutely,* a grade is given based on a teacher's idea of what level of student performances is truly necessary to earn, for instance, an A. Thus, if an English teacher has established an absolute level of proficiency needed for an A grade, and in a given class no student performs at the A-level of proficiency, then no student gets an A. Conversely, if the teacher's absolute grading standards were such that all students had performed beyond the A-level requirements, then the teacher would shower all students with A grades. An absolute system of grading has much in common with a criterion-referenced approach to assessment.

  The major argument in favor of an absolute approach to grading is there are, indeed, legitimate levels of expectation for students which, although judgmentally devised by teachers, must be satisfied in order for specific grades to be awarded. And, of course, it is always the case that people form their absolute expectations based on seeing how folks usually perform. Thus, there's a sense in which *absolutes flow from relatives.*

- *Relative grading.* When teachers grade *relatively,* a grade is given based on how students perform in relation to one another. Thus, for any group of students, there will always be the *best* and the *worst* performances. Those students who outperform their classmates will get high grades irrespective of the absolute caliber of the students' performances. Conversely, because some students will always score relatively worse than their classmates, such low scorers will receive low grades no matter what. This system of grading is somewhat analogous to a norm-referenced approach to assessment.

  As noted earlier, there is a sense in which even a teacher's *absolute* expectations regarding the level of performance needed to achieve an A, B, C, D, or F are derived from years of working with students and discerning how well they're usually capable of performing. But a relative grading system uses the students *in a given class* as the normative group, not all the students whom the teacher has taught in the past.

  The chief argument for a relative system of grading is because the quality of the teacher's instructional efforts may vary, and the composition of a given group of students may vary, some type of class-specific grading is warranted. Teachers who use a relative-grading approach tend to appreciate its flexibility because grading expectations change from class to class.

■ *Aptitude-based grading.* When grading on *aptitude,* a grade is given to each student based on how well the student performs in relation to that student's academic potential. To illustrate, if a particularly bright student outperformed all other students in the class, but still performed well below what the teacher believed the student was capable of, the student might be given a B, not an A. In order to grade on aptitude, of course, the teacher needs to have an idea of what students' academic potentials really are. To gain an estimate of each student's academic aptitude, teachers either have to rely on the student's prior performance on some sort of academic aptitude test or, instead, must form their own judgments about the student's academic potential. Because academic aptitude tests are being administered less frequently these days, in order to use an aptitude-based grading approach, teachers will generally need to arrive at their own estimate of a student's potential.

The main argument in favor of aptitude-based grading is it tends to "level the playing field" by grading students according to their innate gifts and thereby encourages students to fulfill their potential. A problem with this grading approach, as you might guess, is the difficulty of deciding on just what each student's academic potential really is.

As indicated earlier, any of these three grading approaches can be used to assign grades for individual efforts of students, such as their performances on a short essay examination, or for arriving at a student's total-year grade. For instance, thinking back to Chapter 9's treatment of portfolio assessment, it would be possible to use any of the three grading approaches in order to arrive at students' portfolio grades—grades dispensed in letter, numerical, or verbal form.

Hodgepodge Grading

Because of the several grading options available to teachers, how do most teachers actually end up grading students? Well, several researchers have concluded that most teachers assign *hodgepodge grades.* A hodgepodge grade is one based on the teacher's loosely combined judgment of students' (1) assessed achievement, (2) effort, (3) attitude, (4) in-class conduct, and (5) growth.

A teacher who employs hodgepodge grading typically hopes for uniformly high performance in all five areas, and recognizes that *really* poor student performances in any one area might lead to lower grades. Students' achievement, effort, attitude, conduct, and growth, however, are all combined subjectively by the teacher. In hodgepodge grading, there are no scientific-looking quantitative models that, based on students' performances in a variety of areas, obligingly pump out clear-cut grades. Hodgepodge grading is much more mushy. It is, as advertised, a hodgepodge.

In a study of more than 300 teachers and 7,000 students, hodgepodge grading was reported by teachers to be the most common approach they used when dispensing grades (Cross and Frary, 1999). Students confirmed that most of their teachers did, indeed, use a hodgepodge approach to grading. Interestingly, by and large, the students *approved* of their teachers' hodgepodge grading practices. It appears students are willing to risk teachers' subjectivity in combining assessed achievement and other nonachievement factors. Or, perhaps more accurately, students are more willing to run *that* risk than to see teachers consider *only* a student's assessed achievement.

Electronic Record Keeping

Although many seasoned teachers have traditionally kept records of their students' accomplishments by making handwritten entries in a gradebook, the dramatic increase in the use of teacher-friendly computers promises to alter that practice. As more and more youthful, computer-canny teachers enter the field of education, we will surely see marked expansions in the use of computer-based records regarding students' performances.

A number of readily usable programs to help teachers keep track of their students' performances now exist, and more will surely be available in years to come. The mission of these electronic grading programs is to simplify the teacher's tasks so even a rudimentary notion of how to use a computer will allow teachers to save tons of record-keeping time. Some observers of America's classrooms predict, within a decade or so, the use of hand-entered grades in a conventional gradebook will be quite rare.

Parent Talk

Imagine that one of your students' parents, Mrs. Aquino, wants to discuss her daughter's grade in your class. Specifically, she wants to know, "What goes into Mary's grade?"

 If I were you, here's how I'd respond to Mrs. Aquino:

"I'm delighted you want to look into how Mary is graded in my class. What I'd like you to do is look over my classroom information system I've been able to get up and running this year on my lap-top computer. Why don't you come to my class before or after school and I'll show you how I arrive at each of the components contributing to Mary's grade. I'll also show you how I've tried to weight the grade-determination importance of certain tests and other assignments Mary and her classmates complete.

"What you need to understand, Mrs. Aquino, is that any grade given to any student is almost always a teacher judgment based on an amalgam of different sorts of evidence. And, to be honest, because teachers' judgments are involved, and teachers are altogether human, there will invariably be some errors teacher's in grading.

"But I assure you I and the other teachers in our school are trying to do the fairest and most accurate job we can when we grade our students. Why don't you visit and we can review what goes into Mary's grade?"

 Now, how would you respond to Mrs. Aquino's concerns?

Grading's Inherent Imprecision

Wouldn't it be nice if teachers never made mistakes when they grade students? But, as you probably know all too well from having been the recipient of too-low or too-high grades during your own years as a student, teachers make grading errors. Certainly, teachers don't want to make mistakes in the grades they give to their students; however, grading is a judgment-based enterprise in which flawed decisions will surely be made.

Fortunately, in the long haul, such errors tend to balance one another out. Do you recall from Chapter 8 that there are three kinds of rater bias—namely, generosity bias, severity bias, and central-tendency bias? It is true that many teachers are biased in one of these three ways when they grade students. Thus, over the years, a given student will probably be on the receiving end of some undeserved high grades and some unwarranted low grades. What you need to remember is that if you do the best job you can in dispensing grades to your students—that is, if you assign grades carefully and with the kind of deliberateness suggested in this chapter—you'll have done your grading as well as you can. Human judgment, as potent as it is, is not flawless. And it certainly isn't flawless when it comes to grading students.

■ What Do Classroom Teachers Really Need to Know about Assessment-Based Evaluation of Teaching and Grading of Students?

If there ever were two education-related activities in which the results of student assessments play a vital role, those two activities are the evaluation of one's teaching and the grading of one's students. When teachers evaluate the quality of their own efforts, a significant source of data should be the nature of students' performances on classroom assessment devices. When teachers give grades to students, a salient factor should be the quality of students' performances on classroom assessments.

You should realize that when you use students' test results as indicators of your own instructional prowess, a major determiner of how well your students perform will be the particular students with whom you're working. Even using a straightforward pretest-posttest evaluation paradigm doesn't circumvent the problem created because of the dissimilarity of different teachers' students. For purposes of formative evaluation, disparities in students' entry behaviors don't pose all that much of a problem. For purposes of summative evaluation, however, disparities in the abilities and motivation levels of different teachers' students should induce caution in the evaluative use of students' test results. Judgments about the caliber of growth attained by a given teacher must be made in the context of the instructional situation in which the teacher is functioning. A useful way of collecting evidence regarding a teacher's instructional effectiveness is the split-and-switch design.

but what does this have to do with ❓

but what does this have to do with ❓

Teaching?

It is inconceivable to me that an entire profession would allow its members to be judged using the wrong measuring tools. Yet, in education, that is precisely what is going on. And some teachers, largely because they do not understand specifically why certain kinds of standardized achievement tests ought not be used to evaluate schooling, compliantly accept this profound misuse of educational tests. Such teachers may have an intuitive idea that students' scores on some standardized achievement tests don't provide a clear picture of instructional quality, but they can't tell you *why*.

If, as a teacher, you don't help people understand why it is that particular sorts of standardized achievement tests should not be used to judge instructional effectiveness, then you probably deserve what you'll get—thoroughly inaccurate judgments about your skill. But you're not the only one who gets hurt because of this glaring miscarriage of measurement-based justice. Your students will get hurt too. And *that's* why you need to first understand the ins and outs of this important issue, then you need to let others know about the misuse of certain standardized achievement tests to judge educational quality. And it's not just the nationally standardized achievement tests but, quite possibly, a customized test constructed specifically to "better assess a state's content standards." Many of those tests function in exactly the same instructionally insensitive way as a nationally standardized achievement test.

Who are those "others" you need to acquaint with this issue? Well, start off with your colleagues. Few teachers or administrators really understand, at a meaningful level, why some standardized tests aren't the answer for judging schools. Then there are parents who need to understand. And, of course, there are educational policymakers. They definitely need to learn what constitutes solid evidence of instructional quality and what evidence ought never to be used.

In short, if you don't want your own teaching to be appraised using the wrong microscope, then outfit yourself in evangelical garb and start doing a bit of gospel-spreading!

Perhaps one of the most important understandings you should carry from this chapter is the recognition that certain kinds of standardized achievement tests—the kind being used all over the land for purposes of educational accountability—should not be employed to evaluate a teacher's instructional effectiveness. You need to understand *why* such tests are inappropriate for this purpose. And once you recognize why the evidence derived from the wrong kinds of standardized achievement tests is unsuitable for the evaluation of a school staff's quality, then you should see that other evidence, more defensible and more credible, needs to be collected by educators. The public has a right to see how well their tax-supported schools are doing. The public doesn't have the right to do so by using the wrong evidence. It was suggested that *instructionally sensitive standards-based accountability tests* could provide accurate evidence of teachers' success.

Regarding grading, you should know that you need to give careful attention to the isolation of grading criteria and to the weighting of those criteria. However, when you get down to it—that is, when you get down to the dispensing of actual grades—you're more than likely to miss on certain students. Yet, given the inescapably judgmental basis of grading, that's probably as good as it's going to get.

■ Chapter Summary

Having drawn a distinction between *evaluation* as an activity focused on determining the effectiveness of the teacher and *grading* as an activity focused on letting students know how well they are performing, the chapter then tackled the topic of evaluation. *Formative evaluation* was contrasted with *summative evaluation*. Formative evaluation focuses on the improvement of the teacher's instructional endeavors, whereas summative evaluation focuses on such decisions as continuation of the teacher's employment. A preinstruction versus postinstruction paradigm was recommended as a straightforward way of employing assessment results to help determine the effectiveness of instruction. A split-and-switch design for contrasting preinstruction and postinstruction test results was introduced. The use of affective assessment devices was urged, in addition to cognitively oriented assessment instruments, when ascertaining a teacher's impact on students.

The inappropriateness of using students' scores on nationally standardized achievement tests was stressed because of three chief reasons: (1) mismatches between what's tested and what's taught; (2) a technical tendency to exclude from test items covering important, teacher-stressed content; and (3) uncertainty about the extent to which students' scores are attributable to what students were taught at school versus what those students brought to school because of SES and inherited academic aptitudes. Instructionally *insensitive* standards-based tests are those assessments that (1) attempt to measure students' mastery of too many curricular aims and (2) report students' performances in a manner that—from an instructional decision-making perspective—is dysfunctional. Instructionally *sensitive* standards-based tests (1) measure only a manageable number of important curricular targets, (2) describe clearly the skills and/or knowledge being assessed, and (3) report students' performances in a way benefiting teachers' instructional decisions. Teachers were urged to (1) collect more credible evidence of their instructional effectiveness and (2) inform parents and educational policymakers about the need to secure defensible evidence of a teacher's instructional success.

Turning to grading of students, it was recommended that teachers explicate their grading criteria and assign weights to each criterion. Three schemes for arriving at grades were described: ability grading, relative grading, and aptitude-based grading. A hodgepodge approach to grading, commonly employed, was also described. The chapter was concluded with an attempt to offer teachers solace for their task of judgmentally awarding grades to students.

Self-Check

We'll close out this chapter with a fairly short set of self-check exercises. They're also almost dirt-simple easy. Clearly, because this is the final set of these little practice activities you are to complete, I want to send you forth in a thoroughly upbeat mood. Check out the five activities described below in the first set of practice exercises and decide whether each is dominantly *evaluation* (E) or *grading* (G) as these two operations were defined in the chapter. These are, as you know by now, binary-choice items.

(E or G)   **1.** Molly Muggins uses her algebra students' final examination results to determine whether she needs to alter the way she teaches the unit on simultaneous equations.

(E or G)   **2.** Bertram Billings decides which students will receive "exemplary" or "acceptable" labels on their Parent Communication Reports based on students' performances on classroom tests (25%) and, chiefly, on their writing portfolios (75%).

(E or G)   **3.** Sarah Selmo uses her third-grade students' pretest-to-posttest results when conferencing with her principal, who must decide whether to recommend Sarah for tenure in the district.

(E or G)   **4.** Harriet Harris lets her students evaluate all major ingredients in their portfolios, then combines these student evaluations with her own evaluations of the portfolios so interim progress reports, varying from 1 to 10, can be sent to students' parents.

(E or G)   **5.** William Wimzy bases each student's entire course grade on the student's accomplishments in carrying out an elaborate performance test administered during the final three weeks of the school year.

Now, for the last five self-check exercises of the book, grapple with five additional binary-choice items. You've already had some true-false items at the end of an earlier chapter, so as a change of pace please judge each of the following five statements (based on the chapter's contents), as TT (terribly true) or FF (fervently false).

(TT or FF)   **6.** The focus of summative evaluation is on more "terminal" decisions about teachers, whereas formative evaluation focuses chiefly on improving the teacher's instructional effectiveness.

(TT or FF)   **7.** Because of the nature of their items, some nationally standardized achievement tests assess what students bring to school rather than what those students are taught at school.

(TT or FF)   **8.** Absolute grading practices are roughly comparable to criterion-referenced assessment, whereas relative grading practices are somewhat akin to norm-referenced assessment.

(TT or FF)   **9.** Generally speaking, students' scores on any kinds of standards-based achievement test should be the dominant determiner of a teacher's instructional success.

(TT or FF) **10.** Chapter 15, positioned as it is in advance of the book's appendix, glossary, and index—yet close to the book's back cover—is this book's final chapter.

❓ Pondertime

1. Assuming a teacher was committed to the use of students' test results in the evaluation of teaching, do you think those test results would be more useful in *formatively* oriented teacher evaluation or in *summatively* oriented teacher evaluation? And why, pray tell, do you think so?

2. Do you think teachers can "blind score" their own students' tests if those tests are gathered via a split-and-switch design, or should other people do the scoring? Does your answer depend on the kind of test being used?

3. When teachers evaluate themselves (or when supervisors evaluate teachers), various kinds of evidence can be used in order to arrive at an evaluative judgment. If you were a teacher who was trying to decide on the *relative worth* of the following types of evidence, where would you rank the importance of students' test results?

    a. Systematic observations of the teachers' classroom activities

    b. Students' anonymous evaluations of the teacher's ability

    c. Students' pretest-to-posttest gain scores on instructionally sensitive standards-based tests

    d. A teacher's self-evaluation

    Would your ranking of the importance of these four types of evidence be the same in all instructional contexts? If not, what factors would make you change your rankings?

4. If you were devising an assessment scheme to determine how well a reader of this book had mastered its contents, what sort of a procedure would you employ? Would you, for instance, recommend a selected-response test, a performance test, a portfolio, or perhaps selective cranial surgery?

Self-Check Key

1. E	3. E	5. G	7. TT	9. FF
2. G	4. G	6. TT	8. TT	10. TT (Wasn't that easy?)

■ Additional Stuff

Abrams, Lisa M., and George F. Madaus. (2003). "The Lessons of High-Stakes Testing." *Educational Leadership, 61*, no. 3 (November): 31–25.

American Educational Research Association. (1999). *Standards for Educational and Psychological Testing*. Washington, DC: Author.

Cross, Lawrence H., and R. B. Frary. (1999). "Hodgepodge Grading: Endorsed by Students and Teachers Alike." *Applied Measurement in Education, 12*, no. 1: 53–72.

Gardner, H. (1994). "Multiple Intelligences: The Theory in Practice." *Teacher's College Record, 95*, no. 4: 576–583.

Kohn, Alfie. (2000). *The Case Against Standardized Testing: Raising the Scores, Ruining the Schools*. Westport, CT: Heinemann.

Neill, Monty. (2006). "The Case Against High-Stakes Testing." *Principal, 85*, no. 4 (March/April): 28–33.

Popham, W. James. (2001). *The Truth About Testing: An Educator's Call to Action*. Alexandria, VA: Association for Supervision and Curriculum Development.

Popham, W. James. (2004). *America's "Failing" Schools: How Parents and Teachers Can Cope with No Child Left Behind*. New York: RoutledgeFalmer.

Sadler, Philip M., and Eddie Good. (2006). "The Impact of Self- and Peer-Grading on Student Learning," *Educational Assessment, 11*, no. 1: 1–32.

Thomas, R. Murray. (2005). *High-Stakes Testing: Coping with Collateral Damage*. Mahwah, NJ: Lawrence Erlbaum.

■ Nonprint Stuff

Kohn, Alfie. (2000). *Beyond the Standards Movement: Defending Quality Education in an Age of Test Scores* (Videotape #BSMV). Bloomington, IN: Phi Delta Kappan.

Northwest Regional Educational Laboratory. *Developing Sound Grading Practices* (Videotape #NREL-9). Los Angeles: IOX Assessment Associates.

Popham, W. James. *Evidence of School Quality: How to Collect It!* (Videotape #ETVT-13). Los Angeles: IOX Assessment Associates.

PSARAS Foundation and South Carolina Department of Education. (2002). (W. James Popham, Narrator). *Evaluating Schools: Right Task, Wrong Tests* (Videotape SCTV-11; SCTV-26). Columbia, SC: Author.

PSARAS Foundation and South Carolina Department of Education. (2002). (W. James Popham, Narrator). *How to Evaluate Schools* (Videotape SCTV-12; SCTV-27). Columbia, SC: Author.

Stiggins, Richard J. *Report Card Grading: Strategies and Solutions* (Videotape). Portland, OR: Assessment Training Institute.

Stiggins, Richard J. *Student-Involved Conferences* (Videotape). Portland, OR: Assessment Training Institute.

■ Cyber Stuff

■ *The Association for Supervision and Curriculum Development (ASCD)*, established in 1943, is an international organization representing 160,000 educators from more than 135 nations. Its website contains an excellent search-capability focusing on ASCD-distributed products and services. For example, a search for "assessment" produces the top 500 results from more than 2,300 entries. ASCD's considerable array of conferences and training sessions are described on this comprehensive website. www.ascd.org

■ *Education Sector* is a recent arrival in the K–12 debate, and provides an intriguing website where one can often find assessment-related issues addressed by astute observers. Founded in 2006, and funded by a diverse group of philanthropic organizations, Education Sector is an independent, nonprofit education think tank located in Washington, DC. Its co-founders, Andrew J. Rotherham and Thomas Toch, are striving to contribute a dependable source of sound nonpartisan thinking to key education-related debates. Although in existence for only a short time, Education Sector has already carried out several important, highly publicized assessment-related analyses. www.educationsector.org

■ *The National School Boards Association (NSBA),* founded in 1940, is a not-for-profit federation of school boards across the United States. NSBA represents 95,000 school board members who govern nearly 15,000 local school districts serving almost 50 million public school students. Intended to assist those who deal with public school issues, this website contains a search-capability that can isolate substantial numbers of resources related to such topics as assessment. www.nsba.org

Companion
Website

To access chapter objectives, practice tests, weblinks, and flashcards, visit the companion website at **www.ablongman.com/popham5e.**

Where the classroom comes to life!

MyLabSchool is a collection of online tools for your success in this course, your licensure exams, and your teaching career. Discover where the classroom comes to life by visiting **www.mylabschool.com** to access the following resources:

■ Video clips from real classrooms

■ An archive of real-life cases

■ Help with your research papers using Research Navigator™

■ Career Center with resources for:

Praxis exams and licensure preparation

Professional portfolio development

Job search and interview techniques

Lesson planning with state standard correlations

glossary

achievement tests   A measurement of the knowledge and/or skills a student possesses. Although often thought to assess what a student has *achieved* in school, some commercially published achievement tests contain many items measuring a student's out-of-school learning or the students' inherited academic aptitudes.

affective assessment   A measurement of a student's attitudes, interests, and/or values.

alignment   The substantive agreement between two or more of the following: curriculum, instruction, and assessment.

alternate assessments   Meaningfully different tests intended for students with disabilities so that more valid inferences can be made about the students than if the original test were used (even with assessment accommodations).

alternate-form reliability   The consistency of measured results yielded by different forms of the same test.

analytic scoring   A method of scoring a student's constructed responses involving the application of multiple evaluative criteria, one criterion at a time. After having employed the evaluative criteria separately, there may be an aggregation of these separate judgments into a final, overall evaluation.

anonymity enhancement procedures   The steps a teacher takes so that a student accurately perceives his or her responses to self-report affective assessment inventories are truly untraceable.

aptitude tests   A measurement device intended to predict a student's likelihood of success in some future setting, often an academic one. Although formerly referred to as *intelligence tests*, and thought to assess a person's innate potential, aptitude tests often contain a number of the same sorts of items one finds in achievement tests.

assessment   A formal attempt to determine a student's status with respect to an educational variable of interest. Synonyms: *test, measurement*.

assessment accommodations   The techniques used when assessing a student with disabilities or a language-minority student in order to secure more valid inferences about such students' knowledge and skills. Typical accommodations include allowing increased time to complete a test or, perhaps, presenting a test's items in a manner more suitable for the student's limitations.

assessment bias   If an assessment instrument offends or unfairly penalizes a student because of personal characteristics—such as race, gender, ethnicity, or socioeconomic status—the instrument is biased against that student.

assessment description   A delineation, hopefully concise and in teacher-friendly language, of the essential nature of a skill or body of knowledge that's eligible to be assessed.

assessment task   The part of an essay item or performance test that describes what it is the student should do to complete the assessment.

authentic assessment   Performance assessment in which the student's tasks resemble real-life tasks.

binary-choice item   A test item requiring a student to select one of two presented options.

blind scoring   When a student's tests are judged without the judges' knowing whether a test was completed as a pretest or as a posttest.

classification-consistency   A representation of the proportion of students who are placed in the same classification category on two testing occasions or by using two forms of the same test.

cognitive assessment   Measurement of a student's knowledge and/or intellectual skills.

cognitive demand   The essence of the intellectual operation(s) a student must carry out in order to respond successfully to a test's items or tasks.

construct-related evidence of validity   Empirical evidence that (1) supports the posited existence of a hypothetical construct and (2) indicates an assessment device does, in fact, measure that construct.

constructed responses   A student's answers to assessment tasks, such as essay items, that require a response to be generated by the student "from scratch."

content-related evidence of validity   Evidence indicating that an assessment instrument suitably reflects the content domain it is supposed to represent.

content standards   The knowledge and skills that a student is supposed to learn.

correlation coefficient   A numerical index reflecting the nature and strength of the relationship between two variables—for example, between students' scores on two different kinds of tests. The strongest positive relationship is signified by a correlation coefficient (r) of +1.00; the strongest negative relationship is signified when (r) equals –1.00. An (r) of 0.0 indicates no relationship between the two variables under analysis.

criterion-related evidence of validity   Evidence demonstrating the systematic relationship of test scores on a predictor test to a predicted criterion variable.

criterion-referenced measurement   An approach to assessment in which a student's test performance is interpreted according to how much of a defined assessment domain has been mastered by the student.

criterion variable   An external variable that serves as the to-be-predicted target for a predictor exam, such as an aptitude test.

curricular aim   A skill, body of knowledge, or affective outcome that teachers intend their students to acquire.

disparate impact   If test scores of different groups (for example, different ethnic or religious groups) are decidedly different, this is described as an assessment procedure having a disparate impact on test takers.

distractor analysis   Scrutiny of a student's empirical performances on the different answer options contained on multiple-choice and matching items.

distractors   The wrong-answer options used in a multiple-choice test item.

distribution   A term used to describe a set of test scores, such as when one says, "The final exam score distribution from the students in Ms. Hill's class was very homogeneous."

educational accountability   The imposition of required evidence, usually a student's test scores, as a way of holding educators responsible for the quality of schooling.

educational defensibility guideline   A guideline for test preparation stipulating that no test-preparation practice should increase a student's test scores without simultaneously increasing his or her mastery of the assessment domain represented by the test.

empirical item improvement   Improving an item's quality based on a student's performance on the item.

English language learners (ELL)   A diverse group of students whose first language is not English. Such students are often referred to as limited English proficient (LEP) students.

essay item   A test item eliciting a response of one or more paragraphs from a student.

evaluation   An appraisal of the worth of an educational program or, in the case of classroom teachers, either the effectiveness of an instructional activity or the competence of the teacher.

evaluative criterion   A factor on the basis of which the quality of a student's responses to tests can be judged.

extended-response item   An essay item that gives a student few constraints about how he or she is to respond, especially with respect to the length of their responses.

formative assessment   Describes the formal and informal measurement procedures used by teachers and students during instruction to gather information about learning to directly improve that learning. (I have profited from conversations with three good friends and respected colleagues, Lorrie Shepard, Rick Stiggins, and Dylan Wiliam, regarding the precise wording of an appropriate definition of formative assessment. Any shortcomings in this definition are mine, not theirs.)

formative evaluation   The appraisal of a still malleable instructional program, such as a teacher's lesson, for purposes of improving that program.

grade-equivalent scores   An often misinterpreted, estimated score based on the grade level and months of the school year represented by a student's test performance.

grading   An assignment of a quality-designating label (numerical or verbal) to describe the caliber of a student's work.

halo effect   The error of allowing a test-scorer's overall impression of a student to influence any criterion-by-criterion evaluations of the student's response to a test.

high-stakes test   An assessment whose consequences have important implications either for students (such as grade-to-grade promotion) and/or for educators (such as when schools are qualitatively ranked on the basis of students' test scores).

holistic scoring   The method of scoring a student's constructed responses that calls for the synthesized application of multiple evaluative criteria—that is, simultaneously using several distinguishable factors to arrive at an overall judgment about the quality of a student's response.

hypergeneral rubrics   Scoring guides whose evaluative criteria are described in excessively general—hence, dysfunctional—terms.

individualized education program (IEP)   A federally required document describing the specifics of how a child with disabilities is to be educated.

internal consistency reliability   The degree to which a test's items are functioning in a similar—that is, homogeneous—fashion.

item alternatives   The answer options used in a multiple-choice test item.

item-discrimination index   A numerical indicator contrasting, on a particular test item, the proportion of high total-test performers and the proportion of low total-test performers.

item response theory (ITR)   This scale-score approach to reporting a student's test performances takes into consideration not only a student's raw score but also other factors such as item difficulty, the guessability of items, and so on. The computation of IRT scale scores requires considerable computer-based statistical analysis.

judgmental item improvement   Improving an item's quality based on the opinions of student and/or nonstudent reviewers.

Likert inventories   Affective assessment devices organized around a respondent's self-reported degree of agreement with a series of presented statements.

limited English proficient (LEP) *students*   A label, often used in governmental publications, referring to students whose first language is not English. These students are frequently described as English language learners, or ELL students.

matching item   A test-item format that requires students to associate items, as directed, from two different lists.

mean   The arithmetic average of a set of scores.

measurement   A formal attempt to determine a student's status with respect to an educational variable of interest. Synonyms: *assessment, test*.

measurement-driven instruction   An approach to educational reform in which the installation of high-stakes assessments is intended to influence teachers to teach toward the knowledge and skills those assessments purport to measure.

median   The midpoint in a set of scores when the scores are ranked from lowest to highest.

multiple-binary-choice item   A binary-choice item that, along with other binary-choice items, is based on a single, usually somewhat lengthy set of stimulus material.

multiple-choice test item   A test item requiring a student to choose a response from three or more presented options.

norm-referenced measurement   An approach to assessment in which a student's test performance is interpreted relatively—that is, according to how the student's performance compares with that of other test takers.

normal curve equivalent   Often referred to as an NCE, a normal curve equivalent is a scale score representing a raw score's relative position in a distribution of scores that is assumed to be normally distributed. The meaningfulness of this scale-score approach, of course, depends on the degree to which the score distribution involved is, in fact, normal.

offensiveness   A test is offensive when it contains elements that would insult any group of test takers on the basis of their personal characteristics, such as religion or race.

p *value*   An indicator of an item's difficulty based on the percent of students who answer the item correctly. Thus, an item answered correctly by 67 percent of students would have a *p* value of .67.

percentiles   An interpretive score based on the percent of students in the norm group outperformed by a given student. For example, a student whose raw score exceeded the performance of 84 percent of norm group students would have earned an 84th percentile score.

performance assessment   A form of testing in which a student is given a task, typically a demanding one, then asked to respond to the task orally, in writing, or by constructing a product.

performance assessment task   The constructed-response assignment that a performance test presents to the student.

performance standards   The level of proficiency at which content standards should be mastered.

portfolio assessment   An assessment approach centered on the systematic appraisal of a student's collected work samples.

preassessment   A pretest given prior to instruction, typically to (1) determine a student's entry skills and knowledge or (2) employ as part of a pretest-posttest collection of evidence regarding instructional quality.

premises   A matching item's listed elements (on the left) for which a match is sought from a list of responses (on the right).

professional ethics guideline   A guideline for test preparation stipulating that no test-preparation practice should violate the ethical norms of the education profession.

progress map   A description of students' typical progress toward the achievement of a curricular aim.

prompt   The assessment task, typically for a writing sample, that indicates what the focus of a student's composition should be.

psychomotor assessment   Measurement of a student's small-muscle or large-muscle skills.

range   An infrequently used measure of a score distribution's variability that is calculated simply by subtracting the value of the lowest test score from the value of the highest test score.

raw score   The number of items, without any sort of numerical transformation, answered correctly by a student.

reactive effect   The often confounding effect of early assessment on a student's subsequent learning, most vividly seen in the impact caused by preassessment of an affective variable, wherein the student is unduly sensitized to the affective variable with which a teacher is concerned.

regression effect   A well-known statistical phenomenon in which extremely high scorers or extremely low scorers will, when retested, tend to earn scores closer to the mean of the score distribution.

reliability   The consistency of results produced by measurement devices.

responses   In general, a student's answer to an assessment task (or test item). For matching items, responses are the listed elements (on the right) from which matching selections to premises (on the left) are made.

restricted-response item   An essay item that markedly limits the form and content of a student's response to the item.

rubrics   A scoring guide employed to evaluate the quality of a student's responses to performance tests, a student's portfolios, or any kind of student-generated response.

scale scores   Converted raw scores that employ a new, arbitrarily chosen scale to represent a student's performance. A considerable number of scale scores are used in education. (See *normal curve equivalents, stanine.*)

score-spread   The degree to which a set of test scores is dispersed, or spread out.

selected responses   A student's answer to test items that present options from which the student must choose—for instance, multiple-choice or binary-choice items.

self-report inventories   An assessment tool, often completed anonymously, wherein a student's responses reveal his or her values, behaviors, attitudes, and so on.

short-answer item   A test item eliciting a brief response, usually a word or phrase, from a student.

showcase portfolios   Collections of a student's "best work"—that is, the work samples deemed to be of the highest quality. Such portfolios are typically used for celebrating students' accomplishments with parents, policymakers, and so on.

skill-focused rubrics   Scoring guides whose evaluative criteria are applicable for judging a student's responses to any suitable skill-measuring task.

socially desirable responses   Responses of a student that do not represent the student's actual sentiments but, instead, reflect how the student believes he or she *should* respond.

split-and-switch design   A data-gathering design in which a class is split into two halves, each half taking a different pretest. Then, after instruction, the tests are switched so that students take the other test form. Two comparisons are then made between students' pretest-versus-posttest performances on the same test form.

stability reliability   The consistency of assessment results over time. Synonym: *test-retest reliability.*

standard deviation   A statistical index revealing the degree to which the scores in a group of scores are spread out from the group's mean score, larger standard deviations reflecting more score spread than smaller standard deviations.

standard error of measurement   An estimate of the consistency of an individual's test performance(s) represented by an index of how likely it is that another test performance (on an equidifficult test) would yield a comparable score.

standardized test   Any test that is administered, scored, and interpreted in a standard, predetermined manner.

stanine   A scale score based on the division of test scores into nine units of one-half standard deviation distances (on the score distribution's baseline). The highest stanine, number 9, contains about four percent of the scores—as does the lowest stanine, number 1. The middle stanine, number 5, contains about 20 percent of the scores if the distribution is fairly normal in shape.

stem   The initial part of a multiple-choice item—that is, the stimulus to which one of the multiple-choice options serves as the best response.

summative assessments   Tests used to make final judgments about students or the quality of a teacher's instruction. (See *summative evaluation.*)

summative evaluation   The appraisal of a mature instructional program in order to make more permanent decisions about the program, such as continuation or termination.

target instructional domain   A student's cognitive, affective, or psychomotor outcomes that are supposed to be promoted by a teacher.

task-specific rubrics   Scoring guides whose evaluative criteria deal only with scoring a student's responses to a particular task, not the full range of tasks that might represent the skill being measured.

teaching to the test   When a teacher directs instruction toward the assessment domain represented by the test *or* toward the specific items that make up the actual test. Because of this dual meaning, and the confusion apt to result from its use, the expression should be avoided or immediately defined.

test   A formal attempt to determine a student's status with respect to an educational variable of interest. Synonyms: *assessment, measurement.*

test-retest reliability   A synonymous label for stability reliability—that is, the consistency of assessment results over time.

true-false item   A common binary-choice item in which a student's two options regarding the accuracy of a presented statement are *true* or *false.*

unfair penalization   A test item unfairly penalizes test takers when there are elements in the item that would disadvantage a group because of its members' personal characteristics, such as gender or ethnicity.

validity   The degree to which evidence supports the accuracy of test-based inferences (interpretations) about students.

validity argument   A justification of the degree to which accumulated evidence and theory support the proposed inferences (interpretations) about a student's test performances.

working portfolios   Ongoing collections of a student's work samples focused chiefly on the over-time improvement in a student's self-evaluated skills.

writing sample   A student-generated composition intended to allow inferences about a student's writing abilities.

index